Shantytown, USA

Forgotten Landscapes of the Working Poor

LISA GOFF

Harvard University Press

Cambridge, Massachusetts

London, England

2016

First printing

Library of Congress Cataloging-in-Publication Data
Goff, Lisa, author.
Shantytown, USA : forgotten landscapes of the working poor / Lisa Goff.
pages   cm
Includes bibliographical references and index.
ISBN 978-0-674-66045-8
1. Squatter settlements—United States—History—19th century.   2. Squatter settlements—
United States—History—20th century.   3. Slums—United States—History—19th
century.   4. Slums—United States—History—20th century.   I. Title.
HD7287.96.U6G64 2016
307.3'30973—dc23
2015034398

For Steve

Contents

Preface

Ten years ago, as I was researching a conference paper on southern mill villages, I came across a photograph taken at the Olympia Mill Village in Columbia, South Carolina, in the early 1930s. It was my mother as a child, perhaps six years old, standing in front of a vine-choked fence as tall as a man, her feet lost in the high grass and her chin tucked warily away from the camera. Her hair falls around her pale face in loose ringlets, evidence of the previous night's ministrations with strips of rags. The box of family photos where I found this one had several similar photographs of my mother, including one of her modeling her newly bobbed hair, but this photograph startled me. Standing next to my mother, holding her hand, was a black woman as tall as the fence behind them and almost as rigid. This unsmiling character, I later learned, was Sally, who sometimes watched my mother while my grandmother worked a second shift at the mill. She lived in the shanty-town next to the mill village. No one had ever seen or visited her house, and nobody remembered her last name.

Studying mill villages allowed me to excavate my own family's working-class history, a history my mother, the little girl in the picture, had consistently disavowed as an adult; I trace my choice to train as a historian to her decision, after my grandmother died, to omit the facts of her mother's lifelong employment at the mill from her obituary. From my safe perch in the middle class, secured by my mother's career in the federal bureaucracy, I had the luxury to dig into the past she had worked so diligently to escape and, ultimately, erase. Before the mill village, my people had been tenant farmers, and our family stories all took place on one of those two landscapes, the sand hills or the textile mills. Vernacular landscapes gradually became my scholarly focus, and I took pride in knowing my personal history emerged from some of the least auspicious of American landscapes. A family tree full of "lintheads," as mill hands were derisively called, and sharecroppers gave me cover, or so I imagined, from the worst of the heinous racial crimes that disfigured the landscape of the American South. Discovering the photograph of my mother and Sally, however, made me question what I thought I knew about the geography of poverty.

I never found the name of Sally's shantytown, but looking for it convinced me this was a subject of historical importance. I identified two other African-American shantytowns in the same city—Wheeler Hill and Black Bottom—but they were too far from my mother's mill village to be the shantytown my mother remembered. Piecing together snippets—a reference to the mill president who drained swamps behind the mill, a topographic map from the 1930s, and a lone image of an African-American shantytown, marooned captionless in a state archive—I located what I believe to be the site of Sally's neighborhood, on a swath of silty flood plain between my mother's mill village and the Congaree River that shoulders the city, a triangle of swampy land hemmed in by a granite quarry, a cemetery, and some railroad tracks. Now fully in the grip of these unexplored landscapes, I looked further afield and farther back in time, to the nineteenth century, where I found African-American shantytowns with names that evoked black liberation—Hayti, near Washington, DC, or Shermantown in Atlanta—or the suppression of it, such as Kansas, in Chicago. Broadening my focus, I discovered names of Irish and German shantytowns, built often but not exclusively by immigrants, that suggested contests over space and place: Jackson's Hollow, Darby's Patch, Dutch Hill. Some names indicated the occupations of the residents—such as Tinkersville, in Brooklyn—others the condemnation of middle-class critics: Goat Hill, Hog Town, Swampoodle. The mere names of shantytowns illuminated a tangled and intricate combination of American anxieties over race, class, and ethnicity. An editorial cartoon from 1882 captured this brilliantly with a drawing of a drunken Irish immigrant seated in the doorway of his rickety shanty above the caption, "The King of A-Shantee." The Ashanti peoples of west Africa were then at war with Great Britain, and in this cartoon, sympathy for the colonizers fused with antipathy for immigrants and poor people—and, undoubtedly, fears that they might join forces against a common adversary. More compelling yet was my dawning realization that shantytown dwellers themselves used the shanty as a rhetorical device in debates over class, race, and American identity.

My interest in shantytowns accelerated. I left the cookie-cutter confines of mill villages, the subject of numerous scholarly histories, and entered the uncharted landscapes of self-built shantytowns. I started by tracing the first use of the word in print in the United States, a path that led to accounts of the western frontier in the 1820s. The derivation of the word "shanty" proved elusive: the *OED* best estimate is a Canadian corruption of the French *chantier*—literally a work yard or site, which was used in Canada as "chanty" to refer to a log dwelling in the forest where woodcutters assembled. One of the earliest uses of "shantytown" was in 1880, in the caption for a photograph of Manhattan shanties in the *New York Daily Graphic*—the very first photograph reproduced for a newspaper on a printing press.

Next came an excavation of the house form itself, an effort that quickly grew unwieldy as I discovered multiple types of dwellings, from mud huts and teepee-like "pole shanties" to log cabins and salt-box houses, often but not always built by immigrants, Indians, or African Americans, all designated as shanties. Once I started looking for shanties, I found them everywhere. In the inventory for the 1893 World's Columbian Exposition I found a painting called *A Shanty Town in New York,* depicting a warren of sloped-roof shacks inhabited by huddled, rag-wrapped figures pushing carts. At the historical society in Washington, DC, I discovered a series of etchings by an artist obsessed with shantytowns in the District in the 1880s, who documented shantytowns persisting among the towering new mansions being built in the growing federal city. In the archives at the Smithsonian, I found sheet music for songs about shantytowns in the 1930s and 1940s, and then an entire musical comedy from 1882—a minstrel-inspired farce called *Squatter Sovereignty* that charted the rise and fall (literally, in an onstage explosion at the end of Act III) of a real Manhattan shantytown on upper Fifth Avenue. And I didn't just find historical references. I read news coverage of a Miami shantytown erected in 2006 to protest a lack of affordable housing; residents named it "Umoja," the Swahili word for "unity." During the Occupy Wall Street movement, I watched YouTube videos of protestors in Washington, DC, attempting to build a shanty on the Mall, and being blocked by police.

Soon I noticed another phenomenon: shantytowns, unacknowledged by history, often occupied the sites of what are now national landmarks, memorializing whatever replaced the shantytown. Name an iconic American space, and odds are good that a shantytown haunts its early history. The brick boardinghouses of Lowell, Massachusetts, which became symbols of American manufacturing prowess, were themselves constructed by a crew of Boston laborers who lived in a shantytown they built next to the textile mills. Henry David Thoreau built his famous cabin at Walden from the skeleton of a shanty he purchased from an Irish railroad worker. James Fenimore Cooper housed one of his frontier heroes in a shanty, and Walt Whitman rebuked the "shanties of the Emeralders"—Irish immigrants from the "Emerald Isles"—in 1840s Brooklyn. Central Park was freckled with shantytowns, which persisted until the mid-1890s despite multiple campaigns to dislodge them. Shanties and shantytowns appear in the writings of Ralph Waldo Emerson, Emily Dickinson, Louisa May Alcott, and Herman Melville.

As my research continued I found myself awash in shantytowns in popular culture, a stark contrast to their absence from the historiography. Shanties turn up in Civil War photographs, minstrel shows, and American Impressionist paintings. They covered large swaths of major cities, including a twenty-block stretch of Eighth Avenue in New York City, much of the Brooklyn waterfront, and what is now Dupont Circle in Washington, DC. In 1932, World War I veterans built a vast shantytown near the Capitol. John Dos Passos wrote an article about it for the *New Republic,* not long before President Herbert Hoover sent General Douglas MacArthur to burn it down—a decision that contributed to Hoover's defeat at the polls and gave rise to the Depression-era name for shantytowns, Hoovervilles. Shantytowns did not disappear with the New Deal, but tightening zoning and building codes, combined with public housing schemes providing ostensibly better housing for the poor—initiatives we associate, often falsely as it turns out, with liberal progressivism—limited their growth. At the root of some of our most cherished heroes of and narratives about liberal progressivism is a willful quashing of the sovereignty of the poor. By the middle of the twentieth century, with a recovering economy and the dwindling of shantytowns on the landscape, attitudes toward shantytowns grew increasingly sentimental and nostalgic. Movies like *My Man Godfrey,* in which a sojourn in a shantytown humanizes the rich financier played by William Powell, invested shantytowns with the nobility of the common man, an identity that twentieth-century musicians embraced: "In a Shanty in Old Shanty Town" had been a popular tune for almost two decades when Doris Day recorded her version in 1951. The output of popularizers as diverse as Thoreau and Doris Day made me think about shanties' larger cultural meaning, beyond their face value as artifacts of the undocumented landscapes of the working poor. Shanties were not just material objects, interesting in themselves, but cultural signposts leading the way to a deeper understanding of class consciousness in the United States.

Our nation has a long, untold history of shantytowns, stretching from the early days of industrialization in the 1820s through the Great Depression of the 1930s, and persisting in less obvious forms today, including homelessness and FEMA trailer parks. They constitute an alternative vision of American urban space, one that embodies the working class's evolving vision of itself between 1820 and 1940. In *Shantytown, USA: Forgotten Landscapes of the Working Poor,* I restore shantytowns to the central place they once occupied in the nation's imagination and the central role they played in its history. Preserved in the songs, plays, pictures, and movies about shantytowns is a working-poor discourse that resonates with values of hospitality, autonomy, adaptation, and reinvention, but which also reflects bitter inter-ethnic and intra-class conflicts among poor urban laborers. Shantytown residents of all races and ethnicities were keenly aware of economic opportunities and of their civil and property rights, and they acted in ways designed to protect and enhance them—routinely going to court, for example, and often prevailing in their efforts to resist eviction and preserve their occupation of property. This was true of shantytowns built by free blacks, Irish and German immigrants, and their hyphenated-American descendants. But while they claimed the rights and benefits associated with middle-class status—property, privacy, access to the legal system—they rejected the cultural trappings of bourgeois refinement. In the end, they lost the battle over their rights to the city. The history of shantytowns illuminates a direct relationship between the expulsion of the working poor from center cities and developing ideas about public space. Public policy and public works were used to validate and camouflage middle-class fears about the working poor while engraving those fears on the urban landscape. Both the urban public and urban public space have long been "classed," in other words, by the exclusion of certain types of people. Shantytowns open a new site for scholarly conversations about labor, race, urban history, and class formation—a site that unites the material and cultural history of working people.

The material and symbolic history of the shanty and the shantytown date to the earliest European settlement of America. In the 1840s, Henry David Thoreau bemoaned that fact, even while building a shanty for himself at Walden Pond. The story of that shanty, and how Thoreau transformed its social meaning while replicating its form, sets the stage for this history of the forgotten landscapes known as shantytowns.

1

Walden, a Shanty or a House?

Henry David Thoreau's snug cabin at Walden Pond is an American icon. There the quintessential American writer came into his own, finding himself and his distinctive voice through the process of building his own house, growing his own food, and keeping his own company. Today thousands of tourists visit Walden Pond every year, trodding ground that has become a sacred landscape of American self-reliance. The cabin is long gone, dismantled by Thoreau at the end of his 26-month experiment in 1847. Four cement pillars mark the cabin's footprint, but it is the bucolic image of Thoreau's wooden cabin with "no yard! but unfenced Nature reaching up to your very sills" that occupies the collective American imagination. Essential to the cabin's iconic stature is the fact that Thoreau built it with his own hands, a process that he recounts in the pages of *Walden,* the story of his adventure in solitude written between 1845 and 1847.[1]

Less well remembered by the public is the prehistory of Thoreau's famous house. While its mythic status suggests that Thoreau must have felled the trees and hewed all of the lumber himself, pioneer fashion, in fact he bought much of the materials for his cabin ready-made. "I had already bought the shanty of James Collins, an Irishman who worked on the Fitchburg Railroad, for boards," Thoreau wrote in *Walden.* Collins, who paid ground rent for his land, lived in a shantytown beside the Fitchburg Railroad tracks—one of at least four such settlements in Concord—about a half mile from the spot where Thoreau reconstructed Collins's deconstructed shanty to create his famous 10-by-15-foot cabin. Thoreau's exertions have become a cornerstone of American pastoralism and a blueprint for American identity. But the previous home-builder's tale has sparked less interest. Why is Thoreau's reconstituted "cabin" an American icon and James Collins's original "shanty" a forgotten detail? Why does the American public celebrate the self-reliance of a middle-class schoolteacher who dismantled someone else's house and reassembled it as his own, but overlook the self-reliance of the manual laborer who built the progenitor of that famous cottage? At Walden, Thoreau created a template for an idealized version of America with himself in the role of ideal American, a being with the power to make history through sheer force of will. "Wherever I sat, there I might live, and the landscape radiated from me accordingly." In the center of that personal universe he built a house. "I lived alone, in the woods, a mile from any neighbor, in a house which I had built myself," *Walden* begins. Thoreau put the idea and the act of building a home at the core of American identity, where it still resides 170 years later. Thoreau claimed meaning for and through the house he built at Walden Pond, and his exertions have become a fable of American personhood.[2]

Most Americans know the outline of the story. Its essence is ably distilled in the title of a recent children's book, *Henry Builds a Cabin,* which begins, "One spring day Henry decided to build a cabin," and ends with Henry taking refuge in it during a rainstorm. In the spring of 1845, a local schoolteacher named Henry moved to the woods to renounce the harried life of the town where he grew up. He borrowed an axe and cut down trees to build a cabin, carefully notching the beams and corner posts. He kept detailed notes on his daily activities and recorded his thoughts in a journal; many passages recounted his observations of nature. The seasons changed, time passed, and about two years later he moved back into town. His reflections on what he called his "experiment" were published as *Walden; or, Life in the Woods.* He is remembered as self-reliant, frugal, and thoughtful, as a lover of nature who recognized the dangers that cities and manufacturing posed to the American character, and for standing up to the government, for which he spent a night in the Concord jail. *Walden* theorizes an independent, individualistic American character forged by nature. But equally influential is the message that Americans are the sole architects of their own success: that is the unheralded lesson of *Walden.* And its power lies in the distance Thoreau creates between houses like the one he builds at Walden, and shanties like the one he buys from James Collins.[3]

An anecdote from Thoreau's life after Walden illustrates the importance of this dichotomy for Thoreau. In the spring of 1856, he went with his friend William Ellery Channing Jr. to visit an ardent fan named Daniel Ricketson, the heir to a fortune in New Bedford, MA. Ricketson was so taken with *Walden* when it was published in 1854 that he had a replica built on his country estate; he dubbed it "The Shanty" and went there to read, reflect, and entertain Concord's literary elite. Seeing the structure for the first time, Channing conversationally stated the obvious: "That's your shanty." But Thoreau goaded Ricketson with the remark in a letter on March 5: "You plainly have a rare, though a cheap resource in your shanty. Perhaps the time will come when every country seat will have one—when every country seat will *be one.* I would advise you to see that shanty business out, though you go shanty mad. Work your vein till it is exhausted, or conducts you to a broader one; so that C[hanning] will stand before your shanty, & say "That is your house."[4]

At Walden, Thoreau built a shanty. In *Walden,* he persuades readers that it was a house. Thoreau is famous for writing an ode to simplicity, but he was an alchemist, and in the pages of *Walden* he instructs his readers in his craft. Thoreau exiled the shantytowns built by railroad workers like James Collins to the margins, where generations of readers, historians, annotators, and re-enactors have left them. James Collins's shanty, and the shantytowns built nationwide by poor laborers like him, constitute a forgotten landscape of the working poor, an alternative narrative of what it meant to be an American in the early decades of the nation's history. Poor laborers like James Collins did not leave journals or diaries or inventories to explain what they thought of themselves and the nation they were building; their construction of a place to live did not constitute an "experiment." But the houses they built were as rich in meaning as Thoreau's famous cabin, and by interpreting them, one gains access to their perspective on American life and what became known as the American dream. *Walden* is remembered as the tale of one man's encounter with nature, and his commitment to living a simple and above all deliberate life. It is that. But it is also a how-to manual for class formation. Thoreau deliberately reshaped the Walden landscape, and by extension the American landscape, to promote a certain kind of American narrative, a narrative that put middle-class Americans at the center of American history. Restoring the evidence of shantytowns to the landscapes of Concord and the broader American landscape unwinds the lesson *Walden* taught—that the middle class owes no debt to the laboring classes, not even the courtesy of acknowledging their presence. Industrial capitalism as it was practiced by the 1840s depended on the James Collinses of the world, but the progressive narrative of America popularized by Thoreau in *Walden* depended on erasing them from that narrative.[5]

One of the first things Thoreau did after deciding to move to Walden woods was to buy James Collins's shanty. This was not the first time Thoreau had purchased a shanty; the previous fall he and his father bought two from the Fitchburg Railroad to use in construction of a pencil shop attached to the family home. Most of the workers who had built shanties in Concord had moved on when construction on the railroad finished in 1844 and had sold them for a few dollars each to their employer, which in turn sold them at auction. But Thoreau delays the story of buying James Collins's shanty, starting instead with a scene of felling trees to build the frame of his house. Thoreau introduces himself not as a buyer or consumer—roles he eschews in *Walden*—but in the role of a pioneer. "Near the end of March, 1845, I borrowed an axe and went down to the woods by Walden Pond, nearest to where I intended to build my house, and began to cut down some tall arrowy white pines, still in their youth, for timber." The main timbers he hews "six inches square, most of the studs on two sides only, and the rafters and floor timbers on one side." He leaves the "rest of the bark on, so that they were just as straight and much stronger than sawed ones." By the middle of April, Thoreau has built a frame with these timbers, and the house is "ready for the raising," which he does with the help of friends at the beginning of May. He moves in on July 4, "as soon as it was boarded and roofed"—a use of the passive voice that suggests that Thoreau, a scrupulous narrator of his own manual labor, also had substantial help with those tasks. Yet his choice of Independence Day underscores the meaning the house held for him. "[T]he only true America," Thoreau asserts, is the country that provides the liberty to live simply, without luxuries, in the way Thoreau demonstrates at Walden. In the fall he builds a chimney and shingles the sides of the house "with imperfect and sappy shingles made of the first slice of the log," whose edges he straightens with a plane. "I have thus a tight shingled and plastered house, ten feet wide by fifteen long, eight-feet posts, with a garret and closet, a large window on each side, two trap-doors, one door at the end, and a brick fire-place opposite."[6]

Thoreau emphasizes the impermeability of the house: "tight, light, and clean" he calls it elsewhere. Tight, light, and clean it no doubt was, but it was also scruffy, with the bark showing in places and a layer of hand-cut shingles bristling the outside. The image of Walden most people carry in their heads is the flawless vision captured by the drawing used in the woodcut that became the frontispiece for *Walden*, a prim cottage seemingly drawn with a ruler, crisply shingled, with a facade as smooth as a fresh-shaven face, nestled beneath towering trees. But that is a simulacrum. For all the lofty claims Thoreau makes for it, the house he builds is less polished, rougher, with a "sappy" and "imperfect" skin. And unlike the drawing in our heads—or the replica built at Walden Pond State Reservation—Thoreau's house was set close to the slope of the hill; he later asked that the drawing be amended so "that the bank more immediately around the house be brought out more distinctly." Thoreau's friend Channing called the drawing, which was made by Thoreau's sister Sophia several years after she last saw it, "a feeble caricature of the true house." No photograph or reliable drawing exists. But based on Thoreau's description, the actual house was rougher. Over many generations, readers have idealized Thoreau's house, smoothing away the imperfections and memorializing it as a "cabin" or "cottage," not the simple "house" Thoreau most often labeled it. Readers became co-conspirators in locating the meaning of the house Thoreau built as far as possible from the shanty he bought to build it with—as indeed he instructs them to do in *Walden*.[7]

Only a few weeks into his idyll, while he is cutting and hewing the timbers for his house, Thoreau buys James Collins's shanty "for boards." Thoreau presents his purchase of the shanty as a set piece, and the narration sets up a critical tension between the shanty he buys and the "cabin" or "house" he plans to build. "James Collins' shanty was considered an uncommonly fine one," Thoreau wrote. Collins was not at home when Thoreau arrived to inspect the shanty, so he "walked about the outside, at first unobserved from within, the window was so deep and high." He sees a house of "small dimensions, with a peaked cottage roof, and not much else to be seen, the dirt being raised five feet all around as if it were a compost heap. The roof was the soundest part, though a good deal warped and made brittle by the sun. Doorsill there was none, but a perennial passage for the hens under the door board." The owner, Mrs. Collins, sees Thoreau orbiting the shanty, and assures him that "they were good boards overhead, good boards all around, and a good window" of two squares. Thoreau enters the cabin pursued by chickens. Inside, the dwelling was "dark, and had a dirt floor for the most part, dank, clammy and aguish, only here a board and there a board that would not bear

removal." The cellar was "a sort of dust-hole two feet deep." In an astonish-
ingly well-balanced sentence, a sentence you could balance a carpenter's level
on, he notes the contents: "There was a stove, a bed, and a place to sit, an
infant in the house where it was born, a silk parasol, gilt-framed looking-glass,
and a patent new coffee mill nailed to an oak sapling, all told." James Collins
comes home in the middle of Thoreau's inspection, and "[t]he bargain was
soon concluded." Thoreau paid Collins $4.25 for the shanty, which, he discov-
ered upon dismantling it, was held together with nails, staples and spikes.
Thoreau asks that he vacate by 6:00 a.m. the following morning; Collins cautions him to be there even earlier, in order to foil the landlord's demands for
unpaid ground rent. The next morning Thoreau passes the Collinses on the
road, with their possessions tied up in a bundle. "[A]ll but the cat, she took to
the woods and became a wild cat, and, as I learned afterward, trod in a trap
set for woodchucks, and so became a dead cat at last."[8]

The Collinses' shanty would have been one of the few remaining shanties,
or perhaps the last, in what locals called called Shanty Field. It lay about a half
mile from Walden Pond along a stretch of the Fitchburg Railroad known as
Deep Cut, for the rock blasted out to make a passage for the railroad tracks.
Laying explosives was one of the jobs a railroad worker like James Collins
would have performed. Shanty Field was just one of at least four shantytowns
along the railroad tracks, inhabited by roughly 1,000 Irish construction
workers during the building of the railroad in 1843 and 1844. (By contrast, the
official population of Concord was about 2,200 at the time.) At least two and
possibly all four shantytowns were located on small tracts of land owned by
the railroad, abutting the tracks. As Collins's presence makes clear, some of
the laborers stayed to work on the railroad after it was completed, or they left
their families in the shantytowns, leapfrogging to nearby towns to find work
in the mills or on uncompleted stretches of the railroad. Thoreau and his set
were well aware of these Irish laborers, who, it should be noted, may more
likely have been not immigrants but second-generation Irish-American citizens. The route past the Deep Cut shantytown was one of Thoreau's favorite
walking paths to Walden Pond, although he does not mention the shantytown in *Walden*. Young women from Concord traveled "to the farthest corner
of Walden Pond" to provide schooling for children in the shantytowns there,
Thoreau noted in his journal. "The town is full of Irish & the woods of engi-
neers," Ralph Waldo Emerson wrote in a letter to Thoreau in June 1843, as the

railroad was being blasted through the sand-gravel hills west of Concord. Nathaniel Hawthorne took a romantic view of the settlements. In the fall of 1843, after a "solitary walk to Walden Pond," Hawthorne wrote: "In a small and secluded dell, that opens upon the most beautiful cove of the whole lake, there is a little hamlet of huts or shanties, inhabited by the Irish people who are at work upon the rail-road. There are three or four of these habitations, the very rudest, I should imagine, that civilized men ever made for them-selves, constructed of rough boards, with protruding ends. Against some of them the earth is heaped up to the roof, or nearly so. . . . These huts are placed beneath the trees . . . To be sure, it is a torment to see the great, high, ugly embankment of the rail-road, which is here protruding itself into the lake, or along its margin, in close vicinity to this picturesque little hamlet." Shanty Field, whether disparaged or romanticized, was identified both with antiquity and modernity. On the one hand, the shanties represented a barbaric lifestyle marked by primitive construction methods, while on the other, they symbol-ized the pressure of modernity, epitomized by the railroads, canals, and fac-tories that attracted and employed shanty dwellers.[9]

James Collins's shanty was part of one such community, a self-built indus-trial village that made a stark contrast to Thoreau's isolated cabin on the shores of Walden Pond. Thoreau's house, in truth, was more camouflaged than it was isolated. Thoreau says he had no neighbors for a mile, but what he means is that he cannot *see* his nearest neighbors, unless he stands on a hilltop. "My nearest neighbor is a mile distant, and no house *is visible* from any place but the hill-tops within half a mile of my own. I have my horizon bounded by woods all to myself . . . It is as much Asia or Africa as New England. I have . . . a little world all to myself" (emphasis mine). Thoreau deliberately shields his house from view, and the view from his house, because neither contribute to the pastoral ideal he seeks to create, an ideal that depends, ultimately, upon the erasure of shantytowns and the people who build them. Unlike Hawthorne, he cannot imagine the shantytowns as part of a picturesque landscape. To him, Shanty Field was the refuge of the "degraded poor," a class of people he identifies closely with Irish culture. "It is a mistake to suppose that, in a country where the usual evidences of civilization exist, the condition of a very large body of the inhabitants may not be as degraded as that of savages," Thoreau cautions. "To know this I should not need look farther than to the shanties which every where border our railroads, that last improvement in civilization; where I see in my daily walks human beings living in sties, and all winter with an open door, for the sake of light, without any visible, often imaginable, wood pile, and the forms of both old and young are permanently contracted by the long habit of shrinking from cold and misery, and the development of all their limbs and faculties is checked." "But alas!," he writes, after a visit to another Irish shanty in the Walden woods, "the culture of an Irishman is an enterprise to be undertaken with a sort of moral bog hoe." In 1851, after the end of his Walden residence but before the publication of *Walden,* he recounts coming across yet another shanty. "How shiftless—what death in life."[10]

When Thoreau looked at the Collins's shanty, he saw a tomb. No light, no fireplace, enshrouded by dirt, inhabited by animalistic manual laborers: "savages." The Irish themselves were irredeemable, an opinion he repeats after visits to two other Irish residents of the Walden woods: Hugh Quoil, a hard-drinking ditch-digger who lived "in an old ruin in Walden woods" that Thoreau dubs "an unlucky castle," and John Field, a bog digger whom Thoreau tries to counsel in manners of thrift. Chastising Field for spending too much on coffee, tea, and meat, Thoreau encourages him to "go a-huckleberrying" instead, but gives up in disgust at the sight of John and his wife "star[ing] with arms a-kimbo," a gesture Thoreau interprets as incomprehension but, one imagines, could just as easily have indicated dismay. "I tried to help him with my experience, telling him . . . that I lived in a tight, light, and clean house . . . and how, if he chose, he might in a month or two build himself a palace of his own." Here is Thoreau in the role of the social reformer, performing a catechism repeated throughout the nineteenth and twentieth centuries: the middle-class visitor counseling the poor on how to be better poor people, starting with adjustments to their diet and interior decoration. Thoreau echoes anti-Irish sentiments widely held in the 1840s, but his judgments are particularly harsh. He dismisses Field as "born to be poor, with his inherited Irish poverty . . . not to rise in this world, he nor his posterity, till their wading, webbed, bog-trotting feet get *talaria* to their heels." As American literature scholar Dana D. Nelson has pointed out, "Field . . . becomes an essential contrast to the 'only true America' that Thoreau more capably and wisely represents." So does James Collins and his shanty.[11]

The "true America" that Thoreau invokes during his visit to John Field is precisely what is at stake in the distinction Thoreau makes between a shanty and a house. Thoreau lavishes positive attributes on his own home-building, while withholding praise from the home-building efforts of Collins and other shanty-dwellers. Long before he picks up an axe to fell those arrowy pines on the shore of Walden Pond, Thoreau delivers a lengthy meditation on the meaning of shelter in the opening pages of his second chapter. As though preparing the ground for a solid foundation, Thoreau carefully delineates what shelter means, and what it means to build one's own house. Huts, hovels, and shanties pepper the narrative, but serve largely as signposts charting the distance from the ideal house Thoreau plans to construct.

Thoreau carefully supports his analysis of the meaning of shelter by embedding it in historical, geographical, ideological, and mythological contexts. He takes the reader on a journey through space and time, stretching from the prehistoric—"We may imagine a time when, in the infancy of the human race, some enterprising mortal crept into a hollow in a rock for shelter"—to the biblical: "Adam and Eve, according to the fable, wore the bower before other clothes." Indigenous societies from the poles to the plains—the Laplander sleeping in "a skin bag" on the snow, the Indian diving into a wigwam that "was the symbol of a day's march"—provide touchstones for Thoreau's philosophizing about the relationship of the human body to shelter. The ideal shelter is defined as the minimal container separating the human body from the elements. The urge to "clothe himself with the shelter of a home" was "an instinct" man shared with "primitive ancestors," and Thoreau admires what he sees as the impulse toward simplicity shared by ancient and "primitive" peoples. "Our shirts are our liber or true bark," he writes, a comparison that recalls his description of leaving the bark on the rafters in his Walden house—whereas "fanciful clothes" constitute a "false skin." Thoreau champions furnishings that are austere and utilitarian, reproaching himself for harboring three pretty limestone rocks on his desk (he hurls them out the window). He sounds like a harbinger for twentieth-century modernism's "less is more" ethos, chastising "superfluous glow-shoes (galoshes,) and umbrellas, and empty guest chambers" and asserting that "our houses are cluttered and defiled" with furniture. "Why should not our furniture be as simple as the Arab's or the Indian's?" he wants to know. Arguments against excessive exterior or interior frippery bolster Thoreau's diatribe against debt, which for Thoreau is another inexcusable encrustation, needlessly hampering the construction of an authentic shelter. "Most men appear never to have considered what a house is, and are actually though needlessly poor all their lives because they think they should have such a one as their neighbors have," he says, in a tone that bounces between beseeching and accusatory. Whether mortgages or galoshes, the best sort of shelter is unencumbered by their presence. And the goal, for Thoreau, is to be free and unencumbered in order to enjoy nature and learn from it. The "simplicity and nakedness of man's life in the primitive ages," he argues in *Walden,* made him a "sojourner" in nature. "He dwelt, as it were, in a tent in this world," and was wholly satisfied and wholly free.[12]

Thoreau then moves his discussion of the meaning of shelter from the prehistoric realm into the historical time of the colonial era in his own hometown, Concord. He cites three historical accounts of shelter from the seventeenth century, starting with Puritan Daniel Gookin's admiring description of the Indians of the Massachusetts Bay Colony, whose longhouses were "covered very neatly, tight and warm, with barks of trees . . . made into great flakes." Then he introduces the early European occupants of New England, referencing seventeenth-century historian Edward Johnson's description of the first settlers in Concord, who would "burrow themselves in the earth for their first shelter under some hill-side . . . casting the soil aloft upon timber"; and Cornelis van Tienhoven's 1650 description of New Englanders "who hav[ing] no means to build farm houses at first . . . dig a square pit in the ground, cellar fashion, six or seven feet," where they "case the earth inside with wood all round the wall, and line the wood with the bark of trees or something else to prevent the caving in of the earth; floor this cellar with plank, and wainscot it overhead for a ceiling, raise a roof of spars clear up, and cover the spars with bark or green sods, so that they can live dry and warm in these houses with their entire families for two, three, and four years."[13]

Set this beside Thoreau's description of James Collins's shanty, quoted above. Both are small square cabins with dirt piled shoulder-high all around, sided with boards to keep the soil from caving in. Both have plank floors and shallow cellars. Like the seventeenth-century dwelling van Tienhoven described, Collins's shanty has a roof, although it is a "peaked cottage roof" rather than a roof of green spars, or saplings, as in van Tienhoven's example. Both were sturdy enough to shelter a family for three or four years, the colonial dwelling while the farm was established, the Collins shanty while the railroad was built. Thoreau praises the simplicity of just this kind of dwelling and the impulse for simplicity that inspired it. Yet when he comes to the shanty of Irish railroad workers in his beloved Walden woods, the tables turn. Instead of respecting James Collins's shanty as a modern iteration of an American tradition, Thoreau denigrates it in subtle ways, comparing it to "a compost heap," dismissing the cellar as "a sort of dust-hole," and complaining of various inadequacies—the roof is warped by sun, a window pane is broken, the interior is "dank, clammy and aguish." The faint praise that "James Collins' shanty was considered an uncommonly fine one" reinforces Thoreau's scorn for shanties in general. Why this mockery instead of respect?[14]

Honoring Collins's efforts would erase the distance between Thoreau's home-building project at Walden and the shanty-building process practiced by poor immigrant laborers. That is a gap Thoreau wants to increase, not close. "Much it concerns a man, forsooth," Thoreau chides the readers of Walden, "how a few sticks are slanted over him or under him, and what colors are daubed upon his box. It would signify somewhat, if, in any earnest sense, he slanted them and daubed it." When Thoreau wrote that sentence, he was expressing his disgust with the excessive ornamentation of the so-called "cottage architecture" fad that was sweeping the country at the time. Perhaps because Thoreau was writing for his middle-class peers, he did not notice that the shanty builders of Concord were practicing the fundamental art of home-building he espoused, earnestly slanting and daubing the boxes they called home. Thoreau entreats the readers of Walden to focus on what he calls "the substantials"—the foundation and the frame. Doing so immediately classifies James Collins's shanty as insubstantial, since it lacked both.[15]

In *Walden,* time and intention distinguish a shanty from a house. "I made no haste in my work, but rather made the most of it," Thoreau boasts, making a virtue of leisure and reflection. "I went to the woods because I wished to live deliberately, to front only the essential facts of life, and see if I could not learn what it had to teach, and not, when I came to die, discover that I had not lived." Thoreau is famous for his deliberation, and nowhere is that quality more in evidence than in the building of his house. While Thoreau built at a leisurely pace, recording the feelings and emotions engendered by the process, shanty dwellers like Collins built of necessity, hastily, for otherwise they were homeless. The meaning Thoreau attaches to building his own house, in a spot secluded from society, he does not assign to shanty builders like Collins.

The activities of daubing and slanting do not "signify somewhat" when it is a laborer's hand wielding the paint brush or axe, or when it is literally necessity that motivates construction.[16]

Although he knows that laborers build their own houses, it does not signify. Thoreau delegitimizes the efforts of laborers, reserving for the middle class the significance of participating in the construction of one's own home. Virtues of self-reliance and resourcefulness, amply on display in shanties like the Collinses', do not capture Thoreau's attention. Had *Walden* been a less influential book, Thoreau's blindness—certainly no worse than his middle-class peers'—would not matter. But at Walden he created a template for a proper home that proved far-reaching. Whether a house was a shanty like James Collins's or a cabin like Thoreau's depended, ultimately, not on the materials or construction methods, but on who lived there, and what their intentions were when they built their house. It was not the builder but the observer, in this case Thoreau, who declared one handmade house worthy of praise while mocking its near equal. Labeling one house a shanty and another a cabin or cottage claimed for the middle class virtues amply exhibited by the laboring classes, albeit in less self-conscious ways. Ultimately, that distinction would have public policy consequences: labeling shanties as degraded made it much easier to demolish them when they got in the way of new construction or infrastructure improvements later in the nineteenth century. Thoreau's cabin at Walden Pond would qualify structurally as a well-built shanty when compared to the descriptions in contemporary fiction, how-to literature, and art. But Thoreau's intentions render it not a shanty but a cottage, and, ultimately, an icon as powerful and lasting in the American imagination as the log cabin on the plains.

Thoreau's emotional and ideological investments in maintaining a clear distinction between his cabin and Collins's shanty are not peculiar to him, but are deeply engrained in nineteenth-century American thought. As Stuart Blumin and others have shown, the middle classes developed a palette of visual clues for identifying each other. "During the nineteenth century many Americans came to experience class not as part of a national consensus of values but in daily routines and social networks that made their lives visibly similar to those of some people and visibly different from those of others." The urban middle class sorted itself out with major shifts in attitudes that ranged from eschewing manual labor to embracing theater-going and home decoration. The acquisition and display of beautiful things, often in parlors designed for the purpose, illustrated the gentility and refinement of the middle class and aided self-definition. As the standard of living for the middle class rose during the century, the line separating it from the gentry blurred, but that intensified the need to draw a firmer line between the middle and the working classes below. Emerson was forthright on this topic at the time Thoreau was building his cabin at Walden Pond: "Cultivated people cannot live in a shanty," he declared in his journal in mid-1845.[17]

Thoreau's friends bandied about the word "shanty" when referring to the structure Thoreau built at Walden Pond—a structure that he disassembles, much as he did the shanty of James Collins, at the end of his 26-month sojourn in the woods. Thoreau's friend Daniel Ricketson, who built the replica of Walden on his family estate and who is said to have idolized Thoreau, made numerous allusions to Thoreau's "shanty," including a (feeble) sketch of Thoreau that he labeled "A Shanty Man." Another he captioned, "H. D. Thoreau returning to his shanty from Concord." A third sketch pictures Thoreau in a coonskin hat, that emblem of frontier life, and is titled "An Ideal Thoreau." In turn, Thoreau penned an extended description of Ricketson's "shanty" in his journal in April 1857, detailing the size (twelve by fourteen feet) and listing the materials, and making plain that a carpenter, not Ricketson himself, had built the shanty. Thoreau, ever a master of detail, even lists the books on Ricketson's shelves, which he dubs "'*Shanty Books*'" (italics and quotation marks in the original). These include a telling array of titles, including "Drake's 'Indians' . . . Zimmerman on Solitude . . . Farmer's 'Register of the First Settlers of New England,' . . . Downing's 'Landscape Gardening,' . . . Dwight's Travels . . . Virgil," and, buried mid-list, "'Walden.'" In what sense were these "'*Shanty Books*'"? Thoreau acknowledges the ambiguities of shanties and houses, the imprecision of the term and the meanings he has deliberately applied to them. Those italics and those quotation marks insist that readers consider the ironies inherent in the phrase, and by placing it at the end of a long list of varied book titles, as Thoreau does, a list that includes several standard tomes of a classical education, Thoreau winks at his own efforts to distinguish his house at Walden from the shanties that shared the landscape. "Shanty" is an unstable category, and Thoreau knows it.[18]

In attempting to distinguish between his house and other people's shanties, Thoreau creates a dilemma for himself. To make *Walden* more than a personal manifesto, he has to claim a place for it in the chronicle of American history; he has to locate it on a continuum anchored, at one end, by the colonial builders documented in his meditation on the meaning of shelter that forms the prologue to his narrative of home-building. But how can he claim colonial American precedents without acknowledging the shanties that are the direct descendants of the very house-building techniques documented by those foundational historians of the colonial American experiment? He does so by distinguishing the meaning of the shanty and the house on the basis of time and intention. Next, he relocates the terrain of the American frontier from geographical place to interior space, becoming a pioneer of the spirit. That accomplished, he adds a final touch, reimagining himself and his cabin at Walden as the original pioneers on the actual landscape, a feat accomplished with the imagination. In the end, Thoreau creates a tableau—wilderness, happy home-builder, cabin—that requires him to actively erase the Concord shantytowns peopled by laboring families like the Collinses. Shanties and their inhabitants end up shoved to the margins of the national project, while deliberators like himself take center stage, from which they "radiate" a new American landscape.[19]

The figure of the pioneer, and his place in American history, prove challenging for Thoreau. His struggle with the frontier ideal was a familiar one for Americans in the mid-1840s. As the nation became more populous, burgeoning with immigrants as well as native-born citizens more inclined to build and occupy cities, and crisscrossed by railroads, the question of what it meant to occupy a frontier became more complicated. When did colonists become immigrants, and settlers pioneers? Thoreau symbolically strikes out for the frontier, a place closer to nature and removed from urban centers of civilization, when he moves to Walden Pond. But at every turn, he resists the call of the wild, even as he trumpets the supremacy of nature. "It would be some advantage to live a primitive and frontier life, *though in the midst of an outward civilization,* if only to learn what are the gross necessities of life and what methods have been taken to obtain them" (emphasis mine). Repeatedly, Thoreau raises the idea of the frontier only to hedge his bets, skittering away to safer topics. His debates with himself mirror the tensions between improvement and progress, cultivation and wilderness, that were at the forefront of American life in the nineteenth century; these topics generated great anxiety. Thoreau's ambiguity on these issues reflect the very real ambivalence Americans felt at the time. Where was the "frontier"—somewhere on the western horizon? Or was the new frontier an economic frontier, visible in the deep cuts of the railroad tracks and the shanties of the workers who laid them? Should one aspire to occupy one or both frontiers—did they spread civilization, or threaten it?[20]

Thoreau's solution to his frontier dilemma is to reimagine American history with himself as first settler, and Walden as the first hut. In a chapter near the end of *Walden,* called "Former Inhabitants," Thoreau recalls the previous inhabitants of the woods. He remarks on the "dents" in the landscape, the remains of cellars built by the originally enslaved, later free black residents of a shantytown that occupied the woods after the Revolution; he lists several by name, noting that all now occupied "a narrow house," or grave. One, he notes, a barber named John Breed, occupied a "hut" that was "about the size of mine." Other former inhabitants include two Irish laborers, John Wyman, a potter, and his son Thomas; and the ditch-digger Hugh Quoil, a former soldier, who was the last inhabitant before Thoreau himself. "Alas! How little does the memory of these human inhabitants enhance the beauty of the landscape!," Thoreau exclaims. "Again, perhaps Nature will try, with me for a first settler, and my house raised last spring to be the oldest in the hamlet." At Walden Thoreau re-enacts the frontier experience on the long-settled New England landscape, claiming for himself the virtues associated with pioneers while projecting the less desirable qualities onto Irish shanty dwellers such as Hugh Quoil, John Wyman, John Field, and James Collins. One reason for the success of Thoreau's book is that it showed readers how to be a pioneer of the spirit—in the positive sense of civilizing the wilderness—without leaving home. The power of the book's example lies in Thoreau's ability to transform the shanty into a house: his superior intentions turn what had been an uncivilized and barbaric habitation into something beautiful and full of meaning.[21]

This is not, however, a benign reformulation of the American story. Lecturing on the topic of New England to a Baltimore audience in January 1843, Emerson conjured the American classical age of the "Indian in the woods," decried the disappearance of "heroic farming," and expressed his repulsion for "Irish laborers . . . low and semi-barbarous." But the lost pastoral landscape mourned by Emerson was largely a myth, an invention of the fretful elites who lived in the colonial-era villages being bypassed by a rapidly industrializing economy. By the middle of the nineteenth century, Concord was the icon of this romantic interpretation of the American landscape. In the wake of the railroads, factories, and canals that were taking over the landscape, New England elites "glorified New England village ways, creating as orthodoxy the village tradition that served as reflection of both a glorious past and a brimming future." Creating a landscape that in its very hills, dales, and Georgian houses evoked the democratic virtues of America's forebears required a conscious erasure of the manual laborers and the industrial enterprises that employed them. Thanks in large part to writers like Thoreau, Emerson, and Hawthorne, shanty-dwelling Irish railroad workers were left out of the romantic narrative that put towns like Concord at its center.[22]

Shanty dwellers like James Collins, and his counterparts in other eastern Massachusetts towns and cities, were living proof of the changing world against which New England elites mustered their considerable mythmaking skills. The village myth depended as much on ignoring the links to the future suggested by the camps and shantytowns of the floating proletariat epitomized by James Collins, as it did on linking the New England landscape to an imagined colonial past. Just as New England elites erased the memory of the "cramped cottage dwellings" of the "rude, pre-Revolution landscape," they erased the evidence of the crowded shanty dwellings of the rude, early industrial landscape. They erased not a past, but a present—the presence of self-built worker communities in urban areas, factory towns, and along the routes of public improvements like railroads and canals.[23]

Consider Thoreau's first encounter with the "rude" shanty of James Collins from its owner's point of view. Collins returned home one April evening to find Thoreau inspecting the interior of his house. Thoreau, whom Collins had observed recently cutting down some slender pines near the shore of Walden Pond, stood gingerly in the center of the room surrounded by several chickens, Collins's newborn baby, and his wife, whose excited voice Collins had heard when he walked up. "They're good boards overhead, good boards all around, and a good window," she declared, her voice fading on a feeble joke about broken panes making a passageway for the cat. Thoreau, a small man with calloused hands and a nose almost as large as his chin, seemed to be inventorying the contents of the shanty. His eyes skipped across the bed, stove, and bench to linger on the gilt-framed mirror, Mrs. Collins's silk parasol, and the coffee grinder James had nailed to the wall, all relics from the days of steady wages the previous year: 50 cents a day from the Fitchburg

Railroad for laying track and blasting through granite to make the Deep Cut. Collins could see, through the high window, the lighted lamp moving as his wife urged the visitor to notice the peaked roof, the solid walls, and the carefully placed floorboards, warning him not to stumble into the cellar hole. She told Collins later she had seen Thoreau peering through the window and circling the house, waiting for an invitation to step inside.[24]

When Collins greeted Thoreau, he recognized him as the man who burnt down the woods the previous spring by building a fire in a tree stump; the townspeople called him "woods burner." No surprise he was retreating into the woods to get away from those whispers. Thoreau asked Collins if he would sell him the shanty; he called it "an uncommonly fine one" and offered him $4.25. In return for payment on the spot, Collins agreed to be off the premises by dawn the next morning. What a relief the money was, as Collins had found no work once again that day, and the owner of the woodlot was likely to come the next morning to demand payment. The money would be enough to get them to a town further down the line, where the railroad was laying new track, or to Lowell, where Irish immigrants were at last being permitted to work inside the mills. Collins advised Thoreau to arrive early the next morning to avoid the landlord. Thoreau would, he knew, be dismantling the shanty to reassemble it somewhere else; in fact he looked very much like one of the men who had bought the shanties of two friends the previous fall, for building a shop in town. The bargain made, Collins turned his attention to packing the family's belongings. The stove was too big to move, but he thought he could maneuver the bed and the rest of the household goods into one bundle. Maybe the chickens too. The cat would have to fend for itself. At 6:00 a.m. the next morning, Collins and his family, toting their belongings, passed Thoreau on his way to claim their shanty. He was driving a cart, and cast a disapproving glance at Collins as he passed.[25]

The Collinses, and other laborers like them, left no journals or diaries or detailed inventories laying out what their homes and furnishings meant to them, but by reading against the grain of Thoreau's account, and investigating the decisions the Collinses made about their house and its possessions, an interpretation of the shanty from the owners' point of view emerges. Mrs. Collins was proud of the shanty, or at least knew how to emphasize its strong points: "good boards overhead, good boards all around, and a good window." But the Collinses' pride of place came through most clearly in the furnishing of the shanty. The stove, bed, lamp, and bench were efficient and useful; they reflected the Collinses' relative comfort and spoke loudly, although Thoreau did not hear, of the same warmth and light he so valued in a home. But it was the accessories that spoke the loudest. The gilt-framed looking glass, silk parasol, and "patent new coffee mill" were not necessities of life; that was the reason Thoreau scoffed at them, as indeed he disdained most interior furnishings. To the Collinses they would have represented aspiration, luxury, and abundance—three values Thoreau specifically disregarded as unworthy of "the indweller, who is the only builder."[26]

All three objects were also material signifiers for modernity. Parasols were considered a fitting, final touch to a lady's outfit in the 1840s, and though widely available in the United States, they still carried a whiff of European style. By 1845 they were made with collapsible rods, so they represented not only fashion and the means to acquire it—and the brass to display it—but an appreciation for technology as well. Collapsible handles improved portability, a convenience for middle-and upper-class ladies tucking them beneath their chairs, but also a nod to the mobility itinerant workers like the Collinses would have prized. Mirrors and coffee mills were similarly luxurious goods, also highly portable, that also reflected the influence of modern technology. A "patent new coffee mill" in 1845 would have been, quite literally, a recently patented coffee mill, a labor-saving convenience few Americans owned before the 1850s. They signaled both personal indulgence and sensory pleasure, as did the mirror and the parasol. Mirrors were precious objects, and a gilt frame, like a silk parasol, signaled both assertiveness and self-awareness. These were possessions that expressed aspirations, not necessarily to middle-class status, but to the comforts available in a rapidly industrializing America. Owning a parasol, a mirror, and a coffee grinder in a shanty in Shanty Field might also have signaled a status above that of recent immigrants; they may have marked the time invested in steady work on the railroad, or savings accrued bit by bit—or the generosity merited over time from an employer in an affluent household in Concord. Parasols, mirrors, and coffee grinders also connected the Collinses to a wider world beyond Concord, New England, and the United States, a world of European fashion and Brazilian coffee plantations, where identities could be assembled through a collage of consumer goods and the associations they carried. Thoreau sees the Collinses as one thing: Irish. The parasol, the coffee grinder, and the gilt-framed mirror define a wider range of personal identity, not excluding national origin but not confined to it.[27]

These possessions expressed class sentiments as well. Gilt-framed mirrors were a favorite decorative item among middle-class families in the 1840s, intended to show taste and refinement. The availability of consumer items like parasols and mirrors to lower-class people created great anxiety among the middle class, which found it increasingly difficult to tell them apart, especially in growing cities and towns. The Collinses's ownership of these products, which they cherished enough to take with them as they walked to a new destination the following day, reflects not only a certain financial wherewithal but an eagerness to display status that resists the strictures placed on them by their social "betters" in the middle class. Clearly the Collinses aspired to more than survival. They were not living by the rules Thoreau found laudable. Indeed, their possessions indicate that they explicitly rejected the "American" virtues Thoreau championed—austerity, simplicity, abstinence. For them, an American home was not a place to enshrine simplicity and survival, but a space in which to celebrate abundance and indulgence—even in the midst of poverty. In this they were no different from the middle-class readers Thoreau most hoped to convert, those who embraced the elaborately ornamented "cottage architecture" that was sweeping the country at the time through the publication of so-called "pattern books" of cookie-cutter designs that advocated turrets, arches, and the other architectural doodads so appropriately nicknamed "gingerbread." Thoreau lashes out against the superficiality of gee-gaw architecture, and the conspicuous consumption that it represented, in a society increasingly preoccupied with outward display. Instead, he champions inner strength. But these seemingly frivolous possessions mean something different to the Collinses, who, like their middle-class suburban counterparts, embraced symbols of exuberance.[28]

Shanties had a weightier symbolism for people in the Collinses' financial position. They stood for the ebb and flow of available work. The morning after buying the shanty from the Collinses, Thoreau dismantled it and, laying some boards to dry in the sun, hauled several cart-loads to his new home site. He is tipped off "by a young Patrick that neighbor Seeley, an Irishman, in the intervals of the carting, transferred the still tolerable, straight, and drivable nails, staples, and spikes to his pocket." But when Thoreau approached Seeley, he "stood when I came back to pass the time of day, and look freshly up,

unconcerned, with spring thoughts, at the devastation; there being a dearth
of work, as he said." Thoreau paints Seeley as a comic figure, a country rube
upset out of proportion to the "insignificant" dismantling of the shanty and
departure of the Collins family. For Thoreau he represented "spectatordom,"
an audience for the really important drama going on: the first act of Thoreau's
grand experiment at Walden. But for Seeley, the "devastation" of the shanty,
and the relocation of its owners, appears to symbolize the difficulty of finding
a job—"a dearth of work"—and, perhaps, the necessity of forever being on the
move in pursuit of the next one. Rather than acting as chorus to Thoreau's
Greek drama, more likely Seeley was there simply to say goodbye to the
Collins family, to scavenge some nails and staples to use in the construction
or repair of his own shanty, and in passing to express the intimate connection
between a lack of work, the destruction of a house, and the specter of famine.[29]

In *Walden,* Thoreau celebrates house-building as a spiritual, transcendent
activity. "There is some of the same fitness in a man's building his own house
that there is in a bird building its own nest. Who owns but if men constructed
their dwellings with their own hands, and provided food for themselves and
families simply and honestly enough, the poetic faculty would be universally
developed, as birds universally sing when they are engaged?" But such tran-
scendence is only available to the middle-class home-builder; Thoreau finds
nothing of poetry in the shanty. Much of the social meaning of Walden Pond
has derived from Thoreau's account of his artless cabin, which he invests with
American virtues of simplicity and self-reliance. For Thoreau, the crude huts
of the Irish workers expressed their shiftlessness—literally, a lack of resourcefulness, or "shift." But if any meaning is inherent in the shanty, it is the
resourcefulness required for its construction, resourcefulness no less than
that Thoreau expended in the construction of his cabin at Walden. That
potential meaning has been obscured by interpretations such as Thoreau's,
which equated the supposed crudeness of the shanty with the laziness and
lack of resourcefulness of its inhabitants.[30]

Walden induces a sort of cultural whiplash. Thoreau savages poor people's
dwellings, then holds them up as examples for the bourgeoisie: "The most
interesting dwellings in this country, as the painter knows, are the most
unpretending, humble log huts and cottages of the poor commonly; it is the
life of the inhabitants whose shells they are, and not any peculiarity in these
surfaces merely, which makes them *picturesque;* and equally interesting will

be the citizen's suburban box, when his life shall be as simple and agreeable to the imagination and there is as little straining after effect in the style of his dwelling." But when Thoreau encounters actual houses of the poor—shanties—his reaction is quite different. Home-building is not, as he argues, inherently ennobling. Simple homes are transformed, rather, by the intentions of the bourgeois home-builder. Despite its superficial similarities to shanties then being built on the frontier and in his own neighborhood, the house he builds at Walden Pond cannot be a shanty. Thoreau's self-conscious aspirations make that impossible.[31]

In 1851, only a few years before the publication of *Walden,* Herman Melville wrote to Nathaniel Hawthorne from his farm in Pittsfield, MA, that he was "busy building some shanties of houses (connected with the old one) and likewise some shanties of chapters and essays." After much "ploughing and sowing and raising and printing and praying," the author had reached "a less bristling time" in his construction project, yet the book at that point known as *The Whale* remained an "urgent" occupation, being "only half through the press." In comparing the building of his farmhouse to the writing of his novel, Melville counted on Hawthorne to understand the similarities between shanties built of wood and shanties made of words. The term "shanty" indicated effort but not accomplishment. Classifying his work, written or built, as a shanty acknowledged the use of the word to signify work but not status, potential but not accomplishment.[32]

Constructed in haste and of necessity, shantytowns in the first half of the nineteenth century were stubborn reminders of the poverty that accompanied urbanization and industrialization, a pitfall that Americans thought could be avoided, or that would at most be temporary. The persistence of shantytowns ran counter to the American ideal of the small town, the factory town, the big city, even, as time passed, of the western frontier. Like poverty, they were supposed to be temporary, obliterated by progress. Middle-class observers might have interpreted their longevity as proof of a flaw in industrial capitalism. They might have admired the resourcefulness of a James Collins or the resilience of a Seeley, or heard an echo of a middle-class matron's pride in Mrs. Collins's boast that her shanty had "good boards all around." Instead, middle-class observers perceived shanties as degraded and shanty dwellers as deviants. Virtues of independence and self-reliance like Thoreau celebrated at Walden were reserved for citizens with time for introspection, who were able to

self-consciously impute meaning to their choices of housing style and materials. Even when shanties looked strong and secure, the middle class could
condemn them as lower class, as evidence of degradation.

Since at least the 1820s, poor laborers have built houses for themselves
from materials at hand, creating communities that sometimes lasted only
until the canal was dug, the factory built, or the rail laid, but sometimes persisted for decades in the same spots. For at least as long, shantytowns have
been used as rhetorical devices in debates over class, community, and individualism. As much as *Walden* has to tell us about what it means to be an
American, it raises more questions than it answers. Why did Thoreau have
such a visceral reaction to Irish immigrants like James Collins, and, more
specifically, to their proliferation on the American landscape? Why has James
Collins been so thoroughly forgotten, not only by readers, but by historians,
annotators, and re-enactors, who have painstakingly sifted Thoreau's words
and religiously reconstructed replicas of his famous cabin at Walden? James
Collins's shanty reminds us that Thoreau's *Walden* is not the whole story, that
there are other, hidden stories waiting to be found on the American landscape. To find those stories, and the answer to these questions, we have to go
back another generation, to join a Connecticut doctor named Zerah Hawley
as he sets out for the western frontier from his ancestral home in New Haven.
Like Thoreau, he is a son of New England trying to make sense of where
America is going, with a cultural compass firmly aimed at the "true America."

2

Shanties on the Western Frontier

On October 7, 1820, a transplanted Connecticut doctor named Zerah Hawley bumped across the muddy, rutted back roads of Ashtabula County, Ohio, to examine a young patient living in "what is here called a *Shanty,*" which he described to his brother in a letter shortly afterwards. "This is a hovel of about ten feet by eight, made somewhat in the form of an ordinary cow-house, having but an half roof, or roof on one side. It is however, inclosed [*sic*] on all sides." Hawley is surprised by the shanty—a word he has not heard for a kind of house he has not seen before—and he comes back to the subject in subsequent letters home. Hawley's account of his year-long sojourn on the Ohio frontier was published two years later, and his descriptions of shanties constitute the first appearance of the word "shanty" in print in the United States. Since the provenance of the word remains unclear today, Hawley's account, and the circumstances of its occurrence, frame how we understand the presence and the presentation of shanties on the American landscape. The evidence of shanties forces a re-examination of the myth of the American frontier that developed in the two decades following Hawley's tour of the Western Reserve, the roots of the frontier myth in colonial settlement, and the power that the frontier myth continues to wield in popular culture today. Depictions of the frontier in early nineteenth-century travel literature, fiction, and art not only acknowledged the presence of shanties but wielded them as symbols in debates about American history and identity. That discourse starts with Hawley, and his arrival at the physical and imaginative boundaries of the young nation.[1]

The youngest of six sons of a rural Congregationalist pastor, Zerah Hawley graduated from Yale University in 1803 and opened a medical practice in New Haven shortly after. A proud son of New England, Hawley was a direct descendant of a colonial governor of Connecticut; the area where he lived with his wife Harriet and their four children had been occupied by his family since the mid-seventeenth century. But in 1820 he was struggling financially, teaching himself dentistry on the side to augment his modest medical income. How to get ahead? Two of Hawley's brothers had already settled on the Ohio frontier; their examples may have been persuasive. The accounts of outsized success on the Western Reserve—the former "New Connecticut" territory that became part of northern Ohio in 1803—also proved seductive. Land agents and missionaries depicted a promised land of "eminent advantages" where the soil was "naturally fertile," the climate "more mild than the sea-board," and the landscape "smooth and free from stone." "The hand of providence has rarely bestowed a more rich profusion of the necessaries, conveniences, delicacies and luxuries of life, on any portion of the globe," asserted a testimonial printed in the *Hartford Times* in April 1817. But Hawley, cautious, insisted on seeing the frontier for himself before uprooting his family from their ancestral lands. So in September 1820 he set off to visit his brothers Orestes, a doctor, and Timothy, a clerk of court, in Ohio, and evaluate the frontier for himself.[2]

He could hardly have been more disappointed. The journey itself was miserable; the road was stubborn with tree stumps, and at one point the wheels of Hawley's carriage got stuck in the sand on the beaches of Lake Erie. But Hawley expected discomfort. It was the lack of gentility that he found in both the inhabitants and their built environment that alarmed and insulted him, the slackening of manners and abandonment of material comfort that Hawley believed had informed their backgrounds as the sons and daughters, or at most grandsons and granddaughters, of New England. The Western Reserve had been populated largely by New Englanders, and Hawley encountered traces of that landscape in the form of central town greens and protestant churches sporting the solid columns and sleek steeples of Greek Revival architecture. The bulk of the landscape, however, testified to the breakdown of allegiance to New England precedents. Everywhere he looked, Hawley saw signs of degradation, from men's manners ("rude and uncultivated"), to women's clothing ("very ancient") and hairstyles ("uncouth"), and even the weather ("violent"). He documented his observations in a series of letters written to his oldest brother, who remained in Connecticut. Upon his return to New Haven a year later, Hawley published his forthright assessment of the

Ohio frontier, declaring it his duty to "undeceive the community, respecting a portion of the Western country, which has been represented as an earthly Paradise." His detailed reports on the region became a classic of frontier *reportage,* a bracing corrective to the effusive forecasts of government officials, missionaries, and real estate boosters.

> It seemed to me proper, also, and not only proper, but an imperative obligation imposed on me, to give what I know to be a true and faithful account of the privations and disadvantages, under which the inhabitants of that part of the country . . . have to contend . . . with little hope that the succeeding generation can enjoy many of the privileges of an old settled and highly favoured country.[3]

Hawley lingered for almost a year in several different small towns on the eastern edge of the Ohio frontier, earning money as an itinerant doctor. As he visited houses of the poor and the affluent, he recorded the materials, construction, interior furnishings, and characteristics of the inhabitants. Starting with Hawley's first letter home, shanties emerge as a key source of his general disgust and disappointment, and they quickly become prime pieces of evidence in Hawley's prosecution of the American frontier as degraded and degrading. His descriptions of shanties show Hawley grappling with what, exactly, a shanty is and how, in the progressive trajectory of the United States, such unprepossessing housing could persist. From its first appearance in print, the shanty was a venue for the encounter between what was old and what was new in America, both materially and culturally. And from the start, the virtues of resourcefulness, economic aspiration, and domesticity inherent in the shanty go unremarked by a more refined observer, someone presenting himself as an emissary from the real America, the "old settled and highly favourable country" of the eastern seaboard.

Hawley's first encounter with a shanty provoked his description of it as a "hovel," reminding him of a cow-shed. Having gone to the edges of European settlement in North America, Hawley, like many who emigrated from populated areas to the American frontier, believed they would encounter an idyllic landscape, a promised land. The shape and content of that promise varied; in Hawley's case it meant an orderly built environment overflowing with natural bounty—an idealized Puritan New England. With this "cultural grid" in mind, Hawley fully expected to find re-creations of the town greens of New England, studded with emblems of church and state power. His expectations were shaped by his Congregationalist mindset, and his judgment was clouded by the false prophecies of land agents. But Hawley's reactions also speak to the tenacity of the trust Americans placed in the frontier: the confidence that the frontier would deliver outsized expectations was the same as when the first colonists stepped ashore in the seventeenth century. Shanties did not belong on the frontier of Hawley's imagination, primed as it was by the origin stories of his Connecticut forebears, and the exaggerated promotions of contemporary government, real estate boosters, and missionaries. Hawley's physical journey to an economic and geographic frontier, to "the west," was as much a journey into the cultural geography of expectations of progress and development that came to define American identity in the early nineteenth century. Shanties shocked Hawley.[4]

How did shanties, the word and the house form, arrive on the Western Reserve? Etymologies of the word—also spelled "chanty," "shantie," and "shantee"—propose several origins, the most popular being a Canadian corruption of the French *chantier*—a work yard or site—but used in Canada (as "chanty") by 1824, according to the Oxford English Dictionary *OED,* to refer to a log dwelling in the forest where woodcutters assemble during the winter months. ("Chanty-man," a French Canadian term for lumberman, is synonymous with *"homme de chantier."*) Either of those derivations might account for Hawley's encounter with the word used to describe housing in the Western Reserve, for there were, at least by 1824, groups of Irish workers building the Ohio and Erie Canals; and descendants of French colonists occupying areas near the failed late eighteenth-century settlement at Gallipolis and, later, the southeastern part of the state. Hawley's tentative introduction of "what is here called a *Shanty*" shows both his own unfamiliarity with the word and that it is commonplace in northeastern Ohio. Hawley finds it in the Western Reserve, a part of the frontier occupied in the early nineteenth century by several migrant groups: native-born Americans of German and Scotch-Irish ancestry relocating from New England, Pennsylvania, and New York; immigrants from England; and immigrants from Canada, possibly with Scottish roots. It appears that native-born American pioneers adopted a housing form originally imported to the region by settlers with Irish or French origins, and that by 1820 it was a staple on the American frontier. The landscape that Hawley finds is not the copycat New England landscape he expected, but a mottled landscape that was a by-product of transnational ethnic and geographic flux. Hawley could not fit the shanty into a familiar framework of housing styles because it existed outside the settled, eastern framework, and outside the imaginative frontier he had constructed from the contemporary accounts of land speculators and missionaries.[5]

As he visited more shanties, Hawley elaborated on their appearance in subsequent letters to his brother in Connecticut.

> As I did not give you a full description of a Shanty, in my first letter, under date of October 7th, I will do it in this place. It is a tenement, (if so it may be called,) built of logs split through the centre, having the plain surface inwards, and the bark without. They are generally about ten or twelve feet square, with a roof on one side, in the manner that horse-sheds are frequently built; consequently they have no chamber at all.

Hawley struggles to categorize the shanty. He acknowledges that calling it a tenement seems imprecise, as the word "tenement" was synonymous with "house," and by that time associated with brick construction, and used to affirm ownership of real property. Hawley describes a shanty built of logs split in two: based on descriptions of frontier housing in Canada during the same time period, it's possible that what he actually saw was a house built of "slabs," the outermost, waste cut of the log, left shaggy with bark, which would have had a similar appearance. In any case, the logs were not hewn—which distinguished them from the log cabins and "block houses" he saw elsewhere—and they were encrusted with bark. As in his first letter, Hawley notes that the shanty is crowded, with four people occupying one single ten-by-eight room, and that its form reminds him of a slant-roofed shed built to house animals. That slanted roof gave the shanty the look of a freestanding lean-to. Hawley's desire to describe it to his brother fully and accurately shows both its importance on the frontier landscape and its lack of reference in their shared geography. In early-nineteenth-century Ohio, Hawley finds people living in a structure that was unfamiliar to him from his youth and adulthood in Connecticut, and unobserved on his recent trek through Massachusetts, Pennsylvania, and New York, enroute to northeastern Ohio. The wave of factory and canal construction that was to bring shanties and their builders to

New England had not yet begun when Hawley left on his trek in the fall of 1820. The unfamiliar "shanty" suggests Irish or French origins that complicate the historical narratives of the Western Reserve as a land settled by native-born New Englanders, a sort of extension of New England itself. The remix of settlers requires a rethinking of the landscape they made and occupied to include house forms such as the shanty. Not only the population, but the landscape itself was an assemblage.[6]

Hawley documented a number of details about the shanties he visited. None had windows; a hole in the roof admitted light. Some had chimneys, but many did not, and those without were extremely smoky inside. Smoke puffed out through the skylight, or "through the large openings between the logs." These were chinked in the winter with clay, which, drying, shattered into powder on the floor, where it mingled with bits of bark drifting from the split-log roof. Lacking a lock, the single door to the shanty was fastened when the family was out "by a stick of wood leaning against it." That door, hung on wooden hinges, always opened outward in order to preserve interior floor space. Furniture was "much more rude, and less abundant" than in what Hawley described as "ordinary houses," by which he meant the frame houses of New England. All of the activities of the household were carried on in the same single room:

> The bed extended across the end opposite the door within about two feet leaving a space at the foot for a barrel or two, and an area in front of about six feet by eight in which were performed all the domestic operations. I need not give a description of the furniture, as every one can imagine for themselves what it must, or rather, what it *must not* be . . .[7]

In this first printed account of a shanty in the United States, the author followed a pattern that would reappear in descriptions of shanties and shantytowns through the end of the nineteenth century, similar to those we find in Thoreau. The shanty is described in terms of absence, of what it lacks—locks, chimneys, interior walls, adequate floor space, half a roof—in terms of what it is decisively not: a proper house or "tenement." Can it even be considered a house? Is it not closer in form to a shed for animals, a "hovel" for people instead of cows? It is always disorienting to encounter shanties, which are somehow unimaginable and yet thoroughly comprehensible to their elite observers: "every one can imagine for themselves what it must, or rather, must not be." Hawley established a dichotomy between a "real" home and a shanty facsimile that distinguishes descriptions of shanties to this day, while also ascribing to the reader—educated, middling class, eastern, of European extraction—an ability to imagine, without ever seeing, the lives of the poor. The impression is that shanties are imagined by necessity, because they are so out of sync with what the observer knows or assumes about the lives of Americans, even on the frontier.

Hawley's tone is straightforward; he does not strain to demean the shanty or its inhabitants. But he fails to see them as anything but less-than. From their earliest appearance in American literature, shanties are shadows of houses, prototypes but never archetypes, despite their proliferation on the landscape. Hawley's overall reaction to the shanty is surprise that such housing exists in America, a sense of surprise that is redoubled when he visits the homes of the more affluent and "titled" in northeastern Ohio, the judges and legislators and merchants who constitute the frontier elite, only to find them living in log houses and block houses not so much better than shanties. Continuing to live in what Hawley considered substandard housing betrays, he believes, a lack of ambition and initiative, not only on the part of the poor but in the lives of the privileged: "If such are the residences of the Honourable," Hawley writes after a visit to a judge's log house, "what must be those of the vulgar."[8]

Hawley's harangues about the deficiencies of Ohio and Ohioans are somewhat naive, for they ignore the rational reasons for being on the frontier in the first place: the economic payoffs for persevering, struggling and making do. One oft-quoted scene of deprivation involves Hawley's shock at encountering a man so parsimonious that he used the same set of eating utensils for 17 years; in another passage Hawley wrings his hands about the lackadaisical attitude to removing one's hat indoors. But by 1825, with the wave of prosperity that accompanied the construction on the Erie Canal, the frugality of the inhabitants of the shanties, log houses, and block houses of the Ohio frontier was bearing fruit. In a way unimaginable to Hawley, shanties were in fact a harbinger of economic prosperity. In Hawley's equation, the potential financial bonanza did not balance the loss of civility, a decline charted in part by the kinds of houses occupied by the residents of the Western Reserve. But native-born migrants to that frontier were rewarded with economic advancement, a development that fueled a boom in the sort of boosterish frontier literature that Hawley set out to ridicule in the first place.

The housing form that Hawley found so perplexing actually had a long history in the American colonies and the early republic. While it may have been absent from Hawley's reckoning of America's westward movement, it was in fact a staple of that expansion from the very earliest colonial encampments. The first English colonists lived in conical huts of branches, rushes, and turf, modeled on dwellings in rural England. For some these huts were a step down from what they had left behind in England, but not for all. As Fiske Kimball has noted, "although to the gentlemen who were the leaders and chroniclers, their first abodes in the new world were mean enough compared with those to which they were accustomed, to many farm servants and poor people the rude shelters meant no more than a perpetuation of conditions at home." Edward Johnson, one of the early arrivals in Massachusetts Bay (quoted by Thoreau as "Old Johnson" in *Walden*), wrote in 1654 that the settlers "burrow themselves in the Earth for their first shelter under some Hill side, casting the Earth aloft upon Timber . . . yet in these poor *Wigwames* [they stay] till they can provide them houses." The founders of Philadelphia in 1682 built cave-like shelters by digging into the ground about three feet, "thus making half their chamber underground, and the remaining half above ground was formed of sods of earth, or earth and brush combined. The roofs were formed of layers of limbs, or split pieces of trees overlaid with sod or bark, river rushes, etc." The earliest timber construction in the colonies, around 1629, consisted of tree trunks or planks aligned vertically, in the manner of palisades, a method used as late as 1684 by British settlers to New Jersey. Only in Georgia, founded in 1733, were log houses used from the start, and even there the earliest dwellings were unframed "Clap-board huts."[9]

During the 1840 "Log Cabin Campaign" for president, a national myth developed that America's forefathers lived in log cabins. But as the work of architectural historians and archaeologists has shown, the earliest settlers started out not in log cabins, but in what were later known as shanties. "The early chronicles of almost every colony from Massachusetts Bay to the Carolinas clutter the landscape with shantytowns of huts, hovels, tents, cabins, caves, and dugouts," Kimball wrote in his classic study of colonial American architecture. Consistently, these dwellings were labeled temporary by observers, despite evidence to the contrary; often these "wigwams" and "dugouts" housed occupants for extended periods of time. While the expectation was that they would serve for only a few months, Cornelius van

Tienhoven, another historian quoted by Thoreau, described New Netherlands colonists who kept "dry and warm in these [dugout] houses with their entire families for two, three, or four years." Clearly, impermanence was in the eye of the beholder. Even affluent colonists started out in huts, van Tienhoven notes, in order not to waste time building that should be spent planting, and "in order not to discourage poorer laboring people who they brought over in numbers from Fatherland."[10]

But from the moment of landfall, there was pressure on colonists to improve their housing. Just as Hawley applied a standard set in Connecticut to the frontier housing he saw in 1820, early correspondents applied a European or English yardstick to the housing they saw in the American colonies. In the Massachusetts Bay, according to Johnson, by 1654 "[t]he Lord hath been pleased to turn all the wigwams, huts, and hovels the English dwelt in at their first coming into orderly, fair and well built houses"—what Hawley, almost two centuries later, would call "ordinary houses." Even before they left the old country, colonists were taught to imagine a steady progression of housing types that would reflect a predictable rise in affluence. A promotional pamphlet written in 1650 described "six sorts" of dwellings in America: the newcomer's wigwam; the earthfast house; an "Irish" house of posts, wattle, and turf; a log house; a thatched or tiled mud house; and a brick house. Only the last was undeniably permanent, but each represented an improvement over the one before. From a wigwam or dugout, colonists were expected to graduate to a more durable but still impermanent form of shelter known as the "earthfast" house. Common on Anglo-Saxon and medieval sites, "earthfast" dwellings were constructed of timbers embedded in the ground in some fashion. Variations included posts sunk upright in the ground, palisades-style ("hole-set"); or timbers laid directly on the ground or secured in shallow trenches ("ground-standing" or "ground-laid"). One manual described earthfast houses as "a clove board house nailed to posts." A few years after building an earthfast house, colonists aspired to a yet more impressive framed house.[11]

Steady, visible upgrades in housing were important to Puritan leaders who believed their improvement of the land entitled them to possess it—one of the major justifications for taking land, by force when necessary, from Native Americans who occupied it. New England colonists used Native Americans' nomadic practices and collective stewardship of the land, as opposed to individual ownership of it, as excuses for dispossessing them. Indians were not

visibly improving the land and therefore were not entitled to it. The argument
that English settlers were improving the land was made visible by orderly
farms and successive generations of increasingly sturdy houses. Historian
William Cronon quotes Puritan leader Francis Higginson: "The *Indians* are
not able to make use of the one fourth part of the Land, neither have they any
settled places, as Townes to dwell in, nor any ground as they challenge for
their own possession, but change their habitation from place to place."
Cronon argues that New England Puritans used Indians' mobility to deny
their claim to the land that they hunted. "A people who moved so much and
worked so little did not deserve to lay claim to the land they inhabited."
Progress and improvement, reflected in housing, were signs of divine favor. A
colonist's failure to improve his housing was a failure, therefore, to participate
in the collective justification for the repossession of Native American lands.
No wonder colonial leaders nagged settlers to build bigger and better houses.[12]

But clearly, many either could not or chose not to. "One, two, three—hovel,
house, home. In settlement after settlement that was the beau ideal, not for
everyone, of course, and not invariably even for those so minded . . . The
standard was often easier to imagine than to meet." Just three years after
Philadelphia's founding, town leaders tried to put a stop to the construction
of the half-submerged "caves" favored by newcomers, but settlers continued
to build them nonetheless well into the eighteenth century. In 1704 a Boston
woman traveling through the Narragansett country in what is now Rhode
Island was shocked to find a remnant of the earthfast tradition, a windowless,
floorless cottage "enclosed with Clapboards laid on Lengthways." She declares
that "little Hutt *cq* was one of the wretchedest I ever saw a habitation for
human creatures."[13]

That traveler, teacher and businesswoman Sarah Kemple Knight, was surprised to see what she believed to be an anachronism. Wretched huts represented the starting point from which domestic space had presumably evolved.
Huts, wigwams, and dugouts signified the very beginning of the home-
steading process, begun at landfall; their persistence on the landscape was
troubling. No doubt much of the reason was aesthetic: ramshackle huts did
not conform to the Georgian symmetry embraced by tasteful society in the
eighteenth century. But the response also had an ideological component.
These impermanent structures were supposed to be swept away by the march
of progress, just as the transients who occupied them (or were believed to

occupy them) were supposed to transform into rooted, contributing members of American society. To fail to do so was to endanger the entire American colonial (and subsequently, national) project. Colonial and then national leaders and government officials attempted to enforce orderly settlement patterns with some urgency. The belief was common among government officials and policymakers that "compact settlement" and an "orderly frontier" were literally necessary to ensure republican liberty. Policymakers were convinced that "republican institutions would only take root where orderly and industrious settlers were organized in compact settlements." Out of such a commitment to order grew the idea for the Northwest Ordinance of 1785, a vast, abstract gridding of the entire nation. The grid facilitated buying and selling of land, yes, but it was also a manifestation of the idea of orderly settlement as a foundation for American liberty.[14]

The fear of disorder on the physical frontier grew in part out of a fear of disorderly persons, namely the squatters who were by 1780 moving across the Ohio River and forming dispersed, unregulated settlements. Squatters not only located their houses and farms willy-nilly, but built them without securing title to the land. It was difficult in practice for state authorities to distinguish between legal and illegal settlers. Squatters, operating outside of the emerging real estate market, were anathema to the ideal of orderly settlement. Federal surveyors often branded them as undisciplined and savage, "roaming" and "rambling" across the land; George Washington fretted about them in his letters. In 1782, Hector de Crevecoeur warned in his popular *Letters from an American Farmer* that the frontier could cause men to revert to savagery. "There men appear to be no better than carnivorous animals of a superior rank." Squatters—so necessary to the initial repossession of frontier lands from Native Americans and competing colonial powers in the seventeenth century—were by the 1780s the enemies of national expansion. A federal surveyor remarked in 1786 that "this lawless set of fellows . . . are more our enemies than the most brutal savages of the country."[15]

The standardized sale of land enabled by the Northwest Ordinance was designed to block obviously poor, allegedly lazy squatters from the frontier, creating a geographical space that harmonized with the abstract goals of the Ordinance and the ideology of federal policy makers. "The land system itself would teach settlers to 'see' the western landscape—and their own opportunities within it—through the pattern of the grid that specified specific property holdings. Rational, systematic settlement would help create enlightened communities." Early American leaders pinned their hopes for liberty and freedom not on the individual, but on the group, the community, the neighborhood. Squatters were individuals, none more so. But settlement by clusters of settlers, not by individuals or lone families, was the ideal represented by the Northwest Ordinance. To generate development, frontier settlers needed to create neighborhoods, guided by the Northwest Ordinance land system. A methodical national expansion would also ensure the continuation of the Union at a time when East-West fissures were more troubling than North-South divisions, and the threat posed to national expansion by Britain and other colonial powers would not expire until the close of the War of 1812.[16]

In the campaign to impose order on the expansion of the United States, squatters were degraded and demonized for their seemingly haphazard settlement patterns. Squatters' construction of huts, hovels, and shanties, and their continued occupation of these less formal types of housing persisted past the point at which officials expected them to upgrade. As presented by the authors of the how-to literature for emigrants, shanties became a handy means of labeling underperforming members of society. While the imposition of the Northwest Ordinance literally dispossessed squatters, throwing them off land to which they had no legal title, a strict hierarchy of housing types promoted in the emigrant literature set the terms for culturally dispossessing squatters as well: a failure to move up the scale from shanty to house called into question the legitimacy of the builder's claim on not only land, but citizenship.

A special genre of promotional literature developed to instruct aspiring emigrants on how to proceed and what to expect when they arrived on the American frontier. Designed to educate as well as to entice, emigrant literature in English first appeared in the seventeenth century in the form of pamphlets, books, and letters targeting audiences in Scotland, Ireland, and the eastern United States. A genre of travel literature, the emigrant guides functioned as both classified ad and real estate brochure, luring settlers to the North American frontier and preparing them for the journey and transition to new lands. The authors had nationalistic, commercial, and political motivations. Emigration was seen as a way of cementing the home country's claims to new lands, but also as a way of exporting poverty. Emigrant literature thrived, for example, in nineteenth-century Scotland and Ireland following massive agricultural crises, the dislocations of the Industrial Revolution, and the political unrest resulting from both. The language of the guides was declarative, but they brimmed with instruction, and sought to paint the sponsoring organizations, often government agencies or charitable organizations, as benevolent. Authors of emigrant literature, who were often shipping agents employed by the charitable societies sponsoring emigration, covered everything from what to pack to what climate to expect when one landed in North America. As the century progressed, these guides were often written, or at least presented, as first-person accounts by people who had successfully emigrated.[17]

Housing was a focus of every emigrant guide. One of the best-known accounts of emigrant literature, generally referred to by the shortened title of the 1940 reprint, *An Account of Early Settlements in Upper Canada,* was written in 1821—virtually the same moment Hawley set out on his journey to the western frontier—by Robert Lamond, an agent for the Glasgow Emigration Committee. Formed in 1820 to resettle handloom weavers thrown out of work by the Industrial Revolution and the widespread economic depression following the Napoleonic Wars, the Emigration Committee sent several hundred families to the colony of New Lanark, located 200 miles north of Montreal on the St. Lawrence River. The British government granted 100 acres to each adult settler, and according to Lamond's account, 6,281 residents of Lanark and Renfrew Counties applied for passage. The original title of Lamond's report, addressed to the government, tells us much about the intentions of the Glasgow Emigration Committee, the concerns of the emigrants, and the uncertainties involved in undertaking such a transatlantic relocation: *A Narrative of the Rise and Progress of Emigration from the Counties of Lanark and Renfrew, to the New Settlements in Upper Canada, on Government Grant; Comprising the Proceedings of the Glasgow Committee for Directing the Affairs and Embarkation of the Societies—With a Map of the Townships, Designs for Cottages, and a Plan of the Ship Earl of Buckinghamshire. Also, Interesting Letters from the Settlements.* Although directed at a specific audience, the report is a representative example of emigrant literature as a whole.[18]

The designs for cottages mentioned in the title were accompanied by substantial written descriptions and detailed illustrations. Laid out on special plates in the middle of the book, like a spread from a twenty-first-century shelter magazine, the illustrations chart a gradual ascent from "1. A Hut or

Wigwam," described as "generally the first habitation in the woods," through "9. A Plan and Elevation of a Farm Establishment," which encompassed "dwelling-house, barn, loft, stables, and offices." The illustrations are not a menu, but a to-do list: the clear implication is that the emigrant started at the bottom and proceeded, inexorably, to the top. As in the earliest literature of its kind, the "hut or wigwam" is described as either conical or oblong, and made of wooden poles sunk into the ground. "Take, for instance, four poles, of about fifteen feet in length," read one set of instructions. "Place them from eight to ten feet asunder and sink the lower end of each pole about two feet into the ground: with four pieces of timber, form a square sufficient to let out the smoke: incline the poles to the small square at the top; and, if nails are not to be obtained, they may be bound together with *wythe rods*, birch-bark, or by green birch-wood, strung out as ropes; or thick twine may be used for the purpose: the sides can be filled up on the easiest principle, with the branches of trees or spars." A fire was to be "kindled in the centre of the floor, on fire dogs, or cast or wrought iron."[19]

Shanties appear second on the list of cottage designs, and again construction materials and the handling of fire define the structure, designated as "2. A Shade or Shantie." Printed in Glasgow just a year before Hawley's indictment of the Western Reserve was published in New Haven, CT, Lamond's specifications for a shanty differ significantly from those listed by Hawley. Indeed, the two overlap on only one point: the slanted roof.

> A Shade or Shantie—built of rough logs, or boards, and roofed with hollow bas-wood, resembling a tile roof. The fire may be kindled on the floor, or, if it is wished, on the side of the house: the chimney must be built of stone, brick, or such incombustible materials as can be found at hand. Small Canadian stoves, of cast-iron, would be very useful, if the Emigrants could afford to take them along with them. A pit may be made in the floor, for preserving potatoes, &c. from the frost, during winter.[20]

Lamond's "shade or shantie," like Hawley's, is sometimes but not always constructed of unhewn, "rough" logs. And as the illustration accompanying Lamond's text shows, the shanty is distinguished by a slanted roof. The two pages of illustrations show the stark visual difference between a conical hut, a slant-roofed shanty, and a framed house. The importance of the gabled roof,

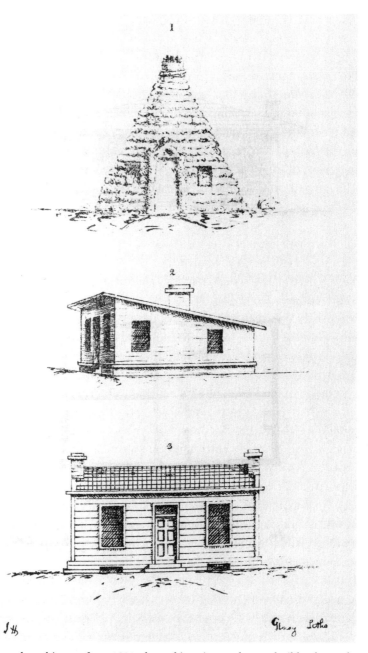

Manuals such as this one, from 1821, showed immigrants how to build a shanty, but warned they should be temporary, not permanent shelters.

and the placement of the gable—at the sides, or at the front of the house—telegraphs status, because it accentuates the height and grandeur of the structure. The shanty did not speak in such clear architectural tones, yet it enunciated a cultural code. The shanty constituted a housing type in its own right, but it was an ambivalent and ambiguous form. In material construction, it was not as specific as "clapboard," for example, and in architectural style it lacked the precision of "Palladian" or "Georgian." A largely overlooked vernacular style of construction, shanties vary in construction materials and techniques and occupy a wide range of visual forms. They are identifiable only in comparison or relation to other, more narrowly defined house forms, generally in terms of what they lack—a pitched roof, an external fireplace, a wooden floor—and even then, the material criteria are malleable. The fuzziness of the shanty form is an essential aspect of its definition, because in the end, shanties are defined in terms of the people who build and inhabit them, not by any particular assemblage of materials in any particular form.

In *The Farmers and Emigrants Complete Guide,* first published in 1845, author Josiah T. Marshall weighs the decision to build a shanty versus a house: "Some will advise a *house* to be first built, others a 'shanty;' but the latter is so expeditiously done, and is so much cheaper, and a comfortable house till the emigrant gets 'acclimated,' that we consider it the best." In the how-to literature, shanties are presented as temporary housing suitable for a temporary condition—the period before immigrants became accustomed to their new surroundings. The construction of a "real" house becomes a sign of increasing affluence, a marker of prosperity. Immigrants should not build houses before they are "acclimated"; neither should they remain in shanties once they are established in the community. To do so, Marshall implies, would send the wrong signal about their place in society. A shanty, therefore, becomes a voluntary yet temporary symbol of outsider status, and its replacement with a house a sign of improving financial and social standing—a condition synonymous with being an insider in American society.[21]

"I incline myself to the regular routine," wrote one English emigrant in 1837; "a wigwam the first week; a shanty till the log house is up; and a frame, brick or stone house half a dozen years hence." Six years may have been an optimistic estimate. Some seem to have been built with a certain amount of care. In 1853, Samuel Strickland and a friend put up the walls and roofed his shanty in one day, but then spent a week "chinking between the logs and plastering up all the crevices, cutting out a doorway and a place for a window, casting them, making a door and hanging it." In Canada, settlers sometimes added a fireplace to their shanties, with a chimney consisting of "a wooden framework, placed on a stone foundation . . . raised a few feet from the ground, leading through the roof with its sides closed up with clay and straw kneaded together." Once a log house was built, shanties were sometimes used to house animals, as were log cabins if a frame house was eventually built.[22]

For writers of emigrant literature, the shanty embodied the tension between progress and backwardness, but it was nothing to be ashamed of *unless it was occupied for too long*. For readers of emigrant literature, the shanty was intended to be a foot in the door, a way to stake a claim. In these works, the shanty is not demeaned, but the imperatives of the how-to genre make it clear that success as a settler was measured by how quickly one advanced from a hut or shanty to a frame house. Success was not to be enjoyed in a shanty. The injunction not to tarry in a shanty was offered as pragmatic advice, as was the injunction to mark your status as a newcomer by beginning with a shanty, not a frame house. In this way, the pageant of American improvement was enacted on the frontier landscape. Writers of emigrant literature stoked the frontier myth with the promise of waves of visible improvements: slant-roofed shanties giving way to milled timber cabins which are then replaced by gabled or hip-roofed frame houses, houses that then acquire, according to Lamond's prescription, not only "proper drains" and plastered facades, but casement windows, porticos, "a rustic railing," a "zigzag fence," and "a live hedge." In his closing remarks to would-be settlers, Lamond expresses the spirit and vision of emigrant literature: "In the designs given, the Emigrant will be able to select the one most adapted to his peculiar circumstances; and, while no person ought to neglect the more important matters of clearing and stocking his farm, a good taste displayed by a few leading families, whose exertions and increasing means may place them in a situation of extending their accommodations and conveniences, will gradually induce others to follow their example." In a land of rustic fences and proper drains, in neighborhoods drawn with crisp geometric precision along the lines of grids extending from the original colonies to the Pacific Ocean, American liberty and freedom would thrive, and the proof will be "good taste." Or so policymakers promised.[23]

But on the ground, whether on the Atlantic coast of the seventeenth century or the Western Reserve in the early nineteenth century, things were messier. As the testimony of emigrants themselves attests, some advanced according to plan: wigwam, shanty, house. Others lingered in shanties far beyond their expiration date. Instead of enacting improvements on the landscape, as policymakers—and the authors of emigrant literature—intended, they stayed in their shanties, symbolically stuck in the squatter stage of American life. We cannot know what the builders of shanties and huts on the one hand, and frame houses on the other, thought of each other. Shanty builders may have consciously thumbed their noses at expectations, proclaiming a sort of oppositional ideology through their refusal to build a frame house. They may have clung to the shanty as a political expression of difference, or resistance. Or their failure to improve their housing may simply have reflected a series of pressing financial concerns and hard choices. But a frontier landscape back-slashed with slant-roofed shanties, as opposed to one rippling with gables, speaks to the tension between settlement and mobility that characterized not only the frontier, but all of America in the first half of the nineteenth century. The mobile shanty—and as the house form evolved, many were built to be literally portable—enacted settlement. Yet the persistence of the shanty on the landscape, a reminder of that mobile tendency in American life, simultaneously threatened it.

American society has always been much more mobile than commonly believed. The ubiquitous shanties on the American frontier testify to values of adaptability, opportunism, and frugality bordering on parsimoniousness. These were virtues of a poor but mobile, not a settled and prosperous populace. In the grand narrative of American progress that developed over the course of the nineteenth century, mobility and its associated values were never promoted as the national ideal. Frederick Jackson Turner's famous 1893 "frontier thesis" reified the frontier as essential to American democracy, yet a landscape built by pioneers did not champion mobility as a national virtue. The frontier is valued as a space for enacting settlement, not as a place in flux. Indeed, transience and transients were systematically painted as threats to progress, whether on the frontier or in towns and cities, where immigrants and African Americans claimed rights to unoccupied land by building shantytowns. Returning shanties and squatters to the places they occupied on the nineteenth-century American landscape—on frontiers both economic and physical—forces the reconsideration of a progressive American ideal grounded in ideas and icons of orderly settlement. The reproduction and representation of shanties reveal not only their geographic range, but insights into the hopes, anxieties, and values espoused by their nonelite builders and their elite critics. Shanties proclaim the values of mobility overlooked or willfully erased in the creation of the progressive American myth. They expose an inability on the part of elite observers to look beyond aesthetics to find evidence of enterprise. The material lives of shanty builders are only part of the story; the shanties they built were expressions of class, race, and ethnicity. They must be seen, re-viewed on the landscape, to be understood.

The tension between settlement and mobility and what they meant to American identity were at the heart, as well, of fiction and art of the first half of the nineteenth century. Two of the most famous cultural figures of the period, James Fenimore Cooper and George Caleb Bingham, explored shifting attitudes and beliefs about squatters and settlers in their work, and both used the shanty as a way of expressing those ambiguities. Who was the real American, the squatter who stayed for a time and moved on, or the settler who put down roots? In a series of novels about the western frontier that became known collectively as *The Leatherstocking Tales,* author James Fenimore Cooper takes on that question. Published between 1827 and 1841, the novels narrate the eighteenth-century adventures of frontier hero Natty Bumppo, the white warrior orphaned as a child and raised by the Mohican Indians in upstate New York, who comes to the aid of British forces during the mid-century French and Indian Wars. (All but the final novel, which takes place in Kansas, are set in New York.) Bumppo, a skilled hunter and fighter whose loyalties are painfully split between his Indian identity and his European origins, embodied the contradictions of American expansion. Cooper's Natty Bumppo is a man caught between his native Indian and Anglophone settler identities, the former representing what Cooper saw as the lost vitality of a frontier wilderness unblemished by massive settlement. Cooper's books pit the destruction of nature against the imperatives of national expansion, justifying the extermination of Indian "savages" even while romanticizing Indian fighters, including Bumppo. The books were so popular that many scholars have credited Cooper with creating much of the frontier ideal himself. Frederick Jackson Turner cited Cooper's work as a source of inspiration for his frontier thesis.[24]

Cooper's last wilderness novel, *The Oak-Openings; or, The Bee-Hunter,* operates as a somewhat melancholy sequel to the swashbuckling adventures of Natty Bumppo. *Oak-Openings* follows the life of a quite different hero, the beekeeper Benjamin Boden, on the Michigan frontier. Although the book was published in 1848, it is set during the War of 1812, a period when the American frontier ended at the Mississippi River Valley and the southern shores of the Great Lakes—encompassing the area of the Western Reserve then known as New Connecticut, where Zerah Hawley was to make his disappointing trek only a few years after the close of the war. While *Oak-Openings* takes up many of Cooper's favorite themes—the primacy of nature, the loss of wilderness—the book also examines other changes overtaking the national identity involving region and class. As in his earlier books, Cooper examines questions of American identity through the lens of national origin and racial allegiance. But in this late book, Cooper also explores how American identity is configured by class, and the anxiety inherent in the burgeoning American cities where his readers lived, of visually distinguishing between people from different classes. Through the character of Benjamin Boden, Cooper explores the shifting social hierarchy of the nation, an investigation that prompts a re-examination of the frontier myth Cooper himself did so much to establish.

The novel opens in a remote forest glade with the meeting of four men, "absolutely strangers" to each other. The time is July 1812, just weeks after Congress declared war on Great Britain on June 18. Three men—two Indians and one European—stand hushed, "grave and silent observers of the movements of the fourth," a second white man named Benjamin Boden, who is looking for bees inside an oak tree that has been struck by lightning. Boden is a man "of middle size, young, active, exceedingly well formed, and with a certain open and frank expression of countenance, that rendered him at least well-looking, though slightly marked with the small-pox." Known throughout the northwestern territories for his superior honey, the Pennsylvania native is a successful entrepreneur with a loyal clientele of settlers. Quickly, Cooper elevates Boden above the other white man in the group, Gershom Waring, a drunken former New Englander with bad grammar and worse manners who lives in a shanty he calls Whiskey Centre—a name that is also used to refer to Waring himself. Boden's physical bearing; his speech, "surprisingly pure English for one in his class of life"; his refinement, suggested by his possession of a spyglass "scarcely larger than those that are used in theatres"; even the extreme purity of his honey, which Cooper mentions several times within a few paragraphs, all set Boden above his companions.[25]

Cooper is careful not to let the reader imagine that Boden is overly refined or elite, however. He carries his bee-hunting tools, "neither very numerous nor very complex," in a covered wooden pail "like those that artisans and laborers are accustomed to carry for the purpose of conveying their food from place to place." His English, while vastly better than Waring's or the two Indians', is not cultured: "Ben used a very pure English, when his condition in life is remembered; but now and then, he encountered a word which pretty plainly proved he was not exactly a scholar." Boden is linked, through his nickname "Buzzing Ben," to the bees, whose industriousness is praised in the hymn fragment that Cooper uses to introduce the chapter:

> How doth the little busy bee
> Improve each shining hour,
> And gather honey all the day,
> From every opening flower!

But like his other, French nickname, "le Bourdon"—the drone—Boden is a laborer. He resembles the green glass tumbler he uses to imprison bees, "a common tumbler, of a very inferior, greenish glass." "[S]ufficiently transparent to answer his purposes," the green tumbler, like Boden, should never be confused, Cooper points out, with the "beautiful manufactures" of "clear transparent glass" available to Cooper's readers by 1848, the year the novel was published. Fear not, Cooper seems to say to his readers, you are more refined than this frontiersman. Even on the frontier, class status is discernible if one takes seriously Cooper's injunction that one's "condition in life" be "remembered." While Boden is of a higher order than his frontier companions, he is not the equal of Cooper's eastern, middle-class readers. Boden's class is discernible through his speech, his occupation, and, the reader soon discovers, his housing.[26]

Boden lives in a shanty. Cooper does not tell the reader how the Pittsburgh native acquired his house-building skills, only that he built the shanty with the help of an unnamed friend. The modest shelter becomes a primary scene for the novel's action, and a vehicle for expressing the subtle class differences that separate Cooper's characters from each other, from the people they left behind in the East, and from Cooper's readers. Boden's "cabin, or shanty" is located on the banks of the Kalamazoo River in what Cooper describes as "literally a wilderness," "unpeopled" (by Europeans) save for the occasional hunter, Indian trader, or adventurer "connected with border life and the habits of the savages." Boden has located his shanty "with much taste" in a grove of oak trees. Several times Cooper mentions the loveliness of the setting—thickets, shade, babbling spring—which makes it superior to Waring's shanty, Whiskey Centre, that "stood on a low and somewhat abrupt swell, being surrounded on all sides by land so low as to be in many places wet and swampy." There are shanties, in other words, and then there are *shanties*. Even as Cooper deploys the word to assign Boden and Waring to a lower class than his readers, he indicates the ambivalence and latitude inherent in the designation. As the shanties reappear later in the book, Cooper demonstrates just how much leeway there is in the gradations of material and form, gaps occupied by unstable yet pronounced implications of class status.[27]

With the precision of emigrant literature from earlier in the century, Cooper describes Boden's shanty. The dwelling itself is 12 feet square inside, with a perimeter that measures a bit less than 14 feet. It is constructed of pine logs, "in the usual mode," with one upgrade that Cooper points out as such: instead of the "common bark coverings of the shanty," Boden's cabin boasts a roof of squared timbers "of which the several parts were so nicely fitted together as to shed rain"—and prevent bears from tearing a hole in the roof to get at the honey. A particular point of pride is a six-paned glass window, transported into the wilderness in Boden's canoe, which opened inward on hinges. This prized symbol of civilization was protected by a row of oak bars set into the exterior logs. Again with hungry bears in mind, the door of the shanty is reinforced with three thicknesses of oak planking, secured on the exterior by a chain and padlock and on the inside by three oak crossbars. Boden christens the shanty *Chateau au Miel*—"Honey Castle"—but twists the French to form the nickname "Castle Meal," a moniker the bears might have liked. The "singularly clean" interior is furnished with "a very rude table, a single board set up on sticks; and a bench or two, together with a wooden chest of some size." Tools hang from hooks on the walls. A pile of bearskins in one corner serves as a bed. The spartan interior, save the bearskins, is reminiscent of Thoreau's sparsely furnished house at Walden Pond, while Gershom's shanty at Whiskey Centre recalls Thoreau's disparaging descriptions of James Collins's shanty.[28]

Cooper describes the shanty as a fitting accommodation for the bachelor bee-hunter, who has become increasingly reclusive during his time in the wilderness—an echo of post-Revolutionary worries that settlers on the frontier would revert to "savagery." In this, Boden recalls Natty Bumppo, whose misanthropy inspired D. H. Lawrence's famous description of the essential white American soul as "hard, isolate, stoic." But Cooper prefaces his description of Boden's shanty with a reproof of shanties in general, which recalls Hawley's comparisons of shanties to animal pens. As the four men leave the glade and walk toward Boden's shanty, Cooper begins an extended aside to the reader:

> [W]e shall digress for one moment in order to say a word ourselves concerning this term 'shanty.' It is now in general use throughout the whole of the United States, meaning a cabin that has been constructed in haste, and for temporary purposes. By a license of speech, it is occasionally applied to more permanent residences, as men are known to apply familiar epithets to familiar objects. The derivation of the word has caused some speculation. The term certainly came from the West—perhaps from the Northwest—and the best explanation we have ever heard of its derivation is to suppose 'shanty,' as we now spell it, a corruption of '*chienté,*' which it is thought may have been a word in Canadian French phrase to express a 'dog-kennel.'

Throughout the rest of the book, Cooper uses *"chienté"* to refer to the shanty (always italicized, always with an accent on the final "e"), in effect calling Boden's home a doghouse. A French doghouse.[29]

Mocking or not, Cooper's account of the word's derivation is specious. One point of entry for the term "shanty" may indeed have been south from Canada, as evidenced by the emigrant literature discussed above and by Zerah Hawley's account of his encounter with the word and the house form in the Western Reserve in 1820. But Cooper seems to have completely invented the idea that "shanty" is derived from the French word for dog-kennel. "Chienté" is not a French word for anything. By suggesting "it is thought [it] may have been" a French Canadian word, Cooper puts himself on a par with Boden who "now and then . . . encountered a word which pretty plainly proved he was not exactly a scholar." Such a blunder would seem worthy of inclusion in Mark Twain's famous rant against Cooper, "Fenimore Cooper's Literary Offenses," in which Twain takes the revered author to task for non sequiturs, invented dialect, and plain bad writing.

The actual roots of the word "shanty" are not Cooper's real concern, however; his point, which he illustrates with the word's imagined derivation, is how cultural meanings are made. Himself the master craftsman of frontier fantasy, Cooper illustrates how "license" and "corruption" combine to manufacture meanings for the word "shanty," which, he points out, has already slipped its semiotic leash to mean both permanent and temporary housing, "throughout the whole of the United States." Then he goes one step further and demonstrates how manufactured meanings give birth to social distinctions, by imaginatively linking Boden, and frontier loners in general, with animals.

Cooper acknowledges the ambiguity of the term even as he defines it, at one point defending the doghouse definition as "the most poetical, if not the most accurate word." He calls attention to his own imaginative process—he winks at the reader repeatedly—and to the process whereby both he, and society, create meaning out of hunches, innuendo, and hope. "At any rate, 'chienté' is so plausible a solution of the difficulty, that one may hope it is the true one, even though he has no better authority for it than a very vague rumor," Cooper writes. Americans—or more precisely, easterners—use the word "shanty" in a "poetical" manner, as a "familiar epithet" that is by its very nature imprecise, with "no better authority than a vague rumor." The fact that the suitability of the term "shanty," Cooper claims, is ultimately up to the speaker's "license" confirms that criteria other than materials, size, durability, and longevity determine whether or not a dwelling is a shanty. The "license of speech" that Cooper mentions in his definition of a shanty describes the process whereby observers, like the author and the reader, override tangible criteria, like size or shape or materials, with more subjective criteria. Like the telltale signs of smallpox that Boden bears on his otherwise handsome face, his class rank—his status as an outsider in the world of Cooper's readers—is revealed by his occupation of a shanty. Shanties are, ultimately, constructed not by their builders, but by the people who view them.[30]

The slipperiness of the term is illustrated by the variation in the actual structures the word "shanty" is used to describe. Boden's cabin is a shanty, but so is Waring's Whiskey Centre, a structure large enough to accommodate the storage and sale of whiskey barrels. At one point in Oak-Openings, Boden shelters a band of displaced Europeans who are running from the Indians. But his "little habitation" proves too cramped for the mixed-gender crowd, and Castle Meal is turned over to the women. The men build a second shanty, which "though wanting in the completeness and strength of Castle Meal, was sufficient for the wants of these sojourners in the wilderness." Castle Meal is considered a shanty despite its timber roof, doors, glass windows, and lovely site. The second shanty Boden builds lacks windows and doors but is twice as large as Castle Meal. Yet both of these dwellings, and the swampy Whiskey Centre, are "shanties."[31]

A location off the grid of civilization is an essential dimension of a shanty. Cooper emphasizes the wilderness setting for Castle Meal, the swampy surroundings of Whiskey Centre, and the proximity of both to the Indian "savages." Cooper also remarks on the ephemerality: shanties are "constructed in haste," to be temporary dwellings. Mobile laborers like Benjamin Boden lived not in cabins, but in shanties, as did itinerant traders like Waring. Whiskey Centre, the name of Waring's shanty, refers to the name given the place by boatmen along the Kalamazoo River who stopped there to drink whiskey, and Cooper distinguishes Waring's shanty by its location, which is both fixed, at the mouth of the Kalamazoo River, and variable, depending on Waring's location. He describes Whiskey Centre—the name, remember, also refers to Waring himself, as though the man embodies the place—as "down our way." "And whereabouts is 'down our way,'" Boden taunts him, "where is Whiskey Centre?" To which Waring replies good-naturedly, "just where *I* happen to live, bein' what a body might call a travellin' name." When Boden "pertinaciously" says he had not seen the Centre when he travelled past the mouth of the river, Waring retorts that he passed by two weeks too early. "Travellin' Centres, and stationary, differs somewhat, I guess; one is always to be found, while t'other must be s'arched after."[32]

Shanties also have an unpredictable form: made from materials "at hand," they accommodate their function rather than replicating contemporary notions of domestic style or architecture, notions that require the importation of materials not "at hand," thereby achieving and indicating a higher social status. Touring the Rocky Mountains in 1847, British explorer and travel writer George Ruxton commented on a settlement: "Scattered about were tents and shanties of logs and branches of every conceivable form." Shanties are made of materials at hand, to serve the need at hand. They did not conform even to vernacular notions, evidenced in the emigrant literature, of what constituted a proper house. Cooper recognized the hierarchy of housing types: in his early novel *The Pioneers,* published in 1823, one character disparages another by saying he's certain the lad "never slept in anything better than a bark shanty in his life, unless it was some such hut as the cabin of Leatherstocking [Natty Bumppo]."[33]

Boden, who Cooper affectionately calls "our hero," may be a relatively cul-tured person with "some of the appliances of civilization about [him]," but as a shanty dweller—a temporary resident, a footloose bachelor with no ties to his community who is more inclined to talk to the Indian "savages" than his white neighbors—Boden's appearance is deceptive. It distinguishes him, first of all, from Cooper's most famous hero, Natty Bumppo, who never builds himself a permanent home—a homelessness that reflects Bumppo's complex embodiment of Indian and British cultures. The inability to reliably label Boden, his social elusiveness, would have struck a chord with Cooper's audi-ence of metropolitan readers, who were at the time experiencing many of the same challenges categorizing the different classes of people they encountered daily on the rapidly changing urban landscapes of growing American cities and towns. They traversed frontiers of their own, urban frontiers, where the search for social cues intensified as populations got bigger and more diverse. Boden's shanty becomes a cultural cue with a social meaning largely indepen-dent of its physical characteristics. "Shanty" is not a neutral term that applies to dwellings that look a certain way; even within *Oak-Openings,* shanties vary significantly in size, shape, and amenities. Rather, "shanty" is a cultural con-struction of temporary housing that helps Cooper's readers locate Boden in the rapidly-shifting geography of class in the mid-nineteenth century.[34]

Looking beyond settled America to the new West, Cooper's novels cap-tured the frontier moment. In "instant histories" of a westward expansion that was ongoing, he provided one of the major contexts for middle-class readers of his period to think about the American frontier. By associating specific house types with various people on the frontier, Cooper presented a picture of what belonged where as a way of understanding the passage of time. His visualizations of what he calls a "shanty" provided a touchstone for middle-class, eastern readers navigating the temporal history of the young nation. But his fictional frontier also provided a guide to contemporary change by charting the shifting landscape of American class formation that his readers occupied in their everyday lives. Cooper unabashedly introduces his own incorrect history of the word "shanty"—the relentlessly italicized and accented *"chienté"*—which foregrounds savagery and underdevelopment. Yet simultaneously, Cooper acknowledges the double role Boden, and the gener-ation of settlers he represents, played in the national imagination, at once the noble pioneer and the suspect squatter.

The meaning of the frontier in American life was also the subject of works by the first American painters to create a national audience for their work, in the 1830s and 1840s. George Catlin's paintings of western landscapes and portraits of American Indians brought visions of the western frontier to eastern audiences eager for an escape from the pressures and dislocations of urbanization and industrialization. On Catlin's heels, George Caleb Bingham attracted national attention for his exuberant renderings of frontier life along the Missouri River in the late 1840s, the same time Cooper was writing *Oak-Openings,* and at the same time Thoreau was living at Walden Pond. Bingham's most famous paintings, such as *The Jolly Boatmen* from 1846, celebrate the hard work and high spirits of the farmers, laborers, trappers, and traders Bingham encountered in his travels up and down the Missouri River. Bingham's renderings of frontier types, not only in his paintings but in hundreds of drawings, further enshrined the American frontier as the crucible of American democracy. Again, the shanty functions as a tool and a site of interpretation for American identity.

Bingham was committed to questions of public policy surrounding national expansion in his daily life as well as in his art: in the 1840s he was active in Whig politics, winning election to the Missouri state legislature in 1848 after losing narrowly two years earlier. In both politics and art, Bingham commented on the status and role of the squatter in American life as a way of debating larger issues surrounding national expansion and the effects of that growth on the development of American identity. By this point, the debate over expansion was inseparable from the debate over the extension of slavery into the former territories, and the question of American identity was one of being a free or a slave nation. Bingham threw himself into that debate as both politician and artist. The shanty appears in his paintings as a distinguishing feature of squatter life, and operates as a tool for comparing squatters unfavorably to settlers—a comparison that cast squatters as not only suspect transients, but as proxies for the proslavery forces determined to move the frontier of slavery in America steadily westward.

One of Bingham's early paintings, *The Squatters,* painted in 1850, addresses head-on the figure of the squatter on the frontier. As in Cooper's frontier novels, a cast of spunky loners and stalwart settlers populate the landscape. Two men, one old and one young, pose in front of a one-room log house. Little of the roof can be seen, but it appears to be made of timbers—the very image of the shanty Cooper both admired and denigrated in *The Oak-Openings,* and a familiar choice from the hierarchy of huts, hovels, and houses promoted in the emigrant literature from the nineteenth century. The squatters themselves convey the confidence Cooper ascribed to his final frontier hero, Benjamin Boden, but also a wariness. The two men, and their dog, gaze directly into the eyes of the viewer. But their body language—the young man's raised knee, the old man's hands crossed on top of a tall walking stick—signals circumspection. In the background a woman is bent over a washtub; two boys play on the ground near a kettle that boils over an open fire. A bright sky warms the spreading valley in the distance, conveying the allure of open lands farther west. The scene mingles admiration with watchfulness, a reflection of the anxiety generated by squatters for many decades. Americans both depended on squatters to extend the frontier, and feared them for the independence, self-reliance, and resistance to government control they exhibited in doing so.[35]

Bingham's own views on squatters were spelled out in a letter he sent to accompany the shipment of the painting to the American Art-Union in New York City, where it was exhibited in 1851. A Whig, Bingham blamed "illegitimate Loco focos," the staunchly Democratic squatters in his Missouri district, for his defeat in the 1846 campaign for the state legislature, and later singled them out as a reason he decided not to run for re-election in 1850:

> The Squatters as a class, are not fond of the toil of agriculture, but erect their rude Cabins upon those remote portions of the National domain, where the abundant game supplies their phisical [*sic*] wants. When this source of subsistence becomes diminished in consequence of increasing settlements around they usually sell out their slight improvement, with their 'preemption title' to the land, and again follow the receding footsteps of the Savage.[36]

Bingham links squatters imaginatively with Indians, recalling eighteenth-century concerns over the uncivilized, "savage" influence of the frontier. Their "rude cabins" identify them, as does their choice to occupy isolated ground. They live outside of community, a choice that, Bingham suggests, threatens community. But while Whig politics may have tempered Bingham's opinions of squatters, his painting does not degrade them. Rather, it notes the ambivalence generated by the role of the squatter in American history and accords them a grudging respect. The title "squatter" is both a tribute and a warning:

the people depicted in the scene compensate for their lack of property by working and taking risks, but still their forthright defiance of civilization is worrisome. So is their political muscle. As Bingham acknowledged in a letter to a political supporter, for all of their transience and unpredictability, squatters exercised power at the ballot box: "These illegitimate Loco focos, whose votes we wish to brush out of our way, have so scattered since the election, over our big praries [sic], that it takes a long time, with a good deal of pulling and hauling, to get them up to mark." Squatters were inferior to farmers, in Bingham's view, but they were not without personal and political power.[37]

The audience for *The Squatters* would have been keenly aware, in fact, of the power of squatters, for by 1851 squatting had become a tactic in the proslavery campaign to let "popular sovereignty" decide whether former territories were admitted to the Union as free or slave states. *The Squatters* triggered not only moral judgments on the desirability of independent squatters versus community-minded settlers populating the frontier—and their role in mythic stories identifying the frontier as the fount of American democracy—but also emotions over the deepening North-South divide concerning the expansion of slavery in the United States. The 1851 debut of *The Squatters* came on the heels of the failure, in 1847, of the Wilmot Proviso, a bill that would have prevented the expansion of slavery to the remaining territories, and the passage of the Compromise of 1850, which amended the Fugitive Slave Act to reaffirm slavery in the territories by asserting that runaway slaves were to be returned to their masters, wherever they were found. The threats posed by squatters, to Bingham's generation, were not only the long-held concerns over "savagery" and regression on the frontier, but also the failure of the Union. As a state legislator, he actively promoted Whig policies opposing the extension of slavery to the territories. The squatter on the frontier in 1851 represented the greatest threat to the nation, in Bingham's eyes: slavery. He blamed the proslavery "Loco focos" for his blighted political career, and in his art, he portrayed them as a powerful but ultimately destructive force.

But the important distinction to make in Bingham's work is not whether he depicts squatters as positive or negative, but that he acknowledges the power they held over the American imagination and the threat they posed to the future of the Union. If Americans continued to imagine squatters as representing something essential about American-ness—a quintessential orneriness or resistance to state power that protected their liberty, an insistence on personal sovereignty above all else—then they empowered the states'-rights forces seeking to extend slavery to the limits of American geography. They imperiled the Union and sacrificed American identity to the slaveholding states.[38]

In his art as in his politics, Bingham argued for a settlement ideal that embraced stability and domesticity and eschewed mobility and individualism. Older questions and concerns—for example, the desirability of orderly settlement, and orderly settlers, as opposed to less organized land development by waves of unregulated squatters—animate Bingham's art and his political rhetoric. But by the late 1840s, the topic of national expansion was no longer waged solely along a continuum of order and disorder: with the growing animosity between northern and southern states over the expansion of slavery, the frontier had become a literal as well as a symbolic space for national debates about slavery. The 1820 Missouri Compromise temporarily staunched the growing regional rift by admitting Maine as a free state and Missouri, the setting for Bingham's most famous paintings of frontier life, as a slave state. But in the late 1840s, U.S. Sen. Stephen A. Douglas of Illinois championed the doctrine of "popular sovereignty," whereby residents of existing territories would vote on whether to legalize slavery in their new states. By the early 1850s, "popular sovereignty" had become derisively known as "squatter sovereignty," a phrase that highlighted the proslavery tactic of squatting in territories ripe for statehood, in effect stacking the deck in favor of a vote to extend slavery. Bingham's painting *The Squatters* rendered a judgment on squatters as a class of people that went deeper than ruminations over the nation's past and how the western frontier had been settled. It raised pressing questions about the nation's future and how settlement on the territorial frontier would shape the American character going forward.

These are questions and debates that Bingham intended the viewers of *The Squatters* to have; they are foregrounded in the painting itself, and supported by details of Bingham's life as documented in his letters and other accounts. But there was another perspective that viewers of the painting would have brought to its exhibition in 1851 that Bingham may not have been aware of, another dialogue involving the builders and dwellers of shanties, not on the western frontier that Bingham painted, but on the urban frontier where his painting was exhibited in New York. On the walls of the Art-Union gallery on Broadway where *The Squatters* made its debut was another painting of squatters occupying contested territory, by a local artist named Charles Parsons.

Irish Shanties, Brooklyn, N.Y., documented the construction of shanties by Irish immigrants living in the Red Hook section of Brooklyn, where they worked on the docks and as manual laborers. A second painting by Parsons, *Negro Huts Near Bedford, L.I.,* showed the conical huts occupied by poor African Americans living in a shantytown near Weeksville, a village founded in 1838 by free, land-owning blacks in what is now the Bedford-Stuyvesant neighborhood of Brooklyn. The huts look like descendants of the humble housing recommended in *The Farmers and Emigrants Complete Guide* or Lamond's *Narrative of the Rise and Progress of Emigration from the Counties of Lanark and Renfrew.*[39]

Opinion of squatters was not a judgment based solely on what people thought they knew about squatters on the western frontier; it was informed by the presence of squatters and their shanties on the urban frontier, settlements they had seen in person, whose influence they felt in their own communities. Real estate development, orderly settlement, and the grid: these were preoccupations of urban life as well as life on the western frontier. The shanty was their logo. Knowing that changes the meaning of Bingham's painting, of Cooper's fiction, of Hawley's reporting. A progressive narrative that demoted squatters on the western frontier from a position at the center of the national drama to one on the sidelines served as a license to degrade and marginalize squatters on the urban frontier. Bingham's painting forced its New York audience to process the meaning of the increasingly noticeable and numerous squatters occupying the growing metropolis outside the Art-Union gallery door. The question of "squatter sovereignty" was not a debate located in a geographically remote area on the western frontier of *The Squatters,* but on the urban frontier of *Irish Shanties* and *Negro Huts.* The presence of shanties united the western and the urban frontiers in the American imagination then, and it prompts us to consider them anew together now. On both frontiers, the people who built the shanties were necessary but ultimately unwelcome pioneers.

3

Shantytowns on the Urban Frontier

In the summer of 1832, a cholera pandemic swept through New York City killing more than 3,500 people—a number equivalent, in today's city of 8 million, to more than 100,000 people. The city was just a bud at the tip of Manhattan Island at the time, its 250,000 residents crowded into the see-saw of streets south of 14th Street; the deaths of so many people in such a small area had a gruesome effect. Most of the deaths occurred in the wooden rookeries and brick tenements around Five Points, including many in what the public record described as "sheds" and "shanties" built of wood and wedged into the gaps between and behind buildings. Packed to bursting with poor Irish immigrants and black laborers, these illegal structures were a response to the severe shortage of affordable housing in the rapidly growing city. Some were built by their inhabitants, others by landlords squeezing profits out of the very streets and alleyways. The lopsided suffering of the people occupying these sheds and shanties fostered the popular but mistaken belief that diseases like cholera were spread by "miasmas," the fetid air emanating from overcrowded housing. John Pintard, a civic leader who founded the New-York Historical Society in 1804, summed up the public attitude when he wrote to his daughter that the epidemic was "almost exclusively confined to the lower classes of intemperate dissolute and filthy people huddled together like swine in their polluted habitations." The best way to prevent further epidemics, civic leaders theorized, was to scrub the landscape clean of "polluted habitations" and replace them with new construction.[1]

So it was that on December 30, 1833, the Board of Assistant Aldermen met to vote on a recommendation to widen Chapel Street, a short stretch of roadway that was spliced onto West Broadway in the 1840s. The minutes show that the three aldermen voted unanimously to approve the measure, a first step toward "cleansing" the neighborhood of the "nuisances" posed by cheap infill housing—"shanties, nearly covering whole lot[s]." But their ambivalence about dislocating scores of poor laborers is clear from the hand-wringing language in the rest of the passage. "The question may arise, where are the poor to go?" Furthermore, the aldermen noted, the dispossessed were the "poor, honest, and industrious class of our fellow citizens, [who] are justly considered the bone and sinew of the nation." The inhabitants of shantytowns were simultaneously an eyesore and an ideal, a paradox that became a template for descriptions of shantytowns as the century wore on. "They must," the aldermen agreed, "be provided for somewhere." But the aldermen quickly wiggled out of the corner they had painted themselves into. "In the opinion of the committee, the question may be answered—go where they may, they cannot do worse." The bone and sinew of the nation would have to fend for itself.[2]

Over the next six decades, thousands of Manhattan's poor laborers built shantytowns north of the settled city and in pockets of ground deemed too rocky or swampy for commercial development. Consistently but often inaccurately referred to as "squatters" in the press, most in fact paid ground rent for their land, inadvertently participating in the development of Manhattan by providing an income stream for speculators. By the 1860s shantytowns freckled Manhattan, coalescing into larger settlements on either side of Central Park. An 1867 *New York Times* article estimated that "twenty-five different settlements" were "scattered all over the upper portion of the City," some "located blocks apart from others, but each bearing a striking resemblance to the sister colony in point of dirt." By that point at least 20,000 "squatters" lived in Manhattan's shantytowns. The largest was Dutch Hill, a "conglomeration of hovels" centered on 41st Street near the East River. Similar "hamlets" of "comparatively insignificant" size—an estimated "twenty-five or thirty shanties" apiece—were sprinkled between Fourth and Tenth Avenues, as indistinguishable, the writer claimed, as particles of ash. Shantytowns also multiplied in Brooklyn, often on land adjacent to factories or the docks, where many shanty dwellers worked. Some 120 shanties comprised a settlement—one of many—in Red Hook, on "an open space of land sunken so far below the city level that all attempts at sewerage have failed." Civic and business leaders, committed to enforcing a gridded plan of development in both cities, painted shanty dwellers as intruders. "Why is this . . . population permitted within the city?" one journalist demanded in 1864. No matter that shanty residents performed manual labor essential to the construction and growth of cities like Manhattan and Brooklyn. As shanties multiplied, and shanty settlements became a typical urban sight, the 1833 aldermens' anxiety over "where are the poor to go?" was replaced with increasingly frantic assertions that shanty dwellers were obstacles to urban development, and indeed, to civilization itself. Such impediments to improvement did not belong in the city at all. The veneer of concern evident in 1833 disappeared as shantytowns became ubiquitous—as it appeared that they might thwart the grid and the logic that upheld it.[3]

The national ethic of improvement encoded in the grid rendered judgments about what, and who, was rightly considered "urban"—and by extension, who and what was considered "American." But the grid had its resisters and refusers in shanty builders, who in confounding the grid signaled a reluctance to succumb to the crushing uniformity and the creeping homogenization of American life it represented. Part farm, part village, part suburb, shantytowns championed ongoing adaptation and transformation. They served the needs of the uprooted but not rootless people who built and occupied them, people whose interests were not served by the grid or the larger principles it represented. The history of shantytowns in Manhattan and Brooklyn reveals an ideology of dwelling that expressed the values, needs, and demands of poor migrant laborers in the nineteenth century, who survived by occupying the territory they staked out in successive shantytowns. Just as the alternate vision of urban settlement represented by shantytowns has been lost to history, so has the ideology expressed by the design and construction of shantytowns. But it lives on in the artifacts of popular culture—songs, plays, illustrations, journalistic accounts. The resulting story of survival in the face of dispossession unsettles the progressive narrative of the formation of cities in the United States in much the same way adding shanties to the western frontier complicates that narrative. Rather than a story of unbroken progress, unfolding in an orderly fashion as the grid marched up Manhattan Island, we see a story of systematic exile cloaked as improvement; alongside that emerges the shanty dwellers' story, a story of survival, adaptation, and transformation. It is not a celebratory one: the evidence of shantytowns exposes deep-seated and often violent ethnic and racial conflict between the poor residents of shantytowns.

One of the earliest accounts of an urban shantytown in the United States was written by Edgar Allan Poe, who arrived in New York with his wife

Virginia in April 1844. Desperate for cash as usual, he agreed to write a series of essays on city life for the *Columbia Spy,* a small newspaper in Pennsylvania. As Poe's assignment attests, the conditions of big city life were of interest to a broad readership living in smaller cities and towns, who found common cause in shared issues of urbanization. For his first essay, he walked north of 14th Street, at that time the limit of dense settlement. A short ramble toward the center of the island took Poe to the edge of the urban frontier, a rugged landscape that fired his imagination as he left behind the nascent grid. "I have been roaming far and wide over this island of Mannahatta," Poe begins, using the Algonquin word meaning "island of hills."

> Some portions of its interior have a certain air of rocky sterility which may impress some imaginations as simply *dreary*—to me it conveys the sublime. Trees are few; but some of the shrubbery is exceedingly picturesque. Not less so are the prevalent shanties of the Irish squatters.[4]

With great economy, Poe evokes the wilderness of the western frontier and the specter of Indian removal during the previous decade. The area north of 14th Street was something of a frontier. The only roads in this part of the island were winding paths established in colonial times. The ground would have been peppered with jimsonweed, a shrub-like bramble with cactus-like pods that is known as moonflower, for the white, trumpet-like blossoms that only bloom at night. Jimsonweed smells, by some accounts, like peanut butter, a savory odor that would have blended with the smell of blood from nearby slaughterhouses. Poe is stimulated by the contrast with the built-up city at the tip of the island: unlike most American cities, which radiated outward from one or two central nodes, Manhattan surged in one direction, northward, at full force. The shantytown Poe visited occupied a swath of land that in 1844 was still owned by speculators holding out for higher land prices; their land-holdings prevented further construction northward, despite a desperate housing shortage downtown.

Poe describes the landscape as "sublime," a word that signified, for his educated readers, an experience of greatness beyond all expression, a moment of possibility and danger that Poe was to return to many times in his work. As articulated in the works of eighteenth-century philosophers Edmund Burke and Immanuel Kant, the aesthetic principle of "the sublime" expressed a sense of delight inspired by awe or even terror, often in the presence of nature. In the nineteenth century the sublime was often associated with natural disasters like earthquakes or volcanoes, or desolate landscapes like the desert or the open sea—or, Poe insists, the boulder-strewn terrain at the center of Manhattan Island, a space that simultaneously marked the edge of the settled city. Having taken the reader into this sublime realm, Poe contrasts the barren but evocative topography with the abundant but vacuous built environment. He notes the sparse trees and the "picturesque" shrubbery, a description that evoked rustic traditions epitomized in English gardening and landscape painting. The picturesque movement, known for celebrating landscapes that were beginning to vanish in the wake of industrialization, was gaining popularity in America. At the heart of the picturesque ideology was the tension between the ideal of nature, which it upheld, and the intricate plans and schemes devised to improve upon nature—an impulse it shared with the grid. Poe both acknowledges and mocks the picturesque by insisting that the most picturesque aspects of the landscape were not natural elements, but the humble built forms that gave it substance: the "prevalent" shanties of Irish immigrants.

> I have one of these *tabernacles* (I use the term primitively) at present in the eye of my mind. It is, perhaps, nine feet by six, with a pigsty applied externally, by way both of portico and support. The whole fabric (which is of mud) has been erected in somewhat too obvious an imitation of the Tower of Pisa. A dozen rough planks, "pitched" together, form the roof. The door is a barrel on end.[5]

The dwelling Poe describes, made of mud and boards, would have been at home in Concord's Shanty Field—Poe wrote this piece the year before Thoreau moved to Walden. The "fabric" of Poe's mud shanties recalls both the dwellings Zerah Hawley encountered 20 years earlier on the Ohio frontier, and the conical huts of African Americans depicted in the watercolor of *Negro Huts* that hung alongside Bingham's painting of *The Squatters* at the 1851 American Art-Union exhibition. The footprint of the dwelling Poe describes, nine by six feet, is much smaller than the one James Fenimore Cooper built for his hero Ben Boden in *Oak Openings,* but in line with the dimensions recommended by the emigrant literature of the seventeenth and eighteenth centuries. Like Hawley, Poe encounters an alien house type on the frontier and tries to make sense of it for himself and his readers. Hawley tried to fit the shanties he encountered into a lexicon of New England housing. Poe locates them in the remote past, spatially and culturally distant from the modern city. Yet this is the terrain Poe turned to when called upon to educate *Spy* readers about the booming metropolis of Manhattan. The "prevalent" shanties north of 14th Street emerge in this rendering as essentially urban. Despite their location on the periphery of the built-up city, they embody ideas central to debates about the future of American cities. The Jeffersonian agrarian ideal, which held sway in the eighteenth and early nineteenth centuries, continued to resonate despite the widespread development of American cities and the growth of American industry. Cities remained suspect, a worry exacerbated by the 1840s by the growing numbers of Irish and German immigrants who were settling in them.[6]

These immigrants were the likely inhabitants of Poe's "sublime" shantytown. Poe describes them as "Irish squatters," but scholarship on Irish immigrants and urban squatters suggests those were imprecise terms; applied loosely, they revealed cultural and social attitudes. Many people labeled "Irish" mid-century, especially before the potato famine of 1845 caused a spike in emigration from Ireland, were in fact more likely to be native-born descendants of Irish immigrants, a fact acknowledged in contemporary newspaper accounts. An "Irish squatter," therefore, was someone of Irish extraction but not necessarily birth. The same was true of the term "German" or "Dutch," used loosely by observers to indicate both German immigrants and their native-born descendants. Similarly, "squatters," a term that indicates living rent-free in the tradition of migrant counterparts on the frontier, was misleading. As a close reading of newspaper coverage of shantytowns during this period makes clear, the term "squatter" was more an indication of a person's social status than his legal rights to land—a fact noted by Roy Rosenzweig and Elizabeth Blackmar, two of the very few scholars to have written about urban shantytowns: "Like the word *shanty*, in mid-nineteenth-century New York the term *squatter* was more of a cultural category than a formal legal designation, a sort of shorthand for the sort of poor people more affluent New Yorkers preferred to remove from their neighborhoods."[7]

Poe calls the Irish shanties "tabernacles," which links them imaginatively with relics of ancient times. His parenthetical explanation that he is using the term "primitively" invokes the original Latin meaning of *taberna*—a temporary, often movable hut made of branches, boards, or canvas. This imposes a reading of shanties as ancient, portable and insubstantial, and therefore out of sync with contemporary New York: a potent choice for Poe's inaugural missive from the front lines of urbanity. Poe calls the shanty a "tabernacle" in jest, to signal the humorous distance between a shanty and a sacred space—and by extension the civilized, improving space of the American city. He doubles the joke by referring to the attached pigsty as a "portico," a place of learning and philosophy as well as the entrance to a classical building. In so doing, Poe charts the distance between shanties and classical models. He completes the caricature with a sarcastic comparison of the shanty to the famously leaning Tower of Pisa, which was excavated between 1838 and 1840 to allow visitors to view its ornate base for the first time. Poe's lofty analogies degrade the shanty. Cosmopolitan references illuminate the cultural divide between shanty dwellers and Poe's readers, while allowing them to identify with the worldly, sophisticated New Yorkers who find shanty dwellers a curiosity.[8]

Poe offers readers two additional ways of distinguishing between themselves and the Irish Catholics who built shanties among the rocks of inner Manhattan. While "tabernacle" had long held a specifically Jewish meaning, in the late eighteenth and early nineteenth centuries it was often used to denote meetinghouses of Protestant Nonconformists, generally Baptists and Methodists. That additional layer of meaning further marginalizes the inhabitants of Poe's shanties: not only are they primitive figures living in mud huts, but as Catholics, they are spiritually suspect. Finally, Poe distances the reader and the inhabitants of the shanties by never introducing them: the shantytown landscape is devoid of human actors. The air of "sterility" Poe ascribes to the rocky landscape more appropriately describes the mood he creates in this passage by omitting human beings, even as parts of speech, by consistently using the passive voice. The shanty he describes "has been erected," the pigsty has been "applied" to its side, boards have been "pitched" to form a roof. Poe's use of the passive voice erases living people from the landscape, disconnecting readers from the shanty dwellers they are judging. That distance would become crucial in the next two decades, as better-off New Yorkers systematically dispossessed poor shantytown dwellers from the landscape to make way for parks, roads, and other public improvements.[9]

In one of the earliest accounts of a Manhattan shantytown, Edgar Allan Poe takes the reader to that uncivilized clime, a land beyond the pale but only a few blocks away. In doing so he sets the tone for mid-century treatments of shantytowns, both visual and written, which place them beyond the bounds of civilization not only geographically but imaginatively, a double exile that enabled observers to deny their palpable presence at the center, the very heart of the metropolis. But Poe's depiction of the shanty, while it encourages readers to think of shanties as out of sync with the "Gotham" of his news-paper reports, recognizes the ambiguity inherent in the presence of "primitive" shanties just a few blocks north of built-up Manhattan. After his description of the shantytown, Poe veers into a lament for the "old mansions . . . (principally wooden)" slated for demolition along the eastern shore of the island. Poe acknowledges that these "magnificent palaces" are nonetheless "neglected— unimproved," and that they present "a melancholy spectacle of decrepitude" that, for all its beauty, is *"doomed."* Here is Poe, the Southern reactionary and master of Gothic literature, who created "The Fall of the House of Usher" in 1839 as an allegory of the doomed South. "The Spirit of Improvement has withered them with its acrid breath. Streets are already 'mapped' through them, and they are no longer suburban residences, but 'town-lots.'" Poe is skeptical of the improvement ethic, but his short article on shantytowns illus-trates how shanties and their builders became rhetorical devices in the pro-gressive American narrative. Shanty dwellers were refugees from the forces of improvement remaking downtown Manhattan in the mid-1840s. They were archaic, insensible, quaint, and doomed.[10]

Poe wrings poetry out of the shantytown and saddles it with sublimity. But his brief dispatch offers practical clues to settlement patterns and housing practices of the residents. Another picture emerges, that allows us to judge the shantytown from the viewpoint of its builders. He mentions the materials used in construction of the shanties: mud, boards, and barrels. All would have been available on-site or at nearby lumberyards and the local docks. Dwellings constructed of materials at hand were a defining feature of shanty-towns. So was an unregimented approach to siting individual dwellings, which took advantage of open space. While a nine-by-six shanty would have provided close quarters, residents would have had room to roam outdoors, as Poe did, over the undeveloped interior of the island. And they could have done so with greater privacy and autonomy than they could have down-town, under the watchful eyes of landlords, police, health inspectors, street-widening committees, and other public officials.[11]

Poe notes the presence of vegetable gardens and pigsties, two reliable sources of inexpensive food not available to tenants of tenement housing. By the 1860s, market gardens kept by shanty residents would become a major source of fresh produce for residents of Manhattan. Evidence of gardens as early as 1844 points beyond self-reliance to free enterprise; shanty dwellers' participation in the market economy matched their involvement in the real estate market, which became more sophisticated as the years passed. Poe's remarks about the layout of the garden signal values of privacy, property, and domesticity, as does the presence of dogs and cats: "A dog and a cat are inevitable in these habitations," Poe wrote, "and, apparently, there are no dogs and no cats more entirely happy." The garden, he notes is "encircled" by a ditch, a large stone, and a bramble. Although Poe uses passive voice throughout his description of the shantytown, someone decided to site the garden along the ditch, drag a stone to mark one corner, and leave the brambles in place along the remaining side in order to demarcate boundaries and claim ownership of space. These boundaries are rooted in the terrain; they do not follow the rigid abstraction of the 1811 grid, which in Poe's description has "mapped" out the land into "town lots." Poe's description foreshadows numerous portrayals of shantytowns in coming decades, in print and in art, that depict large communities of shanties grouped in relation to each other, or conforming to the lay of the land. They are not disorganized, merely ungridded, developing organically, or haphazardly, in the manner of older American cities, including Manhattan itself.[12]

Across the East River, shantytowns were also proliferating in Brooklyn. German immigrants working as ragpickers and later dockworkers built shantytowns near the Gowanus Canal in Red Hook as early as 1843; others developed nearby, including Tinkersville and Slab City, one of the most enduring. The names suggest professions, locations, construction methods, ethnicities, or sometimes political sympathies: Darby's Patch, Sandybank, Bunkerville, Texas. As in Manhattan, the Brooklyn elite interpreted shanty-towns as archaic, backward, and incompatible with urban life, even as their inhabitants occupied jobs and spaces at the heart of the growing city. Researching an article about the future of Brooklyn in the summer of 1847,

Walt Whitman encountered an encampment of shanty dwellers in the vicinity of Fort Greene, the site of a revolutionary-era fort. Located on a swell of ground on the northern edge of the city, Fort Greene was not unlike the interior of Mannahatta island visited by Poe only a few years earlier: charted for expansion according to a gridded plan, but still an expanse of unregulated space bearing the hallmarks of more rugged countryside. And Whitman's perambulations in search of a newspaper story were, like Poe's, an exercise in distancing shantytowns that only served to illustrate just how central they were to urban life. "Descending Fort Greene," Whitman wrote, "one comes amid a colony of squatters, whose chubby children, and the good natured brightness of the eyes of many Irishwomen, tell plainly enough that you are wending among the shanties of Emeralders." The shantytown developed along this stretch of Myrtle Avenue in the 1840s, within view of Potter's Field, and was built, like Poe's Manhattan shantytown, by pre-famine Irish immigrants—"Emeralders"—or their descendants. There are no accounts of what shanties in this specific shantytown looked like; Whitman does not elaborate. But it is likely they resembled the shanties Poe documented in Manhattan in 1844: small huts made of wood planks and mud. Residents on Myrtle Avenue lived undisturbed as long as the land lay beyond the edges of the developing city. But by the time Whitman wrote his account, the land was "all properly laid out on a city map, and the proper grade fixed," and the area occupied by the shantytown had been designated for commercial expansion: it was to be the route for an extension of the stagecoach line connecting with the Fulton [Street] Ferry. Landowners foresaw the creation of a prosperous professional neighborhood nearby, similar to the booming Brooklyn Heights further south, while Brooklyn's business elite hoped to develop Myrtle Avenue into a "wide and extended thoroughfare," in Whitman's words, "answering somewhat here to what the Bowery is to N. York."[13]

But the shantytown was in the way. Business and real estate interests had begun petitioning the city as early as 1844 to remove it. Concerned that the city lacked jurisdiction to do so—the streets, at that point, did not appear on official city maps, "and it was doubtful whether the Common Council have legal control over said sts."—one landowner proposed that the City Inspector be authorized to demolish buildings on the property, "which includes some scores of shanties, pig-sties, cow stables, and paraphernalia of a regular squatter." The city ordered demolitions, but shanty dwellers persevered, apparently rebuilding as quickly as demolitions occurred. In 1845 exasperated local businessmen began to lobby for the creation of the city's first park on the site of the shantytown, as a further enhancement to the neighborhood, and a way to dislodge the shantytown. Two years later the shantytown remained, and plans for Washington Park were stalled.

This was when Whitman took up the park cause in the *Eagle:* "When that noble improvement is consummated, it will elevate the whole standard of affairs in this part of the city . . . for no one with common judgment can fail to see that stretching far and wide the streets here are, in a few years, to be filled with a dense mass of busy human beings. Shall there not be one single spot to relieve the desolating aspect of *all* houses and pavements?" While Poe expressed ambivalence toward "improvement," Whitman was an unreflective booster. In support of the park, Whitman brandishes the popular notion, by then taking hold in American cities, that parks were required to relieve the congestion of urban life, providing the "lungs" of the city, in Frederick Law Olmsted's famous words. Parks also signaled cultural sophistication, an appreciation for manicured nature that had swept European and English cities in the late eighteenth and early nineteenth centuries. As Whitman's campaign shows, parks expressed a romantic ideal of *rus in urbe,* the country in the city. The construction of a park, a Bowery-like shopping boulevard, and a ferry landing along Myrtle Avenue in Brooklyn all reflected middle-class notions of urban progress.[14]

Not long after Whitman's 1847 editorial in favor of Washington Park appeared, the state legislature endorsed the park plan, and construction began in earnest on Washington Park (renamed Fort Greene Park in 1897). But building a park did not solve the shantytown problem. Shanty residents simply relocated a few blocks east, followed by complaints. In May 1849 the *Eagle,* no longer under Whitman's leadership by this time, decried the "intolerable nuisances" that remained on the north side of Myrtle Street, "boundless huts and pens which have so long been permitted to mar this beautiful street by their unsightly aspect." Just two weeks later the *Eagle* reported that "[h]undreds of complaints are made daily by ladies and those passing by in the East Brooklyn Stages." The shantytown literally blocked the path of progress: "I have, besides, heard of instances," the *Eagle* writer confided, "in which capitalists refused to buy lots, or to improve estates already held hereabouts" because no "tenants of respectability" could be expected to rent space "surrounded by such neighbors."

A writer for the Manhattan *Journal of Commerce* lamented "that essentially *floating* population" of about a hundred shanties that despite the imminent threat of removal, refused to budge, instead "living on from year to year and multiplying." In other words, they put down roots, carving out space on the urban landscape where they sometimes stayed for decades, raising families. The shanty dwellers' desire for spatial stability came into direct conflict with middle-class schemes for development.[15]

The campaign against shantytowns sometimes appealed to concerns over public health. In May 1849, the *Eagle* called on city officials to "cleanse and purify" the area designated for the park; the writer uses the words "cleanse," "purify," "filth," or "dirt" eight times in a 300-word article. The author compares the occupants of shanties to the "thief" in the house who steals freedom from disease, "miserable squatters" who are "long time strangers" to cleanliness. Transients, thieves, strangers: shanty dwellers are presented as threats to the public health and obstacles to public improvements. Another article later that same summer gave an inadvertently humorous picture of shanty builders scavenging for lumber. Titled "Depredations on the Fencings of Vacant Lots," the brief article accuses shanty builders of stealing fence pickets from vacant lots around the city; fencing of vacant lots was required by law. "In some cases they had been stolen piece by piece, until the whole had been removed." According to the writer, "[m]any of the huts or shanties about Fort Greene and other places have, in the [landowner's] opinion, been built with the materials thus dishonestly procured." The account sputters off the page, with references to plunderers, marauders, thieves, and "depredators" doing "evil" by stealing fence posts, but the visual image the article calls up, of shanty builders plucking fence pickets in the dead of night and transporting them back to their shanty-towns, is comical. It also testifies to the resourcefulness of shanty builders.[16]

In early 1851 Brooklyn's city council once again authorized the street inspector to clear out the shantytown, by this time referred to as "New Cork" or "Little Ireland," a "cluster of a hundred or more miserable shanties" which persisted in "rendering disgusting by their filth, a large part of the principle thoroughfare, the Broadway of the place." Shanty owners must have resisted that assault, as well, for in April the Council instructed the police to step in and give "the *occupants* of the shanties and *stables* on Washington Park" ten days' notice of eviction. A weary *Brooklyn Eagle* columnist, in a brief item entitled "The March of Improvement," predicted at that point that the police would "hardly succeed short of an *hors de combat* in persuading the inhabitants of the stables to a quiet compliance with the law." Despite efforts to uproot it, New Cork continued inching eastward, settling by the end of the decade on a vast, undeveloped tract known as Jackson's Farm, rechristened Jackson's Hollow by the press after the arrival of the shanty builders—a subtle judgment on their presence. "Hollow," as a place name, indicated the reversion of a cultivated farm to nature, a shift backward from civilization and improvement to a more primitive state. By the end of the 1850s, there were 340 shanties in Jackson's Hollow, housing 1,427 people in an area roughly four blocks wide and eleven blocks deep, centered on Grand Avenue. For the next 20 years, real estate speculators bought up lots for unpaid taxes and "leased portions of the property to the occupants of the shanties that constitute the eyesore complained of." Clearly, shantytowns participated in the larger world of real estate finance: while press accounts routinely demonized shanty dwellers themselves, speculators profited from their continued presence on contested sites.[17]

Meanwhile in Manhattan, another great park scheme was unfolding, another march to improvement that was used to justify the dispossession of thousands of shanty dwellers who made their homes on land that was to become Central Park. Frederick Law Olmsted is remembered as the creator of that great democratic space, a lyrical composition of open fields, ponds, and wooded groves held together by a series of looping pedestrian paths and carriage drives. Central Park today accommodates a diverse array of Mahattanites from all classes, seeking everything from productions of Shakespeare to frisbee tournaments and clandestine meeting places. But this was not Olmsted's vision. He conceived Central Park as a stage for genteel refinement; in his words, the park would "teach" visitors how to use it. Central Park was the very embodiment of the improvement ethic in American life. There, the middle class would refine itself by observing the upper classes, and the lower classes would improve themselves by observing the middle classes. Only the insistent demands of Manhattan's working classes, persisting over many decades, transformed the park into the accessible, multiuse space it is today. Olmsted's disdain for the lower classes was evident from his first action as the park's Superintendent of Construction: the eviction of 300 families from shanties located north of 59th Street, at what would become the bottom of the park. Olmsted saw the working poor as interlopers standing in the way of improvement, and the first thing he did was to order their removal.[18]

As an 1859 photograph of skaters in Central Park shows, poor people were not easily dislodged from this part of Manhattan. Along the top edge of the photograph, a shelf of shanties looms over Fifth Avenue, elevated behind a whirling mass of skaters silhouetted against the icy white of the frozen pond. Numerous magazine illustrations of skaters in the park appeared around the same time, but they all face north, away from the shanties on Fifth Avenue. Attempts to rid Central Park and the avenues surrounding it of shanties, to make way for the costly new residences envisioned by real estate developers, was a slow process. As shanty dwellers resisted, resentment grew among the middle and upper classes eager to secure the park as an amenity and use it to leverage adjacent development. The economic panic of 1857 boiled over in Manhattan with three days of street protests by the unemployed in early November; tempers were quelled, in part, by the promise of construction jobs on Central Park. The contempt for shanty dwellers intensified. Resentment sparked ridicule, which overflowed in an 1857 edition of *Harper's Weekly* featuring an update on the progress of the park.[19]

The article appeared under the straightforward headline, "The Central Park." The text is a workmanlike recounting of the park's design, illustrated with a map. The meat of the article, however, is in the 10 accompanying illustrations of the park's "present condition." The drawings lampoon the grandiose claims made for the park, while denigrating the residents of the shantytowns depicted. "Zoological Specimens Found In The Park" includes drawings of a sow and piglets, billy goat, bulldog, a rooster, and cow. "Present State Of The Carriage Drive" is the caption for a drawing of two rocky bluffs rising, Gibraltar fashion, in front of a shanty draped with telegraph lines—in fact, it is pinioned between the taut telegraph lines and a thick row of boulders at the bottom of the drawing. A shanty emerging from a rocky island, outlined against more telegraph lines, is dubbed "Present Appearance of the Grove." Several shanties, again with telegraph lines overhead, occupy the scene of "The Lake, From A Very Picturesque Point of View." A German family group—mother darning, bearded father with handcart, two sons—are "Fashionable Residents of the Park." An Irish family—darning and handcart replaced by pig and five children—are simply "Fashionable Denizens."[20]

The force of the sneering captions is magnified by the absence of commentary in the accompanying article, which focuses on Olmsted's plans for the park. Some 1,600 people—European immigrants and their descendants as well as African Americans—were living in shantytowns in Central Park when workers began clearing the site in 1857. These illustrations of shantytown dwellers are figures of fun, too "ridiculous" to inspire pity. These "denizens" are harmless, powerless to prevent the conversion of their community into a grove, a lake, a carriage drive. They float disembodied in a sea of text that talks exclusively about the future of the Central Park site. They are vestiges, incapable of influencing the outcome. In the same way that Poe used passive voice to disembody the Irish shantytown he described in 1844, *Harper's* accorded shantytown residents no agency. They did not bear talking about, because they were beneath notice and because, city officials insisted, they would soon cease to exist. Progress had not lifted them out of poverty, but the wrecking ball would dislodge them from its path.[21]

The medium of illustration, showcased in the numerous new magazines launched in the 1840s and 1850s, outperformed print in delivering a blunt condemnation of shantytowns: in a glance, viewers could understand the opposition of retrograde shanty life and forward-looking city life. They did not have to wade through text to get to the point that shanties stood for a lack of civilization—that they were an impediment to improvement. Woodcuts of shantytowns appeared mid-century not only in magazines but in city guide books, another publishing innovation that proved to be very popular with urban residents. Both offered city residents a new way of comprehending the expanding city. The inclusion of shantytowns in these publications testifies both to their ordinariness and to readers' curiosity about their meaning. The annual *Manual of the Corporation of the City of New York,* for example, repeatedly portrayed shantytowns as anachronisms on the urban landscape during the 1850s and 1860s. In the 1868 edition of the guide, a lithograph titled "View in Sixth Ave. between 55th and 57th" shows a row of wooden shanties lining a rocky bluff. In the foreground a few goats graze beneath a line of flapping wash, details that identified shantytowns with rural or village life. Shabbily-dressed shanty dwellers dot the bluff and the muddy patch of ground at the bottom of the image. Against this backdrop of rural references, emblems of progress bear down. Two telegraph poles frame the left side of the drawing and two streetcars anchor the right. Nearby, more telegraph lines lie draped

over a tall frame, ready for installation. Four well-dressed couples, the gentlemen in top hats and the ladies holding parasols, watch the streetcar gallop
past. Intent on their work or on each other, these shanty residents are oblivious to the swinging telegraph lines and the rumbling streetcars, and to their
message of progress. Change is not only coming, it has arrived, and the implication of the lithograph is that shantytowns will soon be flattened in its path.[22]

The scene depicted was located just south of land that in 1853 the city began
acquiring for construction of Central Park. Real estate developers and business leaders assumed that shantytowns such as the one pictured in this
Manual would quickly disappear as residential properties developed around
the park's edges. By the late 1860s, the inevitable disappearance of shantytowns was treated as a *fait accompli* in most press accounts, as it was in the
yearly *Manual.* This assumption applied not only to shantytowns on the edge
of what would become Central Park, but to all shantytowns. In 1859 and 1868,
editions of the *Manual* included illustrations depicting shantytowns as historical anachronisms. In 1859 the featured shantytown was Dutch Hill,
described in the caption as "Squatter Settlement, betw. 1st & 2d Aves. near
38th St. 1858." The artist positions the observer at the very threshold of this
large shantytown. One step forward, and the viewer would step in the large
mud puddle that oozes into the foreground of the drawing. A group of about
15 small shanties sit on a bluff jutting into the East River. Unused planks are
stacked haphazardly near one shanty, giving the impression that construction
is either ongoing or just finished. Chickens scratch for food, and a pig noses
an overturned basket of greens lying on the ground next to a broken pitcher.
Just right of center, two billy goats butt heads. A broom is propped against the
shed. On a hill behind the shanties stands a farmhouse, surrounded by a rail
fence and shaded by a large tree, the only sign of greenery in the picture.
Topped by a cloud-strewn sky, the farm scene is a bucolic counterpoint to the
shantytown below. The overall impression is of foraging animals, crowded
living conditions, and haphazard housekeeping. Although it was located east
of new residential areas that were developing in the middle of the island south
of 42nd Street, the image evokes a village at the edge of civilization, located
somewhere between the city from which the viewer has emerged and the
farmland in the distance—from which, symbolically, the American nation
had emerged. Similarly, an illustration in the 1868 edition of the *Manual*
highlights the disjunction between shantytown and modern city. Called

"View from School House in 42nd Street Between 2nd and 3rd Avs. Looking North," it shows a line of shanties stretched along a rocky bluff. Goats, pigs, and chickens root in the dust at the bottom of the image, where children dart between a trio of abandoned carts. Together children, animals, and carts create a barricade across the bottom of the drawing and between the viewer and the shantytown beyond. In the bottom right corner is a lone streetlamp, a potent symbol of the materially enlightened city that lay beyond the borders of darkest shantytown.[23]

By contrasting icons of rural and urban life, such as goats and streetlamps, these illustrations portray shantytown as out of sync with modern life, barricaded from the enlightened city by geographic and man-made barriers. Almost as potent in the *Manuals* is the absence of any written commentary on the shantytowns. There is no text about shantytowns or squatters beyond the captions, which give only the address and the information that this is a squatter settlement. The *Manual,* a popular guidebook to municipal government and city history, listed information on every aspect of city living, from omnibus routes and property valuations to pawnbrokers' addresses and the names of the paintings hanging in City Hall. Commonly called "Valentine's Manuals" after D. T. Valentine, the council clerk who compiled them from 1842 through 1866, the manuals commissioned artists to depict historic and contemporary New York scenes and maps. Unlike the pictorials

Shantytowns appeared in city guides to New York in the 1850s and 1860s.

popular later in the century, these guides did not gloss over the less laudatory aspects of city life, including, for example, illustrations of asylums,
orphanages, and the tenements of Five Points. The inclusion of shantytown
illustrations in several manuals suggests that these scenes were normal parts
of city life, perhaps even that people would have wondered at their exclusion
from a book devoted to covering every angle of New York's commercial and
civic life. But the Home for the Friendless and the Society for the Relief of
Respectable Aged Indigent Females, both of which appeared in the "City
Institutions" section, and other similar institutions were described in the text.
About shantytowns, nothing was said. Their inclusion is in keeping with the
encyclopedic nature of the guides, but the treatment of shantytowns underscores their paradoxical position as both everyday and aberrant aspects of
the landscape.

In 1854, the year after legislation authorizing Central Park was passed, the
New-York Daily Times published a lengthy article about a large shantytown of
more than 1,000 people on the western side of Manhattan. "If a stranger
should be suddenly set down anywhere in the quarter between Thirty-
seventh-street and Fifty-fifth-street, on the side near the Hudson," the article
begins, "he would hardly suspect that he is in an American city." The shantytown is peopled by Irish and German immigrants, or so the writer identifies
them, "strangers" who live in the "huts," "hovels," and "cabins" they constructed on vacant land. (Again, groups identified as "Irish" or "German"
were frequently not immigrants, but the descendants of immigrants, and
casual references to "squatters" often overlooked the fact that they were actually paying ground rent for the land their houses occupied.) Inviting the
reader to "come down with me now into this little colony—looking like an
Indian settlement," the writer narrates his strange encounter, highlighting the
residents' otherness with comparisons to Native Americans. The fact that
Tammany Hall, the Democratic political machine, was referred to as "the
wigwam" in press articles and political cartoons may have underscored the
political party affiliation of shantytown residents, who were dependable
Democratic voters.

One's first thought is that he is in a collection of wigwams. On every hand
little board or mud huts stretch away, with narrow lanes winding among
them. Some face the street, others surround some interior open ground,

others are planted as if at random in the midst of the lots. Dogs of every size and breed patrol around among them; goats are browsing on the roofs, and pigs calmly repose on the door-sills.

The flavor of a foreign dispatch continues as the writer describes these "Irish shanties, hardly high enough for a man to stand upright within." Goats, pigs, and dogs live in the same room as the family. Beyond the Irish shanties are "neater" huts occupied by Germans. "The yards are swept, there is a little rose-bush under the window, and a well-tilled garden-bed for lettuce behind." Inside he finds "a true German room" furnished with a feather bed and prints of "Bohemian saints," and harboring two "blue-eyed, sun-bloomed little girls, very ragged, with matted hair." "These are the squatters of New-York," explains the writer. With an air of surprise, he notes that despite their poverty, "yet they do not seem an idle set." Nevertheless, he goes on to argue that the children should be sent to the new Hudson River Industrial School on 10th Avenue, where poor immigrants such as these are taught "how to take care of themselves." And yet in the scene he describes, everyone is at work. The men labor "on the docks, or clearing the new houses, or hunting over the streets." The children of the district, which he estimates at between 800 and 900, pick rags and collect ashes, or slop the pigs. Women are singled out for their industry: "Strong, sun-browned women, bundled up in various dirty clothes, come in with little carts of ashes, the children pushing them along; others are cooking in the shanties, and still others are planing off little splinters from blocks of pine for the manufacturers of matches."[24]

Despite this busy scene, the author—who turns out to be Charles Loring Brace, the Children's Aid Society founder who started the odious "Orphan Train" that relocated poor children to the frontier—judges the inhabitants among the "dangerous poor," and warns the reader to take action. "It is from such that come our hordes of thieves and vagabonds and prostitutes . . . They sow seeds of vice and pestilence, amid their hovels of poverty, which scatter wide a terrible harvest among distant abodes of splendor and of wealth." That same year, diarist George Templeton Strong, one of the founders of New York's Sanitary Commission, would refer to the Irish shanties that "[h]ere and there . . . 'come out' like smallpox pustules, along Madison Avenue south of 59th Street. Shanty dwellers were an infection, a foreign object infecting the body politic that had to be eradicated before the innocent affluent, living in "distant abodes of splendor," were contaminated.[25]

Brace's account of shanty dwellers strikes themes that occur repeatedly in accounts of shantytowns for the rest of the century. Animals run amok. Children run amok. Even streets and lanes run amok, resisting the civilizing influence of the 1811 grid. Men are absent. Women are strong and sturdy, often dark-skinned. Domiciles made of boards and mud are "hovels," "huts," "shanties," or occasionally "cabins," but never houses or homes. Inhabitants and their communities are marginalized as foreign; this is not an "American" place. Despite the appearance of domesticity and industry, the scene inspires anxiety in the writer about the spread of crime and disease and acts as a rallying cry for middle-class reformers to teach the poor "how to take care of themselves." In denial of the obvious industry of every man, woman, and child the author encounters in this neighborhood, the "squatters" are declared instruments of vice and pestilence, in need of guidance—nay, salvation—by middle-class reformers like Brace himself. In her famous 1862 poem, "I like to see it lap the miles," Emily Dickinson invokes the specter of a locomotive that careens around mountains to "supercilious peer / In Shanties—by the sides of Roads." Dickinson's train is a straightforward metaphor for industrialization, urbanization, and modernity, which not only dominate the landscape but poke their noses into private domestic spaces with an archly judgmental, "supercilious" air. In just such a manner did Charles Loring Brace and his fellow reformers poke their noses into the shanties of the poor, and find them wanting.[26]

The writers and illustrators who portrayed shantytowns in the mid-nineteenth century suffered from documentary amnesia. Even as they stood in the midst of these communities, chatting with their inhabitants or venturing inside their homes, they presented shantytowns as outside of time and beyond the bounds of community, a historical oddity, or a threat to safety. By the 1850s, the caveat that poor laborers, although an eyesore, were also the "bone and sinew" of the nation—the judgment expressed by the city aldermen who approved the widening of Chapel Street in 1833—had disappeared. That admonition, while condescending, embraced poor laborers as part of the urban citizenry. The aldermen demolished their homes and abandoned them to their own devices, but at least in theory they conceived of them as part of the same urban populus: they winced as they made them homeless. But by

the 1850s, as the discourse of shantytowns makes clear, that tenuous comradeship was broken. Shantytown residents were "strangers" who bred disease and
crime. Brace fears not only the tangible specter of cholera—"pestilence"—but
the scourge of "vice" emanating from shantytown. Poverty, pestilence, and
criminality are collapsed into one category and located on particular urban
landscapes.[27]

Mid-century newspaper articles imaginatively repositioned shantytowns
outside the confines of civilized modern life. In 1858 a newspaper reporter
visiting a large, centrally-located Brooklyn shantytown that covered eight
square blocks described it as "almost an 'unknown land,'" a foreign and exotic
"Constantinople" in the middle of the city, from which a "hegira of the inhabitants" erupted when shanties were demolished. "Gathering up their household
gods, they moved far out of town, where it was supposed the advancing tide of
civilization would never overtake them." An 1867 report in the New York Times
recounted the "marvelous rapidity" of a shanty-raising performed by the friends
and relatives of the settlers. Construction commenced at dawn and was complete, including the erection of clotheslines and placement of "rickety" furniture, by nightfall. "The palaces of the Arabian Nights, built by the Genii at
Aladdin's bidding, were not put up half as quickly as the squatter's shanty."[28]

Another reporter identified shanty dwellers with foreigners in an article
about the trials and tribulations of property owners trying to evict shanty
dwellers from Yorkville, a German-American neighborhood on Manhattan's
Upper East Side; this article pokes gentle fun at the disgruntled rich landlords,
while endorsing their plans to improve their property. "Squatting is a weakness
of Universal Humanity, and squatters are in every land a terror and a scourge."
Pointing to squatter settlements in Australia and Japan, the rant takes a turn:
"You think, good reader, that we talk of distant lands and regions removed by
continents or an ocean. We, too, are a squatter-ridden people." The Yorkville
residents, who the reporter terms "Squatter Sovereigns," are "intruders," located
outside of the circle of "we" rightful citizens. "The owners of lots, especially of
lots around Yorkville, have not taxes only to pay, nor rents to collect, but these
squatters to fight with, and their possession to dispute when they are ready to
improve their property."[29]

By the end of the nineteenth century the forces of improvement had won the
day, and shantytowns were largely eradicated (albeit temporarily) in Manhattan
and Brooklyn. The tale shantytowns tell, of survival in the face of systematic

dispossession, has been largely lost to history. The story we tell about poor immigrants and laborers in New York City is almost always a story about Five Points, the impoverished Lower East Side neighborhood captured by photographer Jacob Riis in the late nineteenth century. Images of an overcrowded, crime-ridden streetscape, encircled by glowering tenements, dominate our visual catalog of poor neighborhoods in nineteenth-century America. A specific intersection of ethnicity, architecture, and urbanity—in which masses of poor immigrants lived in multistory tenements overseen by unscrupulous landlords and terrorized by gangs—Five Points has become the generic landscape of urban poverty in nineteenth-century America. But there were other spaces dominated by poor laborers in Manhattan and Brooklyn, which looked nothing like the tenements of Five Points. Shantytowns constitute a parallel narrative to the familiar story of tenement life. They were not the huddled masses of sheds-and-shanties of Chapel Street, thrown up by unscrupulous landlords to make a quick killing and demolished at the city's whim to make way for more expensive housing. Nor were they the teeming tenements of Five Points, where generations of immigrants and poor workers managed to eke out livings and, gradually, solidify the political power required for economic and social gains. Unlike the tenement districts of the Lower East Side, covered with buildings that were erected, controlled, and surveilled by landlords, shantytowns were self-built communities, constructed by their owners from materials at hand, on plots of land rented from absentee landlords, and delineated according to community standards. They were relatively free of oversight; as one journalist pointed out, shantytown residents lived "a kind of independent life." Like tenement dwellers, they built political alliances and enjoyed a measure of political power. This would have been meaningful, certainly, for residents who had been displaced not only from their native landscapes— immigrants from Ireland and Germany, and African-American migrants from New England—but subsequently evicted during the demolition of sheds and shanties downtown, as happened with the widening of Chapel Street in the 1830s. Doubly dispossessed, they built their own worlds.[30]

In building and occupying shantytowns, shanty dwellers rebelled against the grid, and in so doing, against the middle- and upper-class urban elites who championed it as the model for urban expansion and growth. We unfurl the map of the 1811 grid of Manhattan when we imagine the unfolding of the city northward from its colonial beginnings. But shantytowns provide an alternative narrative of urban development. Shanty builders fashioned not only dwellings but entire neighborhoods that rejected the uniformity of the grid. Shantytowns occupied and domesticated the rocky granite heights, the swampy marshes, and the toxic industrial environs of the growing city. These neighborhoods triumphed over the topography as decisively as the grid; land-use strategies in shantytowns were no more or less "natural" than the land uses organized by the grid. But shantytowns rejected the dichotomy of urban versus rural imbedded in the grid—and the dichotomy of civilized and uncivilized imposed by the grid's advocates. By routinely including agricultural and quasi-industrial uses, shantytowns exploited and damaged the environment as thoroughly as the blasting of streets and the construction of streetcars, els, and apartment buildings, but their footprint was irregular, illegible to outsiders, an encoding of traditions modified by and adapted to the imperatives of modern American urban life. Rather than deploy geometry to control geography, as the grid did, shantytown dwellers evolved a sort of oppositional urban planning that mastered the natural environment without exiling rural uses, while simultaneously preserving traditional practices of single-family occupation that we might describe as sprawl today. Shantytowns sprawled over the urban landscape. They incorporated miniature farms, the keeping of livestock, and on-site small businesses focused mostly on waste removal and recycling—enterprises incompatible with the gridded city.

African-American shantytowns were similarly foreign and strange—figuratively off the grid, despite the long and often legal possession of property by black owners. A minister from St. Michael's Episcopal Church described an African-American shantytown known as Seneca Village, founded in 1825, as a "wilderness" filled with "the habitations of poor and wretched people of every race and and color and nationality." "This waste," he reported, contained "many families of colored people with whom consorted and in many case amalgamated, debased and outcast whites." The white settler strategy of declaring American land a "waste" as a justification for claiming it, despite its obvious use by other populations, dates to the first European settlements. Seneca Village stretched from 81st to 89th Streets between 8th and 9th Avenues, and was home to about 250 people. African Americans owned about half of the parcels of land in the village. Far from being a "waste," Seneca Village boasted two churches and a school, the first in

Manhattan built for black children. By the 1850s many Irish and German residents had built shanties in Seneca Village, and a third church had been founded that served a mixed-race congregation, giving rise to the minister's concern about "amalgamation." Newspaper coverage of Seneca Village, derisively called "Nigger Village" in the press, exoticized it. "The Ebon inhabitants, after whom the village is called, present a pleasing contrast in their habits and the appearance of their dwellings to the Celtic occupants, in common with hogs and goats, of the shanties in the lower part of the Park," the *Times* reported in 1856. The "Ebon" inhabitants were native-born African Americans, hailing from climes no more exotic than New England and the American South. Calling them "Ebon" evoked the foreign air that Charles Loring Brace conjured when he wrote about the Irish and German "strangers" inhabiting the shantytown at 37th Street, or that the visitor to a Brooklyn shantytown meant to invoke by comparing it to "Constantinople."[31]

Newspaper articles painted shantytown residents as "strangers," culturally distant despite their physical closeness. While fanning the flames of nativism, which peaked in the mid-1850s with the formation of the American Party, stories like these offered middle-class readers a comforting cultural geography. An influx of foreign "strangers" may have been building shantytowns just across the street, but they could be placed in a remote social zone. They could be included in a commercial guide to the city, but symbolically excluded by the absence of commentary. A thin sidewalk may have been all that separated shantytown residents from their more affluent neighbors, but cultural barriers offered a greater, longer-lasting protection. Shantytowns existed in another dimension no matter their proximity to the growing city. Even shantytowns imbedded in the urban landscape within the settled portion of the island were depicted as somehow faraway and unfathomable.

Repeatedly, shantytowns were used to illustrate the efficacy and moral rightness of the American ethic of improvement. In one extreme example, an 1853 *Brooklyn Eagle* editorial championed the annexation of Cuba by comparing it to a shantytown standing in the way of urban real estate development, which not only could, but should be grabbed at will. "If a capitalist or a possessor of real estate conceives a desire to improve his property by erecting new dwellings on unoccupied lots," the editorial begins, he should be no more deterred by the presence of poor people than "a projected railway . . . found to run through a farmer's outhouses or cabbage garden." The desire to annex

Cuba, by logical extension, places the United States "just in the position of the builder who wanted the ground occupied by a shanty to erect a marble mansion on its site." There should be no more scruple over annexing Cuba than over demolishing shantytown, the writer insists. "Is there anything dishonourable in this? It has never been so considered." Indeed, the "grasping spirit" of the capitalist is often "an adjunct of a public improvement." A nation should never hesitate in "acquiring a piece of territory when it finds its possession necessary to its safety and progress." In this analogy, shantytown residents are analogous to the "Creole" population of Cuba, beneficiaries of a takeover by the morally superior (and whiter) United States.[32]

Shanty dwellers are Indians, Creoles, or "niggers"; "Celtic" or "Bohemian"; inhabitants of mini-nations within American cities but not part of the great American civilization itself. Quite the opposite, they are obstacles to its progress. Mid-century observers approached the subject of shantytowns with varying agendas and from different viewpoints, some more sympathetic than others. Shantytowns were savage, comic, filthy, orderly, enterprising, and shiftless by turns, or sometimes all at once. But these representations all share one belief, expressed in Poe's pseudo-paean to primitive "tabernacles" in 1844 and reprised thereafter in press accounts and commercial illustrations: shantytowns existed beyond the borders of modern, civilized life. The shantytown was used as an emblem of difference, a marker of the border between civilized us and uncivilized them, a line that mirrored the sides being taken in national debates over Americans deserving of rights and protections of the state and interlopers who tried to grab those rights for themselves. Shantytowns helped middle-class Americans perform the task of deciding who was a citizen, entitled to the rights and protections of American democracy, and who was not. Classifying shanty housing as emblematic of backwardness and a lack of civilization became a way of justifying the repossession of land occupied by shanties, and the exile of the people who lived there—not just from the land in question, but ultimately from the city itself. Evicting families from their homes and razing their houses was much easier if both had been degraded in the public imagination, and painting shanty dwellers as foreign and un-American helped accomplish this. A commitment to improvement, routinely defined in terms of real estate development and property rights, justified the elimination of shantytowns. Improvement, therefore, depended on dispossession—of Indians, African Americans, foreign immigrants. By reducing their homes to eyesores and declaring them "strangers," civic leaders and elites in Manhattan and Brooklyn made the dispossession of shanty dwellers a moral and ethical duty.

Denigration of shanty dwellers sometimes tipped over from labeling them as foreign to debasing them as inhuman. The difference middle-class urbanites perceived between themselves and urban shanty dwellers was summed up in the headline for an 1860 magazine exposé on housing for the poor: "Backgrounds of our Civilization." In 1860, when this piece was published, illustrated magazines were booming, and often featured travel articles that transported readers into unimagined realms. The title of this series asserts the superiority of the magazine's readers, positioning them in the vanguard of civilization, at the front lines of modernity. The illustrations of an East 44th Street shantytown known as Dutch Hill reinforce this hierarchy. In one, two barefooted women, one clasping an infant, face each other on a muddy path. Behind them is a row of shanties made of wooden planks, stretching off into the distance. In the foreground is a trash heap full of rotting vegetation. A goat roots in the garbage and a pig wallows nearby; comically, another pig faces off with a dog at the edge of the muddy slop—mimicking the poses of the two women, who, intent on one another, appear oblivious to the decay around them. The implication is that the women and the animals share this filthy landscape as equals. An editorial accompanying the series interprets these images for readers: "Painful as it may be to dwell upon such scenes, they must not be blinked by society . . . Let the public look at these plague-spots— the dark back-ground of our civilization—and devise measures to remove it, if such a thing be possible." Shantytowns were an older, allegedly primitive form of housing that was an anachronism in the modern city—and cast shadows on the present: shantytowns existed in the background of the expansion and progress of New York City. These backward "plague-spots," literally infected blotches on the body politic, stand apart from "the public" of the magazine readership, a refined, middle-class public, which must "devise measures to remove" the shantytown, "if such a thing be possible." The resignation of the final phrase shows a dawning realization, as early as 1860, that shantytowns were resilient and resistant to removal. Expunging them would not be easy, but it was nevertheless necessary.[33]

The vocabulary for denigrating shantytowns that had been developing since at least the 1830s all came together in an 1869 illustration in *Harper's Weekly*. The full-page image, drawn by prolific illustrator D. E. Wyand, is titled "Squatters of New York: A Scene Near Central Park," and narrates a story of conflict between the imperatives of urban elites and the priorities of shantytown residents. It points toward disputes that animated relationships between shanty dwellers themselves. By the time this illustration, a precursor to photojournalism, was published in June 1869, construction on Central Park had progressed in fits and starts to cover the 863 acres stretching from 59th to 110th Streets. Several million New Yorkers used the park every year, but they were overwhelmingly from the middle and upper classes. Efforts to exclude lower-class users from the park by restricting its use on Sundays, their only day off, persisted, as did the prohibition of sports and many other recreational uses. Arguments over Sunday closings and other efforts to preserve the park for the elite—all championed by Olmsted—came to a head in 1870 when Tammany Hall politicians wrested control away from Olmsted and his backers. When this illustration was printed in *Harper's*, tensions over the future of the park were at a high point.

At the center of the illustration is a heated argument between two residents of the shantytown—in the judgment of the accompanying caption, "Squatters." The woman, who is facing the reader, gestures in the direction of three large dogs sitting a few feet away. She is clearly threatening to sic her dogs on the man. He points angrily over the woman's left shoulder toward the interior of the shantytown, which is shown stretching to the horizon. He stands beside one of many hand carts pictured in the scene, suggesting he may have just parked it in order to debate the woman. This may indeed be a domestic dispute the couple is engaged in, concerning the man's work as a cart-man. Several other women, their faces all drawn with the apelike features commonly used to depict Irish immigrants during the period, watch the public dispute as their children play nearby. The ground is rough, and rows of shanties cling to rocky ridges in the distance. A goat stands atop what appears to be the decapitated roof of a streetcar from the Grand Street Ferry Railroad, perhaps a reference to the imminent conversion to elevated trains: streetcar relics would further identify the shantytown as an anachronism. The argument between the man and the woman is punctuated visually by a tall sign that stands like an exclamation mark between them: on a pole that towers above the rooflines of the shanties, a rectangular sign proclaims "These Lots for Sale." The invitation to "Apply Within" is scrawled below, barely legible in the drawing. Improvements are overtaking this shantytown, as they had those within the park itself.[34]

Central Park was a favorite destination for the middle and upper classes
when this illustration was published in 1869, as conflicts with shanty
dwellers intensified.

The main action of the illustration is internal to shantytown, but the image
provides a social commentary on the clash between the vulgarity of shantytown and the respectable appeal of the expanding city. The paved sidewalk is
positioned as a visual and narrative focal point, marking the tenuous border

between shantytown and the rest of the city. Along the bottom of the full-page illustration, two smartly-dressed young women stride purposefully along, heads together and bonnet ribbons aflutter. Their dresses and their strides are so identical, and they stand so close together that they appear almost as one double-torsoed creature with four feet. A small flock of geese crosses in front of them; to their left sits a goat, that standard-bearer of urban shantytowns. The narrow sidewalk, which one of a group of shanty children has already breached, is too flimsy to serve as a real boundary line between the lives of the young women, obviously coming home from working in a shop or office, and the lounging shanty matrons, who sit in the dirt smoking pipes and talking. The progress of the young women underlines the social barrier represented by the sidewalks, and in shantytown illustrations, the figure of well-dressed women walking the line between shantytown and the city represented by a sidewalk becomes something of a trope. In another *Harper's* illustration from 1881, for example, of "Negro Shanties" in Washington, D.C., a single white woman and her pet dog, a pug with its nose held disdainfully high in the air, traverse the sidewalk between an African-American shantytown and the federal city. The physical distance between the middle-class dog-owner—and, the illustration implies, her dog—and the poor black residents of shantytown is only a few feet. But the sidewalk in these images bisects a vast social distance.[35]

Another drama unfolds in this illustration. The shantytown stretches to the horizon, but the hovering "For Sale" sign foretells its demise. Near the sign, barely visible on a below-grade front porch, a representative of the property owner is pictured, consulting his watch. Time is running out for the shantytown, this detail suggests, and the arguments of residents are little more than antics performed for the entertainment of *Harper's* readers. Or is time on shantytown's side? Here are all of the middle class's fears about shantytowns realized: boundless huts and hovels, stretching into infinity. Signs of progress—the working girls, fresh from work at a new department store or office building; the "For Sale" sign and the attendant real estate broker—offer signs of hope for a middle-class future. But the shantytown dominates the landscape: barnyard animals converge on the fast-paced young women; dirty children trespass on the sidewalk; the sounds of the angry man and woman and, perhaps, the growling of the woman's pack of Cerberus-like dogs mark the gates of urban hell. In this milieu the "For Sale" sign and the clock-watching real estate broker are feeble omens, at best. In this image, shantytown is winning. The drive to remove shantytowns from the urban landscape of New York proved an arduous, lengthy project. More than a decade later, in 1880, *Harper's New Monthly Magazine* published another illustration of the same topic, shantytowns near Central Park, this time captioned "On the Border of Central Park." Another leading magazine illustrator, A. B. (Albert B.) Shults, captured the same narrative with nearly identical stock characters: shanty woman, bedraggled barefoot shanty children, marauding pigs and geese, flapping wash, listing shanties, and an insistent visitor, a top-hatted, waistcoated gentleman leaning on a cane—perhaps a landlord's representative?—who appears to be patiently explaining the coming deluge to the shanty woman. Subtle changes in attitudes toward shanty dwellers are evident in this illustration—the shanty woman, for example, is meek and friendly, and her upturned face, framed with soft blonde ringlets, shows no trace of the demeaning apelike features typically used to depict Irish characters. But the image occupies the same continuum of urban shantytown stereotypes that started with Poe and Whitman in the 1840s.[36]

"On the Border of Central Park" appeared 11 years after *Harper's* 1869 illustration of the "Squatters of New York." A dozen years before that, in 1857, the magazine published its Central Park article poking fun at the "Fashionable Denizens" and "Zoological Specimens" occupying land designated for the park. Three sets of illustrations, evenly spaced over a period of 23 years—in 1857, 1869, and 1880—all on the topic of the shantytowns that persisted in Central Park, all drawing on a vocabulary of backward, rural, "primitive" housing, all made the same point: shantytowns were the antithesis of the modern city, and could not endure. Except they had endured, as these and other images prove. An 1871 article in *Appleton's Journal,* an illustrated weekly that targeted an educated, art-loving audience, described a shanty-strewn region near Central Park, quite possibly the same one depicted in the *Harper's* illustration from 1869: "It is a broken, unkempt, dismantled area . . . It is a place of rocky asperities and high, hard, barren stony outcroppings . . . It is forever being hacked at—shivered by blasts, pried and battered by blows . . . It is as intricate as the Maze at Woodstock," and most worrying of all, "It is everywhere." Far from disappearing, shantytown was everywhere New Yorkers looked. Ultimately, middling- and upper-class elites imposed their wills on urban landscapes. Shantytowns and tenements were forced out of the way by new development and transportation infrastructure in the 1880s and 1890s. But what we now view as a timely, natural progression was at the time undecided and alarming to the middle and upper classes. Shantytowns were a rival vision in the contest to determine what the American city would look like, how it would be used, and who got to decide those questions. Middle-class urbanites wielding the grid, and pursuing public works projects such as Central Park, insisted the right to design the city was theirs alone. But shantytown residents had other ideas about the settings appropriate to urban life. To see what constituted their rival vision, we must piece together popular songs, oil paintings, and the sketchbook of a socialist drawing teacher, and assemble the threads of several chronologies of shanty-towns in Brooklyn as well as Manhattan. The shanty and the shantytown meant markedly different things to the people who built and inhabited them, and while those meanings have been largely lost to history, they have been preserved in popular culture.[37]

4

A Working-Poor Ideology of Dwelling

Throughout Manhattan and Brooklyn, poor laborers took possession of the urban landscape and molded it to their needs. In each instance, their actions presented direct opposition to the encroaching grid and the commodified urban land rubric it inscribed. A land use counter-movement that began in the 1840s, shantytowns thrived well into the 1890s; treated as transients and "squatters," shantytown residents often stayed for decades, establishing businesses and raising families in shanties they built on leased or otherwise vacant land. Histories of Brooklyn and New York go into great detail about the expansion of the grid and the growth of the commercial city, but ignore or set aside the prevalence of shantytowns. Popular songs and art, however, provide a glimpse into the intentions of shanty builders. It is a piecemeal portrait, but an engrossing one. There is also much to learn from elite observations, shorn of their bias and condescension. On close examination, and by splicing these views together, a narrative from the point of view of the shanty builders emerges.[1]

First and foremost, they came to work. Shantytown residents of all races and ethnicities were employed as manual laborers and factory workers, as well as entrepreneurs, providing a range of services to their own communities and to the growing middle-class sectors of the two cities. Social reformer Charles Loring Brace, in one of his several visits to shantytowns, noted that the men labored "on the docks, or clearing the new houses, or hunting over the streets," and that women and children collected ashes and whittled matches. As early as the 1840s, even before famines in Ireland and political uprisings in Germany sparked massive migrations, European immigrants worked on the docks or in factories in industrial Red Hook, building shantytowns in the swampy adjoining land. In 1842, construction workers who lived in a shantytown near the Hamilton Avenue bridge had "a tough fight" with management, and the fierceness of the protests inspired the name of the shantytown, Texas, in honor of the battles that year between the independent state and Mexico. German immigrants, recruited to replace striking Irish workers at the Atlantic Basin, lived in a "row of shanties" along Van Brunt Street starting in 1846. African-American workers, banned or displaced from most factory employment, built a shantytown in a corner of Brooklyn known as Crow Hill, from which they commuted to jobs as domestic servants.[2]

The expansion of textile manufacturing attracted more European immigrants to Brooklyn shantytowns in the 1850s. In 1851, a shanty building boom on Red Hook Point was attributed to the opening earlier that spring of a new cotton factory, which was "confidently expected to afford ample employment to all the inhabitants of that neighborhood during the approaching summer." Shanty dwellers sometimes commuted from Brooklyn to jobs in Manhattan. "A fair proportion of the sun-burned, hard-handed laborers who board the Third-avenue cars, and jump off when nearing an open space of ground covered with shanties of every conceivable shape and dimension, are squatters on their way home," reported one correspondent for the *New York Times*. Other shantytown residents fished, farmed, or scavenged for a living. According to "Ten Thousand Squatters," an 1880 retrospective on the history of New York's shantytowns, the early population was composed of "rag-pickers, pea-nut vendors, street-peddlers, knife-grinders, laborers, idlers, and vagrants." Shanties along Gowanus Beach, in Brooklyn, were occupied by men who hired out boats to fishermen. They padded their income by foraging for timber in the bay, a practice ridiculed by the local newspaper. Peering through telescopes, the shanty men scanned the surface of the bay until they spotted floating logs, then leapt into their boats to collect the booty. "Such a regular regatta as now takes place, beats the prize affairs all to smash."[3]

Contemporary art and illustrations show shanty dwellers pursuing their livelihoods. Carts figure prominently in an 1868 illustration of a shantytown located at 42nd Street and Second Avenue, published in the *Manual of the Corporation of the City of New York*. An 1879 sketch by Fernand Harvey Lungren, called *Shanties on 69th Street*, shows a street vendor pausing in front of a row of shanties. Paintings from the 1860s and 1870s by Ralph Albert Blakelock, by etcher Mary Nimmo Moran, and by an amateur artist named Henreich (later Henry) Metzner depict shantytown laundresses, saloon keepers, junkmen, and market gardeners. An 1869 illustration from *Harper's* shows a shanty woman crouching in the doorway of a shop, manning a display of cakes and coffee for sale; an account from a few years earlier described a woman keeping a cigar and candy store somewhere in "Shanty-dom," a region stretching from Fifth Avenue to the East River north of 44th Street. The leading role in an 1882 musical comedy called *Squatter Sovereignty* belongs to a shanty matron who runs a saloon and sells goat milk on the side. Offal-boiling and piggeries were also popular shantytown businesses. An 1859 newspaper article describes the "onslaught" of police required to demolish "Hog Town," a shantytown rich with piggeries that covered a 10-block area from 46th to 57th Streets between Sixth and Eighth Avenues. The demolition was also celebrated in an article the same year in *Frank Leslie's Illustrated Magazine,* which included a drawing of the shantytown under the headline, "The Great War on the New York Piggeries." In the assault on Hog Town, 87 armed police divided into two columns to surround the fat-renderers. The columns met at the corner of 57th Street and Sixth Avenue, a rocky district "whose summit is crowned by the castle—if it be true that every man's shanty is his castle—of James McCormick, the king of the offal-boilers."[4]

A major source of income for shantytown residents was farming. Residents maintained market gardens and raised livestock for sale and for their own consumption. Poe, for example, commented on the gardens attached to the shanties in undeveloped Manhattan above 14th Street in 1844. They persisted into the 1880s, as artists' renderings prove. As time passed and shantytowns got bigger, some residents raised cows and ran their own dairies, selling milk to customers in more affluent neighborhoods. A November 21, 1864, *New York Times* article complained that some 20,000 squatters enjoyed "the right to free pasture for cows, goats and pigs in the public thoroughfares of the city." Squatters were observed "claim[ing] the right of carrying on the pork and dairy business" in Manhattan. In Tinkersville, a dense shantytown located on a spit of land that stretched into the Gowanus Bay, residents ran a dairy with 10 cows. A newspaper report that judged the Tinkersville residents "lazy-looking" and "indolent" nevertheless recorded that the residents "fat their own pork, raise a few fowls, and supply a portion of Brooklyn with milk."[5]

The goat became the mascot of shantytown, appearing in almost every article or illustration printed about shantytowns in the second half of the century. An 1864 newspaper article applauded the removal of a "goat pasturage" on Third

Avenue a few months prior. Goats are prominently featured in images of shantytowns published in editions of the city *Manual* in 1859 and 1868. Fictional accounts of shantytowns also honored the goat. In *The Age of Innocence,* Mrs. Mingott (a character based on Edith Wharton's great-aunt) stares out at the goats grazing on the motley landscape of shanties, mansions, and bare ground that converged at 57th Street and Fifth Avenue, the site of her new house, built in the late 1860s in what her society friends regarded as "an inaccessible wilderness near the Central Park": "She was sure that presently the hoardings, the quarries, the one-story saloons, the wooden greenhouses in ragged gardens, and the rocks from which goats surveyed the scene would vanish before the advance of residences as stately as her own." In urban settings increasingly configured to accommodate the lives of middle-class consumers, shantytowns provided spaces for the activities of working-poor producers.[6]

Shantytown residents were not the shiftless characters portrayed in the mainstream media. They were laborers and minor entrepreneurs who took possession of the land they needed to establish businesses and house themselves and their families. Portraying them as otherwise required determination on the part of observers. Over and over again, elite observers are caught in a catch-22, inadvertently or begrudgingly acknowledging the thrift and industry of shanty dwellers even as they identify them as lazy and dangerous. An awareness of the disconnect between the disparagement of shantytowns as "dens of vice and wretchedness" and the visual evidence does seep through. The author of an 1858 series on "Homes of the Poor" in the *New York Times* insists that among the "improvident" are scattered "many industrious, temperate, and tidy" residents of shantytown. The men are unemployed but "sober" and eager to work. One example is a blacksmith who travels the length of Brooklyn daily looking for work. Many of the women are good housekeepers: "miserable shanties" on the outside, some of the houses are "patterns of neatness" inside, with religious devotion signaled "in every house" by pictures of Catholic saints or priests. There is even a whiff of prosperity, or at least economic stability: "Some few appear to be comfortably provided for; they own their own shanties, have an occasional job of work, are well, and say they would scorn to beg." A lucky few have "a few dollars in the Savings Bank," a sign that they were not spendthrifts, but valued frugality.[7]

Physically, the form of shanties changed little in the middle decades of the nineteenth century, although they did reflect a variety of styles, and some ingenious repurposing of structures built for other uses. Charles Loring Brace, on a series of visits to shantytowns in 1855, reported that most shanties were either small mud huts or "wigwams," but goes on to detail variation: "Some are of the primitive block form, with a hole in the roof for a chimney; others are arched, others with a sharp Gothic gable. Occasionally, something entirely new in architectural style will meet you in the shape of a rectangular box with diamond lattice work, which, on nearer approach, you discover to be a *Railroad car* banked in, and made into a house." Several descriptions of small boats, or cabins from larger boats, being converted into shanties appear in the media mid-century, and there is artistic evidence of boat shanties as well.[8]

Two artists' renderings, both made around 1850, show the range and the limits of the house form. The first, a sketch by John Mackie Falconer, was made in the swampy environs of industrial Greenpoint. *At Newtown Creek, Long Island* shows a house with a sharply pitched roof, its porch supported by unmilled timbers. The back half of the roof almost touches the ground; a small shed is attached to the rear; and there is no foundation, although the presence of two chimneys suggests long occupation and gradual upgrades. The second, a watercolor by Charles H. Parsons, documents a different style of shanty, one that recalls newspaper descriptions of the "wigwams" observed by Brace in Manhattan, or the "primitive" mud huts discovered by Edgar Allan Poe on his Manhattan rambles in 1844. *Negro Huts Near Bedford, L.I.* depicts an enclave of conical huts, covered with small branches, with walls made of mud and large stones. Rudimentary chimneys protrude from the two shanties in the foreground, poking out of the roofs like small cigars. Wide, squat, perfectly proportioned wooden doors, made of planks, sport hinges and latches. The whole appears to have been whitewashed. One door is ajar, and beside it stands an African-American woman, hands on hips, with her sleeves rolled up and a cotton bonnet or perhaps a tignon on her head. A child sits in the dusty path at her feet, stroking a reclining dog. The woman and child stare out of the picture in the terse manner of the squatter and his son in George Caleb Bingham's *The Squatters,* painted in 1850 and exhibited the following year in the same Brooklyn art show that featured Parsons's *Negro Huts.* The squatter and his son, the African-American woman and her child, and their respective dogs lay claim to the landscapes they occupy, quietly asserting their rights to territory.[9]

Falconer's sketch and Parsons's watercolor reveal shanties on the industrial Brooklyn landscapes that could have been lifted from the woods at Walden, or the Ohio frontier, or the *Farmers and Emigrants Complete Guide* of 1845. Whether in Brooklyn, northeast Ohio, or the interior of "Mannahatta" island, they were small, generally one-room shelters made of mud, stone, sticks, and planks, constructed from natural or man-made materials at hand. They took the form of a conical hut, a lean-to, or an unframed wooden house, often with an attached shed. A description from an 1858 news report could have served as a caption for Falconer's sketch: "With few exceptions, these shanties are of one story, and a very low one at that. Some have an entry, or a porch, around the door, which serves as a protection from the storm, as the original 'front-door' alley enters directly into the main room. Extending back, or attached to one side, is generally a cow shed, in which is kept a horse or cow, and the sunny corners are usually fitted with small 'cubby holes,' which are occupied by the dogs, the goats, and the poultry. There is scarcely a shanty without a few hens about the door; occasionally a goat, instead of a cow, is made to supply milk for the family." The same report described a typical interior: "Nine out of ten of the shanties have only one room, which does not average over twelve feet square, and this serves all the purposes of the family. A bed, a few chairs or benches, a table, a stove and a cradle, constitute the staple articles of furniture; the cradle is seldom empty." Found objects and materials dominated both the structure and its furnishings; the cradle in this account was a soap box with rockers attached.[10]

There was variation in the shanty form. An 1865 survey of 2,000 shanty dwellings in the vicinity of Central Park recorded that while they were usually a single room and "always of moderate extent," the height ranged from 6 to 10 feet; some had one window while others had as many as four; "and its ground area varies much in different cases." A notation that "[t]he better shanties are lathed and plastered" suggests that builders improved their shanties over time. The shanty was a migratory house form come to rest in growing cities, where it inspired a working-poor aesthetic of dwelling that reflected values of reinvention and adaptation.[11]

What was different about urban shanties, exemplified by those found in mid-nineteenth-century Brooklyn and New York, was not the house form, which remained much the same, but the settlement, the shanty *town*. They varied in size, from a scattering to hundreds of shanties, and until the 1870s, were generally referred to as squatter settlements. "A squatter neighborhood comprises an indefinite number of shanties"; they were "everywhere," "multi-tudinous." They took you by surprise. "Some of them are in places where they would never be suspected, and some are so hemmed in and hidden by tall buildings that they can hardly be found. Some of them are just in the rear of elegant brown-stone houses; some rub up against the edges of sparkling Fifth-avenue." A West Side property owner complained in 1879 of having to "grope his way among squatter shanties" to get to the street, "at the imminent risk of being bitten by their vicious dogs." The ubiquity of shanty settlements preoccupied observers, who, struggling to categorize their relationship to the gridded city, dubbed them "villages," or "colonies." Shanty settlements didn't acquire the label "shantytown" until the 1870s, when artists, songwriters, novelists, and journalists all began using the term. At that point the description "shantytown" was applied retroactively to describe shanty settlements founded as early as the 1820s. One observer labeled them "metropolitan hamlets," and although he meant to denigrate the community with a reference to provincial life, the description is apt. Shantytowns were thoroughly metropolitan. But their organization and layout distinguished them from the urban grid taking hold around them. Middle-class observers experienced them as provincial hamlets, adrift in history, but they functioned to promote the very modern requirements of the inhabitants, who needed to live near city jobs while also farming and keeping livestock. Easy access to the built-up parts of the city, and the parts under construction, was essential to shantytown residents, because that is where their jobs or customers were located.[12]

Shantytowns served another, less tangible function for residents: they insulated residents from the prying eyes of public officials, landlords, and social reformers. A system of illegibility, seemingly oxymoronic but highly functional, governed urban shantytowns in the mid-nineteenth century. The location of shantytowns discouraged casual visitation. They were built on the least hospitable urban terrain: the rocky, the barren, the boulder-strewn, the swampy. The first shantytown in Brooklyn occupied a marshy meadow fronting the Gowanus Bay at Red Hook Point. Several more clutched the waterfront along the East River. Some shantytowns were sited on naturally low-lying land, while others were built on land excavated for street extensions; the extreme grading created depressions sometimes 30 feet deep. At a Brooklyn shantytown near the northern tip of what is now Prospect Park, called Darby's Patch in the press, "Pools of water gathered in the Winter and made rare sliding ground for the gamins of the adjacent 'Patch' district, where the shanties of the squatters congregated." Things got worse when streets— including Baltic, Lincoln Place, 4th, and 5th—were cut through, creating sunken lots 30 and 40 feet below street level. Ironically perhaps, the shanty-town residents referred to their neighborhood as The Hill. Similar sunken lots developed in Manhattan as streets were blasted out. Alternately, shanty-towns occupied high, rocky ground. John August Will, an illustrator for *Century* magazine, captured the web of stairways that allowed residents to scale the heights of the boulders and man-made cliffs supporting their dwell-ings. Wills's picture *In Shanty Town,* created during the 1860s, foreshadows a photograph of a shantytown taken in 1896 by Jacob Riis, the famous housing reformer. Both show the steep stairways mounting the small cliffs where shanties "[p]erched on the top of high cliffs, somewhat after the fashion of the Alpine chalets in the picture," as one *Times* reporter wrote. An 1880 account of a shantytown at 43rd Street and Third Avenue detailed the "rickety stairway" leading some 40 feet from the sidewalk to the top of a hill next to a quarry, "here steep, there easy; here made of broken boards with a shaky railing, there made of steps cut out of the rock, or out of the clay between the layers of rock; a well-worn, much-used stairway." Stairs crisscrossed shanty-towns, intersecting with the equally plentiful picket fences, a sign of territory claimed and defended. Picket fences were ubiquitous in shantytown images. Forming enclosures big and small, they girdled market gardens, flagged tiny front yards, and framed domestic and work spaces. Fences and stairways laced the bumpy, sludgy shantytown landscape.[13]

Uneven ground, lunging stairways, careening picket fences: visually, shanty-towns were the opposite of the orderly, uniform mat of the gridded city, where boxes of perpendicular streets, rectangular facades, and evenly-spaced win-dows distilled into a checkerboard of individual bricks and mortar, all drum-ming home the orderly beat of the expanding city. Underlying the grid was a belief that ordered space both reflected and created republican ideals—what architectural historian Dell Upton calls the "republican spatial imagination." Houses and roads in shantytowns, by contrast, meandered and swerved, rose and dove over the ground, eschewing the grid for a more sentient union of site and street. Elite observers interpreted this as a failing; the Legislative Tenement Committee of Brooklyn complained that shanties were "huddled together without regard to regularity, and the eye of the tourist fails to discover any stately avenues of spacious squares, which are elsewhere pleasing to the sense." Another report noted that Tinkersville, also located in Red Hook, was accessible only by a "narrow and serpentine street." This apparently willful lack of uniformity also impressed the reporter from *Appleton's* magazine in 1871: "The buildings back up upon one another in close contact, as if room were scarce; and then others, inconsistently with this idea, stand alone with tottering independence." As a group, the shanties "appear to have been showered by an untasteful architectural pepper-box."[14]

In an era when the grid constituted a universal access code for American cities, shantytowns required initiation. A comic piece in the November 30, 1850, edition of the *Brooklyn Eagle,* recounted an imaginary exchange "between a party of 'Johnny new comes,' who had just arrived from the old *sod,* and their more Yankeefied friends," who together wandered into shantytown. One of the new-comes declares the shantytown a "quare place intirely! Sure, whin one goes from home here at all, they can niver find the way back again." Shantytown was a place where outsiders got lost, the very opposite of the gridded city. (Outsiders included, in this case, newly arrived immigrants; it was the "more Yankeefied" who knew their way around the shantytown.) The judgment of middle-class visitors, especially social reformers, was unequivocal: "All is confused, haphazard, and unintelligible . . . Built of rubbish individually, they hold a rubbishy appearance collectively." In sum, shantytowns were "a spectacle of ideal misery."[15]

Outsiders perceived shantytowns as a labyrinth, but residents navigated them like a maze. Shantytowns were coded for use by their residents. Undulating spaces, "haphazard" streets, and careening homesites served shanty dwellers' practical needs by delineating found spaces—the crannies between the boulders, the solid soil among the marshes—for gardens, cows, ash piles, cart storage, laundry equipment, and the like. Shantytowns accommodated the livelihoods of shanty dwellers by providing work spaces that would not have been available to them as renters living in tenements downtown. Beyond those pragmatic concerns, shantytowns also provided privacy—a rare commodity for poor people in cities. The real estate market was busily producing private domestic spaces for the burgeoning middle class, with the construction of apartment buildings along newly blasted streets surrounding Central Park and in nascent commuter suburbs in

Brooklyn. Poor people, however, lived in overcrowded conditions with no access to open spaces; instead, they commandeered the street for their common use. But in shantytowns, privacy was possible. The "practical possession of territory" was realized to a much greater extent in urban shantytowns, where residents claimed outright control of common spaces and impeded the march of improvement with street patterns designed to confuse. The spaces of shantytowns, geographically imposing and seemingly illegible, unsettled urban expansion.[16]

The seemingly chaotic layouts of shantytowns activated a middle-class anxiety about the legibility of places and persons that was particularly acute in the mid-nineteenth century. Urban elites had an "insatiable need" to see the city clearly; the curlicue byways of shantytowns obscured a clear view. An 1871 magazine article criticized shantytowns for being impure and disagreeable, but also "opaque," and for constituting "a general indefiniteness; an uncomfortable state of beginning and ending." That transgression was all the more vexing given that cities had embarked upon massive and expensive metropolitan improvements in sanitation, transportation, and recreation geared to clean up and sort out urban life. To a middling- or upper-class urbanite schooled by newspapers, architectural pattern books, and illustrated magazines in the particulars of genteel landscapes, shantytowns represented a real threat to the legibility of cities. Perhaps most jarring in a city composing itself along class lines behind uniform facades designed for maximum commodification, the miscellany of shanty housing styles was threatening. While the basic forms were predictable—mud hut, wooden shack, conical "wigwam"—the variations were myriad, and disdained a pattern. "Here is one that overhangs the edge. It was originally . . . a square shanty, built of slabs. Then a west wing was built, the walls made of an old sheet of tin roofing, and the roof made of two big doors laid flat. . . . The next house is very much the same as regards materials, but shaped differently. . . . The next house is built of stone as far as the first low story, and this is surmounted by a tall roof of old boxes, doors, and shutters, with a fragment of an old sail spread over all."[17]

Eschewing the grid for streets that conformed to the landscape, incorporating farming, and privileging a potpourri of housing styles all jumbled up on the landscape, shantytown builders practiced a kind of oppositional urban planning. The narrow lanes and Byzantine streets that signaled chaos to outsiders achieved specific goals for shantytown residents, both pragmatic and personal. But the "architectural pepper-box" of shantytown represented something greater as well, something less tangible. The discursive streets and uneven terrain of shantytowns provided residents with a degree of protection against supervision and surveillance. Social reformers and public officials pushed themselves into shantytowns just as they did into tenements, eager to regulate the habits of immigrants and "improve" their children by assimilation or outright removal from their homes. So-called "friendly visitors" were dispatched by charitable organizations, settlement houses, or churches to survey and analyze the urban poor. Tenements, designed for mass habitation, were efficient to visit, but shantytowns, sprawling and illegible, were not.[18]

The dynamic between shanty dwellers and friendly visitors is explored in the illustrations accompanying an 1860 article in the *New York Illustrated News*. In "Mr. John Bradley's cottage," the friendly visitor stands magisterially in the center of the drawing, as upright as the stovepipe behind him. Clutching a ledger and a pen, he confronts the family: an elderly woman in a ruffled cap, an old man wrapped in a shawl, and a young boy kneeling on the floor. In a hay-strewn corner behind the visitor, an enormous sow suckles four piglets; the pigs are sarcastically identified in the accompanying caption as "fellow lodgers" in the shanty. The visitor's frock coat, wide-rimmed parson's hat, polished shoes, and clipped mustache make a dramatic contrast with the shabby inhabitants of the house. In a second illustration, another young visitor, similarly dressed, interviews "the John Glennan family." While he takes notes on the condition of the four young children, two other men question the fretful mother in the doorway. The father leans against the mantel, disengaged from the action of the scene.[19]

The judgment of the writer and illustrator are harsh; as the title indicates, these scenes are interpreted as primitive and uncivilized. But the condescension of the title, and the renderings themselves, are belied by the unmistakable domesticity of the interior scenes. In Mr. Bradley's cottage, a clock presides on the fireplace mantel, four framed pictures of saints hang on the walls, curtains drape the window, and a tea kettle poses on the stove. Fewer interior details are provided for Mr. Glennan's house, but here also a large stove commands the center of the room, and two pictures are hung high on the wall. These interiors did not comply with the growing nineteenth-century trend toward single-use rooms, each with a specific function, that indicated gentility and refinement, the prime example being the little-used parlor reserved for entertaining guests.

BACKGROUNDS OF CIVILIZATION.—Establishment of Mr. Glennan and his Full-headed Family.—(See Page 195.)

So-called "friendly visitors" monitored the behavior of poor shanty dwellers, as they did tenement residents.

Shanties, like tenements, continued to combine multiple uses in a single room. But the vernacular traditions that governed the spaces of the working poor suggest alternative interpretations of these shanty interiors. The one-room or "single-cell" dwelling continued to be popular in the Irish and English housing tradition (as well as in much of western Europe) well into the nineteenth century. Celtic building traditions were among those employed in the log houses of Appalachia and the sod houses of the Great Plains during the same period. As Henry Glassie notes in his classic scholarship on Irish-American building traditions, "the Irish dimension in the architecture of the American frontier is not a matter of a few discrete forms but of an approach to space generated from social values." The same can be said of the "Irish dimension" of housing in urban shantytowns. While shanties did not simply re-create houses left behind in Ireland, like traditional Irish houses they featured "a welcoming open door that brought the visitor immediately to the hospitable hearth." The crowded, multipurpose main room that distressed nineteenth-century middle-class reformers may have expressed more than its occupants' poverty; it may have continued a tradition of social values that combined family togetherness with a warm embrace of visitors. Those social values were as tangible as the values of privacy, respectability, and refinement espoused by the urban bourgeoisie.[20]

Irish immigrants often fled Ireland because of dwindling opportunities to farm successfully, and they strenuously resisted recruiting efforts to resettle them in farming communities on the American frontier. But shantytowns suggest a desire on the part of immigrants to combine farming with city living. Gardens for private and commercial use proliferate in shantytowns. This land use pattern created an opportunity for residents to farm without relinquishing access to other jobs; indeed, some family members could make wages or conduct small businesses while others farmed. Central Park and other urban parks represented a movement to bring the bucolic open spaces of the country into the city for leisure use by the middle and upper classes. Shantytown residents recombined the rural and the urban in a different way, yielding a practical twist on *urbs in horto:* the farm in the city. Etchings of shantytowns from the 1880s reveal the persistence of large market gardens in shantytowns well past the point when demolitions began in earnest. Mary Nimmo Moran's *Vegetable Garden in Shantytown, N.Y.*, also collected under the title *A City-Farm, New York,* from 1881, shows the market garden of the title slithering down a hill and off the right edge of the picture; it brims with growing crops but is barricaded on two sides by towering walls of apartment buildings. The shanties, gardeners, and especially the horse and cart in the foreground present a rustic challenge to the urban grid of the city, which is recalled in the monotonous pattern of rectangular windowframes on the facades of adjacent buildings.[21]

Images and illustrations of shantytown gardens, owned and operated by the working poor in the nineteenth century, suggest a new context for the current popularity of "urban farms" in major American cities, including Brooklyn and Manhattan. A growing literature on urban farming emerging from environmental and economic development channels argues that food safety and food security depend on expanding the practice, which also dovetails with the organic food and locally-sourced restaurant movement. While the intense interest in urban agriculture arose from sustainability concerns specific to the late twentieth century, urban farming can also be viewed historically, as the working poor's solution to the challenges of linking farm and city on the urbanizing American landscape of the mid-nineteenth century. Current objectives of environmental sustainability—sourcing food in close proximity to the people who eat it, and honoring the nature in your backyard—have analogs in the design and construction of shantytowns in the nineteenth century. Community vegetable gardens and urban farms are rampant today, but the juxtaposition of eggplants and asphalt still gives us pause. We smile at photographs of chicken coops on apartment rooftops in Brooklyn, or goats tied up at the edge of suburban lawns. The effort to reunite farm and city, championed by ecologists, public officials, and community groups, is considered progressive; returning the rural to the urban has become a way of improving ourselves. The campaign to make small-scale farming and keeping of small livestock compatible with urban life is radical because city and farm have been so thoroughly separated in the national imaginary. Ridding the city of the farm—and the rustics who operated it—was a prime project of nineteenth-century city builders, as the evidence of shantytowns attests. The removal of the commitment to the diurnal, the seasonal, the topographical were essential to the triumph of the grid, the clock, the hourly wage. Yet, even as rural practices were being exiled from booming American cities in the mid-nineteenth century, large groups of poor working people struggled to create a hybrid of the rural and the urban that resembles, in practice and purpose, the efforts of the urban farm movement today.[22]

Just as there is a potent political dimension to the urban farm movement today, rallying liberal proponents of sustainability and preservation of public space against conservative corporatists, real estate developers, and climate-change deniers, the farm-in-a-city builders of shantytowns in the nineteenth century coalesced around electoral politics. Shantytown residents preserved land-use policies that benefited their farming enterprises as well as the other, often waste-related businesses they founded—ragpicking, ash hauling, and carting—by voting. They elected officials beholden to them, and those officials looked the other way when shantytown residents broke new laws passed with their dispossession in mind. An attack of sickness in the Brooklyn shantytown known as Tinkersville in August 1856 was "viewed with alarm by the leaders of the Democratic Party in Brooklyn, as an incursion of yellow fever in these parts before the November election would greatly imperil the success of Mr. Buchanan." In state elections two years later, in 1858, the press once again reported that from shantytown, "on election day, whole regiments of Democratic voters find their way thence to the polls." Again in 1862, shantytown residents turned out to vote for Democrats in the municipal elections. "In one ward, which we need not name, [squatters] combined" two years previous "in sufficient numbers, to control the elections for Aldermen and Councilmen. We are not altogether sure that they cannot control the same ward to-day."[23]

Charges of fraud dogged reports of shanty dwellers' political participation, as did insinuations about their right to vote. "Living so irregularly, they are never registered. Ruling the polls, they vote as often as they please, and put their own creatures into office. Decent people are kept away, or stay away, rather than come into contact with them." These "irregular" shanty dwellers nonetheless "hold the balance of power in the Ward. In ordinary times their powers of annoyance are supreme; but their greatest triumphs are on election days." In 1867, a roundup of Manhattan shantytowns mentions their propensity to vote: "The only duty the squatters perform toward the Government is that of voters. The men vote early, and, it is believed, often." For a month before the election, "the rank and file politicians who busy themselves in canvassing the more Democratic wards, are frequent visitors to the squatter settlements." Political organizers sometimes recruited shantytown residents to hand out ballots at the polls. In terms of turnout, shantytown districts often trounced their elite neighbors. Popular tactics for increasing voting in Irish-American districts included fraudulent naturalizations, and, after a voter registration law was passed in 1857, registering to vote multiple times. Tammany Hall politicians actively encouraged immigrants to become citizens so that they could vote.[24]

Sympathetic Democratic officials, elected to office with the help of shantytown voters, dragged their feet on evictions, aiding and abetting shanty dwellers' strategies to retain control over territory by subverting real estate laws and the real estate market itself. Shantytown voters continued to wield enough power at the polls to distress the bourgeoisie as late as 1880. "The squatter population has grown so large in that portion of the City between Sixty-third and Seventy-second streets, Eighth-avenue and the North River, that it has come to be a political power wielding several thousand votes. It will not excite astonishment to any remarkable extent when the fact is announced that a majority of these voters cast their ballots for the Democratic Party."

According to the real estate developers who comprised the membership of the West Side Association, whose interests the *Times* clearly shared, the squatters were "faithful followers of John Kelly," the Tammany Hall boss, who "was protecting them in their illegal usurpation of property rights." City officials apparently looked the other way as shantytown residents flouted laws against keeping livestock within city limits, and pushed back on eviction notices. The same article that hyperventilated about squatters having "control" of municipal elections in one ward also noted they exercised "by favor of the Common Council, the rights of free pasturage for cows, goats, and pigs in the public thoroughfares of the city." In other words, their animals roamed the landscape and the police let them. Landowners, once the land became marketable, wanted to evict residents, but law enforcement dragged its feet for decades. John Kelly served several terms as sheriff in the 1850s and 1860s, which would have given him dominion over imposing laws against livestock and carrying out evictions. In effect, shantytown residents contrived to prevent or at least limit the imposition of laws prohibiting farming practices that they relied upon for their livelihoods, and hobbled an eviction process that depended on the initiative of law enforcement, by actively supporting the election of sympathetic politicians like Kelly.[25]

What did shantytown voting patterns mean? On the local level, voting Democratic during the middle decades of the nineteenth century helped support the Tammany Hall political machine, a thoroughly corrupt regime that nevertheless provided a higher level of city services to poor and immigrant neighborhoods. On the national level, a vote for the Democratic Party was ultimately a vote for preserving and extending slavery, but it also reflected, more generally, a conservative philosophy about federal government. The party had roots in the agrarian vision of Thomas Jefferson, and opposed government intervention (banks, canals) that, they believed, did little to help their base of farmers and artisans; the party also opposed most social and educational reforms on the same individualistic grounds. Debates over slavery fractured the party in 1860, but shantytown residents stuck with the party through the decade and into the 1870s and 1880s. It is unclear to what extent the Irish Americans who rioted in the 1863 draft riots lived in shantytowns, although one of the most scathing articles written about shantytowns in this period cautions, "It will be remembered that from these cabins came the hordes of infuriated demons who formed the main body of the rioters in July, 1863."[26]

In addition to using electoral politics to preserve shantytown land uses, residents gamed the real estate market to prolong their tenure, and went to court to protect their legal rights to occupy property. Harangues about shantytowns in the news media implied that they had no legal claim to the land they occupied, but many "squatters" held ground leases, making them participants in the real estate market at the most basic level, as renters. In Brooklyn's Red Hook shantytown, for example, workers at the Atlantic Dock Co. paid ground rent that by the mid-1850s amounted to between $20 and $30 a year. In nearby Tinkersville, residents paid ground rent of $10 to $15 a year, an arrangement by which "the owner of the land raised a considerable revenue with which to pay taxes and assessments," as one newspaper explained. At the Gowanus Beach shantytown, 60 households paid ground rent of about $30 a year to "a Mr. Woop, of Brooklyn." Bristling at a reporter's insinuation that she was a freeloader, a Brooklyn shanty dweller retorted, "I do not mind tellin' yer I lived at Mr. McCormack's [place], and I paid him twelve shillin' a week." By providing an income stream on property that was at the time unwanted by any other segment of the market, shantytown residents contributed to the city's economy. In effect, they absorbed some of the risk from land speculation. An 1880 overview called "Ten Thousand Squatters" explained how this dynamic developed on what is now the Upper West Side:

> During the years following the Panic of 1873, New-York real estate became a drug upon the market. The owners of land found themselves unable to dispose of their choice lots except at a great sacrifice. They found themselves burdened with heavy taxes. Under these circumstances they were willing to adopt almost any plan which would relieve themselves of this burden. The readiest means of doing this they found to be the leasing of their lots to poor tenants to build huts upon. From scattered hovels there grew up at last whole communities within this district. Some of the more thriving of these squatters became landlords themselves by building whole rows of hovels, which they leased to their poorer countrymen.

The problem, as the article concluded, was that "[s]ome of these squatters have lived in this district a dozen years or more, and they have come to believe that their squatter rights"—which the writer acknowledges included leases and the payment of rent—"are superior to the rights of the owners of the land." Two particular hotbeds for this sense of entitlement, the writer noted, were the Irish shantytown on West 79th Street and the German shantytown at 81st Street, known as Ashville. Dutifully, the author notes that Ashville residents "have their own school-house, their own school-master, and their own priest and chapel"; consistently, shantytowns acquired institutions and functioned as communities. When a landowner wanted shanty dwellers to clear off, "he has usually to resort to the courts, procure an act of eviction against the tenant, and then invoke the power of the law against them." That had been the case for landowner H. H. Camman, who had evicted 200 shantytown families when this article was published on April 20, 1880. "In nearly every case he has had to resort to the courts," for the shanty "inmates resisted the destruction of their homes with all of their might"—and had the tacit support of municipal law enforcement. One evicted shanty dweller refused to leave his shanty at all, to prevent it being torn down. Extreme, even violent measures were sometimes used.

> In one instance the Deputy Marshals . . . bound a squatter, carried him to a distance, and hitching horses to a cable thrown around the dwelling, dragged it to the ground. In another, a hut-owner refused to move out after the necessary legal formalities had been satisfied. The workmen engaged in blasting rock finally approached so near that they were afraid of destroying the lives of the inmates . . . Some men came with pikes, and the house was tumbled from the huge rock on which it stood and broke into fragments 20 feet below.[27]

On another occasion, the Deputy Marshal, distributing eviction notices along 81st Street, "was seized, and a milk-can, half-filled, was turned over his head like a hat." Other deputies were attacked by dogs "kept for the purpose of harassing bailiffs." With some 2,500 shanties occupying the west side of Manhattan north of 59th Street, housing between 10,000 and 12,000 residents, the landowners' association announced its intention to evict them all by May 1, 1880. Although they fell far short of their goal—only a few hundred had been cleared by the deadline—the upper quadrants of the city by 1880 were indeed a war zone, as the secondary headline of "Ten Thousand Squatters" indicated: "A Warfare Begun By West Side Land-Owners." Drummed out of Central Park, shantytown residents flowed into the adjacent land, toward the Hudson River on the west and the East River on the east. Practically all of the area on either side of Central Park was dominated by shantytowns in the 1870s and early 1880s. "They perched on the rocks on the west side, where they built their shanties and exercised, in form at any rate, all of the rights and functions of owners," an 1892 article complained. Over the years, a market in shanty housing developed. "A great many of them had bought the huts in which they lived, having paid for them fully all they were worth, and they produced documents which purported to be deeds of sale and which they supposed to convey to themselves full title to land as well as what had been built upon it." Meanwhile, speculators bought shantytown lands "without actually going to look at the property itself," and were surprised to discover it was fully occupied by people with competing claims to the land, who also had official documents to wave. As the city population swelled in the 1880s, landlords intensified their efforts to evict shanty dwellers—who intensified their efforts to stay on their land.[28]

Shanty dwellers were not just defending their homes but extended communities, a landscape of schoolhouses and chapels, work sites and fenced-in yards, pasturage and piggeries. Newspaper and magazine accounts highlighted the pitched battles, but shanty residents routinely argued their claims not in the streets, but in court. As early as the 1850s, residents of some shantytowns formed legal cooperatives and pooled their money to retain lawyers to represent community members as needed. One 1854 *New York Times* article about the Yorkville shantytown suggested as much: "They say that they are banded together [to] support each other in their mutual defense; that they have their lawyers to defend them when suits of ejectment are brought; that the fees are paid by taxes assessed upon each other." In 1875, eight shanty residents of uptown Manhattan—Michael Stokes, Florence McCarthy, Patrick Hogan, Kate Brean, Michael Donovan, Patrick McClusky, James Ward, and John Ryan—successfully fought their eviction from lots they leased on 108th Street between First and Second Avenues. Some of the residents, whose names point to Irish roots, had leases dating to 1866 in which they pledged to pay landlord John De Groot an annual rent of $20. Each erected a shanty on his or her lot. In November 1874, another man, Patrick Cassidy, claimed that he was the actual owner of the land, and asked the tenants to sign new leases which tripled their rents to $60 a year. When the first month's rent came due, all of the tenants refused to pay, claiming they were illiterate and had not understood what they were signing. It is impossible to know who was scamming whom, but both sides were determined to control the property. When Cassidy filed eviction papers, the residents applied to the Special Term of the Court of Common Pleas to have the leases declared fraudulent and voided, and eviction proceedings permanently enjoined. The court ruled in their favor.[29]

Shantytown residents also benefited passively from the convoluted eviction system. Take, for example, the twisted but not atypical story of Sylvan Place and 121st Street. In 1840 the state legislature gave the city title to this roughly block-square parcel of land. For years it was occupied by a farmers market and firehouse, later becoming a common field where political meetings were held. At that point, squatters built cabins on the site. In 1873 a horseshoer named David C. Carleton bought a building that had previously been erected there by a squatter—proof that shanties themselves also changed hands for money. The enterprising Carleton fenced in the land and built more shanties, leasing them to tenants. A few years later the city, which still owned the land, leased one of the lots to a tenant named Darcey. When Darcey erected his own building, Carleton filed an eviction suit against him. The sheriff ruled in Carleton's favor. At this point the city asserted its dormant ownership rights, and the court went to trial. Carleton won in the lower courts but the Court of Appeals ruled for the city.[30]

Carleton demanded a new trial, and the Superior Court heard his case—along with three other eviction dispute cases—and on November 11, 1885, more than a decade after litigation began, the city won all four cases. Clearly, the city had never sold the land on Sylvan Place to anyone. But just as clearly, the rights to its possession were muddled, a fact that shanty residents, including Carleton, exploited. The newspaper account of the city's ultimate triumph in all four eviction cases was presented as a public triumph over unentitled shanty dwellers. The secondary headline, "Property Worth Over $100,000 Which Squatters Had Enjoyed Possession Of," beneath the headline, "A Verdict for the City," suggests illicit possession of the land by "squatters" who have been "[a]bsolved from the duty of paying house-rent, [and] relieved from the burdens of municipal taxation." But as the details of the case show, shanty dwellers were paying ground rent and their landlord, Carleton, was pursuing his claims to the land through the legal system.[31]

Residents of Brooklyn shantytowns often outsmarted the eviction process without going to court. As landowners and speculators squabbled over legal title to former farms, shanty builders simply occupied the disputed territory, passively resisting official efforts to shoo them off the land. The story of the Jackson's Hollow shantytown along Myrtle Avenue is perhaps the most extreme example. After Walt Whitman's visit in the 1840s, the "Emeralders" regrouped and rebuilt their shantytown several times along Myrtle Avenue. As first Washington Park and then commercial development pushed the shantytown further east, residents hunkered down in the rechristened Jackson's Hollow for several more decades. It was 1873 before the web of lawsuits over legal title to the land was finally untangled, leaving middle-class residents eager for redevelopment of "that eyesore, 'Jackson's Hollow.'" In July 1873 the *Eagle* published a long tirade proclaiming that in the "progressive" order of events the "degenerated" shantytown was destined to "pass away from the present generation"—an assertion the *Eagle* had been making, by this point, for almost 30 years. But still the shantytown did not disappear. Tax arrears exceeded the value of many of the lots, and they did not sell. This impediment to development remained until the mid-1880s, when the courts intervened to settle the tax question. It was 1888—some 45 years after its founding, and 40 years after Walt Whitman first called for its removal—before the Jackson's Hollow shantytown finally dispersed.[32]

Another shantytown for the Brooklyn pantheon: Darby's Patch, known as The Hill to residents. Located at Fifth Avenue and Douglas Street, not far from the northern tip of what is today Prospect Park, it overlapped a much-litigated estate known as the Poole Farm. The original owner, Thomas Poole, bequeathed a life interest in his 100-acre farm to his children in the 1850s. The grandchildren, when they inherited, sued to partition the land. More than 50 parcels were sold at auction starting in 1862, mostly to "well-known real estate dealers." By the time the Poole estate parcels were sold, however, many of them had tax bills in arrears. When the purchasers refused to close the sales, the heirs sued them, creating a legal morass that further postponed development. Meanwhile, Irish-American laborers continued to build shanties on the land, sheltered somewhat from the advance of public infrastructure by the swampy terrain of the old Poole estate, which became a common dumping ground. For the next two decades, lawsuits multiplied, tax bills grew, trash piled up, and shanties proliferated in Darby's Patch.

It took legislation specifically designed to dislodge shanty residents to turn the tide. Things began to change in 1857. In direct response to efforts by landowners in the Red Hook district of Brooklyn to rid Tinkersville of shanties, the legislature passed a law permitting the speedy eviction of tenants "whenever a sudden exigency may arise." The press cheered the law for moving against both "metropolitan and suburban squatters" in a way that "completely upsets the doctrine of 'Squatter Sovereignty' as found in the case of people who pitch their shanties on unenclosed grounds without paying rent, or saying 'by your leave.'" Laws passed in December 1873 declared the tax liens invalid, a ruling that helped clear titles to land in other Brooklyn and New York City shantytowns. The state Supreme Court, in 1885, upheld that law after appeal, opening the way, at last, to the removal of shantytowns. Evictions continued through the 1890s and into the twentieth century—but so did resistance. The *Times* reported on the "final" order to evacuate shanties on the Upper East Side in 1896, some 15 years later. In 1910 it ran a story about Brooklyn shantytowns with the headline "Evicting Squatters is Not an Easy Task," with the telling subtitle, "Some of the Incumbents Had Held the Land for Twenty-five Years." Lady Duffus Hardy, the Victorian travel writer, noted the tenacity of shantytown residents when she visited Manhattan in 1881: "All above Central Park is like a ragged fringe of the great city—long half-finished avenues, straggling sparsely inhabited streets, and skeleton houses; much of the original swampy ground lies still unclaimed. The Irish squatters in their rickety tumble-down hovels still cling to the land; the malarial air may wrap them like a shroud, the swamp with its foul unwholesomeness threaten to swallow them up—they will not stir. By slow, very slow degrees, as the Government reclaims the land, they are driven towards the edge, but wherever they can find a footing they squat again."[33]

What was the source of such determination? Clearly shantytown residents considered possession and occupation of land both an exercise and expression of personal sovereignty. Had social reformers and "friendly visitors" successfully transplanted so-called middle-class values, achieving assimilation through the doctrine of improvement? Did shanties and shantytowns stand for the same American values as brownstone mansions and gridded avenues, or did they express allegiance to a different set of commitments? For those answers, we must turn to popular culture, which preserved in song, comedy, and theater a working-class discourse that included shantytowns, a discourse that resonates with values of hospitality, autonomy, tradition, and adaptation, but also points the way toward a more nuanced understanding of inter-ethnic and intra-class tension among poor urban laborers.

Popular songs from the second half of the nineteenth century, often referred to as broadsides, resound with a working-poor discourse of shanty-towns. A broadside is simply a poem or song printed on one side of a sheet of cheap paper—often a large piece, hence the name—sold in the street by vendors. In the mid- and late-nineteenth century, they were vehicles for songs favored by the working classes, often performed in minstrel shows in music halls or playhouses. Like newspapers of the day, broadside ballads addressed or commented on current events and trends, often in a satirical tone that reflected popular attitudes. Immigrants were frequent topics of broadsides, which poked fun at their dress, manners, and speech. Yet poor laborers, many of them Irish immigrants, comprised a significant portion of the stage audience for broadsides; minstrelsy was popular with the working classes. As the century progressed, the theatrical audience expanded to include middle-class patrons, who fueled a market for more elaborate editions of the ballads printed as sheet music. The fanciful covers, often featuring the stage performers who popularized the song, were given a prominent place in the middle-class parlor, atop the piano. Together they made a tableau of refinement, a domestic triptych that signaled trendiness, classical accomplishment, and condescension all at the same time. It was a quest that defined the urban middle class during the nineteenth century.[34]

Shanties appear in a number of broadsides, starting in the 1850s. The most popular, and the most culturally revealing, was a song called "The Irishman's Shanty." Performed regularly on the minstrel circuit, it was popularized by a Brooklyn-born comedian named Matt Peel, the son of two Irish immigrants who called himself the "Irish minstrel." The song begins with a friendly invitation to step inside and have a look around.

> Did you ever go into an Irishman's shanty?
> Ah! there boys you'll find the whiskey so plenty,
> With a pipe in his mouth there sits Paddy so free,
> No King in his palace is prouder than he.
> (*Chorus.*) Hurrah! my honey.
> (*Spoken.*) Now boys, one for Paddy.
> (*Sung.*) Whack! Paddy's the boy.[35]

From the first note, this song distinguishes itself from newspaper and magazine accounts of shantytowns by inviting you over the threshold; it offers an interior view, an insider's perspective. The very act of invitation sets up the shanty as an open, convivial, social place—the very opposite of the middle-class parlor, a formal space quite separate from the private family quarters. A first-person account of Irish shanty life follows the introduction. Rollicking lyrics paint a fond picture of Paddy, a pipe-smoking, whiskey-drinking "king" of his shanty who lived "proud" and "free" in a wooden hut. Peel, the per-former, hammed up the stage version of the song in typical minstrel fashion, enlivening the choruses with a vocal imitation of the Irish bagpipes. On paper and in performance, "The Irishman's Shanty" expressed a longing for older, traditional expressions of ethnic identity. The lyrics poke fun at Paddy, but avoid the demeaning view popular in the contemporary press. Instead, the song challenges those accounts in ways that flattered Irish Americans and their Irish progenitors. While Peel witnesses the same scene that middle-class journalists and "friendly visitors" did, he interprets it differently. Where they saw deviance, he sees autonomy and sociability. The availability of whiskey and tobacco in this Irishman's shanty, for example, is not evidence of vice and criminality, as middle-class critics insisted, but proof of hospitality. Paddy is sociable. He is also frugal. Self-reliant in a Thoreauvian way, Paddy is the anti-Thoreau by dint of his hospitality.[36]

Subsequent verses describe the meager contents of Paddy's shanty—a favorite theme of journalists, real estate developers, and sanitary inspectors—but without their mocking tone. Like the traditional Irish "single-cell" dwell-ings built elsewhere in the United States, this one is "three rooms in one; Kitchen, bedroom and hall." It is furnished with a three-legged stool "and a table to match," along with a straw mattress lying on the floor and barnyard animals roaming in and out of the house—the very characteristics that had offended the sensibilities of several decades worth of newspaper reporters and magazine illustrators. But details that in other contexts were used to den-igrate shanties here serve to elevate it. Industrious Paddy crafts a "neat little bureau" out of boards left over from building the shanty. Unpretentious Paddy eschews refinement, leaving the bureau "without paint or gilt" and the shanty's walls bare of pictures. A paucity of furniture—"his chest it is three wooden pegs on the wall"—and tattered clothing are not proof of slovenliness, but signs that Paddy has his priorities in order. His wife Biddy is "the jewel that's set in his mind," and his "brats" matter more than "gold that's refined." Unfettered by the demands of wage labor, Paddy is "free"; surrounded by a large, loving family, he reigns supreme. Paddy's lack or avoidance of work has both a positive and a negative aspect: the lyrics simultaneously tease him for being idle and admire his status in the family. His freedom is the outward sign of autonomy; identity springs not from hard work and improvement, but from familial bonds and social engagement. Autonomy is the reward for simple tastes, frugality, and an ability to make do—not a commitment to improvement, evidenced by ceaseless work and toil.[37]

The regard of family and community turns Paddy's modest home into a "palace." Poverty is evident, but is not equated with degeneracy. In this Irishman's shanty, Paddy and his family live the "kind of independent life" that the *Brooklyn Eagle* referenced so wistfully in its 1851 article about the persistence of the Jackson's Hollow shantytown. The independence of shantytowns worried middle-class observers. One reporter opined in 1867 that street extensions in Manhattan and Brooklyn would "raze the squatter's [*sic*] huts, and destroy that somewhat unenviable individuality which distinguishes the tenants." Tenement life—organized, supervised, surveilled by middle-class reformers—was better for the squatters and for the city as a whole. "By seeking a shelter in tenement houses, the squatter will lose, it is true, the privilege of considering himself the monarch of all he surveys, but his descendants will be afforded some insights into the customs of civilized humanity, and the health and appearance of the metropolis will be benefited."[38]

Paddy and his family do not conjure up the specters of disease and criminality raised in mainstream media accounts. They are not dangerous; they are comic. Irish immigrants were frequently lampooned in mid-century minstrel shows. As early as 1843 minstrels parroted the stereotype of "Paddy" as a buffoon who loved to drink and brawl. But the tone was always lighter than nativist political rhetoric, which condemned the Irish as dangerous Papists whose willingness to work for low wages depressed incomes for all laborers. In the 1850s, the Irish fared better in minstrelsy, as stars like George Christy and Matt Campbell broadened the stereotype to include appealing romantic and sentimental qualities. Matt Peel contributed to this shift in attitude with his characterization of Paddy as the proud "king" of his shanty. Peel was born in New York in 1830 of Irish parents and raised in Brooklyn. Like his audience, he straddled the world of Irish immigrants and first-generation Americans. In 1846 he and four other performers founded Campbell's Original Minstrels, which became popular on the minstrel circuit in the late

1840s and 1850s. In the summer of 1857, when a financial panic emptied the theaters in New York, the troupe embarked on a year-long tour of cities west of the Mississippi. A Campbell's Minstrels performance followed a three-part format of comedy and romantic songs, solos by the company members, and a closing farce that usually satirized contemporary fashion or entertainment. "The Irishman's Shanty" would have been performed in the middle of the evening, and if audiences had not liked it, they would have been vocal in their disapproval. The largely working-class audiences for minstrelsy, which included a number of immigrants, were loud and enthusiastic, cheering for performers and sometimes throwing money, but they were merciless when displeased, and just as noisy in their displeasure. Scholars have interpreted this bold behavior as an exercise of power by the frequently powerless. Shantytown ballads support that analysis, but point to more subtle shades of meaning: crowd responses also signaled ethnic allegiances and class tensions—not just with the middle class, but between slivers of the hyphenated working classes and their first- and second-generation offspring.[39]

The fact that "The Irishman's Shanty" was published as sheet music in 1859 suggests it was a crowd-pleaser. The cover of the sheet music version offers clues to the performance that Peel delivered. Dressed in knee breaches, cutaway coat, and a floppy hat, peasant Paddy stands outside a sod shanty surrounded by his family, pig, and cow. Details like the sod shanty imply that the shanty pictured is in Ireland. The tune of the song provides few clues; it was set to an Irish jig that was already a century old when it was first published in 1788 as "Irish Wash Woman." The lyrics, however, explicitly refer to a shanty made of boards; the unpainted bureau, for example, is made of construction leftovers. The shanty has traveled between Peel's stage performance, the publication of the broadside, and the sheet music cover; what started on the local landscape of Manhattan or Brooklyn has retreated to Ireland. Paddy, who starts out an immigrant, reverts to pre-emigration status, and an identity that would have been fluid in Peel's stage performance congealed; it is pinned, geographically, once it enters the parlor as sheet music. This transition may have been a gesture toward the genteel demeanor of the middle-class parlor, where residents would have found a reminder of local shantytowns unpleasant; a sentimental rendition of a rural Irish shanty, by contrast, would have fed their appetite for the picturesque, a style that consistently hid or soft-pedaled the grittier aspects of rural and working-class life. The peasant dress of the characters gathered in front of the shanty further distinguishes them as residents of the countryside, an impression reinforced by the serpentine branches that spring from the first and last letters of the title, entwining it in a woodsy bower. Below, a woman stands in the doorway of the shanty holding an infant; an elderly man sits at her feet, doffing his hat at unseen guests. A young girl peeks over the shoulder of a seated man cradling bagpipes. Paddy brandishes a pennywhistle. The festive mood suggests the end of a work day or perhaps the beginning of a party.[40]

Peel's Paddy appealed to working-class audience members' nostalgia for older traditions, compromised perhaps in the quest for opportunity that accompanied the move to the United States. The impoverished material life described in the verses of "The Irishman's Shanty" is balanced by love of

Matt Peel styled himself the "Irish minstrel." *The Irishman's Shanty* was one of his most popular songs.

family, freedom from responsibility, and the pleasures of drinking and smoking. The peasant family is presented as free from the pressure to improve, to acquire, to get ahead, that Peel's audience was subjected to in New York or Cleveland, Cincinnati, New Orleans, Memphis, Savannah, Ga., or Norfolk, Va.—all cities where Peel performed his act. But the story of Paddy and his shanty is not simplistic; the song is not a superficial endorsement of the life Paddy lives in his shanty. Paddy's provinciality has two sides, and the struggling Irish immigrants in Peel's audience would have viewed him with a mixture of nostalgia and superiority. Paddy prancing in front of his shanty did not represent a past to which the Irish immigrants in Matt Peel's audiences longed to return. Having immigrated, they were more cosmopolitan than the family and friends they left behind, and the simple fact of their attendance at Peel's show was evidence of a certain urbanity. They possessed the self-consciousness necessary to laugh at themselves. Shanty-dwelling Paddy reminded first-generation Irish Americans, like Peel himself, that they had scooted ahead of the "Johnny new-comes" also in attendance.[41]

Laughing at the caricature of the Irish shantyman sharpened the cultural distance from more recent immigrants that the financial circumstances of Irish-American laborers may have blurred. The depiction of Paddy as a provincial rube congratulated Peel's audience on its relative sophistication, while the positive (and romanticized) presentation of Paddy's old-country values reminded them that they could still be proud to identify with that national, ethnic, and rural alternative. "The Irishman's Shanty" honors a past, mythic life that was more carefree and less materialistic, a portrayal that may have provided Peel's audience with a moment of superiority over the grasping, respectability-obsessed middle class as well. Laughing good-naturedly at Paddy was a way to hold him close and at arm's length at the same time.

Shanties appear in a number of Irish comic songs published as broadsides or sheet music, or sometimes both, in the mid-nineteenth century in the United States; they served as a rhetorical device for the working poor, as they did for the middle class. The Paddy of "There's Monny a Shlip" (1874) brags that "My shanty I plashtered wid mud / An shtop't all the howles that I could." Emigrants are evicted from rural cabins in "The Emigrant's Farewell" (1852) and "Must We Leave Our Ould Home" (1890), a fate that by 1903 was being romanticized in songs like "Spare the Old Mud Cabin." An early parody of the emigration ballad, "Teddy O'Neal," published in Boston in 1843, illustrates the twin pleasures of affection and condescension the genre promised, and the symbolic role played by the shanty. As the ballad opens, Teddy's abandoned girlfriend is visiting the Irish cabin of her departed sweetheart. "I've come to the cabin he danced his wild jigs in / As neat a mud palace as ever was seen." She heaps further praise on the shanty: "And, consid'ring it served to keep poultry and pigs in, / I'm sure it was always most elegantly clean." The songwriter's choice to mock typical elements of rural housing—mud and cohabitating livestock—shows that by 1843 these details were already shorthand for peasant life. Irish émigrés were invited to smile at the naiveté of the unworldly narrator, who praises mud huts and equates elegance with cleanliness. (The tripping-over-your-tongue effect of the displaced stresses in the final line of the rhyme, to accommodate the four syllables of the word "elegantly," would have reinforced the joke.) Emigrants, by implied comparison, were cosmopolitans—a distinction native-born Americans might have overlooked, even while laughing along at the backwardness of the ballad's girlish narrator.[42]

In these songs, the shanty serves as a symbol of the supposed provinciality of immigrant newcomers as well as the backwardness of countrymen who remained in their native land. It was a popular symbol, which suggests that it represented a singular tension in immigrant life. In the second half of the 1860s at least four more versions of "The Irishman's Shanty" circulated as broadsides. Publishers included the prolific J. H. Johnson of Philadelphia and H. De Marsan of New York, one of the nineteenth century's most prominent ballad printers; Louis Bonsal of Baltimore, and John Hopkins of New Orleans. Shanties also figure prominently in another broadside called "Uncle Pat's Cabin," also published by H. De Marsan between 1864 and 1878, which like the others paints a relatively sympathetic picture of Irish shanty dwellers. Often re-printings of current hit songs, broadsides generally did not credit a composer; the inclusion of an author's name suggested that the ballad was printed in connection with an ongoing minstrel show or theatrical. Since the De Marsan version credits a composer—George W. Osborn, "of Michigan"— the publication probably coincided with local performances of the song. This version includes three additional verses, possibly the handiwork of Mr. Osborn. The circumstances of this printing, and the publication of the broadside by publishers in four different cities, proves "The Irishman's Shanty" was still popular in the late 1860s.[43]

The new lyrics also suggest a subtle change over time in the symbolic value of the shanty. All four versions tweak the lyrics to make Paddy more foolish than he appeared in Matt Peel's performances in the 1850s and the sheet music version printed in 1859. (To the usual catalog of cohabitating livestock, "Uncle Pat's Cabin" adds the charming detail that "beside him in the shanty / He kept his darling pig.") The standard grammar and spelling of the 1859 sheet music is replaced with thick dialect in these later broadsides, and the borders of the broadside—geometric patterns in the original—are festooned with oafish images of a weeping Biddy and a pipe-smoking Paddy, hands plunged in the pockets of his knee britches. Borders of broadsides were seldom customized for individual ballads, so these unflattering images were probably taken from a stock inventory of benighted immigrant images. But taken in combination with the edited lyrics, the crude representations suggest a hardening of attitudes toward immigrant shanty dwellers in the 5 to 10 years between the publication of Matt Peel's "The Irishman's Shanty" and the H. De Marsan broadside. Perhaps the thick dialect tracked the style of the minstrels who were performing the song at the time of publication.

The three new verses penned by George Osborn for the H. De Marsan broadside, however, focus not on ethnic differences but on class expectations. Paddy is first shown to be oblivious to, then congratulated for being contented with the material discomfort of his life. "He can relish good victuals as ever ye's ate," notes the first line of one verse, but "is always continted with praties and mate." The justification of poverty as good enough for the poor continues: "He prefers them when cowld (if he can't get them hot) / And makes tay in a bowl, when he can't get a pot." In the next verse we learn that Paddy is indifferent to weather as well as food: "He heeds not the rain, though it comes in a flood, / For the roof of the shanty is shingled with mud." The shanty's stovepipe, frequently jeered at by journalists and reformers, becomes "a chimney so neat" that cleverly whisks away the smoke. The ballad concludes with a verse devoted to Paddy's innate generosity:

> The rich may divide their enjoyments alone,
> With those who have riches as great as their own,
> But Pat hangs the latch-string outside of his door,
> And will share his last cent with the needy and poor.
> Arrah! me honey! w-h-a-c-k! Paddy's the boy.[44]

In particular, the final verse turns the shanty-dwelling Irish immigrant into a vehicle for social commentary. The resourceful Paddy does not fuss over his food, taking it cold if he cannot get it hot, or his tea, cheerfully making it in a bowl if he has no pot. Free of pretensions, Paddy is still king of his palace. Furthermore, while the rich only strive to enrich themselves, Paddy opens his pockets, and his shanty, to the needy and poor. The implication is that Paddy is content with his place at the bottom of the social and economic ladder, just as he is with his humble home. Such a sentiment excused a lot of guilt— middle-class guilt over the material wants of the poor, and assimilated immigrant guilt over the impoverished state of more recent immigrants—but expressed admiration as well. To a greater degree than Peel's characterization, it insists that poverty is not an obstacle to Paddy's happiness, because Paddy is blissfully ignorant of what he does not have. Praise for Paddy's charity and domestic bliss mask justifications of self-satisfaction and, perhaps, the guilt associated with getting ahead.[45]

German shantytowns were also the subject of mid-century broadsides. In the second half of the 1860s, H. De Marsan also published a German version of the ballad called "The Dutch Ragpicker's Shanty." A note following the title indicates that it is to be sung to the tune of "The Irishman's Shanty." Gone is any illusion that the shanty in question is in the old country; ragpickers were a fixture on the post–Civil War urban scene, frequently derided in the press. In this broadside, thick with dialect, Hans, the ragpicker of the title, is thoroughly ridiculed. The same modest shanty that is a credit to Paddy (and to his lack of ambition) becomes an indictment when the occupant is a German ragpicker:

> Did you ever shance into a poor Dutchman's shanty,
> Mine Got! dats de place were de lager ish plenty,
> Mit hish pipe in hish mout, sits de Deichter so free,
> No millionare's half ash contented ash he.
> Oora! for Yarmany! un Hans' ish de poy![46]

The verses track those of "The Irishman's Shanty," but the make-do spirit that ennobles Paddy demeans Hans. His shanty is filthy, the walls "papered all over mit rags / Vich every day from de gutter he drags." And unlike the affable Paddy, Hans is a dangerous figure guarded by "two safage togs of muscle

un might" who "knaw all de meat from de bones vich he fins." Hans, meanwhile, is well-fed on "Bologna sausages, hart pred, un de goot sour crout,"
with beer for dessert. The only thing he likes better than beer, in fact, is
Katrina, "hish own shany tear." Like "The Irishman's Shanty," "The Dutch
Ragpicker's Shanty" ends with a closing benediction that commends Hans for
his generosity:

> Should shance pring you past dis poor Deichter's door
> If weary, or hungry, or thirsty or sore,
> He'll give you a shelter mit sometings to eat
> Un not from hish door turn you into de shtreet.
> Oora! for Yarmany, un Hans ish de poy!

But this tip of the hat is halfhearted compared to the ringing endorsement
that ends "The Irishman's Shanty." Also missing is the favorable comparison
of the poor shanty dweller to the greedy, thoughtless well-to-do, for in this
broadside, it is Hans whose grasping ways threaten his urban neighbors. By
the late 1860s, when this ballad was published, the first Tammany mayor,
James Wood, had been elected with the help of the Irish in 1854, and the political power of Irish immigrants was growing. But the German immigrant
population was soaring, accounting for almost a quarter of New York City's
population by 1860; many did not speak English. "The Dutch Ragpicker's
Shanty" is evidence of hardening sentiment against German immigrants on
the part of Irish Americans, who were beginning to flex their political muscles, and who were speaking English widely by this point.

The existence of broadsides about Irish and German shanties, published by
two of the dominant broadside publishers of the period, shows that the shanty
house form was widely understood as a symbol by immigrants, their descendants, and their native-born middle-class neighbors. The fact that broadside
publishers in New York, Philadelphia, Baltimore, and New Orleans all published editions of "The Irishman's Shanty" suggests that the shanty image had
currency beyond New York and Brooklyn. These songs, which originated in
minstrelsy, portrayed shanty dwellers as comic and lumpen, interpretations
that helped more seasoned immigrants and their descendants set themselves
apart from "Johnny new comes" and other ethnicities. Being made fun of
by second-generation immigrants only slightly higher on the economic

ladder could have been demeaning for audience members, but seeing representations, even humorous ones, of oneself or one's family could have been a
positive, affirming experience as well. Descendants of immigrants mocked the
shanty lifestyles of more recent immigrants. Irish immigrants poked fun at
German immigrants. And they all had a laugh at the expense of relatives
left behind in the old country. Showcasing immigrants who continued to live
in shantytowns as ignorant and comical put some distance between aspiring
second-generation Americans and the impoverished countrymen they left
behind. But such distinctions aggravated anxieties about renouncing or
redefining ethnicity. That tension between old and new values is captured in
the overlapping and sometimes contradictory images of shantytowns produced for and by the lower classes in the middle decades of the nineteenth
century. Shantytowns were a tool of working-class formation, as well as
middle-class formation.

The representations of shanties in broadside ballads reveals a critical distance between recent immigrants and established Irish Americans, and
between Irish Americans and German immigrants, but the gap is a space, not
a measure. Instead of calibrating assimilation and resistance, shanty ballads
illuminate a space of exploration and adaptation. Shanty residents and "squatters" did not simply resist assimilation or succumb to it; their performance of
identity cannot be plotted on a scale of cultural compliance or resistance.
Shantytowns show identity in motion. They enshrine mobility and adaptation
as working-poor values. Like middle-class urbanites filling in the grid and
showing off their parlors, the builders of shantytowns were figuring out their
identities on the ground in growing American cities. As these ballads illustrate, tradition remained a virtue, but one that was being thoroughly interro-
gated by the people who inherited it. How much did Irish Americans want to
preserve the model of free-spirited, whiskey-sharing Paddy, and how much
did they want to edit it? How best to preserve hospitality and generosity, and
an open hearth, in the midst of abstraction and commodification of the
domestic urban landscape? In the evolving lyrics set to the ancient tunes of
broadside ballads, immigrants and their descendants weighed their options.[47]

On the minstrel stage, where Matt Peel jigged and sputtered his way through
Paddy's shanty, another performer was making a name for himself as an inter-
preter of immigrant life in New York. Edward Harrigan splashed into Broadway
history in 1882 by writing what many consider to be the first musical comedy:

Squatter Sovereignty, the saga of a Manhattan shantytown under siege. As the boulders fly and the ground splits in the blast zone of the advancing grid, the cast of ethnically diverse characters re-enacted the demolition of an actual Fifth Avenue shantytown, but with songs, humor, and a live billy goat. Here was a whole shantytown world, as told by, if not one of its own—Harrigan grew up on the Lower East Side—then by a near neighbor. It revealed much more about the cultural bargains struck by immigrants and their descendants, and about the interactions between groups of laborers on the working-class landscapes of New York—not only Germans and Irish but Italians, Slavs, Chinese, and native-born workers on their way up the class ladder. Their icon was the shanty—but what would be its fate? While the news media drew an ever narrower view of shantytowns for its anxious middle-class readers, working-class culture produced an expansive, ambitious reading of shanty-town life that delighted its audiences and surprised its critics.

5

Squatter Sovereignty:
Shantytown's Broadway Debut

A s they lost ground on the urban landscape, shanty dwellers infiltrated the dramatic spaces of the musical theater stage, which at that time was just assuming the form we know today. Starting in the early 1880s, musical theater tendered a warts-and-all vision of shantytown that bustled, clanged, came to blows, occasionally exploded. The closer actual shantytowns outside the theater walls got to extinction, the more popular virtual shantytowns framed by the proscenium became. These streetwise comedies of manners, outgrowths of the broadside ballads, constituted a cultural rebuttal to shanty-town demolitions from the working poor. The city's manual laborers and domestic servants, many of them immigrants or their descendants, com-prised the bulk of the audience for these entertainments, and from these ranks many of the lyricists and playwrights who wrote them emerged. Sprung from minstrelsy, these artists portrayed shantytowns as boisterous cultural spaces whose residents had defied and outwitted attempts to demolish their communities street by street. As with broadside ballads, they interpreted shantytowns as spaces of tradition and adaptation, where an ideology of dwelling emerged through the use of domestic space. Musical comedies offered a very different verdict than the thuggish portrayal of shanty dwellers in the press, or the glib indifference of the Paddys circulated in broadside ballads like "The Irishman's Shanty." In the end shantytown residents were unable to save their homes from destruction. But even as they were being demolished, the occupants used their shanties to assert values of personal, ethnic, and national identity. The demolition of actual shanties heightened the use of the shanty as a rhetorical device in debates about class, race, and ethnicity. The shanty as a cultural symbol grew stronger with every shanty-town demolition.

Shantytown's theatrical run got an auspicious beginning on January 9, 1882, when Edward Harrigan's first full-length musical comedy, *Squatter Sovereignty,* debuted to an enthusiastic crowd. There is no theatrical equivalent today for the excitement generated by a new Harrigan musical in late-nineteenth-century New York. If Tina Fey and Stephen Sondheim were partners in a comedy team that wrote and starred in all of its own productions, they might come close to matching the popularity of Harrigan and his partner, Tony Hart. Protégés of Tony Pastor, one of the founders of American vaudeville, Harrigan and Hart performed an assortment of comic Irish, German, and African-American characters drawn from the laboring classes of New York City. They became famous for an 1873 skit called "The Mulligan Guard," a sendup of an Irish neighborhood "militia," or volunteer fire company, which evolved into a long-running series of farcical skits. By the early 1880s the duo were popular not only with immigrants and working-class patrons, but the middle class, which had warmed to music-hall entertainments. As the *Times* review for *Squatter Sovereignty* noted in its second sentence, "The excellent quality of the audience—at least that part of it which occupied the best seats—was sig-nificant." Harrigan played a large part in recruiting middle-class audiences to the theater, concocting story lines that piqued their racial and ethnic biases and integrating musical numbers into the plots. He designed a theatrical space, the Theatre Comique, that catered to a middle-class yen for luxury. On *Squatter Sovereignty*'s opening night, both classes filled the brand new 1,600-seat Broadway theater, festooned with papier mâché friezes and lit by a mas-sive electric chandelier with 22,000 glass prisms—the first of its kind in any theater in New York. The *New York Times* declared the new venue "one of the most beautiful theaters of the City," and praised its departures from tradition, which included a flat oval, as opposed to a horseshoe-shaped hall, an innova-tion that brought the actors closer to the audience members. To the greatest extent possible, the audience for *Squatter Sovereignty* visited, rather than observed, shantytown at the Theatre Comique production.[1]

Set against a backdrop of shanty demolitions, *Squatter Sovereignty* followed the efforts of the Widow Rosie Nolan, the owner of a shantytown saloon, to arrange a marriage between her daughter Nellie and the son of an Irish neighbor, a dreamy sidewalk astronomer named Felix McIntyre, who makes his living selling views of the moon through his telescope "for 10 cents a peep." Patrons enticed by the title of the musical may have expected a play about contested property rights and contested American values, on both the national and the local landscapes. Although the Civil War had been over for 17 years, "squatter sovereignty" summoned antebellum debates over citizenship and entitlement that went beyond real estate. The most vitriolic pro-slavery newspaper in Kansas had been called the *Squatter Sovereign,* and one year after Harrigan's play debuted, in 1883, the term served as a title for a romantic novel about the war. Closer to home, the name recalled the litany of derisive descriptions of shanty dwellers in local newspapers and magazines, where the term "squatter sovereign" was a scornful description referring, most often, to the legal but maddening occupation of now-desirable land by shanty dwellers. A comic painting called *The Squatter Sovereign of Manhattan,* exhibited in Brooklyn in 1869, showed "the 'sovereign,' calmly smoking his 'dudheen' and gazing with apparent unconcern down upon the distant well-built street with its tall churches, French-roofed dwellings and rolling omnibuses." By naming his play *Squatter Sovereignty,* Harrigan, himself an Irish immigrant who grew up on the Lower East Side, converted the menacing overtones of the phrase into parody and defanged the detractors.[2]

The play opens inside the Harlem shanty of the Widow Nolan, who runs a saloon next door to the quarry where many of her neighbors are employed blasting boulders out of the paths of planned streets north of 165th Street. The aging widow is bent on brokering the marriage of her daughter Nellie to an Irish boy, and as the play begins she is meeting with the boy's father, Felix McIntyre, to negotiate dowries. Unbeknownst to the parents, however, Nellie loathes Felix's son Terrence, lately arrived from Ireland, and is scheming to marry instead the son of a middle-class German factory owner who lives south of shantytown. This family drama plays out against a backdrop of even greater domestic upheaval, as the street-paving crew draws ever closer to the Widow Nolan's shack, which lies directly in the path of 172nd Street. As the grid, and earth-moving equipment, close in on the widow's livelihood and her property, she concentrates all the harder on arranging her daughter's betrothal to Terrence McIntyre.[3]

As the curtain rises, the time is 5:00 p.m., one hour before quitting time at the quarry. The widow (played by Tony Hart, in drag) and Felix (played by Harrigan) are hammering out the final kinks in the marriage contract. All that remains is a ritual display of the items each is pledging to their child's dowry—an important step, as both the widow and Felix have promised to forfeit their contributions to the other parent if their own child reneges on the arranged marriage. Felix produces the goods that he is promising to donate to the dowry. Then, with their respective clans looking on, and over the noise of street-blasting outside, the Widow Nolan inventories her contributions. As the item exchange continues, it becomes clear that the widow is contributing all of her accumulated wealth to secure her daughter's future. But she cannot find one crucial dowry item: her beloved goat, Billy. "It's no bargain without the goat," one onlooker hollers. The powwow is about to break into a fistfight when a loud explosion is heard and boulders start falling through the shanty's roof—constructed of paper for the purpose, per Harrigan's instructions. The scene, reproduced on a publicity poster for the play's national tour, ends amid a hailstorm of debris as the Nolan and McIntyre clans run for cover.[4]

Act II moves the action to the Fifth Avenue home of Captain Kline, the widowed father of Nellie's true love, Fred. Having made his fortune with a glue

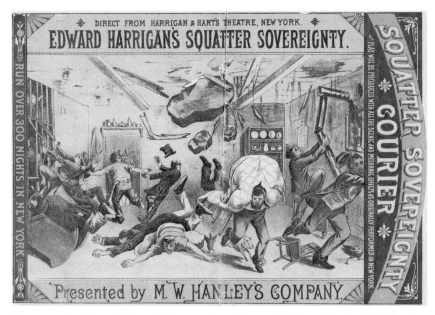

A program for the road show of *Squatter Sovereignty,* which brought the daily life of a New York shantytown to Broadway for more than 300 performances.

factory and built his "brownstone castle" on upper Fifth Avenue, the captain has turned his energies to securing his class position through the marriage of his son to an affluent bride, the daughter of a German brewer who, like Kline, has prospered financially. "I never seed her, but Swartz [her father] is a millionaire and she would make a nice wife for Frederick." Both the captain and the Widow Nolan are eager to marry their children to the most prosperous, ethnically identical candidates available. Nellie and Fred, seeing what Captain Kline has in mind, however, launch an offensive. They decide to pretend that Nellie is wealthy in order to secure the captain's blessing for a match between them—in fact, they decide she will masquerade as Swartz's daughter, the very bride that Kline has chosen for Fred. Throughout the next several scenes, Nellie swoops and curtsies around Kline's parlor, garishly decorated with ceramic busts and spindly-legged furniture, speaking in highfaluting rhythms that mimic her notion of what middle-class people act like. Her clumsy impression of middle-class behavior shows her to be naive, but it also ridicules the affectations of the middle-class patrons in the audience, perched on silk seats especially made for the new theater and basking in the misty glow of the prismatic chandelier as they experienced, vicariously, the life of the underclass.[5]

Act II ends with the successful recapture of Billy, played by a live goat that, at the beginning of Act III, joins the still-feuding Nolan and McIntyre clans on the rocks outside the widow's battered shanty. The widow discovers Nellie has married Fred. The audience is primed for an explosion, but as it turns out, the marriage is perfectly fine with the widow, as soon as it becomes apparent that it accomplishes her main goal: securing Nellie's financial security. Fred, it is revealed, has savings worth $10,000. At this point in the drama, the widow and Felix, who have begun a flirtation, seem poised to act on their flickering attraction. But Felix demands that the widow surrender the dowry, as a penalty for Nellie's breaking her engagement to Terrence. The Widow Nolan refuses. "[A]nd the long-threatened ruction begins," as one reviewer wrote. The contents of the widow's shanty, from feather bed to floppy bonnets, are decanted onto the rocks as the clans tear the house apart board by board. "While geese are flying above the rocks, the warring factions are seen trying to tumble one another from the heights as the final curtain descends," the screenplay instructs. Harrigan used live geese in this scene; on opening night, several flew off the stage and landed on the bonnets of women sitting in the expensive front-row seats.[6]

Harrigan was hailed by contemporary critics for his realism, which went beyond the gimmick of live animals onstage. In the nineteenth century "realistic" indicated a play or piece of fiction about working-class life, still relatively rare compared to works about historical figures or prominent personalities. The topics of "realistic" plays were often ripped from the headlines, and directors delighted viewers with elaborate costuming, special effects— live geese, thundering boulders, and intricate sets. *Squatter Sovereignty* was widely judged to be Harrigan's most socially conscious work to date. In a theater review under the headline, "A Dull Dramatic Season . . . Stupid New Plays by Stupid New American Playwrights," Harrigan and Hart were lauded as "the only persons who have succeeded in putting upon the stage genuine scenes taken from our street life. Our local types have been sparingly used by a few play-makers—poorly, almost invariably. But in the rude plays of Mr. Edward Harrigan the types have proved to be in some cases direct and pungent, and many of the scenes have possessed a peculiarly effective realism."[7]

Harrigan, an Irish immigrant who grew up in a polyglot neighborhood on the Lower East Side, worked very hard at dramatic verisimilitude. He routinely roamed the streets of the Bowery looking for inspiration for sets; the tavern in *McSorley's Inflation,* which also premiered in 1882, was modeled on the actual saloon still in operation today on East 7th Street. Harrigan personally scouted secondhand stores for costumes, sometimes buying articles of clothing from people he met on the street. His characterizations often seemed more like impersonations. "I think your epic of Shantyville is something all by itself. It is, I think, your best," the producer Augustin Daly wrote Harrigan after seeing his portrayal of the shantytown astronomer, Felix, in *Squatter Sovereignty.* "[Y]ou're a living chromo, where on earth did you pick up that walk and those trousers?" Contemporary cultural critic William Dean Howells also approved of Harrigan's efforts: "Mr. Harrigan accurately realizes in his scenes what he realizes in his persons; that is the actual life of this city," Howells wrote in *Harper's* in July 1886. "He cannot give it all; he can only give phases of it; and he has preferred to give the Irish-American phases in their rich and amusing variety, and some of its African and Teutonic phases." Many of Harrigan's skits and plays had clever names—*Cordelia's Aspirations, McSorley's Inflation, Old Lavender*—that touched sentimental chords with his audience. His motto, "to catch the living manners as they rise," was printed on his programs, and he liked to say that his comedy was "planted in the truth."

"The adage 'To hold the mirror up to nature' is as applicable to the swarming myriads of New York as to the Greek warriors before Priam's city, or the lords and nobles who surrounded the Tudors," he declared in an 1886 *Harper's* article. Certainly the description of the Widow Nolan's shanty that begins the typescript of the play suggests an intimate knowledge of shanties, from the horse-blanket covering the piano to the clock on the mantle, to the rag carpet, iron stove, wooden cuspidor, and "neatly covered" table.[8]

In 1881, in preparation for designing the *Squatter Sovereignty* set, designer Charles Witham, who often worked with Harrigan, painted three detailed watercolor studies of a Harlem shantytown known as "Goatville." Now in the collection of the Museum of the City of New York, the watercolors capture many of the stereotypical aspects of shantytown—goats, carts, groaning clotheslines, stovepipes. Scattered people are pictured doing domestic or garden chores, or chatting with neighbors. While lush—gardens and grass blanket the landscape—the presence of taller brick buildings in the near background assure that this urban scene will not be mistaken for farmland. The mood is serene but not picturesque. Not intended for consumption as-is, these scene designs offer a glimpse less mediated, perhaps, than published photographs from the same period. Witham also designed sets for Harrigan plays set on the Lower East Side; the watercolor studies he made for those sets are far from serene. The people, like the buildings, are bent to the point of buckling; refuse clogs the streets; skyscrapers loom over airless intersections. In the *Squatter Sovereignty* watercolors, by contrast, the verdant landscape and open sky provide a less oppressive physical environment for the poor people who live there.[9]

Harrigan refutes a number of stereotypes about shantytown in *Squatter Sovereignty,* starting with the myth that shanty dwellers were lazy and shiftless. Work defines the shanty residents. The middle class, represented by Captain Kline, who owns a glue factory, are industrialists; the lower classes are entrepreneurs and laborers. The captain brags about his business, but is never seen working; his son Fred seems not to work at all. Shanty dwellers meanwhile are always at work. The Widow Nolan not only owns a saloon, but sells goat milk on the side, as a sign on her shanty advertises. Never idle, she is knitting as the play opens. Among her possessions is a washtub, suggesting that at some point she made her living as a laundress. The boys hanging about outside her shanty are "all working boys"; her neighbor maintains a market

garden; her male relatives are identified in the cast list as "hod carriers
(laborers)." Sounds of rock being blasted outside, to make way for a new
street, punctuate the first act; they are produced by shantytown men who
work in the quarry. During the climactic Act III song, "Paddy Duffy's Cart"
("We'd gather in the evening, all honest working boys"), the stage directions
call for a parade of shantytown residents to traverse the stage: a woman lug-
ging a bundle of sticks, workmen toting their dinner kettles, a woman carrying a pitcher, lads pulling a wagon, a blacksmith wearing an apron, a woman
sweeping the stoop of her shanty, a woman taking clothes off the line. All of
shantytown is at work, and unlike accounts in the popular press, which
reported but did not credit the industriousness of shanty dwellers, Harrigan
fastens the audience's attention on the work habits of his characters. The
silence surrounding this pageant of shantytown workers would have been, in
the context of this boisterous comedy, emphatic.

Harrigan bestowed individuality on shanty dwellers; they are not the uniform proles of mainstream news media that middle-class patrons may have
expected. Neither are they the unruly caricatures of mid-century broadside
ballads, safeguarded by the working class. Generally portrayed as indistinguishable in their poverty, the shanty dwellers of *Squatter Sovereignty* are
acquisitive and discerning in matters of taste. The central action of Act I is an
inspection of the dowries pledged by the widow and Felix; it occupies roughly
20 pages of the script and onstage would have taken perhaps 15 minutes to
enact. Harrigan practically shakes the dowry items under the noses of his
audience, which thanks to the innovative floor plan of the Theatre Comique
would have been seated quite close to the action on the stage, and challenges
them to interpret their meaning. After the widow and Felix agree on a list of
dowry items, all of them are dragged into the Widow Nolan's shanty and displayed, game-show fashion, to a gathering of sharp-eyed relatives. This tradition draws gentle criticism from two minor characters, sign-painters named
Salem and Darius, who comment on the ritual: "These old Irish people have
curious ways," notes Salem, to which Darius replies, "Very curious." The ritual
left nothing to doubt, with all the pledged items spread out for mutual inspection by the clans—who, we are told at another point, had traditionally feuded
with each other in Ireland. The dowry items range from the pragmatic to the
sentimental, and signal virtues of change as well as tradition. Harrigan uses
this display of material possessions to challenge middle-class assumptions

about the vulgarity of shanty dwellers, while also illustrating the subtle class snobbery that separated members of the working classes. As suggested by the popularity of broadsides, ethnic minorities who had achieved a degree of financial stability and cultural fluency used the shanty to signal their distance from the newly arrived. Through the pantomime of the dowry, the playwright challenges the prevailing middle-class ideas about shantytown while simultaneously exposing the condescension of working-class people for laborers below them on the economic and social scale.[10]

The Widow Nolan opens the proceedings by donating a feather bed and pillows. In response, Felix contributes two silver candlesticks, two iron skillets, and a painting of the Lakes of Killarney, "from the Louvre." Suddenly, it becomes a competition, a reverse auction with Felix and the Widow Nolan upping the ante with each contribution. The mental accounting (does a feather bed equal a pair of "silver" candlesticks?) challenges the audience to keep score as incongruous piles of goods take shape on stage. When her turn comes, the widow pledges a quilt, a cradle, and a teapot, which inspire Felix to donate two geese and a Harlem Drake (a humorous metaphor for the intended groom, Terrence, or perhaps Felix himself; as the play progresses, the widow and Felix begin a flirtation). This assortment prompts a more generous outpouring from the widow, who donates a cooking stove ("'tis a coke burner") and two items of apparel, a straw hat and a woolen shawl. Felix, not to be outdone on the sartorial front, ponies up a coarse woolen overcoat and rubber boots, and, his most valuable contribution to date, a suckling pig. Egged on by Felix's grandiosity, the widow concludes with a small avalanche of pragmatic and sentimental objects that include a washtub, a piano, a horsehair blanket, and her "own Billy" goat, which she inherited from her husband. The action grinds to a halt when the pet goat cannot be found, placing the entire negotiation in jeopardy; locating the goat, the key to a successful bargaining session, becomes the basis of the action for Act II.[11]

While many of the dowry items are useful, none are simply practical. The pig and the geese were sustainable sources of food, but also emblems of the shantytown economy; the washtub and iron skillets were practical domestic items, but also symbols of self-reliance and domesticity. The cradle, which had been Nellie's, emphasizes a connection to family, ethnicity, and nationality that is as much American as it is Irish: the detail that Nellie laid in it herself suggests she was born in New York, not Ireland. She is first generation

Irish-American, a theme that Harrigan develops in the last act of the play. The lambs wool shawl and "Tuscan bonnet"—a straw bonnet of enduring popularity—had practical uses but also carried a touch of style, like the black silk parasol Thoreau found in James Collins's shanty in Concord. But the scene also provides glimpses of what more status-conscious poor people thought of their less-genteel neighbors and countrymen: when Felix accepts the Wedgwood teapot from the widow, he makes a show of drinking from its spout. Before the stove is added to the widow's pile of donations, Felix strides across the stage and spits into it loudly; the widow passes him a cuspidor, another symbol of her refinement, which he ignores. The widow is proud of her brand names—Wedgwood teapot, Tuscan bonnet, Morning Glory stove—but Felix casually ridicules them. He, however, is proud of his reproduction of a painting "from the Louvre," the Lakes of Killarney. No one in the play is immune to the status that material objects can convey.[12]

Two items, the stove and the quilt, stand out from the rest for their layers of meaning. The bulky Morning Glory stove, featured prominently in publicity posters for the play, has an almost slapstick presence on stage; squat and leaden, it seethes a comic recalcitrance. In its time the Morning Glory was a marvel, a smoke-free stove that could heat an entire house economically. An 1869 improvement on an 1850s design for a "base-burning" stove—a technological leap forward that conserved coal by regulating the air flow at the base of the stove—the Morning Glory was marketed for use both as a cooking and a parlor stove; a special "swinging hearth" allowed easy removal of the ash pan, making it both cleaner and less labor-intensive than older stoves. Famous worldwide, it was so popular in the United States that stores often sold out. The Morning Glory stove affirmed family values in a straightforward way; the stove was literally the hearth of the home, a symbol of warmth and security being passed down from mother to daughter. But it also identifies the widow, a seemingly backward ("old Irish") woman, with modern, labor-saving technology—similar to the way the "patent new coffee mill" that Thoreau belittles in James Collins's shanty actually identifies the Collinses with up-to-date, labor-saving gadgetry. The Morning Glory brand was efficient and clean and powerful, but it also carried an air of refinement, as illustrated by the perky morning-glory blossom pinned to the center of print advertisements for the stove. It promised not only less drudgery, but a touch of gentility. The "two five-iron skillets" that Felix donates recall the introduction of flat-bottomed cast-iron pans in the 1870s, only a few years before the action of the play; more prosaic, they also signal a certain level of modernity. These intimations of modernity press against illustrations in the mainstream press, which audiences for *Squatter Sovereignty* would most surely have seen, which showed stovepipes jutting from the roofs of shanties, askew and discordant on the urbanizing landscape. With the widow's Morning Glory stove and the cast-iron pans, Harrigan offered his audience the view from the other end of the stovepipe, a scene of relatively modern technology and efficient housekeeping imbued with traditional values of hearth and home—signs of achievement and discretion where many in the audience had been taught to expect sloth and backwardness.[13]

Juxtaposed against the relative modernity of the Morning Glory was the wooden bedstead, slats, and bed key donated by Felix, which mark him as, not backward—Harrigan did not sneer at his characters—but less materialistic. Iron bedsteads with metal coil springs had been in use for a decade by the time *Squatter Sovereignty* debuted, although rope beds tightened with keys were in use for several more decades. Similarly, the feather mattress and pillows contributed by the widow harkened back to older practices associated, by the 1880s, with rural roots; audience members at the Theatre Comique would have been eyeing the coil spring mattresses that had only recently debuted, such as the pointedly named Metropolitan Reversible Spring, listed for $12 in a trade catalog published only a few months before the play opened. The feather bed was an iconic article for immigrants, one of the possessions most often transported to America on the long ocean crossing, and therefore linked the proposed marriage and its offspring with older Irish traditions. Social reformers, however, on a joint mission of assimilation and sanitation, tried to separate immigrants from their feather beds and other plush furnishings by arguing that they encouraged vermin. Immigrants resisted. At its most basic level, the bequest of a feather bed and bedstead to the betrothed couple, Nellie and Terrence, carried an endorsement of fecundity and procreation. But the feather bed also represented a rebuke to the social reformers and "friendly visitors" intent on replacing ethnic and immigrant practices with more "modern" middle-class standards. It was a symbol of resistance.[14]

So was the Irish chain quilt pledged by the widow as part of the dowry. It would seem at first glance to be another obvious nod to older Irish traditions of farm and village, family and clan. Quilts were, by 1882, considered rustic, even embarrassingly so, by the burgeoning middle class. An 1874 advice column about beds and bedding published in *The Household* magazine insisted that, "Neither the unhealthful thing called a comforter nor the unsightly covering known as a patched quilt should be seen on a bed in this day." In an 1849 short story in *Godey's Lady's Book,* tastemaker T. S. Arthur, who went on to found his own women's magazine, singled out the Irish chain pattern by name in a passage that dismissed quilts as comically old-fashioned and quaint. People of means and taste bought machine-made blankets; quilts, which cost perhaps a third as much, stamped you as poor, rural, or unworldly. But the Irish chain quilt was a nuanced symbol. The name, and possibly the pattern itself, were not Irish but American inventions. No one knows for sure where the name came from or when it was first applied. According to quilt historians, the Irish chain was one of the earliest patchwork designs developed in America, popular by the early 1800s, but its colonial and post-Revolutionary makers may not have called it by that name. The Irish chain also may have been made in Ireland, but Irish quilters did not label their quilts by pattern names, instead using geographical references to identify different kinds of patched work. "Chain" designs were also common in the weaving industry in Great Britain, where the name refers to the diamond pattern cast by the warp threads of a web; a close-up of a plain-weave carpet, for example, reveals the cross-hatch pattern common to Irish chain quilts. But the name "Irish chain" did not emigrate; it was bestowed on quilts in the United States some time in the first half of the nineteenth century. An Irish chain quilt embodied the amalgamation of old and new that characterized not only the immigrant experience in urban America, but the experience of urbanization generally, as people from rural areas moved into cities, slowly tipping the balance of the nation's population from rural to urban. It spoke to indeterminate origins and muddled identities as much as it did to ethnic traditions; it was an unsettling, ambiguous metaphor. And in the context of the play, that fluidity was celebrated.[15]

Some quilting enthusiasts have suggested, based on their own family histories, that the name "Irish chain" was conferred by immigrant-hating nativists and intended as a slur: the Irish chain was an uncomplicated pattern, and describing it as Irish may have been a way of demeaning immigrants (so easy even the Irish could master it). Others speculate that the term was borrowed from land surveying. The Irish chain was a portable chain used to measure land in the field, superseded in the nineteenth century by the English or Gunter's chain, which also replaced the Scotch chain. (All had 100 hatpin-like links, but of differing lengths.) The Gunter's chain, which was compatible with the decimal system, became the basis for mapping the western frontier following the Land Ordinance of 1785—10 square Gunter's chains equaled one square acre—and in turn it became the standard for the 1811 Commissioners Plan of New York, which laid out the grid according to uniform numbers of chains. The mathematics underlying the Manhattan grid were decidedly *not* Irish. Regardless of origin, the invocation of an Irish chain in a play about shantytown demolitions was a superbly crafted inference. What today is a quilt pattern of indeterminate origin would have been in 1882 a potent symbol of ethnic and cultural conflict, evoking the usurpation of tenanted land and questions of rightful possession that were ongoing in Ireland and in uptown Manhattan—as well as an animus for the elite members of society visiting destruction upon its less powerful citizens. Sentimental moniker or slur, the term "Irish chain" squared off immigrant workers against middle-class elites, and more entrenched first-generation immigrants—like Nellie and Fred— against less Americanized recent arrivals—like Terrence McIntyre.[16]

Because the other Irish chain palpably on view was, of course, the chain of Irish immigrants, people whose passage was paid by relatives already living in the United States—people like Terrence. His fresh arrival is remarked over and over again by Nellie, who finds his rawness repulsive. "I won't marry Terrence McIntyre," she says at one point. "He doesn't even know what ice cream is yet." Chain migration was not a term used when the play was performed; it was coined by historians of immigration in the second half of the twentieth century. But the concept was palpable on the stage of *Squatter Sovereignty* in 1882. The chains under scrutiny were the chains of Irish nativity and tradition, set against the equally persuasive traditions of Irish Americans like Nellie, who as the play unfolds, never wavers from her determination to ignore her mother's wishes and marry the first-generation American man of her choice, Fred Kline, the German glue-maker's son. Nellie is breaking the Irish chain of her family, choosing instead an amalgamated identity made tangible by her mixed-ethnicity, mixed-class marriage. "At home I married the man of my mother's choice," the widow says when Nellie objects to the arranged marriage with Terrence. Nellie replies, "Oh. That was in Ireland where the customs are altogether different." Nellie follows local traditions—American traditions. Nellie's mother bemoans her daughter's interest in dancing and attending "hops" at the local music hall, and her "Yankee ways of going . . . to picnics on the hill above. She's losing all the Irish in her." In the opening scene, the widow comments that Nellie shares a birthday with George Washington, but she gets the date wrong by eight months (Oct. 22 not Feb. 22). That mistake would have elicited a laugh from an audience accustomed to celebrating the first official federal holiday in the United States, established by an act of Congress only four years earlier but commemorated with public parades and general merry-making for many decades. The joke was an opportunity to flatter naturalized and native citizens alike. The errant anecdote underscores Nellie's links to her native country: America. Nellie is fully conversant in American ways that sometimes flummox her mother. Early in the play the widow is distraught when her goat eats her liquor license, because she assumes that means it is no longer valid. She does not grasp the abstraction of the license, but Nellie does, and simply replaces it for her; the widow marvels at the reincarnation.[17]

Harrigan insisted that the audience rethink some of its blunter stereotypes about shantytown domesticity. But he also expressed, in the dowry scene and elsewhere, the ambiguity and ambivalence that the poor and working-class members of his audience felt about reconciling old world traditions with American habits—the same ambivalence voiced in broadside ballads about Paddy, king of the castle in his shantytown kingdom. The audience was torn in its loyalties to traditional ways that older family members were eager to pass down, and the accommodations demanded or presented by urban American life. As the characters' struggles in *Squatter Sovereignty* acknowl-edged, newer ways of life often promised greater comfort, but older traditions carried powerful messages about identity and self-determination that were empowering. Individuality and American identity were not choices between one and the other but a savvy mixture, a self-making that preserved family connections without foregoing the appealing opportunities for change pre-sented by life in urban America. At the same time, Harrigan's sendup of middle-class aspiration tapped anxieties harbored by the middle-class patrons, the persons of "excellent quality" singled out by reviewers as one indication of the play's success. It was fast becoming clear that homogeneity was one of the costs of middle-class status; refinement was a dull business, and the sacrifices it demanded sparked a dramatic re-evaluation of shantytown life in middle-class magazines and art during the early 1880s.

At a time when the urban middle class was obsessed with embedding class status in material objects, *Squatter Sovereignty* undercut class anxieties and presumptions as illusory. Nellie, when she pretends to be the middle-class brewer's daughter, is so transparently *not* what she pretends to be that she raises questions about everyone else. And indeed, they are faking it, too. In one subplot that runs throughout the play, the sign-painters Salem and Darius weave in and out of the action plastering advertisements for "St. Patrick's salve" and "perforated fish-skin undershirts" on the sides of rocks, houses, and "chimbleys" in Shantytown. Salem and Darius briefly pretend to be street surveyors in Act I, because they think a profession with a higher status will impress two middle-class girls, Marie and Belle (interchangeably referred to as "Maria" and "Bella") whom they have recently met. Soon the girls see them at work, and they fret that all is lost:

> SALEM: *(Despairingly)* Oh my, Maria saw me placing St. Patrick's salve on the rocks.

> DARIUS: *(Serio comical)* Oh, Darius, Darius, your Bella has beheld you sticking undershirts on the backs of Shanties.

> DARIUS and
> SALEM: We're lost, lost.

Captain Kline is also revealed to be a poseur, a pastiche of the middle-class refinement he tries to display. His pronouncements of superiority to his shanty-town neighbors are belied by the heavy accent prescribed for the character, who speaks in the stilting faux dialect of "The Dutch Ragpicker's Shanty." His drawing room is drenched in mahogany and decorated with imposing oil portraits but the captain impounds the goat Billy for eating his lace curtains—a standard of immigrant interior decoration. As the play continues it becomes clear that the captain has only recently acquired the wealth that secures his middle-class status. As he describes it, "I am an awful rich man. I make my money by glue. I buy all de old horses in de horse market and melt dem into glue." But he is padding his resume, pretending to be more than he is, as his sister-in-law taunts him when he brags about his Prussian military service, "You were a clerk in a grocery store and rode a truck horse with the Dutch Huzzars." The captain's home address, given as 2595 Fifth Ave.—"just outside of" shantytown, according to the stage directions—mirrors his precarious social position. The house would have occupied the very northern tip of Fifth Avenue, at the time a tendril trailing several blocks past the edge of the grid to meet the Harlem River as it curved toward what would become, two years later, 143rd Street. By middle-class standards this was a hinterland in 1882, but the captain considers himself miles ahead of his shantytown neighbors socially. The farce on the stage of *Squatter Sovereignty* mirrored the farce of class formation being performed on the streets and in the homes of Manhattan, where the middle class built stage sets of prosperity and acquired taste. Like his real-life counterparts, the captain rails against his shantytown neighbors, perhaps all the more because his own financial and social position was so tenuous: they remind him of where he has come from and where he might return, given a financial collapse.[18]

But both the captain and the sign-painters enjoy happy endings. Darius and Salem abandon their ruse of being surveyors, instead bragging to Marie and Belle that "there's $3,000 a year" in the ad-posting business. Quicker than you can say "fish-skin undershirt," they are both engaged to their girlfriends. The brothers of the middle-class girls, whom Salem and Darius fear will be angry when they discover their true class status, are in fact delighted to see their sisters paired with two gainfully employed sign-painters. The captain, meanwhile, reconciles his aspirations by indulging his affections. Embarrassed to discover that he has mistaken the brewer Swartz's wife for his (nonexistent) daughter, the captain impulsively proposes to his cook, Louisa, whom he has earlier disparaged as the daughter of a shantytown squatter. "[D]ot makes it even," he declares after the proposal. His son's marriage to "[d]e daughter of a woman vat lives in a shanty" will be balanced by his own marriage to the daughter of a man who lives in a shanty. These sudden reversals make no sense—and neither, Harrigan suggests, did the con game of class distinction practiced outside the theater (and inside: the cheap tickets sat in the balcony, far from the rustle of the silk seats). The sacrifice of romantic love required by the imperatives of middle-class reproduction, which prompts the captain to marry his son off to an illusory brewer's daughter, are no different than the self-denial demanded by older traditions of arranged marriage, like the marriage contract struck by the widow and Felix without their children's consent.

Squatter Sovereignty is a farce about a farcical system of class formation and reproduction, a long-running engagement on the streets of Manhattan and other growing American cities, and its personal and societal costs. All with live geese, exploding boulders, and rude ethnic jokes.[19]

Much of the humor of the play comes from the class tensions and pretensions that its title reflects. But the classes portrayed in *Squatter Sovereignty* are not so much at odds as they are struggling to merge. Harrigan had written effectively and humorously about immigrant assimilation in the Mulligan skits, which established his reputation as a comedian. But in *Squatter Sovereignty* Harrigan posits a different kind of assimilation—not of immigrants relinquishing their distinctive ethnic traits, but lower and middle classes blending into a less-differentiated whole. Harrigan suggests an alternative future defined by ethnic mingling as well as class diffusion—class as a negotiation, not a test. Or rather, he reflects a present in which that was rapidly becoming the case. Shantytown residents relinquish older traditions, but they do not mutely accept the meanings that middle-class Americans attached to consumer goods, residential addresses, urban occupations, or ethnic difference. The dowries displayed by the Widow Nolan and Felix, for example, reflect a *synthesis* of lower-class pragmatism and middle-class aspiration: a feather bed, but also a painting of the Lakes of Killarney "from the Louvre", two iron skillets, but also a pair of silver candlesticks; an Irish chain quilt, but also a Wedgwood teapot; a goat, pig, and some geese, but also a "piany." The piano, a staple of the middle-class parlor, is wrapped in a horsehair blanket, a homespun covering that the newly affluent reserved for carriage rides in Central Park. The painting of the Lakes of Killarney, described in the script as "a bad looking oil painting or water scene in an old frame," pokes fun at Felix, but it is also a jab at the artistic pretentions of the urban middle class, which was acquiring "art" at a breakneck speed in the late nineteenth century. Indeed, this item in particular foils any effort to see the possessions of shantytown residents as merely aspirational; the true value of the painting to its owner is revealed when Felix's relatives burst into an impromptu serenade about the actual Lakes of Killarney. "By Killarnys [*sic*] lakes and the / Ever winding mountain dells / River streams and flowing wells / Ever fair Killarny." The awkward break between "the" and "Ever" at the end of the first line, occasioning a sharp intake of breath by the singers, would have drawn a laugh from the audience. Harrigan gently mocks the McIntyres' longing for old Ireland, but he also mocks the pretensions of the middle-class patrons he has so skillfully drawn into his swanky new Theatre Comique.[20]

In Harrigan's shantytown, ethnicity is losing ground to class, but ethnic slurs are still part and parcel of everyday life; his presentation would be considered racist today. The Italians and Germans speak in exaggerated dialects, and most of New York's ethnic groups have jokes made at their expense. Ethnic jokes pepper the script: Nellie declares she would rather marry "a Turk" than Terence; Felix makes a joke about the planets, "Uranus, Venus, and Jew-Peter"; Captain Kline threatens to marry "a Chinawoman"; and Felix is teased about being "moon-eyed like a Chinawoman." The play shows ordinary, civil exchanges between members of different ethnicities, and also the brutal biases they hold toward each other. At the very beginning of the play, the Widow Nolan is joined onstage by a workman named Pedro Donnetta, who banters in a thick Italian accent: "Missa No-la . . . Will-a you give-a me one-a drink-a wat." She offers him a drink, and a compliment— "Ye Italians work hard in the quarry beyant"—and he returns the compliment, "I like-a de Irish-a people. Day gotta de good-a de heart-a." As soon as Pedro leaves her house, however, the widow announces her sincere opinion to her daughter Nellie: "Mister Donnetta is a nice Italian. The rest of the gang in the Quarry are savages entirely." Here is a judgment that could have been lifted from the annals of shantytown diatribes, with the names changed to implicate Italians. Late-nineteenth-century popular culture addressed the topic of ethnicity in ways that skewered ethnic minorities without necessarily demeaning them. Building on the minstrel tradition from which it grew, the musical theater could propose a vision of common cause among marginalized groups. As historian W. T. Lhamon Jr. notes, minstrelsy was "one way the working-class knew itself" in the nineteenth century; the performance of cultural gestures by blackface minstrels constituted "useful blazonings of identity" for white and black observers. The characters in shantytown musicals sent up similar cultural flares. Shantytown residents, or at least their avatars, talked back to observers, challenging their assumptions even while putting flesh and bones on some of their prejudices. Audience members were invited to examine these three-dimensional figures for similarities and differences.[21]

Ultimately, prosperity is more important than ethnicity for the residents of

Harrigan's fictionalized shantytown. What appears to be a marriage concocted to preserve ethnic purity is in fact all along intended to secure financial stability; by the widow's own description, she was "endeavoring to marry [Nellie] off comfortable and aisy." Comfort and ease seemed most attainable through a traditional match with an Irish boy, but when it presents itself in the form of a nontraditional match, the widow easily acquiesces. What is the price of her appeasement? A new set of furniture to replace the one repossessed by Felix; in the final moments of the play, Nellie assures her mother that she will refurnish her house in shantytown, and in return receives her mother's blessing for her marriage to Fred. Presumably, that new set of furniture will be purchased at one of the many department stores popping up on Broadway, some 150 blocks south of shantytown; Fred's $10,000 nest egg gives the shantytowners access to middle-class sources of consumer goods. So the Irish chain quilt will be superseded by a machine-made blanket, the feather bed by a spring coil mattress, and the straw bonnet with one of velvet or satin. Other forfeited items, like Nellie's cradle, the pet goat, and the washtub, were disposable relics—not of a backward past, but of earlier stages of the widow's life. Several other objects, the Wedgwood teapot and Morning Glory stove, for example, might simply be replaced with identical copies, because they were already up-to-date. The new furniture is a boon, not a betrayal.[22]

And what of the shanty itself? The most important possession of all, in the lexicon of the play, is a house. It is important both for its financial and its symbolic value. The Widow Nolan begins the play with a monologue about her shanty, and her dead husband's assessment of its investment value: "Rosy says he, when I'm dead and gone there'll be brownstone castles built on this ground and you'll get your own price for it." Now, the widow promises Felix, "my daughter Nellie will come in for the house and ground, that my husband left me by word of mouth." Legal title to the land does not enter into its valuation; possession alone seems to assure compensation. The widow's claims of possession rest on word of mouth, but in shantytown that is a firm foundation. She and her neighbors are proud homeowners. The widow laments her husband's unfulfilled promise to provide her with a "brownstone castle" like the one Captain Kline inhabits, but she's thankful for the shanty and all that goes with it, as she sings in the lilting ballad, "The Widow Nolan's Goat:"

> Oh, I'm a lone widdy, meself and me daughter;
> We live in a house where there's welcome galore;
> My husband he formally [sic] carried up mortar
> From the ground to the third or fourth floor.
> When he died he will'd over the land and the shanty;
> His pipe and his stick, and his frieze overcoat;
> The pig and the goslings, the chickens so banty,
> And his favorite pet, oh my buck Billy Goat.[23]

A decade or so after her husband's death, the widow's shanty is daily in danger of destruction; at the end of Act I, a boulder cut loose by the road-widening crashes through her roof, ending the act with a literal bang. Shantytown is being carved up by real estate developers and blasted to smithereens by municipal wrecking crews, yet the characters seem little worried. Part of their confidence stems from older convictions about the possession of land, as opposed to legal title—the "word of mouth" that assures the widow of a windfall on the shanty she inherited from her husband. But part of it comes from new skills at class negotiation. Why should shanty dwellers worry too much about shantytown demolitions when they are so effectively infiltrating the class that is displacing them? The price of these class *rapprochements,* however, appears to be the shanty. (The widow's goat, that ubiquitous symbol of shantytown, dies early in the third act.) As the physical embodiment of the class divide, the shanty becomes the only nonnegotiable class barrier.

Captain Kline, also house-proud, voices the frustration the middle class felt toward shanty dwellers. He rants against the shanties that cover upper Fifth Avenue. In Act II he vows, "I'm going to tear dem shanties down, build a glue factory and kill every damn goat in Shantytown." Later, when he learns of his son's elopement with Nellie, he threatens to "go get my brewers and tear dese shanties down." He boasts in Act III that he has bought all the houses in shantytown and plans to demolish them to make way for a new factory. The widow retorts, "You don't own my house." Felix and then the assembled clan members chime in, "Nor mine!" The captain's rejoinder, "So move out," starts a riot. On the heels of the tearful reconciliations and surprise nuptials that conclude the play, the captain reminds everyone that he now owns all the houses in shantytown, and he's going to flatten them. He does not get a chance to demolish the widow's house, however. The play closes with a scene that has no dialog, only the sound of boards splitting and crockery smashing as the clans kick apart the widow's shanty, and Felix's relatives triumphantly empty its contents onto the rocks. In *Squatter Sovereignty* the class barriers are permeable, but the shanty has to go. Harrigan put the class conflicts symbolized by the shanty at center stage. And then he blew them up.[24]

After a half-century of portrayals that cast shantytown residents as grotesque throwbacks or dimwitted peons, *Squatter Sovereignty* finally gives shanty dwellers their say. What Harrigan finds inside the shanties of Manhattan is remarkably similar to what Thoreau found inside the shanty of James Collins, but the meanings he assigns to those people and their modest possessions is quite different. Harrigan acknowledges the domesticity of the shantytown scene, the violence of its destruction, and the resourcefulness of its residents even in the face of that destruction. The title of the play, tellingly, is not a geographical marker but a philosophical and legal concept: squatter sovereignty. Do these shanty dwellers maintain their sovereignty even as they lose their shanties? It is an open question at the end of the play. In real life, commercial and residential expansion flattened shantytowns and pushed their residents out of the central city. On stage, the class conflicts crystallized by shantytown could work themselves out in happier, albeit fictional ways.

The "squatter sovereigns" of Harrigan's theatrical shantytown embraced and reimagined that scornful label, defending their rights to urban space even as their houses were being torn down. Their sophisticated solutions to class dilemmas and their forthright scheming on behalf of themselves and their family members exploded an entire array of middle-class presumptions about shantytown residents. The lazy, plodding rubes of mid-century depictions—standards of both middle-class journalism and working-class popular songs—are both given the hook in *Squatter Sovereignty*, and in a series of plays that followed its lead. Harrigan's shantytown residents are not survivors of some rural, European past; they are survivors of middle-class efforts to exile them from the urban landscape that they helped to build. At the final curtain, a spotlight goes up to reveal Darius the sign-painter, who has inexplicably donned a coonskin cap, a flourish that identified the shantytown residents with early American pioneers such as Davy Crockett, or the wary but adventurous folk that George Caleb Bingham portrayed in his 1850 painting *The Squatters*. The phrase *Squatter Sovereignty* recalls Bleeding Kansas and the Civil War, but the play asks the audience to replace that painful association with an earlier vision of determined American pioneers—and to attach the same virtues to the urban pioneers currently being blasted out of their homes in New York's many shantytowns.[25]

Squatter Sovereignty played for 168 performances, about three times as long as the average Broadway musical of the period. "Paddy Duffy's Cart" and "The Widow Nolan's Goat" became two of the most popular songs Harrigan wrote in the course of his very successful career. Harrigan continued to explore more serious, "realistic" topics after *Squatter Sovereignty*—his next musical, *Mordecai Lyons,* was a melodrama about a Jewish pawnbroker—but none were ever as successful as his shantytown tale. He revived *Squatter Sovereignty* for a national tour in 1890 and again on Broadway in 1892. "Mr. Harrigan did well to revive *Squatter Sovereignty,*" one reviewer wrote after the show opened, "for he has done nothing better and not much as good. The old piece has been cordially received, and . . . serves to strengthen our faith in the skill of Mr. Harrigan, which, we confess, was beginning to waver." Immensely popular in his day—George M. Cohan wrote a song in his honor in 1908—Harrigan's name and his works died out in the 1930s.[26]

Through the 1880s and 1890s and into the 1920s, shantytown provided the backdrop, plot line, and characters for a steady stream of stage productions mounted by New York companies, regional and national touring troupes, variety acts, and amateur theater clubs across the country. A spate of shantytown plays and musical comedies followed Harrigan's lead, from *Grogan's Elevation*—a tale of two ash can inspectors—in 1887, through *The Shanty Queen* (1890), *Fun in Shantytown* (1896), and *Shanty Town* (1897), a character sketch written especially for Tom Nawn, a well-known Irish comedian. By then the concept was so worn that the *Shanty Town* publicity poster—a sketch of an Irish cop collaring a wayward boy with one hand and a leering goat with his other, while dodging brickbats—assured skeptical patrons that "The Funniest Farce in the World" featured "Every Thing New." The shantytown locus was still relevant in 1902 when it reappeared in *The Old Reliable McFadden's Flats,* which was made into a movie in 1935; and again in 1914, with *Mrs. Tubbs of Shantytown,* a club play performed by community, high school, and Sunday School groups from Greencastle, PA, to Macclenny, FL, and Hobbs, NM. Shantytown returned to Broadway in 1924 with *Merry Wives of Gotham,* a Laurence Eyre play set in a shantytown at 69th Street and Fifth Avenue during the 1880s, which was remade the following year into the silent movie *Lights of Old Broadway*. The Eyre play concerns twins separated at birth; one, raised by a German-American family, becomes a Manhattan socialite and the other, raised by an Irish family, a shantytown washerwoman. They are thrown together by a land dispute—the socialite's husband owns land in shantytown claimed by the washerwoman's husband—and the plot develops a romantic twist when the son of the wealthy landowner falls in love with the daughter of the shantytown laundress. The lovers are echoes of Nellie and Fred. Few working-class people would have seen the play—by the 1920s, Broadway plays attracted an almost exclusively middle- and upper-class clientele—but many would have seen the movie version in 1925. More than 40 years after *Squatter Sovereignty* debuted in 1882, shantytowns were still useful vehicles for cultural debates about class identity.[27]

Squatter Sovereignty gave a dramatic voice to the residents of New York shantytowns being demolished in the 1870s and 1880s. Shantytown residents spoke for themselves as well, in court and on the streets; very occasionally they got the opportunity to speak out in the press. Addressing a reporter in 1880, a resident of an uptown shantytown decried the shanty demolitions that formed the basis for the plot of *Squatter Sovereignty*. She counted herself fortunate, she said, to live in a shantytown uptown rather than in a tenement downtown, where the "poor creturs" had "no room to stir, and no nothing to that any decent person ought to have." But demolitions, soon to be re-created on the stage of the Theatre Comique with fake boulders and flying papier-mâché, were eliminating the only other option available to poor people. "It's a fine free country, this is, where honest folks can't build a little house to cover their heads on an old rock like this without having the very ground blowed away from under them." As demolitions progressed, middle-class urbanites had to reconcile their culpability in that unjust spectacle. At the same time Harrigan was blowing up the symbol of the shanty on the stage of the Theatre Comique, magazine writers were reimagining shantytown for their middle- and upper-class readers. Shantytown became fertile ground for exploring nagging suspicions that in the race for wealth and position, the middle and upper classes had sacrificed the vital American quality of individuality.[28]

6

Transformed by Art and Journalism

In July 1880 the *New York Times* published a lengthy article headlined "A Visit to Shantytown." Based on several decades of press coverage in which shantytowns were routinely maligned, a *Times* reader might have anticipated the usual tour of mud-caked, goat-infested, irregularly situated shanties teeming with grubby children. But this journey followed a different itinerary. The *Times* writer transported readers to "a quaint little village transplanted from Ireland," located among some granite boulders at 43rd Street and Second Avenue, near Grand Central Depot. Such "villages" as this one were "scattered" across the city, the author continued, indeed "acres and acres of these little shanty houses" were occupied by "thousands of people" in New York. The soothing tone of this introduction signaled a sharp departure from earlier print media harangues. Unlike earlier accounts of shantytowns, which used their ubiquity to stoke middle-class fears, this report treats them as charmed nuggets of the past, cloistered "villages" redolent of the Old Country. The article goes on to admire the work habits of the inhabitants, noting the "spruce" young fellows coming home from work, and the educational accomplishments of the young people, who the author compliments as "civilized"— the very opposite of decades worth of print articles that exiled shantytowns to an uncivilized, backward past.[1]

This supportive and optimistic assessment, with shantytowns cast not as degraded dregs of a primitive past but as survivors of an admirable, traditional way of life, was repeated and magnified a few months later in articles published in two of the leading illustrated magazines of the day. *Harper's* praised the "warmth" and resourcefulness of shantytown residents, systematically refuting the well-worn litany of complaints made against the communities for the previous 40 years, from poor taste to criminality. *Scribner's* went one step further, hailing shantytowns as "the Bohemia of the laboring classes," and urging middle-class readers to look there for positive models for urban life. Together, these articles fostered a sympathetic middle-class attitude toward shantytowns that echoed through popular culture for the next 40 years.[2]

Why the sudden change of heart in 1880? Shantytowns themselves looked much the same in 1880 that they always had, so the impetus was not a change of scene in shantytown. The catalyst was the wholesale and very public eviction of shantytown residents and the demolitions of shantytowns, which began in earnest in the late 1870s and accelerated in the early 1880s. The visible, audible destruction of shantytowns on the streets of New York and Brooklyn prompted a re-evaluation by the mainstream press that produced two different outcomes. One ironic effect was the relief of middle-class guilt over the wrenching evictions and violent demolitions that were happening in many neighborhoods in New York and Brooklyn. With demolitions in full swing, middle-class advocates for city improvements found themselves on the side of sledgehammer-swinging home destroyers, and that was an uncomfortable place to be. It was one thing to champion the parks, French flats, and stately avenues whose construction was blocked by tenacious shantytowns, but it was another to see oneself as part of the forces of homelessness and violence. The print media came to the rescue of middle-class urbanites by reinterpreting shantytowns as quaint remnants of old-world charm, passing naturally from the scene. Demolitions were just another force of nature, no more worth remarking than summer thunderstorms. Inhabitants, however, who had been branded as depraved and craven in earlier media portrayals became in 1880 either folksy and gently amusing, or natural Bohemians living a zesty, earthy life. That interpretation was the cornerstone of a second, new rhetorical use for the shanty: shantytowns and their inhabitants came to symbolize a life of "disreputable freedom" reminiscent of America's founding generations, an identity preferable to the financially more stable but homogenized and shallow existence of the growing middle class. Shantytowns were mobilized as a critique of middle-class urban existence, fading links to authentic—and therefore admirable—cultures that were disappearing from the urban landscape. Once demolitions were underway, the print media reversed its verdict on shantytown, saluting residents for the very characteristics they found lacking in earlier decades. But the imperative that they be wiped from the face of the urban landscape never wavered: the middle-class vision articulated by the print media always placed shanty dwellers on the other side of a physical and social divide.

For both working- and middle-class audiences in the 1880s, disappearing shantytowns became symbolic testing-grounds for future relationships between the classes in urban America. *Squatter Sovereignty,* devised to appeal to working- and middle-class audiences, saw in the rubble of shantytowns a new model for resolving class conflicts with something other than segregation and exile. It individualized shantytown residents and championed their ability to amalgamate rather than assimilate. Journalistic accounts, for all their new-found tolerance and admiration, continued to foretell the disappearance of shantytowns and claim the city as middle-class preserve. The reporter to the "quaint" shantytown clinging to boulders near Grand Central Station set the tone for several accounts issued in the second half of 1880. With a bemused air, the reporter stressed the juxtapositions between new buildings and shanties. "Some of them are in places where they would never be suspected, and some are so hemmed in by tall buildings that they can hardly be found. Some are just in the rear of elegant brown-stone houses; some rub against the edges of sparkling Fifth-avenue; some enjoy, from adjacent hills, the scenery and fresh air of the Park; some are next-door neighbors to brick and stone palaces." In this description, shanties share the urban landscape with skyscrapers and residential "palaces," but they remain somehow unconnected to the city-scape of commerce. They have gone from depraved to "quaint," but only with a great deal of squinting. The *Times* article reports that the 43rd Street shantytown occupied an industrial district that included a stone quarry, brewery, factory, blacksmith shop, and steam boiler-house. Elevated railroads clattered down Second and Third Avenues, the noisy borders of this particular shantytown. As in earlier stories published in previous decades by the *Times,* the reporter criticized shantytown for its "savage" dogs, broken English, and muddy roads.[3]

The writer reported what he saw. But his interpretation departed from convention in two ways. It adopted a grudging respect for the work of the shantytown men, who operate the steam drills and work the quarries that are rapidly devouring their own neighborhood, as the shanties themselves are replaced by tall buildings and graded streets. Earlier newspaper accounts were practically bereft of men, but this one is peopled by "heated men working" and "young workmen coming home." In another shift, the story welcomed the descendants of the Irish immigrants who built the shantytown into the larger communities of the city and the nation, hailing the assimilation of their children and grandchildren with examples of consumption and aspiration. Many of the returning workers observed by the author are "quite as well-dressed as you or I," with "a watch-chain on his vest and money in his pocket." The third generation of Irish Americans to live in this shantytown, their appearance and work ethic prove that "each generation is an improvement on the last." Their grandparents remain in a "wild state," but their parents have grown "a little civilized" after a few years in New York, working hard enough to amass "a little store of money hidden away in some old stocking" and living, by their own measure, better than the "poor creeturs" in tenement houses downtown. The grandchildren, finally, "are very much like Americans' children," thanks to spending several years in public schools where "the peculiarities of their race [were] soon rubbed out." After getting a job and buying some nice clothes and a watch, "they are soon, in their own eyes at least, quite as good as anybody." Unlike earlier newspaper stories that bemoaned the city's failure to civilize shantytowns, this one declares victory. The third generation of shantytowners have been molded by education and steady work, forces as influential in the ultimate demise of shantytowns, the author suggests, as the pneumatic drills—an 1870s innovation—that daily chip away at its physical remains. The author gently scolds them for their squatting ways in a tone that hints at admiration, while openly approving of their education, consumption, and hard work, aspirational qualities that identified them with the newspaper's middle-class readership.[4]

Two months later, the September issue of *Harper's* also reframed shantytown in terms of nostalgia for the Old Sod, and found much to praise in its entrepreneurial spirit. This heavily illustrated article (one illustration per page, often taking up more space than the text) included eight drawings by Albert B. Shults. "On the Border of Shantytown" depicts a landlord delivering an ejectment notice. The villain is not, however, the vituperative, apelike, "sunbrowned" Irish shanty dweller, but the scowling property owner, shown jabbing his cigar at the defenseless woman, who folds her hands demurely beneath her apron. Earlier illustrations pictured shantytown residents as obstacles to neighborhood improvement, but this 1880 image, and others like it published during the ensuing decade, invites the viewer to identify not with the landowner, who has become an intruder from the grim-faced world of commerce and urban development, but with the pliant, overwhelmed shanty dweller. Shults's illustrations reinforce the new interpretation offered by the text, which notes the "softening influence" of the "indistinct reproduction . . . [of] Kerry in the low-lying cottages and the lazy wreaths of smoke" that dapple the sky above the shantytown. Stand "in the hollow" at 86th and Eighth Avenue and gaze at the "long reach of garden, with a weathered old cottage," and "it will seem as if you are in Ireland." Shantytown residents are praised for their home-building and maintenance skills. A man silhouetted against a "violet sky" replacing missing shingles with a bit of "very dilapidated carpet" who would have been mocked in earlier accounts is here tacitly praised, called "a good-natured-looking fellow" who "puffs at his pipe" as he hammers in the nails. Residents are not the threatening layabouts of earlier journalistic accounts, but hardworking homeowners, entitled to readers' respect.[5]

The author, William Henry Rideing, remarks on the size of the market gardens, noting they are a source of much of the produce sold at Washington Market, located on the west end of Fulton Street in lower Manhattan. Rideing points out that gardeners pay between $25 and $50 ground rent annually per lot. Other West Side residents raise geese or make a living as laborers, hucksters, and ragpickers. "[A]nd many of them are rich, having fortunes of between one and sixteen thousand dollars." Again Shults's illustrations support Rideing's praise. In "Garden in a Hollow," a smattering of shanties frame a large garden plot. "Planting" features a striking image of an old woman, impervious to the Ninth Avenue elevated train chugging past a half block away, bent almost double harvesting crops from rows as straight and orderly as the advancing Manhattan grid. "Going to Market" shows the predawn departure of a wagon full of produce headed for the produce market.[6]

Like the July *New York Times* article, Rideing suggests that the metropolis has civilized the shantytown. He does this with a series of contrasts, comparing for example a poised young girl wearing a claret dress and pink boots with her "rough and sour," "ignorant," "brown" parents. Her promising aspect "shows how far-reaching and penetrating the influence of American philo-progenitiveness is, that though barbarians themselves they desire their children to have the benefits of education, and clothe them with a fond generosity." Strolling past a shanty at 68th Street and Boulevard (now Broadway), he contrasts a woman milking a cow on one side of the avenue with the "handsome modern villas" on the other side. The contrast is "not exceptional,"

ON THE BORDER OF CENTRAL PARK.

As shantytown demolitions accelerated in the 1880s, media that had vilified urban shantytowns reframed them as nostalgic reminders of more rural or traditional ways of life.

but characteristic of the entire neighborhood, where "the old and the new, the evanescent and the permanent, that which has been achieved and that which awaits completion, are seen side by side." Shantytown, in Rideing's progressive narrative, is a passing stage in the development of the city, but these "evanescent" locales, visibly moving along the path to "completion," are nothing to fear or loathe.[7]

Rideing repeats this benediction several times. At one point he "peeps" inside a shanty where "a mummy-like old woman is talking Celtic between the puffs of her pipe to a barefooted girl who is kneading bread." Within two minutes he is strolling across the lush green knolls of Central Park, admiring cathedral spires under a saffron sky. Together the "anachronistic interior" of the shanty and the civilized park represent the "realities" of "paradoxical New York." Again the point is underscored by Shults's illustrations. "Old and New" shows familiar boundaries—streetlamp, sidewalk, and small ridge of rocks separating viewer from patch of shanties—but also a wall of apartment blocks rising behind the shantytown. In the background of "Planting" a three-story apartment building rises starkly, as though it too has sprouted from the garden. In "Cliff Dwellings," which shows shanties perched on a ledge of rock high above the graded street level, a well-dressed couple heads up the sidewalk toward the apartment building next door—at five stories, the same height as the ledge of rock that supports the shanties.[8]

Rideing, who wrote several dozen *Harper's* articles on topics ranging from rapid transit and working women to the South Seas, self-consciously reinterprets earlier shantytown depictions. The article is a series of "buts" contrasting earlier treatments of shantytowns with Rideing's more nuanced and cosmopolitan view. Shanty builders have scavenged materials from the dump or bought them cheaply from junk dealers, "But time and the weather have been helped in giving picturesqueness to the nondescript little houses by the vines planted around the walls, and a few flowers." A "dirty" and "dark" interior looms behind a young woman standing in the doorway, "But she wore a fine merino dress" and a gilt necklace, making it "quite evident that she was being brought up with a design of her parents to make some sort of a lady of her." The dogs run wild, snapping at strangers' ankles, and a gang of young boys act like "monsters," "But . . . there is little strife in the neighborhood," according to the local policeman. The ground is an expanse of brown dirt, and the train trestle at Ninth Avenue buzzes as the train rattles by, "But later in the afternoon the crimson splendor of the west is reflected upon the old shanties perched above the level, and their frail and weather-beaten shingles glow with the transmitted warmth." Reappraisals like this one, written for the same illustrated magazines that mocked or vilified shantytowns in earlier decades, presented shantytown dwellers as a mirror of middle-class domesticity. These new shantytown archetypes do not pursue an amalgamated identity, as dramatized in *Squatter Sovereignty,* and their continued occupation of the urban landscape is never seriously considered. This was a rearview mirror image of shantytowns as productive and safe, and shantytown dwellers as resourceful, hard-working, and aspirational: only after shantytowns began to disappear from the city landscape did the middle class see worthy attributes in their working-poor lifestyle.[9]

Earlier writers were repulsed by the dirt and disorder of shantytowns, and incensed by the impudence of shantytown dwellers. But the glowing embers of Manhattan's past that Rideing finds on 43rd Street incite a different kind of passion. He responds not with the outrage of the indignant moralist, or the energy of the eager developer, but with the excitement of the urbane art lover. The standards by which he judges the shanties are not those of the real estate developer or the reformer, but a cultured city-dweller. He might be remarking on the qualities of a watercolor landscape when he notes that weather "has toned the rough clapboards to a soft gray or slate-color," or points out the vines and flowers softening the contours of the shanties. The shantytown is a scene of such "picturesqueness of condition that set [sic] an artist on the edge of desire." Indeed, Rideing goes on to say that he knows artists who are making a living from the same scenes. "It is scarcely safe to let an artist loose among them. They abound with picturesque 'bits', which he declares it next to impossible to exhaust; and not long ago, when I soared into the skyward region where C____ has his studio, I found him black to the wrists with ink, with which he was printing etchings of some things that he had discovered among these shanties." Art is showing the way to a new interpretation of shantytowns, a profitable reinterpretation, but one which, while it does not castigate shantytowns for disarray or disease, ignores almost completely the reality of daily demolitions. Evictions are mentioned only once in the lengthy article: below 70th Street, he points out, shanties are "poorer and denser"; every so often a "nest" of them is demolished by police, "and the occupants are turned out by force and bloodshed."[10]

The November 1880 issue of the *American Architect and Building News*, reporting on an Upper East Side squatter settlement between 67th and 68th Streets, acknowledged it was a "foul village" where the "ground [is] soaked with filth, and the huts unusually crowded and close," and the odor of "effluvium" was so strong that neighbors kept windows shut; nearby Mt. Sinai Hospital feared infection. The Board of Health's order to remove the settlement was entirely understandable, the author admits. And yet. "It may seem hardly becoming a journal which upholds a high sanitary ideal to regret the disappearance of these filthy dens, but we confess that we never pass a village of them without being irresistibly attracted by their extreme picturesqueness. Less gloomy and vicious-looking than city rookeries, the habitations of the squatters, with their white-washed walls of rough boards leaning in all directions, their roofs of rusty tin, torn in a crumpled sheet from some demolished warehouse, their dilapidated stovepipes projecting unexpectedly through roof or walls, and their groups of goats and children climbing about in the sunshine through the circuitous paths among the rocks, have a naive charm peculiar to themselves."[11]

Perhaps the writer from the Boston-based *American Architect* was inspired to visit Manhattan's 68th Street shantytown by the September article in *Harper's,* or by its fraternal twin that appeared in rival *Scribner's* a month later. This article, more than any other, epitomizes the cultural whiplash that characterized interpretations of shantytowns starting in 1880. Written by H. C. (Henry Cuyler) Bunner, the precocious editor of *Puck,* "Shantytown" re-evaluates shantytown life from the perspective of the artist. As Rideing did in his article for *Harper's,* Bunner's report notes the rats, the vicious dogs, the ash heaps, and the one-room shacks that populate shantytown. Yet he counsels the reader to use painterly discretion to edit out material facts and focus on the "chiaroscuro." He describes the shantytown bounded by 65th, 85th, Eighth Avenue and Central Park as "the picture," a landscape that his article frames and focuses for the reader. One of the illustrations that accompanies the story, "Sketching Under Difficulties," shows an artist drawing shantytown surrounded by a group of curious, attentive residents. Bunner's shantytown was a self-conscious product, consumed by a knowing reader, that interpreted subjects who knew they were being documented.[12]

Bunner does not invent new standards by which to judge shantytown; he sticks to the categories of work and housing established by his predecessors. Like them, Bunner assesses shantytown based on its domestic architecture and its arrangement of streets, and how they compare to the orderly, gridded examples that surround it; and by the work ethic of its inhabitants. But where earlier writers found degradation, Bunner spies inspiration. Pointedly mocking earlier views that judged shantytown residents "[p]ariahs of poverty," Bunner praises their good citizenship, noting that their payment of ground rent makes them "lessees of property, and citizens," a title often denied shanty dwellers. Without irony, he notes the occupations of the men—day-laborer, truckman, ragpicker, junkman—and the women, who run beer saloons and shops. He praises them for voting and for obeying the law, gathers recommendations from their Irish and German parish priests and the local policemen. He even chastises the pound for rounding up their goats and other livestock.[13]

Shantytown residents are specifically identified as superior to tenement dwellers. Unlike their counterparts who "gasp out" lives in garrets and cellars downtown or on Baxter Street near the noxious Five Points, shantytowners live in an almost Thoreauvian wilderness, occupying "healthful hovels" close to nature. Their attention to vines and flowers, also noted by Rideing in his *Harper's* article, shows that they possess "A Touch of Refinement," the caption for an illustration of a young woman tending a window box. Choosing shanty-town over the "meanness of small conventionality" and "poor respectability" of tenements allows shantytowners another admirable choice not available to the tenement dweller: ethnic purity. In a repudiation of the ethnic amalgama-tion championed by *Squatter Sovereignty*, Bunner narrates an imagined love affair between "Romeo Guggenheim" and "Juliet Mulvany" that ends with the German's decision to "turn to a maiden of his own people," and renounce his Irish Juliet. Living close to nature, beautifying their surroundings, and sticking to their own ethnic group makes shantytown residents "far supe-rior, as a class, to any tenement-house people," Bunner concludes. Tenements, which would capture the middle-class imagination in the early 1890s with the photographs of Jacob Riis, were already making news in 1880; the first major tenement reform legislation, passed in 1879, mandated the inclusion of interior windows as well as fire escapes, and sparked the ill-fated "dumbbell" tenement design.[14]

But Bunner finds something even more important to praise in shantytown life than civic virtue, hard work, and ethnic purity: individuality. In the "hud-dling host" of haphazardly situated houses that disturbed earlier writers, Bunner discovers the "picturesque irregularity" of "a beggarly Rome," and it is this unconventionality that he finds most admirable about shantytown. "The shanty architect revels in unevenness," practices a "ragged and ruleless architecture" that "scorn[s] a model," uses whatever is at hand, "adapts" to the rugged landscape. "The shanty is the most wonderful instance of perfect adaptation of means to an end in the whole range of modern architecture." Bunner's shanty architect is not merely resourceful; he is "ingenious" and almost perversely creative. Shanties abound with fanciful touches that flout their "irregularity" and mock both middle-class sameness and the numbing predictability of the dumbbell tenement block: "curiously ornate" birdhouses sport "fantastical gables" (illustrated in *Some Bird Shanties'* and one rooftop is adorned with "a coiled and twisted skeleton—a crinoline, that mayhap puffed out of the gorgeous silks of some fair American" who curtsied for the last Napoleon (illustrated in *Odd Bits Here and There*). Shantytown, Bunner proclaims, "is the Bohemia of the laboring classes."[15]

Earlier chroniclers of shantytowns recorded evidence of domesticity and hard work but failed to factor either into their final reckoning of shantytown's worth. Bunner goes to the opposite extreme, papering over the hard facts of shanty life and spinning the superficial details into a picturesque fantasy of "happy poverty"—a view of shantytown that flowered a second time in the twentieth century, in novels and short stories published during the Great Depression. As Rideing did in his *Harper's* article, Bunner sidesteps the reality of what is happening on the ground: in an 8,000-word article illustrated with 14 engravings, the only mention of shantytown's violent destruction occurs literally in a footnote, which laments the fact that since the article was written, shantytown has lost several blocks at each end, "absolutely *lost* them," to demolition. Bunner ignores the destruction of residents' homes, instead employing them for his own purposes, as beacons of originality in an increasingly homogenized city. So while his judgment of shantytown is kinder, Bunner continues a tradition of using reportage on shantytowns to further a middle-class agenda. In Bunner's hands, shantytown becomes a tool for charting the limitations of bourgeois metropolitan life.[16]

In his seminal book *Bohemian Paris,* historian Jerrold Seigel examines the dialectic of Bohemian and bourgeois life, arguing that for all their dissimilarity, the two lifestyles constituted different responses to the same stimuli—revolution and industrialization—which upended centuries of traditional beliefs about the individual and his relationship to society. "Bohemia grew up where the borders of bourgeois existence were murky and uncertain. It was a space within which . . . social margins and frontiers were probed and tested." In his *Scribner's* article about shantytowns, Bunner probes and tests the social margins and frontiers of New York in 1880. He identifies shantytown as a marginal space, as had generations of observers before him. But unlike those observers, who called for shantytown's removal, Bunner holds it up as a model to the culturally emaciated urban middle class. Bunner believed that bourgeois attitudes were destroying city life. In shantytown he found a laboring-class utopia, a place not yet "cityfied" where the residents lived happy lives of "disreputable freedom." When Bunner describes shantytown as a laborer's Bohemia, the distinction is intended to chastise and instruct the city's middle-class residents. Shantytown residents, Bunner writes, were "adventurous," "brave discoverers," "rambling rakes of poverty." They were "wild birds," while the tenement dwellers down on Baxter Street were mere "sparrows."[17]

And the bourgeoisie? Doves, bred for obsequity: "Mr. and Mrs. Doveleigh van Stuyvesant" marry and live in a corner of a parent's house, Bunner writes, "dependent and cramped but unimpeachably proper and 'nice.'" Shantytown residents, on the other hand, had much in common with the Bohemians of Bunner's own acquaintance, who in retreat from "Niceness" rent a room near Union Square, "turn it into a small and cheap palace of decorative art," eat in French restaurants with newspapermen (presumably including Bunner) and artists. They are exiled, "outlawed but happy," "original, independent and comfortable" but "condemned of conventionality." It is this aptitude for originality—for self-making—that Bunner finds most admirable in shantytown dwellers, and which he fears is being submerged by the tide of middle-class conventionality engulfing the city. The ruleless, adventurous, rakish Bohemian inhabitants have not lost their capacity for self-creation, a fact made evident by the numerous examples of their self-expression. Both the generous praise offered by Bunner and the injunction to "know" poor people in their homes justifies intrusion by the middle class, who remain the "supercilious peer" of the Emily Dickinson poem forever poking their heads into the private realms of working people.[18]

Bunner's shantytown residents imitated the innovation and enterprise of the pioneer—a more authentically American way of life, Bunner insists, that the middle class had smothered under a blanket of bourgeois preoccupations. He turns on its head the reform-minded notion that the middle class should teach shantytown residents how to live. Shantytown residents were the teachers, and their classroom was the shantytown landscape, in all its irregular glory. Constrained by convention, Bunner argues, the urban bourgeoisie had lost the knack for individuality—as had laborers confined by tenement life. Both, in conforming to the gridded regularity of urban life, had lost the capacity for self-making.

Bunner urges middle-class conformists to embrace shantytown residents' practice of oppositional urban planning. He turns urban rubes into urban rebels, then encourages his readers to join them behind the barricades. The example of shantytown, Bunner insists, is open to all Americans. "In this country we all belong to, or at least we ought to belong to, the laboring classes," he intones. Anyone, even Mr. and Mrs. Doveleigh van Stuyvesant, could live symbolically in shantytown—that alternative American Eden where everyone builds his own house and plants a vine to caress it artistically—by poking middle-class taste in its collective eye.[19]

This casual recasting of shantytowns as Bohemian enclaves in the 1880s, after 40 years of vilification, shows just how little the representation and interpretation of shantytowns ever had to do with their physical reality. Throughout the nineteenth century and into the twentieth, shantytowns were putty in the hands of social critics, policymakers, and cultural commentators intent on shaping perceptions of poor people by making moral judgments about the landscapes they occupied—or in the case of shantytown residents, that they created. The kinds of dwellings that shantytown residents built did not change substantially in the 1880s, in form or material. But the meaning that middle-class observers assigned to them, once shantytown demolitions began in earnest in the late 1870s, changed dramatically. One year they were dens of vice and criminality, and the next they were rustic retreats reminiscent of our nation's founding. The thrust of the print media for the previous 40 years had been to emphasize the divide between the middle class and residents of shantytowns. As demolitions and evictions began to remove them from the landscape in the 1880s, however, newspapers and illustrated magazines sought to make common cause between the two groups—to bridge the cultural divide that they had helped to create.

A similar transubstantiation was taking place in art. A smattering of artists had produced occasional images of Brooklyn and Manhattan shantytowns since the 1850s, but in the 1870s, shantytown images multiplied. In the hands of the artists who produced them, shantytowns assumed a new role as iconic respites from modernity. Artists generally refrained from harsh moral judgments of shantytown dwellers; rather, shantytowns became an opportunity for moral judgments about urbanization more broadly. The shantytowns featured in late-nineteenth-century art appear as bucolic nubs on the tightening urban fabric. The artists who produced them came from the ranks of the not-yet and the never famous. Ralph Albert Blakelock, in his lifetime one of the nineteenth century's most prominent American painters, obsessively sketched and painted New York shantytowns during the 1870s. Brooklynite John Mackie Falconer located shantytown scenes on a continuum of preindustrial American ruins and relics that elevated them from their previous denigrated state. And a spate of etchers popular in the 1880s, including Eliza Greatorex and Charles Platt, rendered shantytowns as oases of untrammeled nature artistically positioned to refresh the eyes of the elite viewer, even as they were being demolished block by block. Mary Nimmo Moran produced prints of greater complexity, which critique the devastation of shantytowns along with the extermination of Indian tribes, while John Henry Twachtman, alone among his peers, rendered a realistic scene of shantytown as part of an industrial landscape. The work of these artists, and their use of the quintessentially urban shantytown as a rural icon, parallel the development of the market for art and artistic reproductions in the United States. As they pursued the artistic opportunities presented by the image of the shanty, they attempted to shape the burgeoning market for American art.

On the night of September 20, 1873, Ralph Albert Blakelock left his drab studio and headed north, to the shantytowns that dotted the fringes of Manhattan above 57th Street. The 25-year-old painter had only recently returned from a trip to the West, where on several journeys he had executed hundreds of sketches of Indian and frontier life. Blakelock understood the public's appetite for idealized western scenes, and by the end of the decade he would make a name for himself with paintings based on his frontier sketches. But that August and September the artist neglected his trove of frontier drawings, instead sketching the shantytowns that had survived the construction of Central Park and subsequent waves of street paving. It was a volatile moment in the life of the city, and the nation. The day before, the stock market had crashed, ushering in what would become the economic Panic of 1873. The drawing Blakelock made on September 20, a forbidding phalanx of dark doorways and blackened windows, reflected a sense of impending calamity. It is a menacing view of shantytown, literally and figuratively dark. Back in his studio, Blakelock scribbled the address of the shantytown, "58th Bet. 6th and 5th," before ripping the drawing in half. But three days later he returned to the same neighborhood to make another, quite different sketch. This one was a precise, almost draftsmanlike view of residents working on their houses in full daylight. The two views—one passionate but ominous and the other meticulous and serene—express divergent nineteenth-century viewpoints on shantytowns: they could be frightening in their poverty and disarray, but also cheering in their simplicity and pluck.[20]

By 1878 Blakelock had produced a dozen shantytown landscapes. Most were located between 55th and 57th Streets and Fifth and Eighth Avenues, just south of Central Park, or north of 96th Street in Harlem, where plans to expand train lines sparked a wave of speculative development in the 1870s. *Shanties in Harlem,* executed in 1874, may have focused on the same "Goatville" shantytown that scene designer Charles Witham chose for the setting of Edward Harrigan's *Squatter Sovereignty* in 1882. Like the other shantytown views Blakelock painted, it shows prosaic details of daily life. Residents carry sacks and buckets, mend roofs, tend children, and drive wagons. Abandoning the precise naturalism popularized by the Hudson River School, Blakelock wielded his palette knife to create exuberant swatches of color—a bright blue autumn sky, a golden mound of hay, glowering granite boulders. The composition creates a sense of life suspended, or perhaps hanging in the balance. In *Old New York: Shanties at 55th and 7th Avenue* (the nostalgic nickname was probably added later), the almost rigidly geometric built environment of the shantytown balances precariously on the supporting rocks, perhaps, one critic has suggested, a metaphor for the uncertain future the homes themselves faced. Sharply sloping shed roofs create severe diagonals, while the ramrod-straight sides of the wooden houses impose equally assertive vertical elements. Whitewashed rectangles of wall shine in the sun; evenly spaced pickets connect precisely placed gates and stairs. In the painting, from 1870, the exacting lines of house foundations and picket fences defy the swollen boulders and jagged bluffs that surround and support them.[21]

Other Blakelock views of shantytown—*Fifth Ave. and 89th Street, Fifty-ninth Street*—express a similar sense of stability and balance. For all their technical energy, these shanty landscapes are still, sedate, and orderly. Clusters of mostly single-story houses perch on boulders or flank wide expanses of dirt road. Large swaths of sky amplify the breathing room, lending the shantytowns a spacious feeling very different from the claustrophobic woodcuts of illustrated magazines. Dramatic geographic features—boulders, cliffs, sky—dominate the scenes; a glimpse of the sea in the distance might have transformed them into views of coastal villages. Yet the scenes do not seek to inspire the awe of the Hudson River School paintings; there is nothing sublime about Blakelock's resolutely domestic landscapes. As in the Indian scenes he painted from sketches

Artist Ralph Albert Blakelock painted a dozen shantytown landscapes in the 1870s, including this scene of shanties in Harlem.

made during the same period, Blakelock adopted an impersonal tone that dignified his subject. The landscapes emit an air of timelessness.

Shantytown residents dot Blakelock's landscapes, but they are anonymous and almost incidental. The few human beings present, all women save for one child, are portrayed in profile or with their backs to the viewer. They are all at work, often literally burdened by it—carrying water or firewood, hanging up laundry, and toting parcels. Yet they seem to float just above the surface of the painting, as though suspended in midstep. There are no animals; the pigs, chickens, dogs, and cats that journalists and illustrators used as shorthand for the disorder and backwardness of shantytown life are conspicuously absent. By muting the aspects of shanty life that illustrators for journals and newspapers used to mark the depravity of shantytowns, Blakelock understands shanty life as a confrontation and a struggle, not only against the imposing natural elements that dominate the paintings, and against the poverty that marked their existence, but against the forces of urban expansion that slated their homes for demolition. Blakelock depicted a landscape that was, for all its jutting rocks and brooding skies, tranquil and orderly, the very opposite of the unruly "architectural pepper-box" decried by journalists.[22]

Art historians today cite Blakelock's shanty landscapes for social precocity and artistic independence, but in the 1870s, there was little appreciation for Blakelock's radical interpretation. In 1874, snubbed by the National Academy of Design after several years of exhibiting in their annual shows, Blakelock entered *Old New York: Shanties at Fifty-fifth Street and Seventh Avenue* in an exhibition sponsored by the Brooklyn Art Association, which supported less traditional media and subject matter. Critics championed European realists like Jean-Louis-Ernest Meissonier for their craft and visionaries like George Inness for their poetic, self-expressive treatments of nature. And the Brooklyn Art Association, which nurtured local artists, promoted new trends in American art. But none of the half-dozen articles that appeared in the press in the weeks following the Brooklyn exhibit mentioned Blakelock or his painting. The artist would not be invited to participate in another Academy exhibition for five years, during which he finally began to produce paintings based on his sketches of western life. For the rest of his career Blakelock stuck to paintings of Indian encampments, buffalo hunts, and the effect of moonlight on tall trees, and by the end of the century he was one of the most famous living American painters. The robust technique he developed while painting shantytowns endured, but the subject was never revisited.[23]

At the same time Blakelock was documenting Manhattan shantytowns on the brink of disappearance, John Mackie Falconer was recording the shifting shantytown landscape in Brooklyn. Falconer, a loyal follower of the Hudson River School, did two substantive treatments of Brooklyn shantytowns in the 1870s; one survives in the collection of the Brooklyn Historical Society. *At the Foot of Hicks Street,* finished in 1877, is a view of Red Hook from the water. The remnants of the shantytown, founded in the 1840s, cling to the shore of the Gowanus Bay. Wooden shanties line the muddy path of Hicks Street. Some have pitched roofs, others sharply sloping shed roofs. Several residents are shown outside their shanties doing household chores. In the middle ground, two men fish off the side of a houseboat tethered to a buckling dock. To their right, several women hang up wash on a line at water's edge. Behind the row of shanties the brick towers of a factory are visible, spewing smoke. This village-like scene of fishing and household chores is framed by glimpses of the growing, improving city. At the extreme right side of the painting, in the distance above the drying laundry, rises a white church steeple. Two buildings on Hicks Street, also at the right edge of the painting, are not shanties but frame houses with symmetrical facades, their central entry doors flanked by windows. They make an orderly contrast to the crooked angles of the clustered shanties, and serve a similar purpose as the streetlights and telegraph poles that framed the shantytown illustrations in 1850s city guides such as Valentine's *Manual of the City of New York:* change is not only coming, it has arrived. The community teetering at the foot of Hicks Street is out of step, destined to be swallowed up by the improving city in the near distance. But its inhabitants are benign.

Like Bunner and Rideing in their articles for *Scribner's* and *Harper's,* Falconer records a landscape on the threshold of major change. Red Hook was one of the oldest sites of shantytowns in what became the city of New York. In the late 1840s, Irish laborers working for the Atlantic Dock Co. leveled a rise of ground in Red Hook known as Bergen Hill, and carted loads of soil west to the swampy meadow beyond what later became Hicks Street. The laborers built shanties on the infill created along Gowanus Bay, where they—or people of their class—were still living in 1872 when the *Brooklyn Daily Eagle* exclaimed: "the very people who participated in adding these improvements to Brooklyn live today in such a state of barbarism and filth, that the entire aspect of the place is a spectacle revolting in the extreme." Anti-squatter legislation, street pavings, and public health crusades had greatly reduced the number of shantytowns in Brooklyn by that point, and even Red Hook had "almost entirely lost its identity" due to "extensive and important improvements."[24]

When Falconer painted the Hicks Street shantytown in 1877, it was threatened with extinction. The artist locates shanty dwellers on a continuum of American ruins that included crumbling colonial landmarks and the devastation in southern states still rebuilding after the Civil War. Around the same time Falconer produced *Hicks Street,* he was also painting a number of views of decaying historic houses in Brooklyn. One, a meticulous small oil, shows the ramshackle house while it was still inhabited. America was coming to terms with its own ruins for the first time, and artists like Falconer helped Americans interpret them. The influential editor and art historian Sylvester Rosa Koehler praised Falconer's "eye for the poetry of decay," and his ability to see life among the urban ruins.[25]

Like the homes of Brooklyn's founding families, shantytowns were the detritus of an early urban landscape that had outlived its usefulness for the middle and upper classes. Falconer's inclusion of shantytowns with other examples of industrial ruins did not constitute a negative moral judgment of its residents, but it did legitimate the removal elites hoped for. His painting also records relics of another kind: shanty residents. They balance on the line of Hicks Street that stretches from one edge of the scene to the other, creating a thin ribbon of humanity across the middle of the painting. Falconer miniaturizes them in a way that suggests their imminent disappearance. Rather than scorn them, Falconer encourages viewers to think about the values that these humble dwellings and their outmoded landscape called to mind: perseverance, authenticity, simplicity, serenity. There is a sense of loss in the picture, a juxtaposition of the new with the old, which invites the viewer to see shanties as emblems of the nation's rural past. In *Scribner's* and *Harper's,* Bunner and Rideing reclassified shantytowns as quaint or Bohemian; in his paintings, Falconer used them to mark the passage of time in the national narrative. They harkened back to a rural past, which had the effect of eliding the fact that they were in truth relics of an early industrial past. No one was commemorating that past; identifying shanties with the countryside was another way of justifying their removal from the modern city landscape.

Despite the trend toward reimagining shantytowns as harmlessly quaint and admirably rustic, shantytown remained a mutable symbol in the early 1880s. Images of shanties were still occasionally deployed as racist rejoinders. The February 15, 1882 issue of *Puck*—edited by H. C. Bunner, author of the pro-shantytown *Scribner's* article from 1880—featured a cartoon of an ape-like Irish man sitting on an upturned washtub at the door of his shanty, framed by his equally simian wife and the requisite billy goat. He wears a three-legged iron pot on his head as a hat and twiddles a clay pipe, the sinister mirror image of the jovial "Paddy" celebrated in midcentury broadside ballads. The woodcut is sarcastically labeled "Puck's Gallery of Celebrities," and the caption reads, "The King of A-Shantee." It's a crude image, no doubt tongue-in-cheek for the sophisticated readership of *Puck,* a graphic weekly humor magazine that became, under Bunner, a provocative source of social and political commentary with a strong Tammany Hall—and anti-Catholic—bias.[26]

The shanty was also still used to represent the "backgrounds of civilization," as one magazine termed it in 1860. In 1880 the first halftone photograph ever printed in a newspaper was "A scene in Shantytown N.Y.," in the March 4 issue of the *New York Daily Graphic.* The address is not given, and the reference to a generic New York shantytown—a practice repeated in other

PUCK'S GALLERY OF CELEBRITIES.

THE KING OF A-SHANTEE.

The Ashanti peoples of west Africa were at war with Great Britain when this cartoon denigrating Irish immigrants in the United States appeared in *Puck*.

journalism from the period—reflects the ubiquity of shantytowns in New York. The stock photo of snow-dusted sidewalk, boulders, wooden shanties, and brick three-flats could have been anywhere. It appeared on a full page of images rendered with different technologies, including woodcuts and other types of prints. Choosing a shanty, presented here as a relic, as the subject of a photograph printed with a revolutionary technology underscored the modernity of that technology—which was the point of the full-page gallery of images. The second line of the caption brags that the image is a "Reproduction Direct From Nature."[27]

A painter named Alfred Wordsworth Thompson interpreted shanty-towns along similarly generic lines. In 1875, the same year he was honored with induction into the National Academy of Design, Thompson painted *Shantytown, New York City*, another title signaling the pervasiveness and anonymization of shantytowns in the city. Standing in shantytown's main dirt thoroughfare, a large-boned, red-faced woman wrapped in a shawl and apron grips the arm of a sobbing child while gesturing dramatically toward a limp, lifeless cat at her feet. A small boy points accusingly down the road toward a group of carousing older boys; a peddler in a top hat listens nearby. The bottom quadrant of the picture features two goats atop a house-sized boulder that has been painted, *Squatter Sovereignty*-fashion, with an advertisement for liniment; an ad for stove polish occupies the side of an adjacent shanty. References to stove polish and liniment, two products associated with the working classes (specifically, household workers and manual laborers), would have raised a smile from middle-class viewers who led lives unburdened by dull stoves or aching muscles. But the judgment is harsher than that. Only the last letter of the brand name of the stove polish is visible, but the first six letters of the liniment brand are clearly displayed: "CENTAU." While the name could easily and logically be "centaury"—a European herb used as a tonic— the letters suggest just as strongly "centaur," the name of the legendary half man, half beast. Perhaps Thompson was telegraphing of the appropriate attitude toward the hysterical woman at the center of his painting, representing shantytown itself.[28]

Artists, however, largely resisted the use of the shanty as a rhetorical symbol of degeneration and instead followed Falconer's artistic strategy, of repackaging urban shantytowns as reminders of our nation's rural past. In particular, they became a popular subject for etchings, which enjoyed a revival as an art form in the late 1870s and 1880s. Prominent etchers who produced images of shantytowns include Eliza Greatorex, Henry Farrer, Charles Platt, Mary Nimmo Moran, and John Henry Twachtman. Greatorex summed up the appeal of shanties in an 1875 commentary for her pictorial collection, *Old New York, from the Bowery to Bloomingdale,* which itself capitalized on the growing nostalgia for vanishing older buildings: "Groups of what are called, on the outskirts of New York, 'squatters' shanties' are perched on the rocks, or nestled in the hollows, sheltered but malarious; the luxuriance of the vines over those small abodes is a comfort and refreshment to the eyes; grape-vines, trumpet-creepers, scarlet-runners, morning-glories. . . . Streets are rising from the low, irregular hollows; many deep places are being filled in; wagons come and go, the red shirts of their drivers making lovely points of color; the wheels crush through thick beds of weeds, yellow, purple and white." The purple and white weeds recall Poe's description from 1844 of the thorny jimsonweed that covered the rocky shantytown landscape north of 14th Street, while the details of the bright red shirts and other "lovely points of color" prefigure Bunner's praise for the splashes of red, green, and white paint on the shanties he visits in 1880. Greatorex demonstrated her vision of shantytown in her 1884 etching *Shanties West of Central Park,* which pictures a number of substantial shanties surrounded by a picket fence. But the shanties are confined to the background; the foreground and half the picture plane is dominated by a windswept rocky outcrop, which the artist gives more space and more visual weight than the shantytown of the title. Nature battles settlement for control of this landscape, as evidenced by the section of picket fence disappearing into a maw of tangled brush in the foreground. Working in the picturesque tradition, Greatorex edits out the sweat and groan of toil from this landscape, as well as its urban setting, leaving the viewer to contemplate comforting aspects of farm life: luxuriant foliage, colorful flowers, red-shirted peasants. Shantytowns are tapped to provide a wellspring for rural antiquity, a maneuver that reinforces the inevitability of their demise while wrapping them in a cloak of clucking approval.[29]

By the 1880s, the grandiosity of the Hudson River School had given way to more intimate views of nature—not the grand, imposing, sublime nature that had been the theme of mid-century American art, but the familiar and unthreatening nature of childhood memory or an excursion to the shore. As art editor Koehler pointed out in an 1886 essay, the titles of artwork in the 1870s and 1880s told the story: "'Morning on the St. Johns,' 'Morning on the Marsh,' 'Sunset,' 'Near the Coast,' 'The Edge of the Swamp,' 'A Bouquet of Oaks,'—are in themselves sufficient to indicate the change that has come over our art. Twenty or even fewer years ago they would have been: 'The Yosemite Valley,' 'Scene on the Hudson,' 'View on the Housatonic,'—perhaps 'The Old Oaken Bucket.'" Shantytown views played nicely to this new sensibility, eliciting what one historian has termed the "happy-sad" emotions peculiar to picturesque treatments. But the picturesque style had a darker side. Bowdlerized versions of laboring landscapes supported several collective middle- and upper-class delusions about the lives of laborers. In order to "visualize pleasure"—Tim Barringer's apt phrase—on what were actually landscapes of work, picturesque artists ignored the realities of that labor. Picturesque scenes did more than emphasize the positive; they helped viewers pretend that laborers were contented with their lot, and that in turn masked basic truths about the toll physical labor took on workers' bodies.[30]

Shantytowns could be sliced up and excised from their surroundings to produce picturesque slivers of unreality. Henry Farrer and Charles Adams Platt, an exceptionally gifted etcher, also produced shantytown etchings intended as "comfort and refreshment" for world-weary viewers. In true picturesque fashion, they camouflaged their shantytown settings, transforming sites on the busy industrial and commercial waterfronts of Brooklyn and Manhattan into rustic coastal outposts. The Gowanus Bay, the site of Falconer's painting of the Hicks Street shantytown, was one of Farrer's favorite places to sketch and paint; he was best known for marine views with striking sunrise and sunset effects. At least one, *A Seaside Residence,* etched in 1882, portrays a shanty on the shore that has clearly been made from the hull of a boat, easily identifiable in the rounded foundation supporting the gable end of the house. In true shanty fashion, the houseboat sports a stovepipe, but no smoke stirs the air. The Gowanus Bay was one of the busiest commercial harbors in America by 1882, with steamships, barges, and a virtual wall of freight terminals lining the shore north of the Erie Basin. But this tranquil scene belies that daily life.[31]

Similarly, artist Charles Platt edited out the surrounding hubbub when he etched *Shanties on the Harlem* in 1881. This waterside grouping of shanties fronts the Harlem River, an eight-mile tidal strait that connects the East and Hudson Rivers and separates what are now the boroughs of Manhattan and the Bronx. This same neighborhood provided the locale for Blakelock's similarly named painting of 1874, and for Charles Witham's scene designs for the shantytown in *Squatter Sovereignty*. A frieze of city buildings is visible in the far distance, but the grouping of perhaps a half-dozen slant-roofed shanties on the water's edge has the character of a remote fishing village. The wash hanging out to dry and the figures of women performing domestic chores are standard shantytown fare. But the residents' connections to the city hovering in the distance do not disturb the atmosphere. The mood of the scene, like the water in the foreground, is completely untroubled. While it is possible that Platt found an undisturbed bend of the Harlem River to sketch in 1881, the locale was in truth almost as lively as the Gowanus Bay. For at least four decades, the river had been used to transport lumber, fuel, and other raw materials into Manhattan. Since 1848, when construction of the elaborately arched High Bridge extended the Croton Aqueduct across the river, the spot had been a favorite destination for Sunday pleasure-seekers, many of whom promenaded across a pedestrian walkway atop the 1,450-foot span, which rose 140 feet above the river. "Several thousand persons took advantage of the first pleasant Sunday of the season yesterday and made excursions to the upper part of the City," the *New York Times* twittered in April 1881. "All the afternoon the West Side elevated trains were filled with excursionists—men, women and children." The only thing dimming the delight of these "pioneer pleasure-seekers" was the clatter of the railroad along the river's shore.[32]

Those same pleasure-seekers filled the audience for Platt's etching of shanties, and they were not interested in realistic views of a mixed-use landscape. Late-century art consumers, like illustrated magazine readers and sheet-music buyers, preferred picturesque renderings of lives that were no longer present. Artists for the most part steered clear of the challenges of modern life, from racism to industrialization and immigration, instead taking viewers to places "untouched by 'The great magician Improvement'," as one contemporary observer put it. The modern landscapes of city and factory—those that would have included shantytowns—were "scars upon the face of nature which no feeling eye can regard without pain" and inappropriate subjects for art, another critic noted. Vegetables, flowers, villages, waterfronts, Old World scenes, native peoples, and "exotic" locales: these subjects filled late-century art, not factory workers or tenant farmers. For these cultured viewers in "sympathy with nature," a contemporary critic promised, "[s]cenes of rural and pleasant industrial life are permanently enjoyable." As the street grid inched closer to shantytowns, artists interpreted them as remnants of rural life. But they were actually the remains of urban working-poor housing that was deemed inconsistent with the prevailing vision of metropolitan growth. Only by draping shantytowns in the nostalgic veil of the picturesque could Greatorex and others present them as "a comfort and refreshment to the eyes." And only then could they sell them.[33]

Shanties on the Harlem was published as the fifth installment of an etching series—sort of an art-of-the-month club, published in a format similar to sheet music—launched in December 1881. Called *American Etchings*, the series was edited by art instructor and critic Ernest Knaufft. Each issue cost 50 cents and featured one etching, accompanied by a short biography of the artist and "a dash of criticism" by Knaufft. The journal invited subscribers to request signed copies of the featured print at the Manhattan studios of featured artists, thus inviting consumers directly into the art world of the city. The mailing devoted to Platt's *Shanties on the Harlem* included advertisements for art classes in ceramic painting, woodcarving, and embroidery. Editor Knaufft reassured subscribers that Platt's etchings, "remarkable for neatness and delicacy," also possessed a "strongly picturesque character."[34]

In the case of shantytowns, reality and fancy created a subject for art that simultaneously absolved middle-class art-lovers from culpability in the destruction of workers' homes while exercising their newfound skills at art appreciation. Etchings were marketed as a genteel possession, similar to a rented organ or a parlor tapestry, that reflected the owner's appreciation of the style considered appropriate for the middle-class home. They filled a new and growing consumer demand for affordable works of art in the 1870s and 1880s. Purchases of original artwork grew steadily in the United States in the second half of the century, fueled by the efforts of a growing middle class to demonstrate hard-won advances in levels of education and culture by displaying art in their homes. The painterly vision of shantytowns that Bunner, Rideing, and the *New York Times* promoted in articles in 1880 are directly connected to the growing ability, on the part of middle-class consumers, to inhabit that perspective. But the supply of original art was always limited, even in major cities, and it remained out of reach financially for many potential buyers. Etchings were easily reproduced, and when published in limited numbers on luxurious handmade papers, acquired some of the cachet of one-of-a-kind paintings. Yet the ability to produce multiple copies kept prices relatively low, and etchings became a popular way to own "real art" without spending real money. By 1893, largely thanks to the success of the etching movement, the United States was the largest art-buying country in the world.[35]

At the same time that etchings destined for parlors and exhibition galleries signaled the cultural sophistication and refinement of patrons, they also had to conform to middle-class notions of respectability. The decision to obscure the shanty scene's urban context was a conscious one, based at least in part on marketability. Middle-class patrons wanted images that comforted and refreshed, not a confrontation with the contradictions and challenges of contemporary urban life. When etchers found bits of nature in the city, they did not emphasize the clash of city and farms, shanties and apartment building. Out of a cacophonous landscape they extracted a harmonious composition. While the images suggest a feeble resistance to the natural forces of decay—some shanties seem about to be swallowed up by foliage or swamped by rising tides—in fact shanties were being demolished by the more prosaic forces of real estate development and street pavings, which appear in the margins of these images or not at all. Like a city skyline or a harbor filled with freighters, poor shanty residents did not fit the idealized views popular with the art-buying public.

A rusticated refashioning of shantytown life became one emblem the urban middle class used to redefine American labor as picturesque. Shanties on the Harlem River in 1882 were part of a mixed-use landscape of industry, toil, and recreation, but *Shanties on the Harlem* occupied a mythical terrain that expressed the hopes and dreams of the urban middle class. Refinement required not only the acquisition of the "right" tastes, confirmed by the "right" purchases, but a willingness to bear witness to versions of reality that contradicted the evidence of one's senses. The middle class were alchemists. They took the train to amusement parks on the Harlem River one day and displayed rustic etchings of the same location the next. This grown-up game of pretend was played with cultural products, from daily newspapers to limited-edition prints and one-of-a-kind oil paintings. While the charade may have been harmless most of the time, the proliferation of fantastical shanty scenes at the very moment shanties were being demolished and their inhabitants evicted helped convince the owners of uptown property that nothing so terribly bad was going on, and that the evidence of their senses was less reliable than the versions of events inscribed by artists and propped on parlor tables. A similar romanticization informed the representation of American Indians once they had ceased to pose a military threat to the expanding United States.[36]

Few writers or artists expressed the trauma of shantytown demolitions to those who lived there. One who did was Mary Nimmo Moran. Moran was known for incisive, deeply-lined prints of outdoor scenes made largely in the Hamptons. Her images of nature offered viewers a momentary escape from the grimier aspects of late-nineteenth-century city life. But in 1881 the popular etcher departed from her standard views of gloaming fields and Long Island ponds to sketch a shantytown on the very precipice of destruction. *The Cliff Dwellers of New York* shows a remnant of shantytown clinging to the rocks on West 55th Street, not far from Moran's apartment. The shanties were torn down a few days after Moran made her etching, and a sense of catastrophe permeates the picture. *Cliff Dwellers* shows a tight knot of shanties stranded, lifeboat-fashion, atop a swell of boulders. The shanties are deeply lined and heavily inked, in the determined style Moran was known for, and only after absorbing the details of the shanties does the viewer take note of the background: a wall of brick high-rises, lightly etched to fill the sky above and beside the shanties. The drone of the urban grid is repeated in the orderly ribbons of windows, doors, and fire escapes of the backdrop. Nature is already defeated, as a puny, derelict sapling struggling out of the rock attests. And now the city is about to swallow up this shanty atoll.[37]

While the contrasts between the built environments of shanty and city engage the viewer, the title of the etching demands attention for the people living on the landscape. They are barely visible in the center of the print, where several small figures crouch on the boulders that support the shanty. The cliffs resemble those found on the American southwestern frontier. In 1874, the U.S. Geological Survey sent back the first photographs of the cliff dwellings built hundreds of years before by the Anasazi peoples in what is now Mesa Verde National Park in Colorado. Photographs revealed the ruins of an entire stone village etched into the folds of sandstone cliffs, which like the high-rises

These shanties were torn down a few days after the artist made her etching in June 1881.

of New York dwarfed the dwellings below. By likening the few remaining stragglers—humans and houses—in a New York shantytown to the vanished Indian cliff dwellers of the southwest, Moran identifies shantytown residents with an obsolete tribe. The handiwork of shantytown residents did not elicit the awe inspired by the cliff dwellings of the southwest plateau. But both were perceived as ruins, relics of a vanished people. It is as if by venerating them, viewers will be relieved of any complicity in their extermination. Yet there is a mordant strain of ambivalence and self-critique in *Cliff Dwellers*. The craze for apartment buildings, then known as "French flats," exploded in 1875, with the construction of 112 middle-class apartment buildings in that year alone. By 1880 there were more than 1,200 such buildings and the conversion from single- to multi-family living was well underway. When Moran etched her print, middle-class urbanites still had doubts about apartment life; the resemblance to working-class tenements was worrying, as was the relative lack of privacy in flats compared to brownstones. But efforts by real estate developers to rebrand them as more respectable "apartment buildings" were paying off. Moran herself had recently moved with her family into an apartment on 55th Street near Eighth Avenue. She had in effect become a "cliff dweller" herself.[38]

Moran's shantytown, stranded on an outcropping of rocks on 55th Street, was a mirror image of the 43rd Street shantytown "set on a tall rock near the Grand Central Depot" visited by the *New York Times* in July 1880. Moran marks the shantytown residents for extinction, but unlike most period etchings of shantytown, *Cliff Dwellers* is not a picturesque retelling of urban poverty. The cityscape dominates the background, just as the boulders command the foreground. Urban nature, in the form of brick high-rises, is overtaking shantytown, whose residents huddle on the precipice of extinction. The point of view Moran assumes in her sketch is that of the privileged and unthreatened outsider looking on from a safe distance. The shantytown is isolated from the viewer, and hovers above a geographic chasm. There is nothing wistful about this scene of shanty demolition; rather, Moran opens a small window directly onto the fear and isolation that the "cliff dwellers" of New York must have felt as they watched the demolition of neighboring houses, knowing their turn would soon come.

Moran swerved away from the picturesque in *Cliff Dwellers*, but she still viewed the subjects as anomalies in the sweeping progressive narrative of the

American city and the American nation. Only one etcher, John Henry Twachtman, who went on to greater fame as an impressionist painter, did not translate the shantytown landscapes he observed into historical footnotes. Twachtman's *Shanties and Factories,* etched in 1879 or 1880, is one of the few shantytown views that unites shanty residents and factories on the kind of industrial landscape many shared in real life. Twachtman, born in Cincinnati to German immigrants, was one of the first generation of American impressionists, in 1897, to sever ties with the American art establishment. Early in his career he embraced etching—like watercolor, an outsider's art. *Shanties and Factories* is a tiny print, measuring just 2⅜ × 3⅝ inches. The view of the Jersey City, NJ, waterfront shows a woman walking down a sidewalk that edges a ramshackle hut in the foreground. In the distance a line of factories is clearly visible. Smoke pours from one of two towering smokestacks. Originally framed for exhibition with a companion scene, the equally diminutive *Landscape with Footbridge,* the view encompasses shanties and factories on the landscape they occupied together. Pairing *Shanties* with a harbor landscape went one step further, connecting the shantytown to the larger Jersey City landscape and, via the waterway, the rest of the country. Twachtman reverses the direction taken by numerous artists and illustrators before and after him, of either segregating shantytowns from the surrounding city, or excerpting individual shanties to create a faux rural scene. Instead, he integrates shanties into the larger working landscape occupied by the factories and the harbor, likely the places where shanty residents worked.[39]

Twachtman's *Shanties and Factories* reflects the modern life of the harbor at Jersey City, where smokestacks and shanties share the landscape with sailboats and rowboats. These "relics" recall an earlier, perhaps quieter time in the history of the waterfront, but they are shown coexisting with the noisier, modern instruments of industry. Unlike picturesque treatments that shoved laboring people out of the frame or into the shadows, or used their communities as proxies for vanishing rural landscapes, Twachtman's scenes acknowledged the work that was performed there, and the relationship of shantytowns to a larger urban and industrial landscape that stretched beyond the picture plane to the nation and the world beyond.

A counterpoint to the professional artists' views of 1880s shantytowns can be seen in the work of an unknown immigrant artist named Henrich Metzner, who made 14 sketches of the city's German shantytowns, most in the 1870s and 1880s. Here is the viewpoint of a socialist immigrant with strong feelings about the urban landscape, unmediated by middle-class ideas about the progressive American narrative. Listed as a painter in turn-of-the-century city directories, Metzner appears to have emigrated to New York with the wave of German revolutionaries who fled the country after a failed uprising in 1848, and once in New York he made his living as a drawing teacher at the local *turnverein,* an immigrant gymnastic society with socialist roots. He was an avid sketcher of Manhattan buildings and ruins, which he traveled the length of the island to document over the course of almost 60 years. Between 1850 and 1909, Metzner made more than 100 sketches of Gilded Age excess and working-poor life in Manhattan. Metzner's diminutive scrapbook of drawings, now in the collection of the New-York Historical Society, reveals a panorama of urban extremes. In 1872 he sketched the ruins of the Faber lead pencil factory on the shore of the East River at 42nd Street, which burned in May of that year. In 1896, by then principal of the *turnverein* school and editor of the society's newsletter, Metzner sketched the row of tenements that housed the workers at Peter Cooper's Brooklyn glue factory. Like many artists, he also sketched Five Points, although not until the late 1890s. Metzner participated in the fad for ruins that engaged so many artists of the day, including John Mackie Falconer and Mary Nimmo Moran. But the bulk of his sketches, meticulously arranged and enigmatically numbered by Metzner himself, record parts of the city heavily populated by poor workers who built their own homes in the city's sprawling network of shantytowns.[40]

Metzner lived and worked downtown, on the southern end of the island. The addresses of the shanties Metzner sketched, which he carefully noted, chart the progression of shantytowns northward in advance of urban development: 39th Street and First Avenue in 1873; 86th Street and the East River in 1875; 88th Street and the river in 1880; 90th Street and First Avenue in 1884; 94th Street and Second Avenue in 1885. Metzner's sketches feature not only shanties but stores—a saloon on 86th Street and a junk shop on 94th—giving a rare sense of shantytowns as neighborhoods with active internal economies. There is nothing visually startling or unusual to be found in Metzner's shantytown views, although the most elegant of the sketches reveal a sympathetic asymmetry between shanty and terrain. The rudimentary images show mostly individual shanties, some makeshift and askew, others upright and solid. An 1895 image adopts the convention, used in *Harper's* and elsewhere, of depicting a stylishly dressed young woman walking along a sidewalk that separates the viewer from the shanties beyond. The drawings are prosaic, all but a few clumsy and uninspired; they look like the kind of drawing exercises Metzner's students might have produced.

His images are unusual, however, in that they place shantytowns in the context of crumbling Gilded Age capitalism. His egalitarian renderings of old houses, farmhouses, and shanties reflected his own beliefs about class and politics, and offer a unique view of how shantytowns functioned on the urban landscape. The number of shanty drawings picks up in 1873, a couple of years following the *turnverein* manifesto that embraced socialist goals. Metzner recorded a patchwork of urban development in which shanties were more prevalent and as interesting as the summer houses of the city's financial elite, or the crumbling Revolutionary relics of its storied past. For Metzner, shanties are not a vestige of the past, but a part of the present, a matter-of-fact

Henrich Metzner, a German immigrant who worked as a drawing teacher, sketched Manhattan shanties from 39th to 94th streets.

reflection of the living conditions of poor laboring people. If he did not sentimentalize these drawings, it may not have been for lack of talent but in service of different beliefs about class, labor, and the rights to the urban landscape. Only Twachtman comes close to interpreting shantytowns with the same degree of class insight.

Coordinating the locations of Metzner's shantytown sketches with news reports about the progress of street pavings and the demolitions of shantytowns that dictated, it becomes clear that he was tracking them to their last remaining frontiers. Newspaper articles and photographs charted the same path. On the West Side, prolific amateur photographer Robert L. Bracklow shot numerous vivid shantytown scenes, including several on West End Avenue in 1890 and, in 1896, more on 62nd and 63rd Streets just off Boulevard (renamed Broadway in 1899). Bracklow was known for his documentary style, and these photographs are didactic, picturing many of the elements that shanty images had been known for since the 1850s: carts, steep paths, picket fences, hanging wash, boulders, stovepipes, telegraph poles, meandering additions, beacon-like streetlamps. Several focus on what are clearly the last surviving shanties in a developing area of French flats, but unlike similar images, they do not give a cramped impression; these shanty outposts command their landscape, looking down on neighboring apartment buildings from the top of a hill or asserting their possession of land with unbroken stretches of picket fencing; one photograph shows the capacious fenced yard of a shanty dwarfed by an adjacent apartment building, but still in possession of a small stand of trees—one as tall as the new building—that are enclosed within the fenced area. A woman, possibly the shanty owner, stares down the photographer from the sidewalk in front of the shanty.[41]

The work of commercial photographers Edward Wenzel and Hermann Tiemann testify further to the persistence of shantytowns in uptown Manhattan, on land being cleared for development adjacent to Central Park, which was still dotted with shantytowns in its upper reaches. Even as newspapers were publishing headlines asserting that "The Shanties Must Go: Upper Central Park East to Lose a Picturesque Feature," and "Squatters Were Evicted: An Ancient Colony Wiped Out," Wenzel was photographing the dregs of shantytowns along "Upper Fifth Avenue" in 1893 and Tiemann those lining "Fifth Ave. Above 93rd Street" in 1898. The photographs show groups of a dozen or more shanties interspersed with the rocks and large boulders that had so long discouraged new construction visible in the background. Jacob Riis, whose searing but stage-managed photographs focused the nation's attention on the inadequacies of tenement housing in lower Manhattan in the 1890s, also photographed shantytowns during the same period; a half-dozen are in the collection of the Museum of the City of New York. Riis's generic use of the term "Shanty town" to label photographs of different locales follows the same universalizing trend in nonfiction and art. An 1890 view is the only one with an address: "about 69th Street West (Boulevard). Disappeared since." One of several shots from 1896 bears the additional note, "some of the last remnants."[42]

At the same moment, a rowdier "Shantytown" was heralded in several cartoons by R. F. Outcault, the creator of the influential "Yellow Kid" cartoon character and one of the inventors of the modern comic strip. Outcault's "The Great Social Event of the Year in Shantytown," mocking upper-class society weddings, and "The Horse Show as Reproduced at Shantytown," mocking the downward mobility of horse-racing as a leisure-time pursuit, were published in the *New York World*—Joseph Pulitzer's flagship of yellow journalism—in 1896 and 1895, respectively. With their sassy, savvy shanty-dwelling denizens and their incisive send-up of middle-class pretension, Outcault's "Shantytown" echoed Edward Harrigan's indictment of the self-deluding lunacies of class distinction.[43]

Middle-class tastes, however, almost certainly animated the choice of two views of generic Shantytown selected to hang on the walls of New York state's exhibition hall at the 1893 World's Columbian Exposition in Chicago: *In Shanty-town,* an oil painting by Robert V. V. (Van Vorst) Sewell, and *A New York Shanty,* an etching by Charles A. Vanderhoof. No copies of Sewell's painting survive, but examples from his oeuvre—*A Silver Sea, Sea Urchins, Exhausted Bacchantes*—suggest his picturesque orientation, which one critic praised for its "pure and refined sentiment" which "caught the true decorative spirit." A copy of Vanderhoof's etching, *A New York Shanty,* resides in the Museum of the City of New York. It is a dreamy, rustic image of a particularly overgrown shanty with a woman standing in the doorway, her features as unspecific as the landscape; oddly, a turkey with splayed tail feathers is sitting in the yard. There is no hint of the city landscape; the only visible structure is the roofline of another shanty. The "New York" shanty of the title might well have occupied a rural corner of the state, indicating the wished-for banishment of urban shanties from the city landscape. The etching would have hit a demure note amidst the sea of art works on the walls of the New York State Building, itself a Beaux Arts exclamation point between the subtler colonial caesuras of the neighboring Massachusetts and Pennsylvania buildings. On walls festooned with neoclassical garlands, scrolls, and pilasters, *In Shanty-town* and *A New York Shanty* acknowledged the reputation New York City had gotten for shantytowns, while simultaneously confirming their exile from the modern city. The attributes heralded by H. C. Bunner and William Rideing in 1880, who reimagined shantytowns using a painterly vocabulary of violet skies, Irish hamlets, and "ruleless architects," permeate the images of shantytowns chosen to represent New York's once ubiquitous, but by 1893 virtually extinct shantytowns. Cloaked in a fog of manufactured nostalgia, New York's shantytowns became a quaint logo for the thoroughly modern city, which by the end of the nineteenth century had colonized shantytowns for middle- and upper-class use.[44]

In 1896, an article in the *New York Times* reported that the "last stronghold" of shanties were holding on "like Periwinkles" on north Fifth Avenue, including one on the rocks at 99th Street "known locally as 'The Widdy's' shanty." Artists documented this disappearing urban frontier. Magazine illustrator John M. August Will sketched a "squatter village" at 67th Street and Ninth Avenue in 1887, and then a lone shanty outpost at 116th Street and Fifth Avenue in 1890; while Louis Oram, also an illustrator, contributed a final flourish in 1898, with several jewel-toned watercolors of individual shanties filling the nooks and crannies of upper Fifth Avenue. Oram's *Old Shanties* and *Bit on the Boulevard* are parlor-ready decorative art, yet they also depict the menacing slabs of apartment blocks towering behind the shanties. By the end of the century, a quickened pace of real estate development uptown, especially on the Upper West Side, increased transportation options, and several additions to the zoning and building laws pushed the last remaining shantytowns to the very edges of urban development. Most significant for shanty dwellers, new building laws prohibiting wooden exterior construction, in an effort to prevent fires, had been extended to 140th Street by 1882. Still more restrictive laws, for the first time enshrined in an official building code, took effect in 1901. Surface train lines were electrified on Amsterdam and Broadway in 1898, and in 1904 subway stops were opened between 72nd and 96th Streets. This, along with the running of electrical lines to the Upper West

Side, had the lopsided effect of squelching residential construction at both the high and the low end, as single-family shanties and single-family mansions were pushed out by taller elevator hotels and apartment buildings.[45]

A fitting coda for Manhattan's vanishing shantytowns appeared in 1904, in a newspaper column headlined "True Story of an Eviction." The column spotlighted a letter to the editor from a distressed landlord who claimed that he had been unfairly implicated in an earlier *Times* story, which ran under the provocative headline, "Evicted Crippled Widow Carried Out of Old Landmark House Despite Crowd's Protests." The landlord of the property, located at 125th Street near Claremont Avenue on the Upper West Side, challenged the headline, pleading that the evicted woman was a squatter who had been given nine months notice of eviction. "Like a great many other squatters, possession, in her eyes, had apparently convinced her that she owned the land, and she was persistent, pertinacious, and pugnacious"—as generations of shanty dwellers before her had been. Further details give this anecdote an iconic stature. According to the aggrieved landlord Mrs. Jones was not poor (in the course of eviction several bank books were turned up); not a lone widow (she had married daughters living nearby and a son rumored to be a magazine writer); and not a cripple (her broken leg was healing and she refused the offer of an ambulance). She was also a landlady herself, renting a shanty near her own to a local photographer; and had allegedly refused to pay ground rent once the property occupied by her shanty was sold to a new owner several years before. She had hired a lawyer to defend her claims to the land, and succeeded in delaying the eviction proceedings for a full eight months, a period extended, the landlord admits, simply with entreaties for more time. The only truth in the original headline seemed to be that she had, in fact, been evicted, but even in this she exhibited a level of real estate savvy that would have made her nineteenth-century counterparts proud: as her possessions lay piled on the sidewalk in front of her shanty, she negotiated a half-month's free rent on an apartment in the same neighborhood, and free transportation there for herself and her belongings, in exchange for leaving quietly. "I personally agreed to pay $17 for half a month's rent," the landlord concluded, "and then Mrs. Jones left in our carriage." It was an exit worthy of the Widow Nolan, with neighborhood associations intact, a new residence nearby, and grown children moving up the ladder of social stratification. There is no doubt that shanty dwellers were victimized by real estate developers, Central

Park visionaries, bourgeois social reformers, French-flat-seeking members of the middle class, even the reporters and "special artists" who interviewed and sketched them for the waves of retrospective articles that appeared every few years in magazines and newspapers. There is also no doubt that far from being the dumb rustics of those imaginaries, they believed that possession was as good—better—than legal title to land, and they persisted in their determination to stay in their homes.[46]

The history of shantytowns on the urban landscapes of Brooklyn and Manhattan—and many other growing American cities in the nineteenth century—has been largely forgotten, but the traces remain in popular culture. Assembling them produces a patchwork of social meaning, revealing the intricacies of class formation and the progressive narrative of urbanization and modernization in the nineteenth century. One important aspect remains to be examined: African-American shantytowns. They thrived in Manhattan and Brooklyn, in places like Seneca Village, which occupied land that became Central Park, and Crow Hill, an antebellum shantytown on the site of what is today the Bed-Stuy neighborhood in Brooklyn. There and elsewhere, they played an important role in the life of African-American residents before, during, and after the Civil War through Reconstruction and the early twentieth century. Just as immigrants developed shantytowns that simultaneously positioned them to take advantage of economic opportunities while accommodating evolving traditions, African Americans created landscapes that nurtured personal autonomy, cultural continuity, and economic advancement in an era of disenfranchisement and violent repression. To explore shantytowns fully we must shift our gaze south, to Washington, DC, and Atlanta, GA, where shantytowns provided both independence and refuge to African-American citizens struggling for survival and civil rights on a landscape designed to systematically exclude them.

7

African-American Shantytowns, 1860–1940

In Margaret Mitchell's *Gone with the Wind,* after surviving the war and returning to find her beloved Tara in ruins, Scarlett O'Hara runs into her former slave, Sam, in an Atlanta shantytown. She is surprised to see Sam in this part of town. "What on earth are you doing in a nasty place like Shantytown, you, a respectable darky?" she asks him. Sam responds, "Law'm, Miss Scarlett, Ah doan lib in Shantytown. Ah jes' bidin' hyah for a spell. Ah wouldn' lib in dat place for nuthin'. Ah nebber in mah life seed sech trashy niggers." Scarlett uses Shantytown to convey her high opinion of Sam and her condemnation of the former slaves who did live there: if "respectable darkies" like Sam did not live in Shantytown, those who did live there lacked both self-respect and the good opinion of whites. Sam hastily agrees, and distances himself from the people Scarlett refers to as "Shantytowners" by insisting that he is merely "biding" there and has plans to return "home" to Tara, the plantation where he was enslaved by Scarlett's family. This provided a comforting vision for white readers, of African Americans secretly yearning to return to the days of white supremacy. But Sam is dissembling; he is indeed living in Shantytown, hiding from the police because he has killed a white Yankee. Although Mitchell presents this as evidence of Shantytown's degeneracy, it is also proof that Shantytown was a reliable refuge from white surveillance and oversight, a place where Sam could successfully evade white pursuers.[1]

Mitchell's zeal for historical detail is well known, and the shantytown she locates "out the Decatur Road" was probably Butler Street Bottoms, sometimes known as Darktown. It is possible Mitchell heard firsthand descriptions of the shantytown from local residents she interviewed during her 1922–1926 stint on the "Old Inhabitants Beat" at the *Atlanta Constitution,* for which she compiled the reminiscences of elderly white residents. Like the historical Butler Street Bottoms, the Atlanta shantytown Scarlett drives through consisted of "cabins in the creek bottoms." A "dirty sordid cluster of discarded army tents and slab cabins," shantytown "had the worst reputation of any spot in or near Atlanta, for here lived in filth outcast negroes, black prostitutes and a scattering of poor whites of the lowest order," Mitchell wrote. At one point Mitchell describes Scarlett approaching a "group of shacks squatting in the hollow"—a phrase that conflates shanty residents with the shanties themselves, depicting both humans and hovels as crouching animals. Scarlett smells a mixture of wood smoke, fried pork, and overflowing privies, which she finds repulsive. Mitchell's "Shantytown," possibly a composite of several historical Atlanta shantytowns, embodied white fears of black autonomy, which though suppressed by Jim Crow remained potently visible.[2]

Shantytown makes a dramatic appearance in the film version of *Gone with the Wind,* released in 1939. Scarlett, rebounding from the war with a new husband and a new lumber business, encounters Rhett Butler on the street by chance, and impresses him with her determination to drive through Shantytown on her way home. "Through Shantytown, alone?," Rhett asks sarcastically, watching Scarlett nestle a gun into the folds of her lap rug. "Haven't you been told that it's dangerous to drive alone through all that riff-raff?" "Don't you worry about me," Scarlett snaps. "I can shoot straight if I don't have to shoot too far." As she tears across the Shantytown bridge in her wagon, lashing her horses to speed her passage, two men, one white and one black, accost her. From the sea of destitute squatters, Sam rises up to rescue her, sweeping her off to Tara after wrestling both the attackers to the ground. And so, Sam does indeed return home to Tara, in the role of loyal protector.[3]

At the same time Mitchell's book and movie were exciting white audiences, another Atlanta artist, painter Hale Woodruff, was delivering a very different perspective on the city's black shantytowns. Hired in 1931 to create a fine arts department at Atlanta University—itself constructed on the site of a black shantytown demolished for the purpose in 1869—Woodruff routinely took his art students to an impoverished area bordering the southern edge of the campus, where they sketched the wooden houses and unpaved streets of a shantytown known as Beaver Slide. "We painted shacks and outhouses to the extent that we were dubbed the 'Outhouse School' of painting," one former student recalled. Woodruff was commissioned by the WPA to paint a large two-panel mural on the interior of the university's new School of Social Work, the first such school at a black university in the United States. In this epicenter of African-American "firsts," against a backdrop of controversial rhetoric of racial achievement and uplift, Woodruff painted *Shantytown* and *Mudhill Row,* two large panels depicting the Beaver Slide shantytown in a brawny, modernist style. They were unveiled in 1934. Within a few years, Beaver Slide was demolished to make way for University Homes; the era of public housing projects, which ended so ignominiously in the 1970s, had begun.[4]

At a moment of radical reformation of the landscape, Woodruff memorialized Beaver Slide and other Atlanta shantytowns, which constituted the earliest settlements of emancipated African Americans on the southern landscape. Commonly called "bottoms," they occupied the lowest-lying, least desirable sites in Atlanta, Richmond, Charleston, and other southern cities. Some, like those in Washington, D.C., Alexandria, and Arlington, predated the war, populated by free blacks or hired-out slaves. But African-American shantytowns surged after the end of the war, as waves of migrating blacks relocated from southern plantations. Some moved to nearby rural areas, others to towns and cities in the South and elsewhere; some settled in the Freedmen's Villages built on the site of former army encampments, or populated short-lived model towns in the North and Midwest. But many thousands built and inhabited shantytowns. Shantytowns in places like Atlanta, in fact, were the first places many emancipated African Americans experienced physical freedom—and simultaneously, the efforts of whites to limit and ultimately erode that freedom.

Stretching from the 1840s to the 1930s, African Americans first freely assembled *en masse* in shantytowns in Atlanta and Washington, D.C., and used vernacular forms to express personal sovereignty. They largely ignored the advancing urban grid in order to build communities that served their practical and expressive needs. Rather than abide by the urban geometry, they constructed clusters of houses built in styles and laid out in patterns that repudiated the oppressive regularity and uniformity of the slave quarter. These communities embodied the personal, familial, and domestic privacy that had been withheld from African Americans until the end of the Civil War. Building shantytowns, they seized the opportunity to individualize and particularize their houses in ways that spoke to postwar identities and racial renegotiation.

In 1867, a white resident of Atlanta named Mr. Hoyt called his neighbor, a young black woman named Mary Price, a "damned bitch." She objected. Hoyt, offended, called the police, who went to her house to reprimand her. At that point her mother, Barbara Price, stepped in: "I replied that I would protect my daughter in my own house, whereupon he pulled me out of the house into the street," she told police. The policeman called out to another man to help him, and together they "jerked and pulled" Barbara, who was pregnant at the time, down the street and into the guardhouse. The city council acquitted Hoyt, but convicted Mary and Barbara Price for foul language and fined them $350. It took the sustained intervention of the Freedmen's Bureau to reverse the judgment and extricate the Prices from this miscarriage of justice.[5]

This story of abuse of power in the Reconstruction-era South is one of thousands, if not hundreds of thousands, that illustrate the uninterrupted practice of white supremacy following the defeat of the Confederacy and the emancipation of enslaved blacks. It provides insight into the meaning African Americans attached to their houses and, by extension, to their neighborhoods. The context of Price's story makes it clear that she is living in a shantytown. The aggressive policeman pulled Price out of her house and "into the street," a display of brute power but also a tacit acknowledgment that she had sovereignty over the space of her house in a way she had not before. The policeman stops short of bursting *into* her house, a sign that his power was circumscribed. Home, in the form of a humble shanty, had become a refuge for African Americans—not impregnable, but fortified. Frederick Ayers, one of the more sensitive and empathetic missionaries stationed in Atlanta by the American Missionary Association after the war, noted the connection between the abstract notion of freedom and the material possession of a house: "The idea of 'freedom,' of independence, of calling their wives and their children, and little hut their *own*, was a soul animating one, that buoyed up their spirits." When Barbara Price stands up to the white policeman, she is no longer just her body; she is her house. Her legal rights take up space; they are grounded. Price's assertion that her daughter is protected in her "own home" conveys a similar communion between owner and home. Freedom had become a spatial reality.[6]

Personal sovereignty created power of place, and in turn, place conferred sovereignty—in the shanty, as in the plantation house. Changes in African-American status were literally taking place in shantytown. Place always had meaning for blacks, enslaved and free: the difference after emancipation was not the creation of meaning, but the injection of power into that meaning. If Irish and German immigrants claimed "squatter sovereignty" in northern cities, formerly enslaved African Americans gained and wielded black sovereignty in southern shantytowns. Reconstruction was under way and had not yet been successfully sabotaged by whites. While enslaved workers expressed identity and agency through their organization and use of slave quarters, those spaces did not express personal power. Shantytowns occupied by emancipated African Americans following the war were the first places where that was possible.

Of course, the story of Barbara Price's fight with the Atlanta police does not end with her assertion of domestic dominion. The policeman responds to Price's claim of spatial sovereignty by physically pulling her out of her house and into the street. The street was a contested space, the shantytown a new frontier of racial power relations—a space where poor whites and emancipated blacks competed for scarce resources, under new rules of engagement. The policeman who accosts Price embodies the sentiments of whites in general when he defies the changes wrought by Reconstruction. He pulls Barbara Price from backstage to center stage, hurling their conflict into the public sphere, where he quickly attracts the support of a white accomplice. Her pregnancy makes her an especially potent symbol of newfound black sovereignty: the child she carries, unlike the child Mary, who spat back at the white man who called her a "damn bitch," will be born free. The spectacle of two white men dragging a pregnant African-American woman to the guardhouse is a chilling illustration of white supremacists' determination to revoke the fledgling freedoms of emancipation; they literally re-house her in a space guarded by whites. When she publicly asserts her right to domestic space, they return her—and her unborn child—to bondage.

Although white supremacy ultimately triumphed during Reconstruction, at the moment when Mary Price asserted her power over her shanty in Atlanta, that future was not decided. What was unfolding was a future in which whites and blacks—Prices and Hoyts—occupied the same neighborhoods. It was nothing new for white and black bodies to occupy the same spaces; white owners and black slaves lived in often intimate proximity to each other. The postwar period, however, was the first time large numbers of blacks and large numbers of *poor* whites had shared a landscape on something like equal footing. While hired-out slaves working in cities had a degree of autonomy, they were always subject to their owners' or employers' whims. And very few African Americans, whether free blacks or hired-out slaves, lived in Atlanta (or anywhere other than a farm or plantation) before the end of the war. Almost everyone in Atlanta was a newcomer. Shantytowns facilitated the changing geography of race in Atlanta, as African Americans shifted from living in proximity to employers—house servants living behind a masters' house—to peopling new communities. A shantytown was a relatively modern place in the late 1860s.[7]

Newspapers, missionaries' letters, and Freedmen's Bureau records paint a picture of early Atlanta shantytowns as the first postwar integrated urban neighborhoods. Articles in the *Atlanta Constitution,* the more liberal local paper, track the establishment of black neighborhoods in the "bottoms," a term that meant both low-lying land, and, in postwar Atlanta, the bottom floors of integrated buildings. Often, basement doors opened onto alleyways located below grade at the rear of houses or tenements, and these lower floors were occupied by African Americans. As housing shortages got worse, landlords capitalized on the crisis by renting out the lower floors of existing tenements to African Americans, creating a physical hierarchy of spaces above and below street level. Bottoms or "bottom" also appears to be the name that African Americans themselves used to describe their neighborhoods, as opposed to the glib and often demeaning nicknames proposed by white elites: Happy Hollow, Pigtail Alley, Bone Alley, Darktown. Some landlords built shanties to rent out, while other shanties were self-built by inhabitants on rented or vacant land. Rebecca Craighead, a teacher with the American Missionary Association in Atlanta in the 1860s, referred to houses African Americans constructed "on rented parcels of land."[8]

African Americans inhabited at least five shantytowns across Atlanta after the war. More affluent white residents segregated themselves in the northern part of the city, but other quadrants included at least one shantytown: Jenningstown, in the hillier western area of the city, and the adjacent Beaver Slide; Shermantown in the northeast; Summerhill in the southwest; Butler Street Bottoms—the site of Scarlett's fictional attack in *Gone with the Wind*—along Decatur Street north of the Georgia Railroad; and Tanyard Bottom, where 80 years later the very first public housing project in America, Techwood Homes, would be built on a site that was still, at that point, largely a shantytown. Mechanicsville, located in the southwest quadrant of the city, developed in the 1870s. The two largest postwar shantytowns, Shermantown and Jenningstown, had roughly 2,500 inhabitants each; Summer Hill (later Summerhill) had about 1,500 residents. All of these areas were prone to flooding and sewage overflow, except for Jenningstown, where in 1869, in an ironic landscape twist, a number of shanties were razed to make way for what became Atlanta University, the first African-American university in the city.[9]

The population of the city doubled in the 1860s, to slightly more than 21,000 people in 1870, as did the population of Fulton County, to just over 33,000. The black population, 20.5 percent in 1860, was 45.7 percent a decade later. Because of the level of segregation verging on apartheid in the city in the twentieth century, the degree of racial integration in Atlanta's early shanty-towns can be surprising. Shermantown, in the 1870s, was 22 percent white, Summerhill 25 percent. All three of the largest African-American settlements had easy access to schools and churches, usually African Methodist Episcopal (A.M.E.) and Baptist. Shermantown had a number of multifamily residences that included boarders, as well as tenements then known as "apartments." Summerhill and Jenningstown, which had the fewest white residents, were mostly one-person households or small families headed by one or two parents. There were pockets of black residency all over the city except for the northern rim, where the few black residents were mostly domestic servants living in the homes of white employers.[10]

There were a number of shantytowns dubbed "Shermantown" in the Reconstruction South. The name indicated a settlement built on the site of an encampment by the Union army. Often, these encampments attracted dozens and sometimes hundreds of still enslaved African Americans; Shermantowns were in a sense refugee camps, at least to begin with. After the war ended, some became sites of Freedmen's Villages, where African Americans found basic shelter and access to education but endured continued oversight and surveillance. A local newspaper in 1868 described Atlanta's Shermantown as an area containing "small stores, shops, and other places where the neces-saries of life . . . are sold to enterprising inhabitants," but noted that flooding and sewage overflow were common problems. Acknowledging the racial integration of the neighborhood, the writer resisted the idea of Shermantown as a "black district," pointing out that the community had fewer African Americans than many settlements of the same size, and "very many white men 'native and to the manor born,' who reside upon the picturesque heights above the reach of 'de African scent.'" The following year, in a letter to the editor of the *Constitution,* another white Atlantan praised the "intelligent contrabands" living in the Shermantown neighborhood, which boasted a free school, several churches, and housed "more of the better class of negroes in proportion to number than usually fall to the lot of suburbans." While white liberals were damning Shermantown with faint praise, they were commending the creation of Brownsville, a largely black suburb around Clark University where the developers would "only sell lots to a decent class of negroes." Just as the Freedmen's Bureau itself was committed to moving African Americans out of Atlanta and other southern cities where they had congregated, white Atlantans pined for an urban landscape without poor black residents. Shermantown was a site of both white and black class formation in the postwar nation.[11]

Reconstruction ended in Georgia in 1872, and a new constitution passed in 1877 paved the way for the Jim Crow era. By the late 1870s, magazines like *Harper's New Monthly Magazine* were reporting on the new stately buildings and nascent cultural institutions rising from the rubble of postwar Atlanta. Shantytowns, however, persisted, and were presented as proof of Atlanta's inadequacy. In 1879, *Harpers* sent reporter Ernest Ingersoll to explore "The City of Atlanta" for readers. For the travelogue, one of many written about growing cities during the decade, the magazine commissioned illustrations of the ornate U.S. Courthouse and the lofty, gaslit interior of the city library, hung with portraits of Confederate leaders. Although the author sniffed that Atlanta's public buildings, while new, were "not imposing," Ingersoll's story connected Atlanta's fledgling efforts at high culture with promising signs of economic growth, regional reconciliation, and racial segregation. He praised Atlanta's education system, noting that it included two private black "'universities,'" demeaned by quotation marks, and titillated his readers with a visit to an African-American shantytown. "A feature of the city to which no well-ordered resident will be likely to direct a stranger's attention," he confided, "is 'Shermantown'—a random collection of huts forming a dense negro settlement in the heart of an otherwise attractive portion of the place."[12]

Emancipated African-American women established laundries in Atlanta shantytowns.

Brave adventurer Ingersoll sets out on a voyage of discovery. "After dinner, I take a cigar and saunter out." Hearing music down a "dark alleyway," he finds "five laborers, each black as the deuce of spades, sitting upon a circle of battered stools and soap boxes, and forming a 'string' band, despite the inconsistency of a cornet. The whole neighborhood is crowded with happy darkies, and though the music is good, I choose the enchantment of distance. Not far away I strike another circle of freedmen," this time playing a banjo and guitar. Walking further, he encounters a vendor hawking patent medicine, and a pair of black minstrel performers, "but corked in addition to make themselves blacker," playing music, dancing, and "reciting conundrums" to an audience of 200–300 "delighted darkies." An accompanying illustration captioned "There's Music in the Air" portrays the vivid scene. Ingersoll does one more "saunter," to the train station, to watch the trains pass from the north and the east, as if to remind himself he is still connected to civilization, before ending his sojourn, and the article.[13]

Ingersoll noted that in Shermantown, the women "'take in washin', and the males, as far as our observation taught us, devote their time to the lordly occupation of sunning themselves." Illustrating this comment is a drawing that affords a deeper look into the economic functioning of African-American shantytowns. Captioned simply, "Shermantown," the illustration shows a work yard ringed by wooden shanties. At the center is the communal laundry, an enterprise also referred to in a *Constitution* article two years later, about the Beaver Slide shantytown. The laundry is open to the air but covered by a pitched roof. Six women are working in the laundry, either washing clothes or hanging them up to dry. All are wearing the headwraps known as tignons, which originated among Creole women in Louisiana but spread throughout the South, and became a marker of African-American identity and resistance. Four of the five men depicted are all lounging—literally leaning against door frames, railings, or walls—while watching the women work; the fifth is filling a bucket at a pump. A pig and a few chickens meander in the yard. The shanties, some free-standing and others that appear to be part of a barracks, are constructed of vertical boards; pitched roofs are covered with tar paper. The shanties have short brick chimneys. Unframed entry doors without sills are elevated slightly above the ground, accessible by short ladders. Behind them, on the crest of a small hill, are several larger buildings, possibly the remnants of the Union barracks, or perhaps buildings associated with Atlanta University.[14]

Although *Harper's* aimed to portray idleness, the scene emanates enterprise and activity. The writer, Ingersoll, comments on the "tall, straight negro girls marching through the streets" with bundles of laundry on their heads. He mines the image for exoticism, but laundresses were in fact early community leaders and labor pioneers. In Atlanta, twenty African-American laundresses formed the Washing Society in July 1881, and by October they had recruited more than 3,000 members. A strike won them higher wages and self-regulation as a trade, and the Washing Society—called the "Washing Amazons" by detractors—created an early model for collective bargaining.[15]

Several of the article's other illustrations reflect the industry and enterprise of African-American residents, although the magazine does not frame it that way. In "The Chair Vendor," an African-American man carries half a dozen splint-bottom chairs like a bundle of laundry on his head. In the text, the author notes the presence of ragpickers, "troops of little black boys" who gather up rags. Another illustration, "Street Auction," shows the consequences of poverty, as essential household goods—stoves, saddles, tables—belonging to "negroes, 'poor whites,' and loungers" are auctioned off. Elsewhere the author mentions the iron mines, tobacco trade, guano production, and of course cotton industry that fueled economic growth in Atlanta, largely with the labor of African-American workers who lived in shantytowns.[16]

Harper's illustration of the communal laundry reveals shantytown as a domestic landscape characterized by modern construction techniques and laid out as a residential fortress. It is clear that the shanties ringing the laundry are examples of what was known as a "box house." A box or boxed house, sometimes called a "plank house," was an economical if uncomfortable house form that proliferated nationwide from the middle to the end of the nineteenth century. A box house has no framing; boards are simply lined up and nailed to each other and to internal supports. They rest in the ground, leading to the classification of these houses as "earthfast." Such earthfast houses were among the earliest structures built by European colonists on the North American continent. But in the late nineteenth century, they also proliferated as manufactured housing assembled by the owners, especially popular in boomtowns where housing shortages were the norm. Inside, box houses were usually three rooms, possibly organized in what is known as a "single pen" or "center-chimney saddlebag" layout. The thin walls were generally papered with newspapers and magazines for insulation and decoration. Constructed of rough planks of irregular width and length, a box house was not as comfortable as a frame house, which was built of finished lumber, weatherboarded, and painted, with more and larger windows. But a box house marked an improvement over a tent, in terms of comfort. And over a slave cabin, in terms of everything else.[17]

Perhaps ironically, log cabins built for enslaved workers, especially in the decades preceding the Civil War, were much more comfortable than the shanties, tents, and tenements they occupied in the decades following the war. But the layout of shantytowns were an explicit rejection of the uniformity and pernicious order of the slave quarter, with its rows of identical log cabins. Inside, box houses, while often of flimsy construction, offered a very different arrangement of space than the slave cabin, which often crowded several families into one room. The three interior rooms of the "saddlebag" design may have appealed to ex-slaves who previously had to share one room with family and non-family. Despite their shortcomings, box houses offered a measure of privacy.[18]

The identification of box houses on the postwar Atlanta landscape demonstrates values other than those espoused by the middle class about "good" and "bad" housing in America. Permanence, stability, and prosperity, prized by the middle class, were not the only virtues worth expressing in the building of a house. Looking closely at the everyday housing built or inhabited by ordinary people can reveal qualities that point to alternative values that are as true of shanties in postwar Atlanta as they are of the suburban tract house, the pueblo, or the single-room occupancy hotel. In southwestern North Carolina, white former residents and builders of box housing have recorded what it meant to residents of rural Appalachia who could not afford to build frame houses but nevertheless had a choice between building a log or a box house, and they chose to build box houses. Plank houses had the virtue of lasting no more than the builder's lifetime, as they weren't being built for posterity. African Americans living in Atlanta during and after Reconstruction may also have seen pragmatism, not posterity, as a virtue in housing. A box house offered a visual alternative to typical slave housing, and an interior arrangement of space that accommodated both the nuclear family and the boarding of related or unrelated others.[19]

The box house connected its builders to a wider, national identity closely aligned with industry, as opposed to plantation agriculture, and with the mobility of labor. Vertical plank or "box" housing was a popular form of construction in coal-mining towns by the late nineteenth century—as popular in Appalachia, and just as prevalent as log houses. Box housing has been traced to lumber towns, plantations, and railroad camps. Box housing was built by individuals with materials at hand, but they were also manufactured and sold in kit form to large construction sites, delivered around the country by train to be assembled as company housing. Box housing was mobile housing, and fitting for emancipated labor, which was mobile as well. It was unmoored, in its manufactured form, from a specific region, and was affordable housing. To live in a box house in Atlanta, or anywhere else, was to subtly declare your mobility and, by extension, your ownership of your own labor, and your own body.[20]

Just as important, box houses were occupied by African Americans who were *refusing* to move around in search of jobs. The Freedmen's Bureau, established in 1865 to distribute rations and relief to emancipated African Americans, aggressively tried to move them out of urban centers, either by returning them to plantations, where farm jobs were going unfilled, or further west or north, where manufacturing jobs might be available. While many were compelled to move, many thousands of African Americans resisted the pressure to relocate—and to sign onerous labor agreements. African Americans were able to stay in Atlanta because they had established themselves in quickly built, easily assembled shanties, arranged in fortress-like shantytowns like Shermantown. The Freedmen's

Bureau forced African Americans out of "contraband camps" and steered them toward the fringes of town, not just in Atlanta but as a general policy. African Americans hunkered down in shantytowns. White elites tried to control where African Americans lived after the war, while shanties facilitated choice.[21]

Shanties were indeed "products of poverty," but they also represented connections to tradition and alternative values that the builders, whether rural whites or urban blacks, embraced in the final decades of the nineteenth century. Hear Barbara Price, confronting the policeman at the threshold of her shanty in 1867, asserting that she would protect her daughter in her "own house." Box houses were drafty, saggy, visually incoherent, and ephemeral. But they were home to poor laborers in the decades after the Civil War, including African-American laborers who settled in huge numbers in places like Atlanta, and as homes, they sent messages to the powerful that the world had changed. Like Mary and Barbara Price, in their "own house" African Americans did not expect to be molested or trifled with. The performance of the African-American homeowner imbues the box house with its social meaning. It was not a fortress, but it was a place African Americans could call home.[22]

Shantytowns emerged as a center of African-American life in other southern cities as well. As early as 1865, the news media was reporting on settlements of former slaves housed in small cabins covered with slabs and tar in areas of Washington, DC. "On K, L, and M streets south, between Second and Fourth streets west," the Washington Post reported in 1865, "is a settlement containing some thousands of inhabitants, called Fredericksburg, and here the occupants own the homes, paying one dollar per month ground rent. They have created a church of their own, and support a colored pastor. Here may be found more evidence of comfort and independence than in any other large settlement of contrabands in the city. They have shops, and streets, and little gardens, and seem contented with their lot. Many of their houses have attained an altitude of two stories, and paint and verandahs ornament not a few of them." The writer goes on to point out similar settlements of occupant-owned cabins further west and north, "all sorts and sizes of them . . . wedged in every conceivable shape into vacant spaces and yards and alleys."[23]

An 1866 report by the commissioner of police described some of the less comfortable settlements, with extended families of African Americans crowded into "mere apologies for shanties" barely six or eight feet square, packed densely into the triangle of land where the southeast corner of the

White House grounds touched the northwest corner of the Mall. Many rented but "the more enterprising have erected cabins of their own." As the city government undertook an ambitious scheme of public works projects in the 1870s, under the leadership of legendary Alexander "Boss" Shepherd, new construction impinged on pre-existing African-American settlements. As a columnist for *Atlantic Monthly* reported in 1873: "The great houses of millionaires or of high government officials will, more likely than not, have a tumbledown tenement, a mean grocery, or a negro-shanty not a block off, and not seldom they are next-door neighbors."[24]

As late as 1882, amateur artists captured examples of shanties only a few blocks from the Capitol. The titles of several sketches made that year by Charles Deforest Gedney, a photographer who participated in the Wheeler Expedition to the American West in the early 1870s, tell the story: "Cabin behind rowhouses"; "Negro cabin near U.S. Capitol"; "Cabin within three squares of the Capitol." Outside the city's core, shanty settlements flourished along the waterways, in areas long occupied by African Americans working as enslaved laborers on nearby plantations or on the canals and the wharves, warehouses, and lumber yards that lined them. Settlements were catalogued at 11th and P Streets, Vermont Ave. and 12th.Street, and 22nd and M Streets. Derisive names for these and other settlements—"Hell's Bottom," "Murder Bay"—telegraphed the judgments of white elites, who took residents to task for insufficient architectural splendor. "The present places are of the rudest possible construction, few having any sashes in the window aperture, a board shutter closing out the cold winds, light and ventilation together, when shut," wrote one reporter, who observed the men and the women smoking "short, black pipes." Shanty settlements also developed on the outskirts of the capital. An 1869 article in *Atlantic Monthly*, titled "Spring in Washington," takes the reader on an excursion "through the woods and over hills. [I] went directly north from the Capitol for about three miles. The ground bare and the day cold and sharp. In the suburbs, among the scattered Irish and negro shanties, came suddenly upon a flock of birds."[25]

Birds in flight, landing *en masse* on the Washington landscape is an apt if unintended metaphor for the development of African-American shantytowns in the nation's capital during and after the Civil War. For the first time free to move about, to congregate, to form communities outside the oversight of white owners, emancipated African Americans made their way to

Washington, DC, where the shifting legalities of spatial freedom were taking form on the urban landscape. Enslaved workers carved out spaces of relative freedom for themselves in both rural and urban locations even before the war; hired-out slaves living in cities, in particular, were able to craft spaces and strategies for moving through them that afforded them degrees of autonomy and even independence. But the landscape that opened up after emancipation had opened up a bit earlier in Washington, DC. In April 1862, President Lincoln signed the District of Columbia Emancipation Act into law. Coming less than a year before the Emancipation Proclamation freed slaves in all of the Confederate states, the law—though controversial—cemented Washington's reputation as a relatively safe and prosperous haven for African Americans. From Maryland, Virginia, and states further south, fugitive slaves gravitated to the nation's capital, where long-established neighborhoods of enslaved and free blacks swelled with newcomers.[26]

After the war officially ended, migrants arrived at an even faster rate. Between 1860 and 1870, more than 29,000 African Americans—half of the total number of newcomers—moved to the District, which at that time did not include Georgetown, bumping the total city population to 109,000 and making the city home to the fastest-growing black population in the nation. As they did in Atlanta, a number of these newcomers originally settled in Freedmen's Villages established by the federal government, often on the sites of Union army encampments. The large Freedmen's Village constructed on the grounds of the confiscated Robert E. Lee estate, now the site of the Arlington National Cemetery, survived into the 1880s, long past the demise of most other such settlements, a testimony to the determination of its formerly enslaved residents. But Freedmen's Villages did not, could not absorb the thousands of African Americans who migrated to the places where they were built. Moreover, Freedmen's Villages were explicitly organized as places of transit and transition. They existed in order to provide temporary accommodations to African Americans presumed to be on their way west, north, or back to the rural south, or so the Freedmen's Bureau hoped. Even as it doled out food, clothes, and temporary lodging, the Freedmen's Bureau hustled African Americans down the road. It was a rare settlement that persisted, as the one at Arlington did, past the end of Reconstruction. Freedmen's Villages were essentially at odds with the long-term needs of most of the African

Americans housed in them, who resolutely resisted relocation from the cities where they congregated. This was as true in Washington as it was in Atlanta.[27]

Unlike Atlanta, where the prewar black population was scant, Washington had long been a center of free and enslaved black life. Many African Americans settling in Washington joined longstanding settlements, with internal economies designed to serve the needs of African-American residents. Free black settlements in Alexandria, Georgetown, most significantly Herring Hill, and the southwest quadrant of D.C., known locally as "The Island," all boasted long traditions of black political power and civic leadership. Thriving churches and pioneering schools for black students, established by African Americans, provided strong institutional support. On these landscapes, African-American migrants could largely circumvent confrontation with whites. But these neighborhoods could not accommodate all the migrants, and many African Americans either chose or were forced by circumstance to live in new communities near the city's core, adjacent to traditionally white areas. Where before the war blacks would have lived surreptitiously in these areas, in owners' back yards, or if hired-out, in alley dwellings, after the war they came into direct confrontation with whites, a conflict that escalated as the value of land occupied by black migrants soared.

One such contentious shantytown developed along K Street. In the spring of 1867 Gen. Oliver Otis Howard, the commissioner of the Freedmen's Bureau, was summoned to a stretch of "rough structures" along K Street, only a few blocks north of the White House grounds. There he conferred with the owners of city lots located between 13th and 17th Streets, carved out of the former site of Union army barracks and sold at auction after the war to speculators who were seeking to eject the "large, troublesome crowd" of African Americans who had built a welter of makeshift shanties along the street. "A few industrious negroes were cultivating small gardens on the vacant lots, but the majority were that crowd of helpless refugees that were living hand to mouth, nobody could tell just how," Howard wrote in his autobiography. There were thousands of people in the same condition throughout the city, former slaves and freedmen who had migrated during or just after the war from Virginia, Maryland, and further south. This "floating colored population" of men, women, and children had "seized and occupied" the land after the departure of the army, but now that the war was over, real estate in the capital was soaring in price, and the new owners were eager to resell the lots at higher prices. The capital was a morass of dirt streets and wooden sidewalks at the time, so unsanitary that some members of Congress suggested moving the federal capital further west. What chiefly distinguished this stretch of K Street was not its condition, which was no worse than most of the city's core, but its investment potential.[28]

As Howard narrated the story, he addressed the residents of K Street, telling them they had to move on. But they yelled back: "Where shall we go, and what shall we do?" He responded, rhetorically, by asking what would make them self-supporting? They answered, "Land!" While Howard found some of the crowd "saucy" and some "stupid," he judged "the greater number appeared anxious somehow to earn their way." He appropriated $52,000 in government funds to buy land to resettle the population of the entire eight-square-block area—more than 250 families—on one- and two-acre lots on the other side of the Anacostia River. It was not prime real estate: the land, known as the Barry Farm, abutted the Government Hospital for the Insane (later called St. Elizabeth's), and the misleadingly named Uniontown, a working-class suburb that expressly prohibited the sale or lease of land to black or Irish tenants. On a visit to Barry Farm a few years later, Howard noted that the residents, who had fully repaid the government for their property, had built a church and a school, and that many had found work "grading Capitol Hill and in their neighborhood"—ironically helping to build, like shantytown dwellers in New York, the very infrastructure that would ultimately displace them.[29]

Howard, like many narrators after him, told the story of the K Street settlement as a parable of Reconstruction, in which the caring but canny federal government rescued the rough, unschooled, destitute freedmen with a scheme that only coincidentally benefited white speculators and landowners. The landowners eager to evict former slaves from K Street are solicitous of their welfare. The African-American inhabitants themselves "seemed to realize they could not much longer stay there in the heart of the capital on that costly ground." Howard of course intervened on K Street in order to clear the land for development while disguising it as white benevolence. Howard was no cardboard bad-guy: he fed and housed indigent black migrants and later helped found Howard University. But on K Street as elsewhere in the nation, the priorities of white landowners came first. Even before the end of

Reconstruction, the federal government set in motion a pattern of removing blacks from the core of the city, often at government expense, in order to facilitate development by and for whites.[30]

It was significantly cheaper to live in a Freedmen's Village than in rental housing, yet residents of Freedmen's Villages were required to follow a spate of rules governing personal conduct, and were regularly monitored and inspected. Shantytowns offered an alternative to surveillance and oversight of Freedmen's Villages. Officials were often struck by just how vigorously freed people resisted leaving the capital, but also, equally, how little they trusted the government. Living in a shantytown may have created a greater sense of confidence, security, and privacy. As part of its campaign to move African Americans out of Washington, the Freedmen's Bureau fretted over the conditions of freed people's housing. They worked with the metropolitan police, for example, to clean, whitewash, and if necessary raze shanty housing in the core. As time passed and the scores of poor black residents remained, in 1868 they recommended demolishing the remaining "small tenement houses occupied by the poorer class of colored people" and "scattering the occupants." William F. Spurgin, a Freedmen's Bureau official in charge of cleaning up freed people's housing, felt they were unjustly singled out for filth; his reports also emphasized the filthy conditions at white settlements. Efforts to clean up housing, however, focused on neighborhoods of "contrabands" and not of poor whites, normalizing a situation in which government officials scrutinized and pronounced judgment on African-American homes.[31]

Shanties were often Exhibit A in efforts to evict African Americans from the city's core. The *Daily National Intelligencer* in 1865 noted that shanties were "generally made of the cheapest lumber, covered with felt and tar" and divided into overcrowded apartments. J. V. W. Vandenburgh, an officer of the Freedmen's Bureau, in an 1867 report noted a number of freed families "living in the most miserable of shanties" and "literally wallowing in filth" in parts of "the Island"—the local name for the large triangle of land that drooped from the bottom of the Mall to the fork of the Potomac River, bounded by the Washington Canal on the east. He declared it the Five Points of D.C., "where sin and misery steeped in licentious amalgamation is allowed to exist." An 1866 report by the commissioner of the metropolitan police, A. C. Richards, described windowless shanties subject to the "miasmatic effluvia" of the stagnant swamp upon which Washington was built. Shanties one story in height were erected within three or four feet of each other. "These openings lead in so devious a course that one with difficulty finds his way out again," the commissioner wrote, echoing anxieties about the unseen, and therefore uncontrolled and unknowable. An area of 50 square yards located at 13th Street and the Washington Canal (dramatically dubbed Murder Bay) housed 100 families; another at Rhode Island Avenue and 11th Street housed 213 people on 200 square feet of land. The renters among them were exploited, as a traveling Welsh industrialist observed in 1868: "It was found that from five to eight dollars per month are paid for the rent of these miserable shanties." But others had beaten the system, paying instead "a ground rent of three dollars per month" in an area subdivided into tiny squares, also crammed cheek to jowl. Those who chose or were able to build their own shanties saved money and had more space. A shanty settlement at 14th Street at Ohio, for example, boasted small back yards.[32]

Washington elites insisted repeatedly that spaces occupied by migrant refugees did not constitute a legitimate part of the city, and Democratic politicians went so far as to demand their removal from the city landscape altogether. D.C. Mayor Richard Wallach offered to find space for local poor African Americans who were permanent residents, but not for migrant refugees. The Democratic *Constitutional Union* demanded that the city's "contraband camp" be moved "to some backwoods." While in fact they were the nation's newest insiders, contrabands, even by dint of that label, were defined as outsiders. It is significant that absorption into the spaces or life of the city was not offered as a credible outcome by anyone in authority at the time—not the mayor, or the press, or the Freedmen's Bureau. Significantly, the 1862 law that emancipated blacks in the District a full year before the Emancipation Proclamation included a commitment to make every effort to support colonization in Africa. So the very act of remaining in the city's core—in the shantytown along K Street, for example—amounted to an assertion of rights. Claiming a right to the city in Washington, DC, was in effect a performance of national identity as well—both personally, in the form of individual African-American shanty dwellers creating their identities as urban citizens in space, and on the level of the nation. The incorporation of a free, African-American identity into the nation's capital marked a shift in the national identity, from a slave state to a nation of free citizens.[33]

By 1870, the total population of D.C. had grown to 131,700, from just over 75,000 in 1860. Affluent whites, squeezed by a shortage of housing, gradually moved north of the city core, increasing pressure on poor residents to get out of the way. A series of infrastructure improvements in the 1870s literally paved the way for gentrification, caused the demolition of hundreds if not thousands of shanties, and created a patchwork of rich and poor houses along many of the city's avenues. The encroachment of white residential development on poor black neighborhoods is captured in an 1881 illustration from *Harper's,* captioned "Negro Shanties." It shows a pair of one-and-a-half story houses sandwiched between four-story brownstones on a steep sliver of land. A long flight of steps leads from the front door of the shanty to the sidewalk below, where a well-dressed white woman, gazing forward, walks her dog. Several children occupy the steps. At the top of the stairs a black woman in a headdress lugs a basket of laundry, half-hung on a short length of clothesline nearby; she pauses to stare down at her white counterpart. The laboring woman, encumbered with too many children, shackled by poverty, studies her white counterpart across an abyss of race and privilege. They are separated as well by a historical chasm, the scraps of freedom seized by blacks during Reconstruction all but obliterated by the relentless march of white real estate development. The African-American woman in the illustration is still holding her ground. But as the haughty pug dog and his unblinking owner attest, she will not prevail. The title of the article, "A Nation in a Nut-shell," encourages analogies between the capital and the nation. White middle-class elites were squeezing out poor laborers, African Americans in particular, on the urban landscape.[34]

By the time *Harper's* published its assessment of "Negro Shanties" in 1881, African-American shantytowns in Washington were being demolished in the waves of infrastructure improvements undertaken in the 1870s. Several escaped demolition, primarily those that occupied the fringes: the ends of newly paved streets, the low-lying areas earmarked for infill, the banks of moribund canals. These shantytowns were documented by a young, poor, aspiring artist named DeLancey Walker Gill, who sketched Washington's disappearing shantytowns in the early 1880s. Gill achieved minor fame later in his career as a photographer for the Bureau of Ethnography, taking thousands of portraits of visiting Indian delegations that are still exhibited today. But in the early 1880s he was an apprentice draftsman, an avid watercolorist, an eager member of the amateur art community in D.C. While his artistic skill was modest, his pen-and-ink drawings of shantytowns are astonishing in their detail: both the exteriors and, in one case, the interior of shanties are painstakingly rendered, as are the landscapes they inhabit. There is perhaps no better visual record of how African Americans lived in D.C. during the 1880s than Gill's largely neglected shantytown sketches.

Plotted on a map, Gill's shantytown sketches stake out the edges of 1880s Washington. His images depict mostly African-American shantytowns, but include a few settlements inhabited by Irish and German immigrants, and a couple that housed both black and immigrant residents. The African-American shantytowns sketched by Gill clustered in three areas: near the Potomac, west of the White House grounds; in the vicinity of K Street; between Dupont Circle and Rock Creek; and on Meridian Hill, past the northern limits of the city on W Street, on the site of what is now Malcolm X Park. The shanties are all earthfast structures with no foundations, made of boards nailed either horizontally or vertically (or both) to wooden studs. In this they resemble closely the shanties built by Irish and German immigrants in New York and Brooklyn, as well as the shanties built in Atlanta by emancipated African Americans—and, indeed, the shanties built on the American frontier during the colonial and early republic eras. These African-American residences have annexes and els, as well as small additions clearly intended for animals. But their additions proliferate to an even greater degree. Some shanties have just one room but many are a conglomeration of rooms, tacked onto each other like wayward train cars. Aggregated houses that combine rooms of various sizes zigzag across the landscape, defying a standardized model. Vertical siding is as common as horizontal siding, and sometimes a single residence employs both, adding to the patchwork appearance of both individual shanties and entire shantytowns. Brick chimneys with tall, tapering ceramic chimney pots burst from the centers of the largest room, indicating the presence of modern stoves in the interiors—as opposed to the open fires or fireplaces common in antebellum slave cabins and quarters. Some houses have two chimneys, suggesting, as do multiple doors to the outside, the presence of several unrelated families or individuals inside.

Like newly free tenant farmers on the rural landscape, urban residents built housing complexes in tight clumps and clusters. African-American

"Meridian Hill," DeLancey Walker Gill, 1883.

shanty dwellers didn't sort themselves into separate, predictable units evenly distributed on the landscape; they bundled their houses together. Like shanty dwellers in New York and Brooklyn, they lived off the grid, building communities that often presented an obstacle to the advancing urban geometry. Households were dense with people, in various relationships to each other, and the shoved-together nature of the structures themselves reflect that.[35]

This urban landscape of small housing nodes offered African Americans the protection of group living, and the economies of scale that provided the domestic privacy that had been withheld from them until the end of the Civil War. Shanties were built in pieces, as families grew or as unrelated boarders were taken in as a source of income or additional labor. But adding on rooms also created the opportunity to individualize and particularize the houses in ways that would have been impossible during the last decades of slavery. Uniform housing was an expression of owners' power and the social control they exerted over slaves. Gill's drawings offer clues to the multiple strategies African Americans used during and following Reconstruction to mold the urban landscape for their own purposes, both practical and symbolic. With

their shanties, African Americans in post-Reconstruction Washington signaled their individuality.[36]

Gill's drawings provide further evidence of postwar African Americans'
efforts to use the domestic urban landscape to declare their sovereignty.
Fences are ubiquitous—diminutive picket fences, splitrail fences, tall privacy
fences—but they seldom enclose anything. Rather, they stake out private territory around the shanties, reinforcing the boundaries of the homesite. Often
shanties have more than one fence, neither of which encloses anything. They
are both decorative and symbolic, establishing or re-emphasizing property
boundaries, but they are seldom utilitarian.

Topographical details reinforce ideas of sovereignty. The shantytowns have
dirt streets, but the orientation of the houses follows the lay of the land, not
the grid or its radial accomplices. Shanties are often perched high on bluffs or
hills; loosely girdled by fences, they have the air of domestic fortresses. That
effect is reinforced by the body language of the residents who appear in
almost every sketch Gill made, standing like sentinels in or near doorways.
Gill most likely invited this display of ownership, as he maneuvered through
the back yards—never the main streets—of African-American shantytowns,
making sketches or perhaps just taking photographs to sketch from later as he
is known to have done. The placement of the many add-ons—el kitchens,
lean-to rooms, partially enclosed work spaces—also served to insulate the
main room (or rooms) of the house, which held the prized stoves. Someone,
friend or stranger, proceeding all the way to the hearth would pass through
numerous adjunct spaces—up a hill, past a fence, through a gate, across a
porch or stoop, through the front door, and then perhaps through an ante-
room before reaching the main living space. Even the notion of a main living
space bears interrogation, as the massing of shanties points to multiple primary users of the indoor space.[37]

Just as the fences operate as decorative and symbolic elements, so do, in
many instances, doors, porches, and entryways. A number of Gill's drawings
show the incorporation of louvers, latticework, verandahs, and inset porches
into shanties built in African-American neighborhoods. A view of a shanty in
Meridian Hill, located near the northern border of the District in 1883, shows
a pair of louvered exterior doors. The same shanty, a combination of a side-
gabled unit and a lean-to addition, features an inset porch located in the
crook of the two structures. Three other shanties in Meridian Hill, including

two along gentrifying Champlain Avenue, have latticework porches or louvered doors, or both. Uncovered verandahs, more like balconies than porches,
appear on shanties at 22nd and N and at P Street near 18th—both near Dupont
Circle—and on a shanty near 18th and B, not far from the White House
grounds. A two-story shanty at 26th and N has a lattice-covered window, a
louvered door, an inset porch, and a verandah. Here, and in two other drawings, a succession of propped-up ladders lead all the way to the roof; possibly
they provided access for repair and maintenance, but they may also indicate
that people were sleeping on the roof, above the reach of mosquitos, positioned to catch a rare breeze crossing the humid marshy landscape. One of
the most fanciful uses of latticework occurs on a shanty in Dupont Circle
located next door to the then-new Stewart Mansion, which rises cathedral-
like across the street; another new mansion, mansard tower hovering menac-
ingly, abuts the rear of the shanty.[38]

Lattice and louvers serve practical purposes: they regulate heat, dappling
the sunlight without restricting the flow of air. Inset porches similarly offer a
place to escape the sun, while verandahs provide a place to step out of the
house and catch a passing breeze. These elements also speak to values of privacy and property. Latticework, flimsy in itself, creates a distinction between
public and private spaces—requiring an invitation to come into the house
itself; the same is true of porches in general. These architectural elements also
signal African-American identity. All are associated with Caribbean architecture in general and Jamaican architecture in particular. They appeared frequently in New Orleans and elsewhere in Louisiana and along the Gulf Coast.
Their recurrence in Washington in the early 1880s does not signal a direct
importation from the Caribbean; long before that point such practices had
been diffused throughout the East Coast by migrating African Americans,
both enslaved and emancipated. They would have seeped into black southern
culture by the 1880s. But their use in shanties in Washington did communi-
cate racial identity: while they had Caribbean, not African, origins, by the
1880s they were quintessentially African-*American*. Similarly, the headdresses
worn by every African-American woman pictured in Gill's drawings of shanties express African-American identity—in this case, the origins of the head-
dress, also worn in the Caribbean, were indeed African. By the 1880s, the
head-wrap, like the louvered door or the latticework window, was a marker of
African-American identity.[39]

The formation of postwar African-American identity is evident not only in the details of these shanties, but in their very form, and in the way they relate to the landscape. A close look at an image of a shantytown located west of the White House grounds, on what became Constitution Avenue, illustrates this claim. Gill drew several pictures of shanties in this area. One particularly striking image features a distinctive clapboard shanty at 18th Street and B Street NW (now Constitution). Several one-room shanties, placed at angles, face a narrow dirt street lying roughly parallel to the river. In the foreground, a large shanty rests atop a small tsunami of land, peering over its neighbors to the Potomac River beyond. The shanty has a very steep roof, so steep that a second story has been created on the back half of the house. The rear wall plummets like a cliff face into the swell of ground below. House and ground together look like a giant wave that has been sucked out of the placid river.

The 1880 census shows a substantial African-American population living near 18th and B Streets. Several women worked as nurses, a number of men in the fishing industry: Albert Powell, 41, from Virginia; Henry Harris, 39, and John Barseo, 35 both from Maryland; all worked on a sand boat. Thomas White, 22, was a sailor. For these residents, this house design had both practical advantages and expressive capacities. The exterior walls are constructed out of three lengths of shorter boards, perhaps two to four feet long, laid horizontally end to end and nailed to vertical wooden supports on the interior of the building. The short lengths of the boards and the fact that they are riven, or split from logs, as opposed to milled, suggests that the builder scavenged them from a nearby lumberyard; there were several along the Potomac. Two vertical seams run from ground to roof, reflecting the presence, inside, of wooden studs. The roof has been constructed in three sections as well, each more precipitously pitched than the one before. It is ski-slope steep. By stitching the house together in this way, the builder creates a second floor space without framing or foundation. On the two-story facade that overlooks the river, verandahs are visible, another extension of livable space wrought from thin air. These creative siding and roofing techniques produced a significant amount of additional space, both in the depth of the house and its height, even extending off the rear wall.[40]

Gill sketched a number of shanties of this design, in several areas of Washington, interspersed among shanties with more conventional lean-to roofs and single-story designs. Another was located at 18th and D Street

N.W., only a few blocks away. These distinctive shanties resemble a design called a "flounder house"—so called because of its tall, often windowless side. Flounder houses were a popular form of infill housing in nearby Alexandria, where housing shortages and rising land prices inspired people to wedge new buildings into the narrow parcels between existing houses. Flounder houses have the appearance of a front-gabled house that has been sliced neatly in half along the ridge line, turned sideways, and jammed hard into an urban lot. They were also popular in Pittsburgh, Baltimore, Cincinnati, St. Louis, and Charleston, SC. The entrance door is generally located on the angular, pointed side facing the street. While surviving examples are brick, frame flounder houses were also built in the nineteenth century. It is possible the African-American builders of "flounder shanties" adapted the urban form, but there are key differences. The main entrance is not cut through the triangular side, but placed in the low-slung, first-floor facade—at the foot of the ski slope, as it were. The flounder shanty, unlike the flounder house, is not windowless, just the opposite: shallow porches on both the first and second floors over-look the river, presupposing the presence of both windows and doors on the large expanse of that side.[41]

Only one Gill drawing includes a sketch of the interior of a shanty. Interior views of poor people's housing are exceedingly rare, and Gill's rendering offers a valuable amount of detail. The sketch shows the inside of the main room of a shanty near 22nd and O Street N.W., where a woman stands tending a pot on the stove. A small child holding what appears to be a poker for the stove stands beside her, looking out at the viewer. As in all of Gill's sketches, the facial features of the people are illegible. The details of the furnishings are distinct, however. The kitchen stove has pride of place in the middle of the floor. A large stovepipe, perfectly straight with one crisp perpendicular bend, ascends through the roof. A small table and several ladder-back chairs sit flush against the wall, which also holds a kerosene lamp on a small shelf, next to a clock. High on the wall above the woman's head hangs a painting or an illustration of some kind, quite large and prominently displayed. In a niche near a high window of four glass panes are three shelves holding a variety of plates, cups, bowls, and other kitchenware, hutch-like, and a few groceries; beneath the shelves are a large barrel that may have held flour and what may be a bread box. Baskets and pans hang on hooks. Walls, floor, and ceiling are made of wide, bare boards; some sort of covering, perhaps tar paper, covers portions of the walls behind the stove and underneath the window. Every object has a place and the effect is orderly and precise. It is a utilitarian space, animated by household chores and family relationships, with a well-scrubbed appearance and precisely placed furnishings that signal a high degree of domestic pride. The picture, presiding high on the wall, and the clock, poised on its own shelf, point to efforts to personalize the space and lift it above the quotidian. While the layout of shanties on the landscape, and the massing of units into aggregated houses gave African-American shantytowns an idiosyncratic appearance, interiors like this one point to the primacy of family life that scholars have documented among both enslaved and emancipated African Americans.[42]

People appear in many of Gill's drawings, sometimes simply standing in front of their houses or in their yards, but sometimes participating in activities related to work and domestic life. Women are often depicted carrying marketing baskets. One Gill sketch portrays a group of about a dozen women crouching with their baskets on a hillside, harvesting something from low

"22nd and N Streets," DeLancey Walker Gill, 1883.

bushes. Women often wear ankle-length white aprons and invariably a head-dress that imparts a lingering Africanism. Children are pictured in almost every sketch Gill made of shanties and shantytowns, a poignant reminder of the transition from slavery to emancipation. Men appear less frequently, usually as aproned figures standing in a work yard. One sketch is a close-up of a handcart operator, in a top hat and vest, pushing a two-wheeled cart with a "For Hire" sign on the front. Another shows an African-American store-keeper in a bulbous hat staring out from the doorway of a grocery store at 15th and L Streets. The signs advertise the culinary indulgences—Ice Cream, Milk Pie, Select Oysters, Ice, Cool Beer—that often accompany leisure time.

The landscapes of African-American life presented in Gill's sketches and watercolors leave a markedly different impression than images of African Americans published in the media or painted by artists during the same period. In the early 1880s, when Gill was sketching shantytowns, magazines and pictorials were celebrating the growth and gentrification of Washington, DC, in the wake of a series of public works projects in the 1870s that included the paving of many of the previously unbuilt streets and alleyways designated in the L'Enfant plan of 1791, and the construction of major water and sewer infrastructure projects. In 1884, *Century Magazine* reported on the transfor-mation of Washington in the preceding dozen years: "Costly improvements were undertaken and miles of expensive pavements and other works were laid across swamps and streams, and through vast waste places where nothing but frame shanties and government stables of the war period had yet pene-trated." Yet in 1884 the city retained "a very incongruous and ludicrous appearance." The article lamented that "everywhere there are superb resi-dences looking out upon fields of red clay and weeds, and flanked on either side by such shanties as perch on the rocks in the upper part of New York. This incongruity reaches its height on the principal street of the town, Pennsylvania Avenue." There the author found grand mansions interspersed with "dilapidated and wretched little houses of ancient date, which look singularly out of sympathy with their surroundings." Shanties were used rhe-torically to signal both progress and the greatest obstacle to it: poor people, especially poor black people.[43]

One of Gill's most compelling images, *Dupont Circle* shows an extrava-gantly tarpapered shanty in Dupont Circle, hanging onto its spacious corner lot even as massive mansarded mansions rise around it. Grand brick houses, including the Stewart Mansion, an early gentrifying pioneer, rise cathedral-like among the shanties, transforming the area from an African-American settlement into a fashionable white residential district. The shanty bears the marks of African-American identity: unpredictable massing, delicate lattice-work, lopsided roofs, and a tapering chimney pot atop a sturdy chimney, diverting sparks from the flammable house below. The juxtaposition of board shanties with the palaces of Washington's elite in areas like Dupont Circle created a rhetorical dichotomy that observers found irresistible. In 1883, newspaper columnist Frank "Carp" Carpenter, put the two house forms in conversation with each other. "The shanty says to the palace, 'This is a free country. We are equals. My master may be bigger than yours during the next administration; then perhaps I shall be built up, and you'll be sold for that mortgage which you know very well is now on your roof." For middle-class arbiters like Carpenter, the shanty perhaps did represent a democratic correc-tive, a tonic for the increasingly grandiose character of the federal city. The sharp contrast of white wealth and African-American poverty impressed Gill, who scrupulously recorded the minute details of shanty architecture and shantytown landscapes.[44]

Gill's views of shantytowns provide a perspective on a type of African-American landscape that is seldom analyzed: a self-built landscape. Other artists portrayed African Americans on landscapes of slavery. Gill's drawings

"Dupont Circle," DeLancey Walker Gill, 1883.

show the spatial choices African Americans made for themselves, albeit within a range limited by financial and political realities. These choices reflected African Americans' attempts at racial renegotiation on the landscape. The drawings document the spatial changes inherent in the end of slavery, and accompanying efforts of African Americans to establish themselves as independent citizens.[45]

Gill's fascination with African-American life in D.C. didn't end with his sketches and watercolors. Among Gill's papers at the Historical Society of Washington are a number of spirituals along with sentimental songs about African-American life, all handwritten in what is presumably Gill's hand. One, "Negro Camp Meeting Song," evokes a land "way over yonder by Zion's hill / Where de fields are green and de waters still." The number of songs suggest that collecting them was yet another hobby of Gill's. With these songs, and with his shantytown sketches—which he did when he could have been earning commissions for pretty pictorial scenes of the capital—Gill was working out for himself the racial identity of a post-slavery nation. That conclusion is given a chilling confirmation by the presence, inserted without comment among the sheaves of Gill's papers, of a startling artifact: a photograph of four African-American men hanging from the branches of several trees in a patch of woods. There are no marks on the photograph to indicate the location of the scene; the heavy cardstock suggests it may have been printed as a postcard, a grisly but not unusual souvenir of lynchings in the South. Lynchings of African Americans were hovering around 50 per year nationwide during the period Gill sketched black shantytowns, a figure that more than doubled over the next decade. A lynching in Washington, DC, was threatened in February 1880, and in July 1919, white mobs wounded several dozen African Americans in street violence, killing five. The photograph of a lynching in Gill's papers shows that he understood the threats African Americans faced from white supremacists as they tried to maintain their claims to the D.C. landscape in the late nineteenth century. So does a later watercolor, done in 1887, of Fort Monroe in Hampton, VA, the site of the first self-created mass settlement of African Americans in the United States, where the word "contraband" was coined in 1861. The camp's nickname, Slabtown, suggests it included a significant number of self-built shanties.

Later in his career, Gill would become well-known for his studio portraits of visiting Indian delegations, including photographs of Goyathlay (Geronimo) and Chief Joseph. Those photographs, between 2,000 and 3,000 studio portraits made between 1890 and 1920, also documented a vanishing people in exquisite detail. They profess a similar absence of overt authorial interpretation—although of course to document, preserve, and archive in this fashion is in itself an interpretive and curatorial move, signifying hierarchies of class and race. The photo-realism of Gill's Indian portraits surfaces in his scenes of shantytowns. There was little if any artistic license taken with these images; Gill faithfully documented the length of boards, the textures of materials, the slant of pickets, even the tufts of grass in the yard. Gill captured his subject matter with draftsman-like precision, avoiding the picturesque impulse that informed most artistic depictions of African Americans and their landscapes. His drawings are not nostalgic or sentimental, but they are studies of a vanishing landscape. His drawing of the shanty persisting in the midst of mansions in Dupont Circle, for example—reminiscent of etcher Mary Nimmo Moran's etching of the lone surviving shanty in her 1881 *Cliff Dwellers of New York*—does not wrap the shanty in nostalgia, or hail the mansions as beacons of progress, but it does assert what white elites deemed inevitable, and did indeed come to pass: the erasure of self-built African-American housing from the nation's capital. Gill does not demean the shanties; if anything, he seems to revel in their individuality: the insouciance of a flounder house high on a hill, the tracery of latticework or louvered shutters piercing a coarse and prickly tarpapered wall. But his views do not argue for the right of shanties to exist and persist in the growing federal city. Like other artists who documented shantytowns, he captured a vanishing phenomenon for posterity.[46]

The shanty was used as a rhetorical device by the emerging black middle class, most memorably by Booker T. Washington, in debates about strategies for racial "uplift" and the correct uses of political activism. Washington used the shanty to signal a sort of prehistory of African-American citizenship, identifying rudimentary housing as an obstacle to the betterment of the race. In 1893, Washington asserted that students of industrial educations, such as those offered at Hampton Institute, would build a "comfortable, tasty, framed cottage" to "replace the log hovel that had been their abode for a quarter of a century." A change in housing signaled an uptick in education and status. Washington's analogy echoes the authors of emigrant housing guides in the early nineteenth century, who prescribed frame houses as the natural progression from unframed shanties.[47]

Washington used the shanty to similar, if more ambivalent rhetorical effect in his first autobiography, *The Story of My Life and Work*. Written for a black audience and published in 1901 shortly before the more famous *Up From Slavery*, which targeted a white audience, Washington distinguishes between three forms of African-American housing: the slave cabin, the shanty built by newly emancipated blacks, and a proper frame "house," built by better educated and more aspirational members of the race. The introduction to the narrative, written by J. L. M. Curry, an officer in the Confederate army who became an advocate for African-American education, laments that "six millions of our Negroes are living in one-room cabins," and commends Washington's "earnest crusade against 'the one-room cabin.'" The quotation marks around the phrase attest to its popularity as a slur used by whites to denigrate blacks—living in one room indicated a lack of not only money, but morals and education. Equal to Washington's accomplishments as an educator, Curry added, was his campaign of "pacification and good citizenship" among African Americans. He goes on to commend the industrial training offered at Tuskegee University, which "stands conspicuous . . . for intelligent productive labor, for increased usefulness in agriculture and mechanics, for self-respect and self-support, and for the purification of home-life." Tacitly, the one-room cabin stands for the opposite: for idleness and sloth, for a lack of self-respect, for impure home life, whatever that may be, and possibly for rebelliousness rather than "pacification." As in the cultural judgments rendered by the white middle class, the "tasty, framed" single-family home becomes the standard for comparison. Good citizens eschewed the one-room cabin and embraced the tasteful framed cottage and the pure home life that it ostensibly made possible. A failure to progress was attributable not to systemic problems—slavery, the failure of Reconstruction—but to personal attributes and environmental choices.[48]

Washington himself wields the symbols of the framed cottage and the unframed shanty in the text of his autobiography. Three homes from Washington's childhood are featured in the text, each accompanied by a photograph. The first, identified as "The house in Virginia where Booker T. Washington was born. (Still standing.)," shows a rectangular cabin of one story plus a loft, made of roughly hewn logs held together with mud. The roof is barely visible but appears to be made of planks. A door to the loft, accessed by an exterior ladder, and the openings for several small, paneless windows, apparently boarded up, can be seen, as can a workbench under a large tree that shades the house. There is a chimney of what appears to be brick, and stretching to the edge of the frame, a picket fence. An entrance door is not visible but presumably occupies one of the other sides. Washington reminisces about his birthplace:

> I remember very distinctly the appearance of the cabin in which I was born and lived until freedom came. It was a small log cabin about 12 x 16 feet, and without windows. There was no floor, except one of dirt. There was a large opening in the center of the floor, where sweet potatoes were kept for my master's family during the winter. In this cabin my mother did the cooking, the greater part of the time, for my master's family. Our bed, or 'pallet,' as we called it, was made every night on the dirt floor. Our bed clothing consisted of a few rags gathered here and there.[49]

From Washington's recollections, it seems likely that the building where his family lived also served as a kitchen for the big house; it was not unusual for slaves to live in outbuildings. In size and form, cabins built for housing closely resembled structures built as kitchens, dairies, smokehouses, or toolsheds. Whether free-standing or combined with work spaces, slave quarters were generally "bare, geometric expressions—square or rectangular boxes with roofs," that "signaled that a strict hierarchical order was in force."[50]

Two other photographs of houses appear at the end of the first chapter, juxtaposed with each other: "The house in which Booker T. Washington's family lived in West Virginia at the time he left for Hampton Institute," and below it, "The cabin in West Virginia where Booker T. Washington lived as a small boy." The visual differences are striking. The house Washington occupied when he left for college was a simple but solid clapboard house with a shingled roof and a stone foundation. The facade is reassuringly symmetrical, with sash windows of 12 panes framing a central doorway capped by a 3-pane lintel. Two brick chimneys are visible at either end of the house. Two unidentified men occupy the front stoop, peering into the camera. The composition would be perfectly balanced if not for the jagged bits of picket fence protruding from the bottom of the frame, which the photographer clearly tried to minimize. The well-balanced house, with its refined touches—shingles, windowpanes, two chimneys signaling the warmth of the interior—fills the entire frame. The domestic environment that produced the Booker T. Washington who got himself to Hampton Institute, this photograph suggests, was the product of a humble but orderly home that announced its aspirations toward higher standards of European domestic architecture. This house is congruent with the educated, cultured civic leader that Washington would style himself.[51]

Directly below this photograph, insisting upon comparison, is a photograph of "The cabin in old Virginia where Booker T. Washington lived when a small boy." The cabin, which Washington calls a "shanty" in the text, resembles a sardine can with one edge pried open; did the shed roof collapse, or was a corner of a flat roof torn off in a storm? The structure makes no visual sense. Photographed off-center in deep shade—unlike the previous photo, taken with full sun hitting the front of the house—the cabin is presented as a chaotic assemblage of mismatched parts. Doors, barrels, wheels, bins, ladders, sticks, logs, cans, rails, and carelessly draped bits of fabric (clothing? linens?) form an indecipherable maelstrom. The cabin sits in a large but chaotic work yard; other outbuildings can be seen to the sides and rear. The image of the cabin serves as an eyebrow-raising counterpoint to the vision of domestic self-control inherent in the house above. The autobiography presents the cabin as backward: it occupies a prehistorical space, an "old Virginia" landscape that hardworking and forward-thinking African Americans like Washington abandoned in favor of a more socially acceptable and progressive house.

At the same time, the miserable cabin adds an ambivalent note to Washington's fable of progress. The hardships it conveys, of deprivation, overwork, and desolation, a life defined by the small compass of the work yard, establish Washington's credentials as an achiever, a self-made man. The shanty conveys the authority of shared experience that Washington required in order to speak on behalf of his race. He had suffered; he had struggled. True to Washington's philosophy of self-help, the deprived boy who lived in that cabin grew into the self-assured young man that ushered into the world from the tidy house in West Virginia. Readers learn that Washington, who worked as a child in the salt furnaces and coal mines, eventually got permission from his stepfather to attend the public school, rising every morning at 4:00 a.m. to do so. His work ethic lifts him out of the shanty where he grew up and leads him to Hampton Institute, where he resolves to expand African-American access to higher education, an ambition that leads him, surprisingly, to yet another shanty.

As Washington narrates the story, he arrived at the Tuskegee Institute in

Alabama in 1881 to find that "there was no land, building, or apparatus" set up for the school he had been hired to run. Undeterred, he "opened the school, however, on the 4th of July, 1881, in an old church and a little shanty that was almost ready to fall down from decay." Just as Washington himself began in a shanty, so does Tuskegee, with the same successful results. The shanty—and Washington's ability to shake free of its symbolic meaning—becomes a rallying cry in the origin narrative he crafts about Tuskegee. Even as the school's finances begin to improve,

> all the while the farm was being paid for we were holding school daily in the old church and shanty. The latter at least was well ventilated. There was one thickness of boards above and around us, and this was full of large cracks. Part of the windows had no sashes and were closed with rough wooden shutters that opened upward by leather hinges. Other windows had sashes, but with little glass in them. Through all these openings the hot sun or cold wind and rain came pouring in upon us. Many a time a storm would leave scarcely a dry spot in either of the two rooms into which the shanty was divided to make room for separate classes.

Later, in 1899, Washington secures funding from Andrew Carnegie to build a library. "Our first library and reading-room were in a corner of a shanty, occupying a space of about five by twelve feet." Once again the shanty charts the distance Tuskegee has come, while also reaffirming its roots.[52]

Washington invoked the shanty to indicate progress and improvement, but also to claim authentic blackness; his birth and childhood in a shanty were shorthand for the shared experience of deprivation and oppression required to represent African-American aspirations with authority. But like the representations of the shanty by white artists, writers, and assorted other cultural spokespersons, Washington's shanty is a thing of the past, a relic of a former, less desirable way of life. Washington appreciates the tension between the cabin, the shanty, and the house, but he does not credit the shanty as a symbol of viable virtues. The sense of the shanty as a relic of African-American life comes across vividly in a 1916 painting by William Edouard Scott, an internationally known African-American painter and muralist. One of the first black artists to include scenes of everyday African-American life in his paintings, he memorialized the shanty as an icon of African-American history in *It's Going to Come.* A tignon-wearing African-American woman stands, as though rooted, in the dirt yard of a plank shanty; hands on hips, her body pivoting slightly, she both confronts the viewer and presents her shanty for inspection. The shanty, made of vertical planks with a mud and daub chimney, appears to be a single room. It occupies the bulk of the frame, but the bright white of the woman's apron, and the figure of a child crouched behind her, command the viewer's attention.

It's Going to Come could be a pre-emancipation scene—the war is going to come, but so is emancipation. Or it could be a contemporary scene, in which case it invites speculation about what, exactly, is going to come. The artist, who painted several portraits of Washington, shared his philosophy of racial uplift: perhaps a better future is going to come. The scene was likely painted near Tuskegee, suggesting that the better future that is coming would be ushered in by the education and doctrine of personal accountability promoted by Washington and his colleagues. Regardless of what is coming, the shanty is going: it harkens to a past of slavery followed by exploitation and disenfranchisement. But the woman stands defiantly before her shanty; while the artist used it to convey destitution, her rooted stance suggests a more complicated relationship to her surroundings, which include a washtub and, behind the shanty, a line full of drying clothes. She is clearly a laundress, earning her own living and raising her child. Scott left us with a clear indication of the social meaning of shanties, proof of their use as a rhetorical device in debates about working-class formation and racial identity well into the twentieth century.[53]

Shantytowns continued to be a material reality for African Americans. Often referred to as "suburbs" in the media, these suburban shantytowns represented a rejection of multifamily urban options offered by the private and the public sector. One such African-American shanty-suburb was built south of Chicago in what is now Robbins, IL, in 1892, on the site of a failed scheme to build housing for the 1893 World's Columbian Exposition. Like many shantytowns, it was built on bottomland, "level terrain dotted with four park-like lagoons." Restrictive zoning and segregation made it all but impossible for African Americans to find decent housing near their jobs in Chicago, so Robbins represented a rare opportunity to own one's own home. In 1910 a developer started selling settler's lots, charging as little as $90 each and offering a monthly payment plan. By 1917, some 300 people lived in the four-square-mile village southwest of Chicago. Like the tenement dwellers who upgraded to shantytown, many of the residents of Robbins who moved there in the 1910s and 1920s were former apartment dwellers leaving "Chicago's teeming south side" in search of "a humble dwelling with a small plot of ground to raise corn, carnations, cabbages, and carrots; a few chickens; a luscious goose or two; and perhaps a shoat to fatten for next winter's larder." Many residents were employed in the building trades, and a twentieth-century chronicler of Robbins noted several former Pullman porters as well as "many common laborers, a few college graduates, and a sprinkling of sharecroppers and plantation hands fresh from the south" among early Robbins residents.[54]

In June 1939, Alfred O. Phillipp, from the Federal Writers' Project, visited Robbins and submitted a handwritten report to the WPA Folklore Project. While some bought modest ready-made houses, "many could only muster the down payment for a lot. As there were no building restrictions these latter suburban aspirants haphazardly gathered a quantity of second-hand lumbers (perhaps some old car siding) some sheet tin, same cheap roofing paper, and assembled what was merely intended to be a temporary abode. Later, when they worked and saved a little money, they would build 'real' homes. Certainly it was not their fault that these fond hopes were but infrequently consummated." Phillipp shared *Scribner's* writer H. C. Bunner's admiration of the shantytown builders' resourcefulness, as well as Bunner's tendency to romanticize the community constructed by outcasts from middle-class white society. He places the shantytown dweller in a distinct category. "The tenement dwelling city Negro and the plantation Negro are alike comparatively well known. Then there in the village or small town Negro who lives in a hovel on the ragged edge of a small community entirely controlled by white officials. But the dweller in Robbins is a true Negro suburbanite."[55]

By the time Phillipp visited Robbins, it was a town of 2,250 people, 70 percent of them on relief and many living in "shanties and dilapidated houses" that Phillipp had to admit "mar[red] its potential beauty." But Phillipp took issue with a previous WPA writer who implied "that shabby houses and shanties are Negro characteristics. Let me repudiate this insinuation most emphatically. Shanties and dilapidated houses are not racial characteristics, but economic factors. Poor people all over the world (regardless of race or color) live in hovels and inferior dwellings; while rich people live in fine houses." Phillipp is clearly moved by the resourcefulness and hard work of the African Americans he interviews in Robbins. Like Bunner 60 years before, Phillipp is not only educating his reader into the mysteries of shantytowns, but validating their existence. His argument for their intrinsic worth includes their inhabitants' triumph over long odds, the value they place on home and land ownership, and their sophisticated system of self-governance. At the time of his 1939 interviews, Phillipp noted that a large part of the "labor gang" digging drainage ditches for a nearby township was made up of African Americans from Robbins, showing that residents of this shantytown-cum-suburb were providing the labor for public improvement projects.[56]

As part of his investigation, Phillipp attended a meeting of the Village Board of Robbins, "a civic-political assembly unique in the Chicago region. It is the only incorporated area in Illinois administered exclusively by Negros." Here Phillipp touched on a point raised in descriptions of 1930s shantytowns: they often provided their residents a greater degree of participation in the political process than they could get in the larger society. Southerners unable to vote at home because of poll taxes had more say in the running of Hoovervilles and shantytowns outside their region than they did in their own hometowns. Transients who no longer had resident status anywhere, and therefore also could not vote, were at least able to participate in the governing of their makeshift, self-built communities.[57]

Robbins was one of a number of so-called African-American suburbs founded in the late nineteenth and early twentieth centuries. At least three others also started, or had self-built sections that qualified as shantytowns: the Cherry neighborhood founded outside of Charlotte, NC, in the late 1880s; Herring Hill in what is now the Georgetown neighborhood of D.C.; and the shantytown at Cumberland, MD, called Walnut Bottom. Architectural historian John Michael Vlach has identified similar African-American shantytowns in New Orleans, Mobile, AL, and Charleston, SC.[58]

A poem titled "Shanty," published in *Poetry* magazine in November 1927, distills the white elite view of African-American shantytowns. The ellipsis in the first line is in the original:

> This is a nigger shack . . .
> Walls held together by two pins,
> Sagged like a drunkard front and back;
> Roof made of old tomato tins
> Picked from an ash-heap, hammered flat;
> A chimney like a stove-in hat;
> Crates, coops, old boards and empty bins.

The "nigger shack" of the poem is a purely aesthetic experience; the poet is uninterested in the life of the inhabitants, although the adjective "drunkard" identifies them as morally suspect. The shanty is there to be consumed by a white viewer. As in many descriptions of shanties, reading against the grain yields insights, in this case a glimpse of the determined builder who picked through ash heaps and hammered tomato cans into siding, cobbling "crates, coops, old boards and empty bins" into a shelter. But in this image, the shack personifies the African-American builder.[59]

The opposite calculation animates several images of Beaver Slide produced a few years later by Hale Woodruff. In these striking images, human figures inform the viewer's response to the ramshackle buildings. Familiar elements—crooked houses, rocky wasteland, meandering stairways, muddy streets—recall iconic shantytown scenes. But Woodruff forces a more nuanced critique, insisting that the viewer weigh the force of the shanty inhabitants' personalities against the decrepit architecture of the shantytown. In *Shantytown,* the muscular figure of an African-American woman mounts the drooping stairway leading to a row of shanties. She wears high heels and a large hat, decorative elements at odds with the flimsiness of the stairs she climbs. In *Sunday Promenade,* an image from the same period printed posthumously, a wave of striding, smiling African-American men and women sweep down a Beaver Slide street lined with stores and a church. An aspidistra plant in a window signals the domesticity of the interior.[60]

In a laudatory review of Woodruff's 1934 murals *Shantytown* and *Mudhill Row,* the editor of the *Atlanta Constitution,* Ralph McGill, praised their modernist style but missed the nuance of the renderings. "Both of them hurt with garish poverty and their stark bleakness," he wrote. In *Mudhill Row,* "[t]he climbing hill of raw, red clay, eroded and twisted is a vista of ugliness and harshness. It speaks with a thousand silent tongues." They did speak with a thousand tongues, but their message was not merely bleak. Viewed through the lens of the people who live there, the meaning of the shantytown is transformed. The fractured shantytown roofline is defiant, not defeated. The facades are ratty but imposing, towering over the busy street. Like his contemporaries, Woodruff acknowledged the disappearance of shantytowns like Beaver Slide as inevitable; he titled one 1935 linocut, of a mule standing in front of a shanty, *Relics.* Like Edward Harrigan, who blows up the shanty at the end of *Squatter Sovereignty* in 1882, Woodruff did not argue for its survival. But at a time when Atlanta

"Going Home" 7/10 Hale Woodruff 35

Hale Woodruff and his art students were dubbed the "Outhouse School" for their renderings of poor Atlanta neighborhoods, such as "Shantytown" from 1934.

shantytowns were being demolished on his very doorstep, he took time to differ-
entiate between the buildings and the people. The people in Woodruff's shantytown images are not relics; they throb with modernity. Amid decay and destitution, Woodruff located humor, style, and optimism. Even as Scarlett O'Hara
drove her carriage across the movie screen and into the dangerous depths of a
postwar Atlanta shantytown, Woodruff commemorated the complexity of
African Americans living in its twentieth-century present.[61]

8

Depression-Era Shantytowns

I t's only a shanty in old Shanty Town," the singer croons, drawing out the vowels as the melody dips a full octave to land longingly on "town." "The roof is so slanty it touches the ground." The performer, his face smudged with charcoal and sporting a crumbled top hat, hobo-fashion, fixes his gaze on an invisible byway from the nation's past, located somewhere in the middle distance between the dance floor and the bar of the nightclub. Pressed and dressed couples smile from their tabletops, swaying to the familiar refrain. The swing band chugs along tunefully as the sentimental vista unfolds, inviting the listener to travel with the singer to a land, and a time, where a "tumbled down shack by an old railroad track, like a millionaire's mansion is calling me back." He finishes the song on a high note, emotionally and musically:

> I'm up in the world,
> but I'd give the world to be where I used to be,
> A heavenly nest, where I rest the best,
> means more than the world to me.[1]

The performer, Ted Lewis, was known for his sentimental renditions of ballads, often performed in costume as a lovable tramp. Released as a single in 1932, "In a Shanty in Old Shanty Town" reached number one on the charts and stayed there for 10 weeks. During that time, unemployment was well on its way to a high of more than 20 percent, reached the next year; some 1.5 million people were already homeless. The Depression was in full swing and would persist until 1939, when the country's entry into World War II ushered in an economic recovery; even that year, unemployment stood at 17 percent. Yet the song that captured the imagination of the public during the height of the

Depression was a nostalgic embrace of poverty. In this reimagining of the life of the poor, the shanty operated as a central icon. The rickety shack by the railroad track was something to revere, something to aspire to. It was more valuable than "the millionaire's mansion," despite its material inferiority. The singer, who is "up in the world," wants to return to the "heavenly nest" of the shanty: only there can he find rest. And, as the last verse informs us, his "queen" is waiting there for him, "with a silvery crown." Shantytown, the singer concludes, "is more than a palace . . . it's my everything." It is a metaphorical heaven.[2]

If this wistful 1932 recording were an isolated instance of shanties being used in this romantic, nostalgic way at the height of a crushing Depression, one might dismiss it as an example of the middle-class elites pulling the wool of "happy poverty" over the eyes of a suffering nation. (Ted Lewis, who called himself "the high-hatted tragedian of song," was known for starting his live performances by asking the crowd, "Is everybody happy?") But the song was recorded more than three dozen times over the next four decades, by many different types of performers, and the shanty icon resonated with multiple meanings. Belle Baker, a ragtime singer known for her Yiddish-themed torch songs, also recorded it in 1932. Alice Joy, an old-time singer with a distinctive chesty voice, sang it so often on her radio show that an edition of the sheet music featured her on the cover. The song appeared in two movies and two more recordings in the 1930s and inspired a holiday spinoff, a six-minute animated cartoon called *The Shanty Where Santy Claus Lives,* in 1933. ("They're making toys / for little girls and boys / in the shanty where Santy Claus lives . . ."). Seven more versions of the song appeared in the 1940s, and a dozen more in the 1950s—including a silky-smooth version by Doris Day in 1951 and a rockabilly rendering by Jerry Lee Lewis in 1958. Fats Domino recorded it. Dizzy Gillespie recorded it. It appeared on a collection called *Songs Everyone Knows* in 1960 and another collection, an oddity that proved it had truly permeated popular culture, titled *51 Popular Organ Skating Favorites* in 1964. It was recorded in swing style, doo-wop, honky-tonk, cha-cha, jazz, and country. Its vogue across four decades, in forms popular with a wide variety of American tastes, proves the enduring power of the shanty and the shantytown as emblems of fortitude and resilience in the twentieth century; poverty itself became a badge of honor during the Depression—perhaps even a mark of patriotism—and the shanty was one of its logos. It became a symbol of resilience in the face of poverty, dislocation, and even war.[3]

Shantytowns became familiar points of reference in fiction and movies as well. Depression-era novels such as *Shanty Ann* and *A Tree for Peter*, both written for children or young adults, were idylls of happy poverty narrated by resourceful and philosophical unemployed people, and their equally plucky offspring, living in shantytowns of their own making. Hollywood also discovered the shantytown. Joel McCrae in *Sullivan's Travels* and William Powell in *My Man Godfrey* remember what really matters in life when they land, down on their luck, in Depression-era shantytowns. These novels, movies, and songs turned the specter of eviction and homelessness on its head starting in the 1930s. They located values of resourcefulness, community, and hard work in the shantytowns built and occupied by displaced Americans. This cultural representation of the shanty, shanty builders, and shantytowns persisted through the 1950s and into the 1960s. It was taken up by hillbilly and country stars, including Johnny Cash, and acquired a hardscrabble, rebellious sheen.

During the Depression, however, shantytowns represented both the material condition of the poor, as dispossessed and unemployed workers moved between shantytowns looking for work; and a radical alteration in the nature of self-built housing. On a landscape of economic collapse, the shifting meanings of the shanty tracked the collision of individualism and collectivism in American culture. In 1932, the same year that "In a Shanty in Old Shanty Town" was making its way up the charts, a destitute but determined band of World War I veterans converged on Washington, DC, and built a vast shantytown along the Anacostia River, within view of the Capitol. The troops, who called themselves the Bonus Expeditionary Forces, had marched to Washington from as far away as Portland, OR, gathering members and strength as they progressed from one city to the next. Their goal was to personally ask Pres. Hoover and Congress to pay them their war bonuses early, because their entreaties so far had been rebuffed. They needed the money to weather the deepening economic depression. The bonus was not in dispute, only the timing of it; they wanted it immediately, instead of 1945, as legislation promised. Some 20,000 people from 22 states marched in the spring of 1932. Some could not make it all the way to Washington, and congregated in shantytowns they christened "Hoovervilles" in honor of Pres. Hoover. "Hard times are still Hoovering Over Us," read one explicit protest sign. Hoovervilles sprouted in cities and towns across the country, from Seattle to Brooklyn, some as big as small towns.[4]

As the Depression worsened, dispossessed families built shantytowns in cities and towns across the nation, such as this one in Seattle, WA.

The stalwarts arrived in Washington in mid-June, assembling for a mass rally on the steps of the Capitol on July 5. But they did not convince Pres. Hoover to change his mind. Days turned into weeks. To house themselves and their families, the war veterans built a shantytown across the Anacostia River. They called it Camp Marks in honor of the police captain, S. J. Marks, whose district included Anacostia. Marks, along with D.C. Chief of Police Pellam D. Glassford, refused to follow Pres. Hoover's orders to disband and demolish the encampment, and instead befriended the veterans. Shacks and shanties erupted on the landscape as the soldiers built shelters more lasting and comfortable than the tents they started with. Following military protocol, they erected shanties in straight rows, uniformly spaced, marked with street signs. They built central kitchens and dining areas, and as the weeks of protests stretched into the summer, a post office, a barber shop, and library. Drinking and begging were prohibited. The residents of Camp Marks collaborated on vaudeville nights and other family entertainments. Classes were held for children, and the protesters published their own newspaper, the *BEF News*. At the height of Jim Crow, housing and other activities were integrated.[5]

Camp Marks soon become a tourist attraction, with Washington residents pouring over the bridge on weekends to visit the shantytown; enterprising vendors sold food and postcards of Camp Marks. Several show shanties decorated with patriotic slogans or images. John Dos Passos vividly described the vast shantytown in an article for *The New Republic*. "[T]he men are sleeping in little leantos built out of old newspapers, cardboard boxes, packing crates, bits of tin or tarpaper roofing, old shutters, every kind of cockeyed makeshift shelter from the rain scraped together out of the city dump." Yet the shantytown was orderly and busy, reminiscent of a boot camp "with its bugle calls, its messlines, greasy K.P.'s, M.P.'s" and rows of latrines the men dubbed "Hoover Villas."[6]

On July 28, a resolute Pres. Hoover finally prevailed. Chief Glassford, persuaded to disband the camp, arrived with 100 troops to execute the president's order. But the anxious president had called in the U.S. army. Under the command of Gen. Douglas Macarthur, tanks rolled through the streets of the capital. Troops, who he had been training secretly in riot control, charged across the Anacostia Bridge on horseback, sabers aloft, tear gas canisters flying, and set the entire shantytown on fire. In one vivid image, taken by an Associated Press photographer, a flaming shanty is silhouetted against the dome of the Capitol, wordlessly illuminating the tragic irony of enlisted soldiers burning down an encampment of World War I veterans who had come to beg for their war bonuses. It was the end of what is perhaps the most famous shantytown in U.S. history.[7]

The Bonus March did not get the veterans what they wanted, but it played a decisive role in shaping federal policy during the Depression. The moniker "Hoovervilles," attached to shantytowns across the nation, denounced Pres. Hoover's policies visibly on the landscape and helped Roosevelt win the election. The rout of Camp Marks rallied support for the poor and dispossessed nationwide and helped lay the groundwork for public support of Pres. Franklin D. Roosevelt's New Deal policies. The 1932 construction of Camp Marks was not the first time a shantytown had become part of a larger orchestration of sustained protest: unemployed workers calling themselves Coxey's Army, after leader Jacob Coxey, built encampments on two protest marches to Washington, DC, in 1894 and 1914; and Streeterville, the shantytown George Wellington "Cap" Streeter developed on a sandbar in Lake Michigan, became a site of protest against real estate developers in the 1880s.

The depression and droughts of the 1930s swelled the ranks of the homeless poor across the country. Many slogged from town to city or field to orchard looking for work and a place to live. Families, youths, and single women crowded into inner cities, renting rooms in lodging houses and tenements or, if penniless, bedding down in the shelters and missions run by cities or charitable organizations. Transient men, romanticized in the 1930s as hoboes, often lived in "jungles" at the edges of cities or near railroads or ports, or in flophouses on the edge of downtowns. Out West, families traveled from cheap auto camp to cheaper auto camp, in an exodus memorialized in John Steinbeck's *Grapes of Wrath*, speeded on their way by donations of gas and oil from overwhelmed relief agencies whose solution to transients was to keep them moving past the city line. But an estimated 100,000 under- or unemployed people spent the 1930s not in hobo jungles, center-city lodging houses or auto camps, but in the dozens of American shantytowns known as Hoovervilles.[8]

Although shanties in the twentieth century, like those in the nineteenth, were generally constructed mostly of wood, they sometimes reflected the availability of geographically specific natural resources. Migrants built log shanties along the Iron River in Michigan. A writer for the Federal Writers' Project saw "palmetto-thatched huts with floors of rough boards or hard

Troops under the command of General Douglas Macarthur set fire to the shantytown built by the Bonus Army on the Anacostia flats in Washington, DC, in 1932.

packed dirt" in the Florida Everglades in 1938. After the 1920s, car and truck parts appear regularly in shanties, sometimes forming the basis of the structure. As the Farm Security Administration photographs of the 1930s and 1940s demonstrate, some shanty builders showed great creativity in the matter of siding, roofing, front doors, and general decoration. One FSA photograph shows a shanty completely sheathed in old license plates, while others attest to the popularity of metal advertisement panels for use as siding. Some shanties have covered porches; some have fences that delineate private space around the house. One shanty sports a front porch laced with ginger-bread latticework. The efficacy of the shanty form is suggested by one of the more remarkable FSA photographs, which shows the "minimal house" prototype constructed in 1938 in Arvin, CA: a slant-roofed two-room shed with a protruding metal stovepipe that looks remarkably like a shanty. FSA designers seemed to consciously be imitating the style chosen for self-building by many of the people it hoped to house.[9]

Field workers, particularly those employed or commissioned by the National Travelers Aid Societies, reported on the independence and ingenuity of shantytown dwellers, who often confounded the efforts of relief agencies to move them into alternative housing. The governor of California suggested to a congressional committee in 1940 that the best solution to the migrant housing problem would be to provide services to the self-built shack towns: "If a framework had been provided for these communities, in the sense of adequate roads, proper sanitation, water and sewer facilities, then even if the housing was makeshift and improvised, the community might still have shown definite development and improvement over a period of years." But policymakers in Washington did not take seriously such alternatives; officials at the Works Progress Administration (WPA) did not even read many of the reports they commissioned on the status of homeless transients from 1935–1940. The alternative model for housing the poor that shantytowns presented was never considered.[10]

In the early years of the Depression, shantytowns were often a better option than the other alternatives open to transients looking for work: municipal lodging houses, flophouses, or the mission. Many resented the mandatory attendance at religious services demanded by missions. A 1933 article in *The New Republic* recounted the municipal lodger's experience: standing in long lines monitored by the police; reciting personal information to strangers; stripping for medical exams, showers and delousing; surrendering their

clothes and personal possessions for fumigation; bad food; lights out at
6:00 p.m.; communal sleeping rooms that smelled of disinfectant and human
odors. "Men were fed and housed in large numbers in one building without
even the privacy of cattle kept in separate stalls." These disadvantages recall
the drawbacks of Freedmen's Villages experienced by African Americans
after the Civil War, with the federal government again filling the role of disingenuous shepherd, prodding transients on to the next town with promises of
available jobs or more appropriate housing. Shantytowns, which offered privacy and conviviality, were often a cut above not only municipal lodging
houses and missions, but hobo "jungles" on the edges of cities, where transient men (for the most part) bedded down in tents or shelters made of cardboard and bits of scrap lumber.[11]

There were numerous Hoovervilles in New York City during the 1930s.
Commissioned to paint murals of New York life on the ceiling of the rotunda
in the U.S. Customs House in New York City, artist Reginald Marsh made
sketches for a panel called *Soup Kitchen [East River Shanties]*. Now in the collection of the Museum of the City of New York, the watercolor sketch shows
homeless African-American men gathered around a fire in a trash can, and a
woman clutching a baby in front of a wooden shanty as her husband forages
for materials nearby. Several other artists, including Louis Leon Ribak,
Samuel Thal, and Charles Bayley Cook also painted Hoovervilles in the 1930s.
One of the largest shantytowns in New York was Hoover City, located at
Henry and Clinton streets in Brooklyn. By 1933, there were 600 people living
in the 200 or so shanties in Hoover City, including a new baby. In addition to
the usual scrap lumber, old pipes, and ash cans used to build shanties in previous decades, the Hoover City homes incorporated discarded truck bodies
and floors made out of newfangled materials like linoleum. The moribund
shipping industry also provided useful refuse: one resident made a bed out of
two old metal sailors' bunks.[12]

But Hoover City had much in common with its historical antecedents.
Furnishings were salvaged from the dump and repaired, and residents planted
vegetable gardens. One-room shelters were added onto a room at a time, and
improvements were made to original shelters. There were no city services, but
residents got water from a nearby hydrant. Neighbors visited each other and
seemed to welcome new settlers without remark. Unemployed residents were
actively looking for work. The police patrolled the area frequently but did not

(a)

(b)

(*c*)

Depression-era shanties reflected the creativity and resourcefulness of their destitute residents.

consider the shantytown a problem. The population was relatively stable. "Few people moved out after they established themselves," even in winter. If they did decide to move, they sometimes sold their shanties to newcomers for as much as $50. And when asked, residents professed their preference for shantytown life over the available alternatives, citing a "sense of personal freedom," independence, and the very practical advantage of being able to return home after looking for work in the mornings—a choice not open to residents of missions, flops and lodging houses, which prohibited daytime occupancy. The residents boasted that shantytown dwellers had resisted even the "Reds" who had attempted to organize them. That is quite a scene to contemplate: reformers trying to convince desperately poor people that they had a right to complain, then being treated as agitators who had tried "to break their spirit."[13]

Far from the urban environs of Brooklyn, residents of Arizona and California shantytowns were living in strikingly similar circumstances and expressing similar preferences for shantytown life over the alternatives. A Phoenix shantytown beneath the Central Avenue Bridge on the outskirts of town was the refuge of cotton-pickers who could no longer afford the rent for cabins at the nearby auto camp in 1931. Concrete piers provided one ready-made wall for each shanty. Frances G. Blair, the executive secretary of the Tucson Red Cross, found the living conditions so bad they were almost "indescribable," yet she did a thorough and compassionate job of it in her report to the President's Organization on Unemployment Relief. Between 50 and 60 concrete piers supported the bridge, and families constructed shanties against the piers, using "pieces of cartons, old tin, bits of carpet or gunny-sack—anything that can be had is used to build a bit of shelter." The residents, which ranged between 50 and 85 or so families depending on the season, numbered the piers and their shacks accordingly, using them as "addresses" when they applied for public relief. Some stayed a few days or weeks, others several months. The river spanned by the bridge was dry most of the year, and drinking water had to be carried from the auto camp. Yet the out-of-work pickers preferred their shantytown to the admittedly limited alternatives. "When the floods came last winter the county authorities moved the families to the fair grounds, but as soon as the place was habitable they moved back under the bridge."[14]

The 1933 Federal Employment Relief Act (FERA) funded a Federal Transient Program that at its peak served 300,000 transients in 44 states.

The program established several hundred labor camps to house transient workers—a drop in the bucket of the housing problem. While the camps were physically more attractive than the municipal shelters, they were unpopular with some transients and many local residents. "[C]ritical voices complained that the shelters, recreational facilities, and three square meals a day were nothing more than a government dole that supported and encouraged transiency at the taxpayers' expense." The inhabitants were not the unemployed in search of work, but "a motley group of fugitives, misfits, handicapped, bums, hoboes and tramps," as a former director of one camp attested in a two-part feature for *The Saturday Evening Post*. City leaders also cited the negative impact on property values. In Saratoga Springs, city leaders worried about the proximity of a camp to the new Saratoga Spa resort and requested its closure, even though it housed men who had worked on the construction crews that built the spa.[15]

While some transients found the camps helpful, many others complained about the food, the harsh discipline—including incarceration—and poor management of the labor camps, including embezzling of camp funds and food rations. A more widespread problem was the distance from the camps to cities, where transients needed to go to look for jobs. As one participant explained, "They cared for us first in city shelters, raising the standard of physical care. Then they shunted us away from the cities into isolated camps on the fringe of civilization, when most of us were city workers and city dwellers." A state commission appointed to study the problem in New York recommended that in the future, transient camps be located not in the countryside but on the periphery of urban centers—the same prescription for exiling African-American shanty dwellers prescribed by the Freedmen's Bureaus in cities like Atlanta and Washington during and after Reconstruction.[16]

The self-built artistry and self-governance of shantytowns reflected that requisite New Deal virtue, self-reliance. The individualism of shantytown dwellers might have resonated with New Deal efforts to provide jobs instead of cash payments, which reformers saw as fundamental to preserving Americans' independence. But the government did not perceive it that way. After only two years, the Roosevelt administration canceled the Federal Transient Program, making transients eligible for work relief programs instead. But transients found it hard to compete with local residents for scarce WPA jobs, and in the second half of the decade, the transient problem intensified. Families took to the road, often heading for the Southwest and California, and roadside shanty-towns proliferated. Their experience was captured by Carleton Beals, the writer of a January 1938 article in *Forum and Century*. He set out to catalog shanty-town conditions in the San Joaquin Valley, inviting readers to join him on his fact-finding mission in much the same way H. C. Bunner had done on his visit to a Manhattan shantytown in 1880. On a visit to the Hooverville outside Bakersfield, CA, Beals noted typical features of the shantytown landscape: shel-ters made of "flattened oil tins, burlap, cardboard and rags" sprouting "tilted rusty smokestack[s]," one with a front door fashioned from a cardboard Montgomery Ward refrigerator box. Several hundred families lived in this "foul slough" located, notably, across the street from the Chamber of Commerce. The Bakersfield "jungle" was typical of dozens of such communities across the West and Southwest, Beals wrote, where transient labor camps erected by the federal government were only "a step above" such Hoovervilles.[17]

Yet these Hoovervilles seem also to have coalesced into functioning com-munities. Beals recounts the story of a federal aid worker who went out to a Hooverville to distribute rare federal relief funds, but could not find several qualified recipients at home. Not to worry, she reported: "they always divvy up everything anyway." And Beals notes the prevalence of Pentecostal reli-gion in the California Hoovervilles, many of which had biblical names: The Angel, The Burning Bush, The One God, The Crusaders. Beals notes the fre-quent sight of itinerant pastors in Packards with "Jesus is Here" printed on the side, traveling to preach at Pentecostal churches erected by the residents of many Hoovervilles. Where they lacked church buildings, he says, pastors provided tents for the services. One pastor even rented out home sites to Hooverville residents, who were required to pay a tithe to his church as well. Beals notes a 1930s innovation in shantytown living, the "elaborate home-made trailers" that some transients pulled behind their cars, often "stacked high with dirty bedding, cots, belongings, tents, an iron stove." Running boards supported battered trunks, galvanized tubs, sometimes a dog or accordion. Dismantled and discarded, cars and trucks were used as building supplies for stationary shanties like Hoover City in Brooklyn. Out West, they transported shantytown trappings from place to place as their owners fruit-lessly looked for work.[18]

Bell Gardens, in Los Angeles, provides another glimpse of shantytown life in the late 1930s and early 1940s. Typical of the "Little Oklahomas, Little

Arkansas's and Little Texases" ringing the outskirts of California cities, Bell Gardens had boomed between its inception in 1934 and 1941, when it was cited in testimony given to the House Select Committee to Investigate the Interstate Migration of Destitute Citizens. As they had in Hoover City, market principals operated in Bell Gardens. According to Henry Hill Collins Jr., chronicler of the congressional hearings, migrants paid $200 to $375 for microscopic "garden farms" in this "mushroom community," paying a few dollars down and a few dollars each month. (Since this scheme at least held out the hope of eventual ownership, it may have compared favorably to doling out $1 a month in rent to the Oklahoma City health department for a similarly microscopic lot at the Elm Grove Community Camp.) Bell Gardens was peopled by recent arrivals, but the housing they built and the obstacles residents faced were much the same. At first they erected "flimsy and insubstantial" shelters of scrap lumber and tin, but soon residents could be found "gradually 'improving' as best they could" without the benefit of streets, water, or sanitation. Other similar shantytowns were to be found in the Southwest, often along rivers or near dumps. Oklahoma City, Collins declared, housed "the largest and worst congregation of migrant hovels between the Mississippi River and the Sierras." Bell Gardens was one of the largest shantytowns, by 1940 "a vast suburban slum" of 26,000 residents—making it larger than the capitals of 14 states at the time.[19]

Because of shifting definitions and methods of counting shantytown dwellers, it is hard to pinpoint how many there were in the 1930s. Two studies from 1933 provide the best sources for estimating the size of the shantytown population. In January, the National Committee on Care of Transient and Homeless (NCCTH), an independent group of social workers, academics, and concerned citizens, conducted a census of 809 cities in 48 states and the District of Columbia. It found that 370,403 people had been served by transient or homeless relief agencies in the cities polled, and from this number extrapolated a national homeless population of 1.5 million. Of that total, about half were transients and half were "local homeless," suggesting a non-transient homeless population of about 750,000 people. The study, the first of its kind to distinguish between local and transient homeless, did not specify how many of either group were living in shantytowns. Just three months later, in March, the Federal Transient Program conducted its own census and found slightly fewer homeless people—201,596 transients in

765 cities polled—from which it extrapolated a homeless population of about 1.25 million people. Noting an alarming increase in the number of homeless families since the previous December, the FTP broke down its findings according to types of shelters occupied by the homeless. Some 15,658 people were living in shantytowns, another 18,039 in "jungles, box cars, etc." Using the same multiple the FTP used to arrive at the total transient population, that extrapolates out to about 94,000 people nationwide living in shanty-towns in 1934. That number may be conservative. The FTP created a separate category for families, so it is impossible to know how many of the approximately 19,000 homeless families (or roughly 86,000 people) nationwide were living in shantytowns. Also, only people who had appealed to agencies for relief were counted, a flaw that led to undercounting in every category. Finally, the census admits that the numbers of people listed as living in "jungles, caves and shanty towns" are "only general estimates," a phrase that makes the whole project suspect as a source of shantytown population estimates. But it is the best estimate available.[20]

The next time the federal government took a close look at the transient population, which was the only context in which shantytown residents were studied, was the 1941 congressional hearings on destitute migrants, called the Tolan hearings after its chairman, Rep. John H. Tolan of California. The investigation covered agricultural and non-agricultural transient labor, and investigators collected more than three million words of oral and written testimony, including interviews with transients and migrants. Housing continued to be a major problem after the demise of the Federal Transient Program, the report concluded, with many unemployed transients living in shack towns in the suburbs. "In the words of a witness before the committee, 'poor housing is without question one of the worst results of interstate migration.' Thousands of migrants throughout the country still live in shack towns, usually in suburban neighborhoods." But as the nation mobilized for war, the hearings were quickly reoriented away from the problems of transient housing and care and toward the sudden shortage of housing for defense workers; the committee changed its name to Select Committee Investigating National Defense Migration. Shantytowns did not disappear, but they did shrink in number, especially in the Southwest and California, as people got defense jobs. The expansion of cities and the growth of suburbs in the 1940s also eliminated shantytown locations, and the construction of public housing for the nation's poor may have absorbed former shantytown residents. But the denouement of shantytowns was hastened by demolition. Demolition of shantytowns and squatter settlements in the 1930s and early 1940s were, in fact, the dress rehearsal for the urban renewal of the 1950s.[21]

In the 1930s, shantytowns were reconceptualized as slums, a sleight-of-mind that required policymakers to ignore much of what field workers and journalists were telling them: shantytown dwellers were resourceful, self-reliant people who valued work and wanted to live in communities of single-family dwellings near their places of employment. Historians were similarly distracted. Contemporary accounts from the 1910s through the 1930s offered detailed descriptions of shantytowns that are seldom if ever incorporated into the historiography. While historians have written copiously on the culture of tenement dwellers, hoboes, and ghetto residents, they have not shown the same interest in shantytowns. As a result, the historiography lost sight of a viable alternative to public housing, and helped perpetuate a one-dimensional view of the poor as helpless, disorganized people trapped by their environments in a "culture of poverty" from which only liberals, experts, and bureaucrats could deliver them. The shantytown model might have been preserved, at least, in the historiography. The loss of that model—a space in which poor people constructed their own homes and communities—makes it difficult to picture poor urban people today in any other landscapes than slums or public housing projects.[22]

The identification of shantytowns as permanent slums in the 1930s was a key step toward the historical and cultural amnesia surrounding shantytowns today. The often inaccurate idea that shantytowns were temporary communities had never saved them from the bulldozer's wrath, but it had insulated them somewhat from the intrusion of local governments. Once shantytowns were declared permanent slums, however, they were vulnerable not only to residential or infrastructure development but to the large-scale clearance that eventually became known as urban renewal. By the 1930s, researchers had been insisting for several decades that people, not economic conditions, created slums. "The slum harbors many sorts of people: the criminal, the radical, the bohemian, the migratory worker, the immigrant, the unsuccessful, the queer and unadjusted," wrote a 1929 housing expert of a shantytown along the Chicago River. Dangerous levels of "freedom and individualism"—by which the writer meant lack of trust and neighborliness—thrived in these areas, populated by "marooned families" and transients. These "dregs," the writer concluded, "are not really a part of American life." Once a group of people is declared un-American, tearing down their houses gets a lot easier. Two years later in 1931, the committee studying slums for President Hoover's Conference on Home Building and Home Ownership summed up the professional wisdom on slums, based on three decades of housing surveys conducted in major American cities: "The slum is more than an economic condition. It is a social phenomenon in which the attitudes, ideas, ideals and practices play an important part."[23]

The reform position on the causes of slums shifted in the late 1930s under the influence of urban planners such as James Ford, whose classic 1936 treatise, *Slums and Housing,* became a key text of urban renewal. Ford rejected the notion that residents were to blame for slums, insisting instead that slums were economic phenomena identified by "age, neglect, and low standards or practices of sanitation," not the perceived moral stature of their residents. While rejecting the moralistic definition of a slum, Ford continued to champion government intervention to protect public health and safety. That included greater powers for the police and widespread demolition authority. Ford's redefinition of a slum recalls a Supreme Court justice's famous definition of pornography: you know it when you see it. "Shanty towns and squatter settlements, even though new, are also slums," Ford added near the end of his first chapter, entitled "What is a Slum?" By the time of the 1941 Tolan hearings on the migration of destitute citizens, the equation of shantytowns with slums was complete. "In California . . . shack towns have developed. Without plan or civic supervision, they develop into small communities surrounded by gas stations, stores, and beer parlors." One might have reasonably predicted that such small communities would improve over time, but that was not the conclusion reached by the congressional committee: "They are the beginnings of permanent rather than temporary slums."[24]

Urban planners in the 1930s removed the protection that their perceived transitoriness had previously provided shantytowns, tying their fate to that of inner city slums. The consequences were soon visible. The FSA and its precursor, the Resettlement Administration, evicted squatters from condemned land in the Southwest and West, sometimes building new migrant housing on the same site. Public money was sometimes used to demolish shantytowns standing in the way of waterfront parks and other public improvements, as a reporter for *Survey Graphic* discovered in 1935: "Directly in view from the dock site was Dayton shantytown, one of the most depressing small town slums in this section of the country. Not a pretty beginning for a waterfront park. TVA agreed to buy this land . . . The slum was demolished. Now the zoning board and the men from the State Plan Commission are trying to clean up things in the part of town where residents of the old shantytown have gone."[25]

The most famous invocation of a shanty settlement in popular fiction appeared in 1939 in Laura Ingalls Wilder's book, *By the Shores of Silver Lake*, the fifth in the series of nine Little House books based on the Ingalls family's pioneering experiences on the western frontier in the 1880s. *Little House on the Prairie* and its companions caught the imagination of the suffering 1930s public by extolling the virtues of hard work, perseverance, and frugality in the face of economic distress, with family ties and teamwork triumphing over all obstacles to create meaning on a landscape of poverty. In the earlier books, the Ingalls family does not live in shanties, but they do live in several very modest houses, including a log cabin, that establish simple, self-built houses as an American virtue—along with the mobility that made frontier settlements possible. In the fourth book, *On the Banks of Plum Creek*, published in 1937, the family lives in a "dugout" house in Minnesota. Essentially a sod shanty, in that it was self-built out of materials at hand, the dugout house is an ancient type of mud hut built into the side of a hill or river bank, or sometimes dug out of the very earth; in photographs of dugouts, often only the roofs are visible. (In 1935, in the midst of the Little House books, the song "Little Old Sod Shanty on the Claim," was released, leveraging both the popularity of the books and of "In a Shanty in Old Shantytown.") The walls of dugouts were frequently made of sod, cut out of the prairie in rectangular patches. Sometimes called "soddies," they were sturdy if damp, and very popular on the prairie where wood was scarce. The description of the Ingalls' dugout indicates its front wall was made of sod. Interior walls of earth, carved out of the ground itself, were whitewashed, and the earth floor was kept smooth. Grass grew on the roof, further camouflaging the house. In the book, the mother remarks that someone could walk over the house "and never know it's here." The family planted morning glory vines around the front door, and made makeshift window panes out of greased paper.[26]

The family occupies more shanties in the next book, *By the Shores of Silver Lake*. After moving yet again, this time to De Smet, SD, they live at first in a railroad camp, essentially a shantytown, and then in a tar paper claim shanty—so-called because it advertised the family's legal claim on the land—they build on their homestead. "The little house and its half a slanting roof were built of rough boards with cracks between. There were no windows and no door in the doorway, but the family is thankful for a floor." The shanty looked "like a yellow toy on the rolling prairie." Claim shanties were made with widely-spaced vertical studs, rudimentary boxed windows and doors, and a layer of tar paper held on with lath (thin strips of wood). Looking something like a train box car, they resembled the simplest urban shanties, including the one-room shanties often visible in the background or on the edges of DeLancey Walker Gill's shantytown drawings of Washington, DC, in the early 1880s. In Wilder's book, the mother says their claim shanty looked like "half of a woodshed split in two." While the Ingalls are building their claim shanty, Almanzo Wilder—Ingalls's future husband—and his brother are shown building sod shanties on their Silver Lake claims.[27]

The family is still living in the shanty, not yet weather-proofed, at the beginning of the next book in the series, *Little Town on the Prairie,* published in 1941. As in the earlier books, the shanty is presented as something to be proud of, a product of risk undertaken not only for the good of one's own family, but the nation as a whole. The shantytown community is also presented in a positive light, full of individuals fiercely pursuing their own opportunities but cooperating and supporting their neighbors, and especially newcomers like the Ingalls, at every turn.

A similarly wholesome ambiance fills the shantytowns at the center of three movies made in the mid-1930s: *Man's Castle, My Man Godfrey,* and *Sullivan's Travels. Man's Castle,* 1935, starring Spencer Tracy as the shantytown swell who takes in homeless Loretta Lynn, got a "dismal" reception from the public. *Sullivan's Travels,* a 1941 Preston Sturges comedy starring Joel McCrae, got mixed reviews but has entered the pantheon of critically acclaimed Depression-era films. *My Man Godfrey,* a shantytown fable released in 1936, was successful with both critics and movie-goers, garnering six Academy Awards and going down in movie history as the first film to be nominated in all four acting categories. The movie charmed audiences with its depiction of a "forgotten man" played by William Powell, who is plucked out of a Manhattan shantytown by Carole Lombard's character, a flighty heiress named Irene Bullock, who is participating in a decadent scavenger hunt with her boozy high-society friends; in addition to a "forgotten man," players must bring back a goat. The movie opens with Irene and her friends converging on the shantytown, where Irene spots Godfrey, who is dressed in the dirty, disheveled clothing of a hobo. Within minutes, however, having won the game for Irene, he is clean as a pin and serving as the family's butler. The almost menacing frivolity of the Bullocks is enacted in various bits of business involving stolen pearls, tea parties, smarmy Lotharios, and lots of drinking; through it all Godfrey stands erect, literally and figuratively. His presumably inferior social position combines with his obvious rectitude and good sense to embarrass his wealthy employers in the eyes of the audience, who suspect there is something Godfrey is not telling us.[28]

And there is: Godfrey's secret is that he, too, is from the upper class, and was cast into shantytown by a bizarre series of misunderstandings. Godfrey saves the Bullock family fortune in the end, gaining the love of Irene, which he doesn't quite seem to want. The shantytown—a settlement of tin and board shanties along the East River—appears twice more, each time marking an important turn in the plot. About an hour into the movie, Godfrey makes a mysterious visit to his former shantytown, later revealed to have been a fact-finding mission in his scheme to transform the site. His former mates greet him enthusiastically, and Godfrey, standing beside a trash heap with the Queensboro Bridge looming behind him, delivers a soliloquy on honorable poverty and the men who personify it: "Here," he says, taking in the landscape, "we have some very fashionable apartment houses, over there is a very swanky nightclub, while down here men starve for want of a job." He sums up what he learned during his time living in the shantytown: "One thing I discovered was that the only difference between a derelict and a man is a job." We see what came of Godfrey's soul-searching the next time we see shantytown, at the very end of the film. The bridge is there, and the river, but all else is changed. The dump has been transformed into "The Dump," a glamorous nightclub on the site of the swampy, trash-strewn settlement where Godfrey had his epiphany. In theme park fashion, the former shanty dwellers park the cars, serve the drinks, and wait on tables outfitted in tuxedos. Presumably, they live somewhere else now.

My Man Godfrey affirms the resilience and the work ethic of the dispossessed poor, one of many such movies to do so during this period. Like those, it valorizes the poor without seeking to inconvenience the affluent. But the demolition of the shantytown, and the clumsy transformation of the shanty dwellers into valets, barmen, and food servers—essentially the transformation Godfrey himself undergoes as a result of the dissolute scavenger hunt that opens the film—argues for a more pointed reading. For all its validation of honest poverty, and its skewering of the vain and shallow rich, *My Man Godfrey* is a capitalist fantasy. Poverty is cured not by government programs or systemic change, certainly not by a moral accounting of the rich and powerful, but by the largesse of high society: it is Godfrey, who turns out to be a financial wizard as well as a Harvard graduate and descendant of the Mayflower, who "saves" shantytown by building a nightclub and then hiring the former denizens of the shantytown to work there. The destitute men are no longer "forgotten," but not due to any sort of class reckoning. For most of the movie, Godfrey acts as moral barometer, embodying qualities of common sense, wit, and fortitude that the film locates in the lower classes—they emerge, quite specifically, from the shantytown in the form of Godfrey. Efforts to humiliate him fail, again because of his superior character. Yet the film unwinds itself by championing Wall Street, not Main Street, and charity, not entitlement. The shantytown's transformation into "The Dump" is played for laughs, but it mocks the very people it pretends to honor, in the fictional world of the film and on the streets of Depression-era America.[29]

Sullivan's Travels, which appeared in 1941, hit many of the same themes but with a heavier cudgel. Joel McCrae plays John L. Sullivan, a movie director disgusted with the shallowness of his own successful movies, who resolves to make a serious, socially relevant film based on a novel called *Oh Brother, Where Art Thou*—a title adopted by the Coen brothers for their sardonic 2000 film of the same name. Against the advice of the only working people he knows, his butler and his valet, Sullivan disguises himself as a "forgotten man" and sets off to experience first-hand the lives of the dispossessed. Trailed by a double-decker bus kitted out with all mod-cons, at his studio boss's insistence, Sullivan accomplishes little until he slips the leash and hitchhikes back to Los Angeles, where he befriends a failed young actress played by Veronica Lake. Known only as "The Girl," Lake soon discovers the truth about Sullivan but joins forces with him nonetheless. A hopelessly tangled plot ensues, ending with a case of mistaken identity that first lands Sullivan in prison, and then gets him out—and into the waiting arms of The Girl. Along the way the audience watches Sullivan tramp through soup kitchens, homeless shelters, railroad yards, and a labor camp; one long montage takes place largely in a Hooverville.[30]

Sullivan sets out on a disingenuous errand to experience—to consume, really—poor people's hardships. His scheme is no less self-serving or decadent than Irene Bullock's scavenger hunt at the beginning of *My Man Godfrey*: they are both spoiled rich kids too self-absorbed to understand how condescending their games are. Irene ends the film no wiser than she started; Godfrey is inspired by his shantytown stint to reclaim his role as lord of the manner. Sullivan, however, is genuinely changed, but only because his game gets away from him, and he is thrust into the actual lives of the poor and dispossessed. The Hoovervilles in *Sullivan's Travels* are not the affable places they are in *My Man Godfrey* or "In a Shanty in Old Shanty Town." They are always uncomfortable and occasionally dangerous. But Sullivan is a better man at the end for having been poor, as is Godfrey. The movie stymied patrons looking for the belly laughs Sturges usually delivered, although over time critics recognized it as one of Sturges's best films, perhaps his masterpiece. Appearing two years after the book *Grapes of Wrath,* and the same year as *Let Us Now Praise Famous Men,* the movie tapped into a darker vein of national sentiment.[31]

The rhetorical use of the shanty in songs, novels, and movies produced in the 1930s and 1940s points to something more than collective guilt and denial on the part of the middle class. In these works, there is not a trace of the traditional trope of blaming the poor for their poverty that runs through so much of American history. Maybe it took something as dire as the Depression to dislodge that narrative. "In a Shanty in Old Shanty Town," reverberating through the four decades that linked the Depression to the civil rights movement, rejected the notion that shanties and their residents are "not a part of American life" by locating values associated with shantytown at the center of American identity. The upper classes are the outsiders in shantytown, for their character has been eroded by contact with "the world." The middle and working classes have united behind common values, evinced in the shanty and the shantytown. For the space of the Depression, no one is expected to "improve," just hang on. Shanties connected both the working poor and the middle class to a nostalgic rural past, to the frontier settled by hardy pioneers like the Ingalls family.[32]

That happy place is, however, completely white. The implied comradeship between the classes is only available to white Americans. Shantytown, the imaginary shantytown of the past, is a sundown town, a Jim Crow paradise. A racial pattern governs the popular culture responses to shantytowns starting in the 1930s: the nostalgia they generated, and the sense of shared values emerging from both a shared past and a common resolve to get America going again, are resolutely white. The inhabitants of white shanty-towns were quaint and folksy. The residents of black shantytowns, on the other hand, were dangerous; for them, deprived still translated as depraved. A dichotomy between poor white and poor black neighborhoods hardened during the Depression, in which poor whites were participating in "happy poverty," and poor blacks were threatening it. Poor white shanties could be homey; poor black shanties could not. The *Gone with The Wind* shantytown where Big Sam hid out was fearsome; the "old shanty town" of "In a Shanty" was endearing. Whites could be proud of impoverished pasts; blacks could only be ashamed. When Ted Lewis crooned that the shanty was "calling me back," the speaker is white and the forgotten landscape is, too. Subtly but unmistakably, "In a Shanty" invokes a Jim Crow, possibly even a pre-Civil War past. Nostalgia, itself, was used as a tool of white supremacy, invalidating the experiences of poor African Americans while inscribing the past of white shantytowns as legitimately American.

The denigration of African-American shantytowns was reinforced, or at least not disputed, by leading African-American intellectuals and civic leaders, including W. E. B. Du Bois. Although he disagreed with Booker T. Washington on many issues, Du Bois agreed with Washington that better housing was essentially a civil right, and considered a commitment to improved housing a measure of racial progress. In 1893, Washington bragged that graduates of Tuskegee University would replace the "one-room hovel that had been their abode for a quarter century" with a "comfortable, tasty framed cottage." Du Bois concurred. In *The Crisis,* the NAACP publication he edited for 24 years, Du Bois sometimes published "before and after" photographs of housing, with cabins representing the race's past and houses or even man-sions pointing the way to its future. He championed new apartment blocks as an advance over the "old type of Negro alley," and in 1920 devoted an entire issue to the subject of domestic architecture. Bungalows, pictured in a 1913 article, were among his favorite styles.[33]

In his 1899 study of Philadelphia, and in his 1908 study, "The Negro American Family," Du Bois advocated separation of rooms by functions, glazed windows, exterior walls painted white, and tasteful furniture, including feather mattresses and parlor tables. He lamented the lack in the South of "an ideal home-making to which the better class of freedmen could look," such as the New England cottage provided in the North. While he emphasized that "among the mass of poor homes there is growing up a strong beautiful family life," Du Bois saw the "tasty framed cottage" as proof of personal worth. A failure to aspire to one was evidence of personal failure that inhibited the advancement of the entire race. While black middle-class artists like Hale Woodruff promoted on occasion a more nuanced, ambivalent interpretation of black shantytowns, incorporating aspects of shared culture and community in depictions of neighborhoods on the verge of demolition, the dominant discourse about African-American shantytowns coming from middle-class and elite spokespersons rejected them and preached "assimilation via architecture." The black shantytown that stuck in the white public's mind was the one in *Gone with the Wind*, home to ex-slaves and murderers, and a clear threat to whites. The one presented by black leaders, while it acknowledged the family life that had managed to thrive there despite destitute circumstances, sought to erase black shantytowns from the history of the post-Civil War era.[34]

During the economic boom years of the 1950s and early 1960s, shantytowns ceased to be of primary interest to government officials and, for the most part, social reformers. They continued their run in popular music, however, with multiple recordings of "In A Shanty" reminding listeners of the joys of virtuous poverty. As before, the shantytowns conjured by the song continued to be white shantytowns, even when African-American artists were doing the recording. The black musicians who recorded the song in the 1950s and early 1960s, including Dizzy Gillespie, Fats Domino, Big Bill Broonzy, and the Ink Spots—were all extremely popular with white as well as black audiences.[35]

Shantytowns returned to the public landscape and the public consciousness during the Civil Rights era, as social protest accelerated in the late 1960s. The shantytown was overtly embraced, in May 1968, as a symbol of poverty by the Poor People's Campaign, which built a large encampment called Resurrection City on the grounds of the Mall. More than 3,000 protestors staged nonviolent demonstrations in keeping with the vision that the Rev. Martin Luther King Jr. had articulated in his final sermons before his assassination the previous month. As riots erupted across the country in the aftermath of King's murder, the Resurrection City encampment became a symbol of continued commitment to King's nonviolent strategies. Protestors—led by Jesse Jackson, who became mayor of Resurrection City—staged demonstrations demanding that Congress pass anti-poverty legislation. Their goal was to remain in their tent-like Resurrection City shanties until such bills were passed. Heavy rains, however, turned the shantytown into a muddy, sodden expanse, which became a fitting backdrop for the muddled agendas of the activists in charge of the protest. Reminiscent in spirit of Camp Marks, built by WWI veterans along the Anacostia River in 1932, the Resurrection City shantytown was defeated by forces beyond its control: the assassination of Robert Kennedy on June 5, 1968, was the final blow. Disheartened, protestors disbanded, but not before Jackson had created one of the most lasting refrains of the civil rights movement: trying to rally the discouraged protestors, he led them in cries of, "I Am Somebody!" In a tribute to the activists massed on the Mall, the hearse bearing Kennedy's body was driven through what remained of the chillingly misnamed Resurrection City.

At the same time Resurrection City was claiming the shantytown as a symbol of American poverty, shantytowns were becoming a global symbol of abject poverty in the Third World, as it was then known. The identification of shantytowns with the urban slums of Africa, South America, and India disqualified them as emblems of white working-poor culture in this country. While the incidence of shantytown coverage in the American press skyrocketed in the second half of the twentieth century, virtually all of it concerned shantytowns in developing countries, which were depicted as squalid and vast—always vast. The message was that these shantytowns, home to thousands, threatened social order—a reading that located poor shanty dwellers resolutely outside of society. The shantytown, used to illustrate backwardness and a lack of civilization in nineteenth-century urban shantytowns in the United States, played a similar rhetorical role in the late twentieth century, as a sign of global backwardness. Photographs of teeming slums in Lagos or São Paulo shocked viewers, arousing sympathy as well as disgust, but they also summoned an unspoken comparison that reified the United States: we had no such landscapes here, in our land of capitalism and democracy. The shantytowns of poor countries, published and broadcast routinely in the U.S. press starting in the 1960s, indicted their respective nations. The lack of shantytowns in the United States was something to be proud of—an accomplishment, of course, that could only be asserted in ignorance of our own country's long history of shantytowns.

One of the last popular cultural examples of a working-poor shantytown came in the song "Shantytown" in 1967. Recorded by Johnny Cash and June Carter, "Shantytown" owes a clear debt to the longtime hit, "In a Shanty in Old Shanty Town," which continued to appear on oldies collections and recordings by novelty bands, such as the Harmonicats in 1965. Cash and Carter's song, which unites the shanty and the town in a single word, is a harsher, edgier version of shantytown. It is a hardscrabble place, the kind that might have given rise to a hardscrabble hero like Cash. In the song, Cash's character taunts the affluent society woman voiced by Carter, asking why someone who lives on "solid ground" is dallying in shantytown. Cash mentions several times the "pride" he feels for his shantytown origins. Like shantytowns in earlier songs and movies, this one is a place of pure virtue, unsullied by materialistic concerns, where the rich are taken to task for their decadence. The society woman of Carter's narration both craves shantytown and, according to Cash's character, condescends to it. What, Cash asks, keeps her "coming back" to shantytown? The lament at the center of "In a Shanty in Old Shanty Town," that the shantytown is "calling me back"—is repurposed here as an erotic metaphor. But the sentiment remains. Shantytown summons something deep in the American being.[36]

But the rhetorical use of the shanty and the shantytown as symbols of the white working-poor American experience came to an end in the 1960s. At the height of the Cold War, in a decade marked by civil rights and antiwar activism, global shantytowns captured the attention of scholars in the West. Their landmark studies of *favela* settlements in South America refuted the conclusions of 1930s housing experts such as James Ford, who justified demolitions by concluding that shanties were not "real" homes, which made residents of shantytowns "not a part of American life." "The favelados and suburbanos do *not* have the attitudes and behavior supposedly associated with marginal groups," insisted Janice Perlman in her celebrated 1976 study of the Rio *favelas*. "Socially they are well organized and cohesive and make wide use of the urban milieu and its institutions. Culturally, they are highly optimistic and aspire to better education for their children and to improve the condition of their houses . . . Economically, they work hard, they consume their share of the products of others . . . and they build . . . Politically, they are neither apathetic or radical . . . In short, *they have the aspirations of the bourgeoisie, the perseverance of pioneers, and the values of patriots*" (italics in original).[37]

In the 1960s, urban planner and theorist John F. C. Turner made similar observations, comparing *favela* residents with ghetto residents in the United States. The conclusion that South American shantytowns—*favelas, barriadas, colonias,* and *ranchos*—were slums "varies between a half-truth and an almost total untruth," Turner wrote. Working against the conventional wisdom on slums galvanized by Oscar Lewis's influential 1968 book on the so-called "culture of poverty," Turner insisted that South American shantytowns were "a considerable improvement on [residents'] former condition, whether in the city slums from which they moved to the Barriada or in the villages from which they moved into the city slums." Shantytown dwellers were the much poorer "equivalent of the Building Society house-buyers of the suburbs of any city in the industrialized world." Turner recognized the importance of the intangible qualities of shantytowns. As Turner explains: "though the official world did not recognize it, housing was more than a material product, it also provided people with existential qualities like identity, security and opportunity, which quite transformed the quality of ordinary people's lives." Living on their own terms gave them "optimism." "If they were trapped in the inner cities, like so many of the North American poor," Turner concluded, "they too would be burning instead of building."[38]

In the late nineteenth and twentieth centuries, the slum and the ghetto became "ideological sites" where reformers, planners, and researchers established links between economic inequality, social heterogeneity, and the urban landscape. In order for this triangulation to work, shantytowns had to be the equivalent of inner city slums. Considering them separately revealed not the "pathology" reformers saw in the inner city, but the middle-class values supposedly embodied by the suburbs—privacy, property, and individualism. Shantytowns could have shown New Deal liberals the flaws in their public housing strategy, if they had looked. In the same time period, liberal reformers were largely responsible for wiping out two inner-city housing alternatives— lodging houses and single room occupancy hotels (SROs)—that were popular with poor people but did not meet the housing standards created and imposed by the liberal establishment. These vanished housing models insist that we search diligently for what has been erased from the American landscape, and the American consciousness. The history of shantytowns, like that of SROs, reveals a deep and abiding distrust for poor people on the part of liberal reformers. The shantytowns built by the poor argued for a decentralized, self-built, market-based solution to the affordable housing shortage. Like suburbanites, shanty dwellers wanted a single-family house with room for a garden located close to but not in the central business district. Today, along the U.S. border with Mexico, shantytown dwellers still want the same things, and urban planners, city officials, and social reformers are still insisting that they know better.[39]

Epilogue

Shantytowns, if they ever left, are back. Since the 1950s, shantytowns have proliferated along the U.S.-Mexico border, and in recent decades their numbers have soared. Called *colonias* because of their Hispanic population (*colonias* is Spanish for "neighborhood"), these shantytowns appear in the media as Mexican or South American imports, unconnected with the American shantytowns of the previous one hundred years. Scholars analyzing the rapid growth of *colonias* in the United States note the "unprecedented social formations" they represent, comparing these "highly visible poverty pockets" to Third World settlements. Identified as slums in the 1930s, U.S. shantytowns ceased to have an independent existence or, it seems, a history in the United States. They are now universally treated as a symptom of "global south" industrial development with no roots in American history. Meanwhile, more than two thousand of them flourish on the Texas-Mexico border, housing some four hundred thousand people. While these *colonias* bear unmistakable likenesses to the *favelas* of South America and the shantytowns of South Africa and India, they also look and function a lot like American shanty-towns of previous generations.[1]

Contemporary journalists, even sympathetic ones, are unaware of this connection to our own history. In January 1996, Philip True, a reporter for the *San Antonio Express-News,* set out to investigate the approximately five hundred thousand people living in 1,400 *colonias* between Brownsville and El Paso—a number strikingly close to the number of "local homeless" polled by relief agencies in 1933. True defined *colonias* as "unregulated subdivisions that lack piped drinking water, sewerage, electricity, and other basics most Americans take for granted." He described a typical abode in El Cenizo, a sprawling shantytown on the banks of the Rio Grande about fifteen miles south of Laredo: "a one-room structure the shape and sophistication of a large packing crate," a twelve-by-twenty wood frame building with one door, one window, and no plumbing. The scenario he recounted of the *colonias* is a replay of shantytowns from the 1880s through the 1940s: poor people migrating in search of work, often to the city, and building shelters for themselves out of materials at hand. A shortage of affordable or desirable urban housing in Brownsville and El Paso spawned a shantytown on the worst land available—in this case desert land takes the place of "bottoms" land—which was sold in tiny portions for as little as $130 down and $100 a month. Since the developer held the paper, one missed payment could mean a total loss for the homeowner. Yet *colonia* plots sold as fast as developers could print contracts. Residents built their own homes, True writes, "one board at a time, improving as they went. And that's what they did. After years of work, many older homes now would fit into a lower-middle-class development anywhere in the United States."[2]

Colonias residents interviewed by True "envision a time when life will be better," if not for themselves then for their children. "We live here because there is no other way to do it," explained one resident. "When we moved here in 1990, there was nothing—no water, no sewer, no electricity, no telephone. We lived like the first people who ever came to the United States. But little by little, we built our own house. Then came electricity, telephone, and now we have cable television. Through our own efforts, we are beginning to have our own life." That last sentence could be the shantytown dweller's motto. And the comment True elicited from the then-attorney general of Texas, a moderate Democrat, could be the slogan for the historical opposition to shantytowns: "I don't agree with people that we should have slums like in India in Texas simply because people have no money." The question posed by the unsympathetic Board of Aldermen in New York City in 1832, as they prepared to order the demolitions of shantytowns in downtown Manhattan, remains: where are the poor to go? Poor people insist upon living somewhere—a great inconvenience to politicians, urban planners, and middle-class property owners—and many of them refuse to go where government officials tell them to go.[3]

In the developing world, a number of nations have adopted a model called "sites and services" to address the inadequacies of shantytown housing without mandating its demolition. Rio de Janeiro and Mumbai, for example, have cleared sites for self-built communities and provided infrastructure in the form of water, sewers, streets and electricity. That approach, imperfect but promising, seems almost impossible to implement in this country. At the time of True's story about the Brownsville *colonias,* the state of Texas earmarked

$300 million, much of it from the Environmental Protection Agency, for water and sewage treatment plants in the *colonias* region. But because the *colonias* were not legally platted, they could not receive the aid. And because state subdivision rules made paved streets and other improvements prerequisites for platting, it seemed unlikely that the *colonias* would ever be platted. Frustrated, Texas officials tried to outlaw their sale and development— legislation that *colonias* residents organized to fight. For as flawed as the *colonias* are, they are often the only affordable housing option available. "For residents and their advocates, the question remains: if people stop selling lots in the [*colonias*], where will the poor live?" The *colonias* continue to thrive today, despite the efforts of urban planners and government officials to stifle them. Residents recently organized a "Right to Light" campaign to pressure government officials to install street lights in their pitch-dark neighborhoods. They still lack running water and other basic utilities. One *colonia,* Cameron Park, has been identified as the poorest neighborhood in the nation.[4]

Shantytowns persist in other forms in twenty-first-century America. You see them in the temporary encampments built or inhabited seasonally by itinerant workers who follow the circus, for example, or the laborers who work at NASCAR racetracks. The trailer park is in many ways the modern shantytown. Contemporary homeless encampments echo shantytowns, as do informal migrant labor camps. And we see the ghosts of shantytowns in protest encampments. In Miami in 2006, residents erected a shantytown they dubbed Umoja— Swahili for "unity"—on a vacant city-owned parcel downtown. They were protesting the failure of the city to provide affordable housing for its poor residents. Umoja Village lasted six months before a mysterious fire burned it to the ground. The activists created a nonprofit called Take Back the Land, which is now helping to place homeless people in vacant foreclosed homes. Shantytowns have emerged on the post-Katrina landscapes in New Orleans, despite federal and state efforts to prohibit them. As shantytowns of old, these are communities of houses built by their poor inhabitants, for themselves.[5]

Because shantytowns have been overlooked systematically or ignored in American history and historiography, today when they reappear on the national landscape, Americans regard them as an unfortunate import from the developing world. In 2008, as the national economy spiraled downward, shantytowns and "tent cities" were built in several U.S. cities, including Seattle, Portland, and San Francisco. Major newspapers and magazines rushed to investigate this new American phenomenon, the shantytown. A reporter for *The Nation* dug deeper, and traced shantytowns back to what looked like their beginnings: 1989. "[S]hantytowns have been a periodic but permanent feature of American urban life for at least the past two decades," he wrote. "They are what connects us to São Paulo, Lagos and Mumbai, physical manifestations of our growing inequality and societal neglect." In their enactment of economic inequality, the shantytowns lately built in American cities do indeed connect the United States to impoverished peoples everywhere. But shantytowns have been a feature of the American landscape for more than 175 years. They connect us not only to the struggles of the poor in other countries, but to our own past.[6]

NOTES

ACKNOWLEDGMENTS

CREDITS

INDEX

Notes

Abbreviations

BDE   *Brooklyn Daily Eagle*
NYT   *New York Times, New York Daily Times* (prior to 1857)

1. Walden, a Shanty or a House?

1. Henry David Thoreau, *Walden: A Fully Annotated Edition* (New Haven: Yale University Press, 2004). All subsequent citations from *Walden* are from this edition. *Walden* was originally published in 1854 by the Boston publisher Ticknor & Fields, as *Walden; or, Life in the Woods*.

2. Thoreau, *Walden*, 41, 78, 1. Critical approaches to Thoreau and *Walden* have focused on Thoreau as a nature writer and amateur scientist, or emphasized the transcendental aspects of his prose. See Alan D. Hodder, *Thoreau's Ecstatic Witness* (New Haven: Yale University Press, 2001); Alfred I. Tauber, *Henry David Thoreau and the Moral Agency of Knowing* (Berkeley: University of California Press, 2001); Laura Dassow Walls's introduction to *Material Faith: Henry David Thoreau on Science* (New York: Houghton Mifflin, 1999); and William Gleason, "Re-Creating Walden: Thoreau's Economy of Work and Play," *American Literature* 65, no. 4 (December 1993): 673–701. The psychosocial literary history by Robert Milder, *Reimagining Thoreau* (Cambridge: Cambridge University Press, 1995), considers Thoreau's relationship to antebellum Concord but does not mention shanties or James Collins. Two more recent volumes make the case for Thoreau as an archaeologist and student of material culture: David F. Wood, *An Observant Eye: The Thoreau Collection at the Concord Museum* (Concord, MA: The Concord Museum, 2006); and William E. Cain, ed., *A Historical Guide to Henry David Thoreau* (New York: Oxford University Press, 2000).

3. Thoreau, *Walden*, 39; D. B. Johnson, *Henry Builds a Cabin* (Boston: Houghton Mifflin, 2002), not paginated. Literary scholars have long analyzed Thoreau's relationship to the Irish; they usually note James Collins but concentrate on the other Irish figures in *Walden*, Hugh Quoil and the Field family. See Frank Buckley,

"Thoreau and the Irish," *New England Quarterly* 13, no. 3 (September 1940): 389–400; George E. Ryan, "Shanties and Shiftlessness: The Immigrant Irish of Henry Thoreau," *Éire-Ireland: A Journal of Irish Studies* 13, no. 3 (Fall 1978): 54–78; Helen Lojek, "Thoreau's Bog People," *New England Quarterly* 67, no. 2 (June 1994): 279–297; and Shaun O'Connell, "Boggy Ways: Notes on Irish-American Culture," *Massachusetts Review* 26, nos. 2 and 3 (Summer–Autumn 1985). Most recently, Laura Dassow Walls has argued that Thoreau had a "deep, complex, and profoundly sympathetic involvement in the lives of his Irish neighbors." See Walls, "'As You Are Brothers of Mine': Thoreau and the Irish," *New England Quarterly* 88, no. 1 (March 2015): 5–36; quote on page 6 note 1.

4. Thoreau to Daniel Ricketson, March 5, 1856, *The Correspondence of Henry David Thoreau*, eds. Carl Bode and Walter Harding (New York: New York University Press, 1958), 412.

5. Thoreau, *Walden*, 9. While Thoreau put the middle class at the fulcrum of American history, he also sought to reform it by criticizing its materialism and superficiality. See Lawrence Buell, "Downwardly Mobile for Conscience's Sake: Voluntary Simplicity from Thoreau to Lily Bart," *American Literary History* 17, no. 4 (Winter 2005): 653–665; and Cecelia Tichi, "Domesticity on Walden Pond," in William E. Cain, ed., *A Historical Guide to Henry David Thoreau* (London: Oxford University Press, 2000), 95–122. While Thoreau distinguishes himself from the Collinses' shanty, he does not embrace the typical gentility and refinement of the acquisitive middle class.

6. Thoreau, *Walden*, 39, 41, 43, 198, 47.

7. Ibid., 198; W. Barksdale Maynard, "Thoreau's House at Walden," *Art Bulletin* 81, no. 2 (June 1999), 307; quoted in Frederick Benjamin Sanborn, *Recollections of 70 Years Volume II: Literary Life* (Boston: R. G. Badger, 1909), 390.

8. Thoreau, *Walden*, 41–42.

9. On Irish railroad workers, see Brian C. Mitchell, *The Paddy Camps: The Irish of Lowell, 1821–1861* (Champaign: University of Illinois Press, 2006), 24. For descriptions of Thoreau's walking paths, see Maynard, *Walden Pond: A History* (New York: Oxford University Press, 2005), 52, and maps on pages 44–45, 110, and 150. Thoreau, *The Journal of Henry David Thoreau*, eds. Bradford Torrey and Francis Allen (Boston: Houghton Mifflin,1906), 12:215, quoted in Maynard, *Walden Pond,* 53; Ralph Waldo Emerson, *The Letters of Ralph Waldo Emerson,* ed. Ralph L. Rusk (New York: Columbia University Press, 1939–1995), 7:456; Nathaniel Hawthorne, October 6, 1843, in *American Notebooks,* ed. Claude M. Simpson (Columbus: Ohio State University Press, 1972), quoted in Maynard, *Walden Pond,* 54.

10. Thoreau, *Walden*, 126, 34, 198; Thoreau, *Journal*, 2:314, 4:336, 4:343. For an opposing interpretation of this last shanty, occupied by the Riordan family, see Walls, "'As You Are Brothers of Mine'," 23–27.

11. Thoreau, *Walden*, 254, 199, 198, 201; Dana T. Nelson, "Thoreau, Manhood, and Race: Quiet Desperation Versus Representative Isolation," in Cain, *A Historical*

Guide to Henry David Thoreau, 84. Talaria are the wings commonly seen on the feet of Greek god Hermes, in artists' renderings.

12. Thoreau, *Walden,* 26–28, 34–36. On the idea of the primitive hut in history, which stretches back to Vitruvius and which clearly preoccupied Thoreau, see Joseph Rykwert, *On Adam's House in Paradise: The Idea of the Primitive Hut in Architectural History* (Cambridge, MA: MIT Press, 1981).

13. Thoreau, *Walden,* 29, 38.

14. Ibid., 41–42.

15. Ibid., 46. On Downing see David Schuyler, *Apostle of Taste: Andrew Jackson Downing 1815–1852* (Baltimore and London: Johns Hopkins University Press, 1996), and Amelia Peck, ed. *Alexander Jackson Davis, American Architect, 1803–1892* (New York: Rizzoli, 1992).

16. Thoreau, *Walden,* 41, 88, 46.

17. Stuart M. Blumin, *The Emergence of the Middle Class: Social Experience in the American City, 1760–1900* (Cambridge: Cambridge University Press), 297. On refinement, see Richard L. Bushman, *The Refinement of America: Persons, Houses, Cities* (New York: Alfred A. Knopf Inc., 1992), 404, xv. Emerson, *Journals,* 195.

18. Ricketson's sketches are reproduced in Thomas W. Blanding, "Daniel Ricketson's Sketch Book," *Studies in the American Renaissance: 1977,* ed. Joel Myerson (Boston: Twayne Publishers, 1978), 327–338; Thoreau, *Journal* 9: 322–323.

19. Thoreau, *Walden,* 78.

20. Ibid., 11.

21. Ibid., 255, 247, 250, 256. For a thorough discussion of the free black inhabitants of Concord, see Elise Lemire, *Black Walden: Slavery and Its Aftermath in Concord, Massachusetts* (Philadelphia: University of Pennsylvania Press, 2009). See also Robert A. Gross, "Thoreau and the Laborers of Concord," *Raritan* 33, no. 1 (June 2013): 50–66.

22. Emerson, *Later Lectures, 1843–1871,* eds. Ronald A. Bosco and Joel Myerson (Athens: University of Georgia Press, 2001), 1:23. On the myth of the colonial New England village see Joseph S. Wood with Michael Steinitz, *The New England Village* (Baltimore: Johns Hopkins University Press, 1997), 2, 134, 136, 162, 163.

23. Wood, *New England Village,* 2, 162.

24. Thoreau, *Walden,* 42. Thoreau notes a "place to sit" among the items in the shanty; I have designated it a bench.

25. Thoreau, *Walden,* 41–43. In April 1844, Thoreau made a campfire in a tree stump while camping in the woods outside Concord and started a fire that burned down approximately half the woods, some three hundred acres, and nearly ignited the town of Concord itself. For a description of the event see Rebecca Beatrice Brooks, "Henry David Thoreau: The Woods Burner," *History of Massachusetts: The History of the Great State of Massachusetts,* http://historyofmassachusetts.org /henry-david-thoreau-woods-burner/.

26. Thoreau disdained interior furnishings: "Furniture! Thank God, I can stand

without the aid of a furniture warehouse . . . the more you have of such things, the poorer you are" (*Walden*, 63).

27. On parasols, see Joan Severa, *Dressed for the Photographer: Ordinary Americans and Fashion, 1840–1900* (Kent, OH: Kent State University Press, 1995), 5, 49. On coffee-grinder patents in the early 1840s, see Joseph Edward MacMillan, *The MacMillan Index of Antique Coffee Mills* (Marietta, GA: Cherokee Publishing, 1995), xxv–xxvi, xxxi, 519, 1279.

28. On consumption patterns as they relate to middle-class formation in the nineteenth century, in addition to Blumin and Bushman, see Elizabeth Donaghy Garrett, *At Home: The American Family 1750–1870* (New York: Harry N. Abrams, 1990); Katherine C. Grier, *Culture and Comfort: Parlor Making and Middle-Class Identity, 1850–1930* (Washington: Smithsonian Institution Press, 1988); and Karen Halttunen, *Confidence Men and Painted Women: A Study of Middle-Class Culture in America, 1830–1870* (New Haven: Yale University Press, 1982). On middle-class formation more generally, see Burton J. Bledstein and Robert D. Johnston, eds., *The Middling Sorts: Explorations in the History of the American Middle Class* (New York: Routledge, 2001), especially the essays by Debby Applegate ("Henry Ward Beecher and the 'Great Middle Class': Mass-Marketed Intimacy and Middle-Class Identity," 107–124) and Sven Beckert ("Propertied of a Different Kind: Bourgeoisie and Lower Middle Class in Nineteenth-Century America," 285–295).

29. Thoreau, *Walden*, 42–43. The first reports of the Irish potato blight appeared in the fall of 1845, after Thoreau buys the shanty from James Collins, but the famine had crested and receded by the time *Walden* was published in 1854.

30. Thoreau, *Walden*, 44, 197; *OED Online*. According to the *OED*, "shiftless" means "lacking in resources; incapable of shifting for oneself; hence, lazy, inefficient," as well as "ineffective, futile," http://www.oed.com/view/Entry/178096?redirectedFrom =shiftless#eid.

31. Thoreau, *Walden*, 46.

32. Herman Melville to Nathaniel Hawthorne, June 29, 1851, quoted in Hershel Parker, *Melville: A Biography, Vol. 1, 1819–1851* (Baltimore: Johns Hopkins University Press, 1996), 847.

2. Shanties on the Western Frontier

1. Zerah Hawley, *A Journal of a Tour through Connecticut, Massachusetts, New-York, the North Part of Pennsylvania and Ohio, Including a Year's Residence in That Part of the State of Ohio, Styled New Connecticut, or Western Reserve* (New Haven, CT: S. Converse, 1822), 31.

2. "A Description of New Connecticut," *Connecticut Herald*, December 5, 1816, reprinted in the *Hartford Times*, April 8, 1817, reproduced in Richard Buel Jr., ed., *Peopling of New Connecticut: From the Land of Steady Habits to the Western Reserve* (Middletown, CT: Acorn Club, 2011), 60. On anti-emigration sentiments circulat-

ing in the press, see Buel, 113–120. On the Western Reserve generally see Robert A. Wheeler, ed., *Visions of the Western Reserve: Public and Private Documents of Northeastern Ohio 1750–1860* (Columbus: Ohio State University Press, 2000); Harry Forrest Lupold and Gladys Haddad, eds., *Ohio's Western Reserve: A Regional Reader* (Kent, OH: Kent State University Press, 1988); and Stuart A. Stiffler, "Books and Reading in the Connecticut Western Reserve: The Small-Settlement Social Library, 1800–1860," *Libraries and the Cultural Record* 46:4 (March 2011): 388–411.

3. Hawley, *Tour*, 55, 48, 50, 67, 31. As the son of a Congregationalist minister, Hawley would have seen the positive descriptions of New Connecticut written by missionaries-cum-land-agents in denominational publications such as the *Connecticut Evangelical Magazine* and pamphlets published by the Connecticut Missionary Society.

4. Amy DeRogatis, *Moral Geography: Maps, Missionaries, and the American Frontier, Religion and American Culture* (New York: Columbia University Press, 2003), 129.

5. Hawley, *Tour*, 31; "shanty, n.1," *OED Online*. Widespread speculations that "shanty" is derived from joining two Irish words, "sean" and "tigh," with the proposed meaning "old house," are not supported by scholarship; http://www.oed.com /view/Entry/177491?rskey=AGxLIa&result=1#eid.

6. Hawley, *Tour*, 55; "tenement," *OED Online*, http://www.oed.com/view/Entry /199111?redirectedFrom=tenement#eid.

7. Ibid., 31, 55.

8. Ibid., 47–48.

9. Fiske Kimball, *Domestic Architecture of the American Colonies and of the Early Republic* (New York: Charles Scribner's Sons, 1922), 4. On construction techniques in early American houses, see also Cary Carson, Carl Lounsbury, and Colonial Williamsburg Foundation, eds., *The Chesapeake House: Architectural Investigation by Colonial Williamsburg* (Chapel Hill: University of North Carolina Press, 2013). Edward Johnson, *Wonder-Working Providence of Sion's Saviour in New England* (1654; repr., Andover: W. F. Draper, 1867), 83, quoted in Kimball, *Domestic Architecture*, 5; J. F. Watson, "Annals of Philadelphia" (1830), 65, 159–60, quoted in Kimball, *Domestic Architecture*, 5–6; "State of the Province of Georgia" (1740), quoted in Kimball, *Domestic Architecture*, 7.

10. Cary Carson, Norman F. Barka, William M. Kelso, Garry Wheeler Stone, and Dell Upton, "Impermanent Architecture in the Southern American Colonies," *Winterthur Portfolio* 16, no. 2/3 (Summer–Autumn 1981): 139–140.

11. Johnson, *Wonder-Working Providence*, 174, quoted in Kimball, *Domestic Architecture*, 8; Carson et al., "Impermanent Architecture," 136; Edmund Plowden (Beauchamp Plantagenet), *A Description of the Province of New Albion* (1650), quoted in Carson et al., "Impermanent Architecture," 155.

12. William Cronon, *Changes in the Land: Indians, Colonists, and the Ecology of New England* (New York: Farrar Straus Giroux, 1983), 55, 53.

13. Carson et al., "Impermanent Architecture," 141; Kimball, *Domestic Architecture*, 6; Malcolm Freeberg, ed., *The Journal of Madam Knight* (Brookline, MA: David R. Goodine, 1972), 13, quoted in Carson et al., "Impermanent Architecture," 160.

14. Peter S. Onuf, *Statehood and Union: A History of the Northwest Ordinance* (Indianapolis: Indiana University Press, 1987), 31.

15. All quoted in Onuf, *Statehood*, 32: "Extract of a Letter from a Gentleman at Ft. Harmar . . . to His Friend in Town [Boston]," *New Haven Gazette and Connecticut Magazine*, October 5, 1786; George Washington to N. C. Read, November 3, 1784, in John C. Fitzpatrick, ed., *Washington Writings*, 27:486; J. Hector St. John de Crèvecoeur, *Letters from an American Farmer* (1782; repr., New York: E.P. Dutton & Co., 1957), 42–43.

16. Ibid., 39.

17. For an overview of emigrant literature in the early nineteenth century see editor Elizabeth Helen Thompson's introduction to Robert MacDougall's 1841 work, *The Emigrant's Guide to North America* (Toronto: Natural History/Natural Heritage, 1998), xi–xxiii; and Marjory Harper, "Image and Reality in Early Emigrant Literature," in *British Journal of Canadian Studies* 7, no. 1 (1992): 3–14. Charlotte Erickson, a leading scholar of British emigration, touches on emigrant literature post-1850 in *Invisible Immigrants: The Adaptation of English and Scottish Immigrants in Nineteenth-Century America* (London: London School of Economics and Political Science; Weidenfeld and Nicolson, 1972); and *Leaving England: Essays on British Emigration in the Nineteenth Century* (Ithaca, NY: Cornell University Press, 1994).

18. Robert Lamond, *A Narrative of the Rise and Progress of Emigration from the Counties of Lanark and Renfrew* (Glasgow: Chalmers and Collins, 1821), 69, https://archive.org/stream/narrativeofrisepoolamo#page/no/mode/2up.

19. Ibid., 66–68, and following five pages of illustrations (unpaginated).

20. Ibid., 66.

21. Josiah T. Marshall, *The Farmers and Emigrants Complete Guide* (New York: D. Appleton & Co., 1845), 51–54. On log shanties see also Robert Scott Burn, *A Handbook of the Mechanical Arts* (Edinburgh: William Blackwood & Sons, 1854), 43–46.

22. W. A. Langton, *Early Days in Upper Canada: The Letters of John Langton* (Toronto: Macmillan Co. of Canada, 1926), 20, quoted in Brian Coffey, "From Shanty to House: Log Construction in Nineteenth-Century Ontario," *Material Culture* 16, no. 2 (Summer 1984): 64; Samuel Strickland, *Twenty-Seven Years in Canada West* (London: 1853), 92, quoted in Coffey, "From Shanty to House," 63.

23. Lamond, *Narrative*, 50.

24. Richard Slotkin notes Cooper's "pre-imminence among mythologizers of the frontier" in *Regeneration through Violence: The Mythology of the American Frontier, 1600–1800* (Middleton, CT: Wesleyan University Press, 1973), 468.

25. James Fenimore Cooper, *The Oak-Openings; or, The Bee-Hunter* (New York: Burgess, Stringer & Co., 1848), 12, 14, 23, 16.

26. Ibid., 15, 14, 17, 9, 12, 16. The author of the hymn lyric is Isaac Watts (1674–1748).

27. Ibid., 11, 28, 97.

28. Ibid., 29, 28, 31.

29. D. H. Lawrence, *Studies in Classic American Literature, The Cambridge Edition of the Letters and Works of D. H. Lawrence* (Cambridge and New York: Cambridge University Press, 2003), 65; Cooper, *Oak-Openings,* 26.

30. Cooper, *Oak-Openings,* 26.

31. Ibid., 200.

32. Ibid., 26, 29–30.

33. George Frederic Ruxton, *Wild Life in the Rocky Mountains* (New York: McMillan, 1916), 37; Cooper, *The Pioneers* (New York: Penguin Books, 1988), 111.

34. Cooper, *Oak-Openings,* 28, 11.

35. George Caleb Bingham, *The Squatters,* oil on 23⅛ in. x 28¼ in. canvas, 1850, Museum of Fine Arts, Boston.

36. George C. Bingham to American Art-Union, November 19, 1850, *Letters from Artists vol. 6,* American Art-Union Papers, New-York Historical Society. Pre-emption, or squatters' rights, allowed people who had settled on unsurveyed public lands to purchase the land they had improved without bidding at government auction; a series of laws passed in the 1830s preserved pre-emption rights, but they were limited by the Pre-Emption Act of 1841, which made government foreclosure easier. The Homestead Act of 1862 restored many of the squatters' rights lost in 1841.

37. George C. Bingham to Maj. James R. Rollins, November 2, 1846, *Letters,* 15. Bingham does not use the word "shanty" in his comments about squatters, but the house in *The Squatters* fits the descriptions of shanties in emigrant literature and frontier novels, specifically the unmilled timbers and a sloping lean-to roof.

38. Art historians have divided on the question of what *The Squatters* means in the context of Bingham's other work. Nancy Rash argues that the painting depicts squatters negatively, as unentitled despoilers of land; while others, including Elizabeth Johns and Barbara Gloseclose, read the portrayal more sympathetically. See David M. Lubin, *Picturing a Nation: Art and Social Change in Nineteenth-Century America* (New Haven: Yale University Press, 1994), 94–95.

39. "Catalogue of Pictures and Other Works of Art, the Property of the American Art-Union. To Be Sold at Auction by David Austen, Jr. at the Gallery, 497 Broadway, on Wednesday, the 15th, Thursday 16th, and Friday 17th, December, 1852. At 11 O'Clock, a.m.," *Bulletin of the American Art-Union* No. 10, Supplementary Bulletin (December 1, 1852): 6; "American Art Union, Second Day Sale," *NYT,* December 17, 1852, 3.

3. Shantytowns on the Urban Frontier

1. John Pintard, *Letters from John Pintard to His Daughter, Eliza Noel Pintard Davidson, 1816–1833* (1832; repr., London: Forgotten Books, 2012), 4:72–73.

2. "Document No. XXIII, Board of Assistants, Dec. 30, 1833," *Documents of the Board of Assistants, from May 21, 1832, to May 12, 1833* (New York: Common Council), 151–152.

3. "Local Intelligence: Our Squatter Population," *NYT,* July 15, 1867, 8; "The Charter Election: A Crying Evil," *NYT,* November 21, 1864, 4. On the history of the grid see David M. Scobey, *Empire City: The Making and Meaning of the New York City Landscape* (Philadelphia: Temple University Press, 2003), 120, 217–219.

4. Edgar Allan Poe, "Doings of Gotham: Letter I," *The Columbia Spy* (Columbia, PA), May 18, 1844, reprinted in *Doings of Gotham,* Thomas Olive Mabbott, ed., (Pottsville, PA: Jacob E. Spannuth, 1929), 23. General information on the *Spy* essays is from Kevin J. Hayes, ed., *Cambridge Companion to Edgar Allan Poe* (Cambridge: Cambridge University Press, 2002), 16.

5. Poe, "Doings of Gotham," 23. On the picturesque see Ann Bermingham, *Landscape and Ideology: The English Rustic Tradition 1740–1860* (Oakland: University of California Press, 1989), 84–85; and John Conron, *American Picturesque* (University Park, PA: Pennsylvania State University Press, 2000).

6. The classic analyses of the interplay between the urban and the rural in American culture are Thomas Bender, *Toward an Urban Vision: Ideas and Institutions in Nineteenth Century America* (Baltimore: Johns Hopkins University Press, 1982); and Leo Marx, *The Machine in the Garden: Technology and the Pastoral Ideal in America* (1964; repr., New York: Oxford University Press, 2000).

7. Roy Rosenzweig and Elizabeth Blackmar, *The Park and the People: A History of Central Park* (Ithaca, NY: Cornell University Press, 1992), 77. On the influence of Irish immigrants on American urban culture, see James R. Barrett, *The Irish Way: Becoming American in the Multiethnic City* (New York: Penguin Books, 2013). On shanties in Manhattan see Rosenzweig and Blackmar, *Park,* 65–77; John Atlee Kouwenhoven, *The Columbia Historical Portrait of New York: An Essay in Graphic History* (New York: Harper & Row, 1972), 271; Catherine McNeur, *Taming Manhattan: Environmental Battles in the Antebellum City* (Cambridge, MA: Harvard University Press, 2014), 137–138, 184–188, 209, 219, 222; and Jason Jindrich, "The Shantytowns of Central Park West: Fin de Siècle Squatting in American Cities," *Journal of Urban History* 36, no. 5 (September 2010): 672–684.

8. Poe, "Doings of Gotham," 23.

9. Ibid.

10. Ibid.

11. For details on construction materials in nineteenth-century Manhattan, see Richard Howe's articles on the *Gotham History Blotter* (blog), published by the Gotham Center for New York History at City University of New York's Graduate

Center, especially "Hovels or Holes?" http://www.gothamcenter.org/blotter/?p=855, and "Notes on Invisible Wood," http://www.gothamcenter.org/blotter/?p=945.

12. Poe, "Doings of Gotham," 23.

13. "Myrtle Avenue," *BDE,* August 16, 1847, 2; "Common Council," *BDE,* July 9, 1844, 2. In 1884, with money saved from royalties on *Leaves of Grass* and a loan from his publisher, Walt Whitman bought the only house he ever owned, which he described as "a little old shanty of my own." The two-story frame house in Camden, NJ, was badly in need of repairs and lacking a furnace when Whitman bought it. He lived there until his death in 1892. Whitman to Anne Gilchrist, April 20, 1884, quoted in J. R. LeMaster and Donald D. Kummings, eds., *Walt Whitman: An Encyclopedia,* Garland Reference Library of the Humanities, vol. 1877 (New York: Garland Publishing Inc., 1998), 429.

14. "Myrtle Avenue," *BDE,* August 16, 1847, 2; Rosenzweig and Blackmar, *Park,* 4. As architectural historian Dell Upton has pointed out in his study of the antebellum American city, middle-class urbanites in this period pursued the "twin goals of civilization and urbanity," busily "inventing physical settings appropriate to the new models of urban life." Dell Upton, *Another City: Urban Life and Urban Spaces in the New American Republic* (New Haven: Yale University Press, 2008), 3.

15. "Myrtle Avenue," *BDE,* August 16, 1847, 2. According to an article in the *Brooklyn Daily Eagle* in March 1872, the Jackson Farm—from which the shantytown, which became known as Jackson's Hollow in the late 1850s, took its name—occupied sixty-six acres bounded by Myrtle, Classon, Greene, and Grand Avenues. Articles in the 1850s give Gates Avenue, two blocks south of Greene, as the southern boundary. Taking those boundaries into account, I have estimated the size of the shantytown in the 1850s at seventy acres. "Female Pugnacity," *BDE,* June 27, 1851, 3; "The Board of Education and the Great Increase of Shanties," *BDE,* March 22, 1872, 2.

16 "The Public Health," *BDE,* May 30, 1849, 3; "Depredations on the Fencings of Vacant Lots," *BDE,* July 6, 1849, 3. See also "Brooklyn," *BDE,* September 26, 1849, 1.

17. "The March of Improvement," *BDE,* April 23, 1851, 3; "Jackson's Hollow," *BDE,* February 5, 1873, 2.

18. Rosenzweig and Blackmar, *Park,* 91.

19. Untitled photograph, 1859, Museum of the City of New York; reproduced in Abraham A. Davidson, *Ralph Albert Blakelock* (University Park, PA: Pennsylvania State University Press, 1996), 118. By contrast see Winslow Homer's several illustrations of skaters for *Harper's Weekly* and other magazines, e.g., "Skating on Central Park" from 1861.

20. "The Central Park," *Harper's Weekly,* November 28, 1857, 756–757.

21. Ibid. For a timeline of Central Park history, see http://centralparkhistory.com/, compiled from Rosenzweig and Blackmar's *The Park and the People.* Robert Moses, parks commissioner in the 1930s, also ordered the demolition of shacks and shanties constructed on a strip of land between the railroad tracks to the west of

Riverside Drive and the shore of the Hudson River, in order to extend the park from 125th Street to 152nd Street.

22. "View in Sixth Ave. between 55th and 57th," *Manual of the Corporation of the City of New York* (New York: Common Council, 1868), facing p. 536. On the discourse of magazine illustrations see Joshua Brown, *Beyond the Lines: Pictorial Reporting, Everyday Life, and the Crisis of Gilded Age America* (Berkeley, CA; London: University of California Press, 2006), 86, 136–137.

23. "Squatter Settlement betw. 1st and 2nd Avs. Near 38th St., 1858," *Manual of the Corporation of the City of New York* (New York: Common Council, 1859), facing page 420; "View from School House in 42nd Street between 2nd and 3rd Avs. Looking North," *Manual of the Corporation of the City of New York* (New York: Common Council, 1868), facing page 526; Richard Plunz, *A History of Housing in New York City: Dwelling Type and Social Change in the American Metropolis* (New York: Columbia University Press, 1990), 54.

24. Charles Loring Brace, "Walks among the New York Poor," *NYT*, April 19, 1854, 2.

25. Ibid.; George Templeton Strong, *The Diary of George Templeton Strong*, eds. Allan Nevins and Milton Halsey Thomas (New York: Macmillan, 1952), IV, 155 (October 22, 1867).

26. Emily Dickinson, "I like to see it lap the miles" (1891; repr., Ralph William Franklin, ed., *The Poems of Emily Dickinson, Vol. 1*, Cambridge, MA: Harvard University Press, 1998), 408. Scholars estimate the poem, not dated by Dickinson, was written in autumn 1862.

27. Contemporary accounts of this viewpoint include George G. Foster, *New York by Gas-Light and Other Urban Sketches* (1850; repr., Berkeley: University of California Press, 1990); and James Dabney McCabe, *Lights and Shadows of New York Life; Or, The Sights and Sensations of the Great City* (1872; repr., New York: Farrar, Straus and Giroux, 1970). See also Upton, *Another City*, chapter 3, "The Smell of Danger," 54–63.

28. "Homes of the Poor," *NYT*, February 24, 1858, 3; "The Public Health," *BDE*, May 30, 1849, 3; "Our Squatter Population," *NYT*, July 15, 1867, 8.

29. "Homes of the Poor," *NYT*, February 24, 1858, 3; "City Squatters," *NYT*, July 2, 1854, 4.

30. "Female Pugnacity," *BDE*, June 27, 1851, 3.

31. John Punnett Peters, *Annals of St. Michael's: Being the History of St. Michael's Protestant Episcopal Church, New York, for One Hundred Years, 1807–1907* (New York: B. P. Putnam's, 1907), 445–446, quoted in Rosenzweig and Blackmar, *Park*, 67; "The Present Look of Our Great Central Park," *NYT*, July 9, 1856, 3. On Seneca Village, see Rosenzweig and Blackmar, *Park*, 64–73. Seneca Village was subsequently the subject of a popular 1997 exhibit at the New-York Historical Society, "Before Central Park: The Life and Death of Seneca Village." Although the majority of residents were African Americans, by 1854 some 30 percent of the 264 residents of

Seneca Village were Irish Americans, with a sprinkling of Germans. In 1853, Manhattan won the right to use powers of eminent domain to clear land designated for the park, but when black landowners in Seneca Village were told they had to move they resisted. "They have been notified to remove by the first of August," the *New York Times* reported, but the "policemen find it difficult to persuade them out of the idea that has possessed their simple minds, that the sole object of the authorities in making the Park is to procure their expulsion from the houses which they occupy" ("The Present Look of Our Great Central Park," *NYT,* July 9, 1856, 3).

32. "Annexation," *BDE,* November 16, 1853, 2.

33. "Backgrounds of Civilization," *New York Illustrated News,* February 11, 1860, 200–201.

34. D. E. Wyand, ill., "Squatters of New York: A Scene Near Central Park," *Harper's Weekly,* June 26, 1869, 412. The presence of two streetcar remnants labeled "Grand Street" is intriguing, since the closest that line came to Central Park was 42nd Street, twenty-seven blocks south. Perhaps this was a testimony to the scavenging practices of shanty dwellers.

35. A. B. Frost, ill., "Negro Shanties," *Harper's New Monthly Magazine,* May 1881, 544.

36. A. B. Shults, ill., "On the Border of Central Park," *Harper's New Monthly Magazine,* September 1880, 564.

37. Albert Webster Jr., "A Strange Border," *Appleton's Journal,* May 20, 1871, 574.

4. A Working-Poor Ideology of Dwelling

1. In his history of real estate development in New York City, David M. Scobey notes, "One important gap in my reconstruction of uptown development is the lack of attention to shanties and squatters' communities; clearing them was a perennial thorn in the side of real-estate developers." See Scobey, *Empire City: The Making and Meaning of the New York City Landscape* (Philadelphia: Temple University Press, 2003), 301 note 60.

2. Charles Loring Brace, "Walks among the New York Poor: The Squatters of the City," *NYT,* April 19, 1854, 2; "Red Hook Point: Thirty Years in the Slums," *BDE,* December 2, 1872, 4.

3. "The Sanitary Condition of the City," *NYT,* August 22, 1856, 6; "Red Hook Point," *BDE,* March 1, 1851, 3; "Ten Thousand Squatters," *NYT,* April 20, 1880, 8; "Our Squatter Population," *NYT,* July 15, 1867, 8. On the history of the working poor in the United States, see Seth Rockman, *Scraping By: Wage Labor, Slavery, and Survival in Early Baltimore* (Baltimore: Johns Hopkins University Press, 2009); and Billy G. Smith, ed., *Down and Out in Early America* (University Park, PA: Pennsylvania State University Press, 2004).

4. "Red Hook Point," *BDE,* April 11, 1851, 3; "Ten Thousand Squatters," 8; "View from Schoolhouse in 42nd St. between 2nd and 3rd looking North," *Manual,* 1868,

facing page 526; Fernand Harvey Lungren, *Shanties on 69th Street,* 1879 (New-York Historical Society, inv. no. 1930.71); D. E. Wyand, "Squatters of New York: A Scene Near Central Park," *Harper's Weekly,* June 26, 1869, 412; "Squatter Sovereignty . . . An Inside View of Shanty Life," *NYT,* July 12, 1865, 5; Edward Harrigan, *Squatter Sovereignty* typescript, Edward Harrigan Papers 1871–1984, New York Public Library for the Performing Arts, Series III (Scripts), box 2, folder 8; "The Offal and Piggery Nuisances," *NYT,* July 27, 1859, 1; "General View of the Piggery District, Situated on Fifty-Sixth and Fifty-Seventh Streets, between Sixth and Eighth Avenue," *Frank Leslie's Illustrated Newspaper,* August 13, 1859, 166. A city ordinance in 1859 prohibited piggeries south of 59th Street. On piggeries, see Catherine McNeur, *Taming Manhattan: Environmental Battles in the Antebellum City* (Cambridge, MA: Harvard University Press, 2014), chapter 4, "Hog Wash and Swill Milk," 134–174. As McNeur points out, Tammany Democrats supported piggery owners.

5. John M. August Will, *In Shanty Town,* black ink and wash and graphite on 6 in. x 8 in. paper, undated, Drawings and Works on Paper, New-York Historical Society (likely for *Century Magazine* in the 1860s); Mary Nimmo Moran, *A Vegetable Garden in Shantytown, N.Y.,* etching, undated, Museum of Fine Arts Boston, 1887; "The Charter Election," *NYT,* November 21, 1864, 4; "The Sanitary Condition of the City," *NYT,* August 18, 1856, 6.

6. "The Squatter Population of New York," *NYT,* November 25, 1864, 4; "Squatter Settlement between 1st and 2nd Aves. Near 38th St.," *Valentine's Manual,* 1859, opposite p. 420; "View from Schoolhouse in 42nd St. between 2nd and 3rd Looking North," *Manual,* 1868, opposite p. 526; Edith Wharton, *The Age of Innocence* (New York: D. Appleton, 1920), 10, 24–25. Hoardings were screens of boards enclosing a construction site.

7. As art historian Elizabeth Johns has pointed out, the middle-class response to the growing phalanxes of urban poor and immigrants reflected a dizzying "mixture of blame, projection, and attempted amelioration." Johns, *American Genre Painting: The Politics of Everyday Life* (New Haven: Yale University Press, 1991), 183. "Homes of the Poor," *NYT,* February 24, 1858, 3. Depicting the poor as tantalizingly salvageable may also have been a fund-raising strategy for social reform organizations.

8. Charles Loring Brace, "Dutch Hill," *NYT,* March 21, 1855, 2–3.

9. John Mackie Falconer, *At Newtown Creek, Long Island,* painted porcelain 1¼ x 9½ x 9½ dinner plate, ca. 1876, Brooklyn Museum, Luce Center for American Art; Charles Parsons, *Negro Huts Near Bedford, L.I.,* watercolor on 8 in. x 12 in. canvas, 1851, in private hands.

10. "Homes of the Poor," 3.

11. *Report of Citizen's Association Council of New York Council of Hygiene and Public Health upon the sanitary condition of the City* (New York: D. Appleton & Co.), 1865, quoted in Richard Plunz, *A History of Housing in New York City: Dwelling Type and Social Change in the American Metropolis* (New York: Columbia University Press, 1990), 54.

12. Albert Webster Jr., "A Strange Border," *Appleton's Journal*, May 20, 1871, 574; "Our Squatter Population," 8; "A Visit to Shantytown," *NYT* July 11, 1880, 5; "Street Openings and Squatters," *NYT*, December 7, 1879, 5.

13. *BDE*, August 23, 1885, 1; Jacob A. Riis, *Shanty Town*, gelatin silver print, 1896, Museum of the City of New York; "Our Squatter Population," 8; "A Visit to Shantytown," 5.

14. Upton, *Another City*, 9, 137; "Red Hook Point," 3; "A Strange Border," 574. For example, the Manhattan block bounded by East 42nd, the East River, East 37th, and Second Ave.; see William Perris, *Maps of the City of New York*, plate 76, Early Real Estate Atlases of New York, 1857, New York Public Library, http://digitalcollections. nypl.org/items/510d47e0-bf82-a3d9-e040-e00a18064a99.

15. "Fresh Arrivals," *BDE*, November 30, 1850, 3; "A Strange Border," 574.

16. Elizabeth Blackmar, *Manhattan for Rent, 1785–1850* (Ithaca: Cornell University Press, 1989), 180. My understanding of unsettlement is shaped by Anna Brickhouse, *The Unsettlement of America: Translation, Interpretation, and the Story of Don Luis de Velasco, 1560–1945* (New York: Oxford University Press, 2015).

17. Upton, *Another City*, 86. Upton's theory of the importance of spatial legibility conforms with conclusions drawn by other scholars on the growing middle-class anxiety over physical legibility, as reliable markers of class—dress, manners, etc.— grew unreliable. See Halttunen, *Confidence Men and Painted Ladies*; John F. Kasson, *Rudeness & Civility: Manners in Nineteenth-Century Urban America* (New York: Hill and Wang, 1990); James W. Cook, "Seeing the Visual in U.S. History," *Journal of American History* 95, no. 2 (September 2008): 432–441; and Brown, *Beyond the Lines*, 272 note 46; "A Strange Border," 574; "A Visit to Shantytown," 5.

18. Historian Paul S. Boyer describes the "urban moral-control tradition" that united reformers from the Jacksonian period through the Gilded Age. Boyer, *Urban Masses and Moral Order in America, 1820–1920* (Cambridge, MA, and London: Harvard University Press, 1992), ix, 277–283. On reformers and social control, see also Lori D. Ginzberg, *Women and the Work of Benevolence: Morality, Political and Class in the Nineteenth Century* (New Haven: Yale University Press, 1992); Daniel Eli Burnstein, *Next to Godliness: Confronting Dirt and Despair in Progressive Era New York City* (Urbana, IL: University of Illinois Press, 2010). On the role of the friendly visitor, see Roy Lubove, *The Professional Altruist: The Emergence of Social Work as a Career, 1880–1930* (New York: Atheneum, 1973); and Karen Whitney Tice, *Tales of Wayward Girls and Immoral Women: Case Records and the Professionalization of Social Work* (Urbana: University of Illinois Press, 1998), especially chapter 1, "I'll be Watching You: The Advent of the Case Record."

19. "Backgrounds of Civilization," 201.

20. Henry H. Glassie, "Irish," in Dell Upton, ed., *America's Architectural Roots: Ethnic Groups That Built America* (Washington, DC: National Trust for Historic Preservation, 1986), 76.

21. Mary Nimmo Moran, *A City-Farm*, 8¹¹⁄₁₆ in. x 12⅛ in. etching, 1881,

Metropolitan Museum, New York; also collected as *A Vegetable Garden in Shanty-town, N.Y.*, Museum of Fine Arts, Boston.

22. Natalie Jeremijenko does some of the most compelling work on city/farm issues today, combining science, technology, and environmental art with community implementation. See her X Clinic and Farmacy projects: http://www.environmentalhealthclinic.net/ and http://environmentalhealthclinic.net/farmacy/.

23. "The Sanitary Condition of the City," *NYT*, August 22, 1856, 6; "Homes of the Poor," 3; "The Charter Election," 4.

24. "Squatter Sovereignty," 5; "Our Squatter Population," 8. A voter registration law was passed in New York State in 1859, one of the nation's first, but political operatives subverted it. On voter fraud among Irish Americans in antebellum New York, including fraudulent naturalizations, see Tyler Anbinder, *Five Points* (New York: The Free Press, 2001), 321–327.

25. "John Kelley's Squatters," *NYT*, April 29, 1880, 8.

26. "Squatter Sovereignty," 5.

27. "Red Hook Point: Thirty Years in the Slums," 4; "Homes of the Poor," 3; "The Sanitary Condition of the City," 6; "Spring Moving in Darby's Patch," *BDE*, March 25, 1884, 2; "Ten Thousand Squatters," 8. See also "The Rights of Squatters," *NYT*, February 8, 1892, 10, a retrospective overview of history of laws regarding squatting ground leases and title fights.

28. Editorial, *NYT*, September 7, 1880, 4.

29. Brace, "Walks among the New York Poor: The Squatters of the City," 2; "Suit to Eject Occupants of Shanties," *NYT*, October 13, 1875, 5.

30. "A Verdict for the City," *NYT*, November 12, 1885, 2. Shanties were also built in the suburbs of Brooklyn. A classified real estate ad for "Mechanics' Home Lots" that ran repeatedly in the *Brooklyn Daily Eagle* during 1868 urged readers to "save rents: build a shanty, always a home," on graded ground that was "one hour distant" from the city but close to churches, stores, and schools—and, at $17 and $25 per lot, "cheap as paper" ("Real Estate for Sale," *BDE*, August 5 through December 5, 1868, usually page 1).

31. "A Verdict for the City," 2; "The Charter Election," 4.

32. "Homes of the Poor," 3. According to the *New York Times* the shantytown covered the area bounded by Flushing and DeKalb on the north and south, and Classon and Ryerson on the east and west, with some settlements extending as far north as Fulton Avenue. "Jackson's Hollow," letter to the editor, *BDE*, Feb. 5, 1873, 2; "Jackson's Hollow, Ways and Customs of Its Fast Fading Occupants," *BDE*, July 23, 1873, 3. On tax arrears and final clearing of shantytowns, see "The Title To Be Taken," *BDE*, August 23, 1885, 1; and "Going at Last," *BDE*, April 19, 1888, 2.

33. "Public Lands—Official Regulations," *NYT*, June 22, 1857, 5; "The Title to Be Taken," 1; "Ten Thousand Squatters," 8; "Squatters' Shanties Torn Down," *NYT*, April 17, 1881, 16; "The Shanties Must Go," *NYT*, May 31, 1896, 21; "Evicting Squatters Is Not an Easy Task," *NYT*, November 20, 1910, 67; Lady Duffus Hardy, *Through*

Cities and Prairie Lands: Sketches of an American Tour (London: Chapman and Hall Ltd., 1881), 66–67.

34. On the popularity of minstrelsy with the working classes, see David R. Roediger, *The Wages of Whiteness: Race and the Making of the American Working Class* (London: Verso, 1991); and Walter T. Lahmon Jr., *Raising Cain: Blackface Performance from Jim Crow to Hip Hop* (Cambridge, MA: Harvard University Press, 1998). On the popularity of broadsides, see Charles Hamm, "The Tin Pan Alley Era and Its Antecedents," in *Irving Berlin Early Songs, I. 1907–1911* (Madison: A-R Editions Inc. for the American Musicological Society, 1994), xx; and Irving Howe, *World of Our Fathers: The Journey of the East European Jews to America and the Life They Found and Made* (New York: Galahad Books, 1994), 556–573. For an overview of broadsides in the nineteenth century, see the online finding aid to the New York State Library's Broadside Ballads Catalog, http://www.nysl.nysed.gov/msscfa/broadsides.htm.

35. Henry Tucker, *The Irishman's Shanty* (New York: Firth Pond & Co., 1859). The front of the sheet music advertises it as "A Favorite Comic Song, with imitations, as sung by Matt Peel." Hear an instrumental version at http://www.pdmusic.org/tucker/ht59tis.mid.

36. The classic work on Irish hospitality is Glassie, *Passing the Time in Ballymenone: Culture and History of an Ulster Community* (Philadelphia: University of Pennsylvania Press, 1982).

37. On single-cell and other vernacular housing forms, see Glassie, *Pattern in the Material Folk Culture of the United States* (Philadelphia: University of Pennsylvania Press, 1971); and Glassie, *Vernacular Architecture* (Bloomington: University of Indiana Press, 2000). On the evolution of Irish folk housing forms, see Peter Ennals and Deryck Holdsworth, *Homeplace: The Making of the Canadian Dwelling over Three Centuries* (Toronto, Buffalo: University of Toronto Press, 1998).

38. "Our Squatter Population," 8.

39. On the Irish in minstrelsy, see Robert C. Toll, "Social Commentary in Late-Nineteenth-Century White Minstrelsy," in Annemarie Bean et al., eds., *Inside the Minstrel Mask: Readings in Nineteenth-Century Blackface Minstrelsy* (Hanover, NH: Wesleyan University Press, 1996), 96–97. "Irishman's Shanty" was performed on the road; a notice in the *Chicago Tribune* on December 14, 1863, noted the song was scheduled to be performed that evening at the Varieties theater. On the history of Campbell's Minstrels, see John Franceschina, *David Braham: The American Offenbach* (New York: Routledge, 2002). "First generation" is used variously to refer to immigrants, and to children born to immigrants; I use it here in the second sense, to indicate the first generation born in the United States. See Robert C. Toll, *Blacking Up: The Minstrel Show in Nineteenth-Century America* (New York: Oxford University Press, 1974), 12.

40. In his influential book on minstrelsy, Eric Lott used sheet music covers (along with many other sources) to examine the cultural meaning of blackface in the nineteenth century. See Lott, *Love and Theft: Blackface Minstrelsy and the*

American Working Class (New York: Oxford University Press, 1993); see also Stephanie Elaine Dunson, "The Minstrel in the Parlor: Nineteenth-Century Sheet Music and the Domestication of Blackface Minstrelsy," in *American Transcendental Quarterly* 16 (December 2002): 241–256.

41. Roediger argues that one of the appeals of blackface minstrelsy was that it "assuaged the tension between a longing for a rural past and the need to adapt to the urban present" in mid-nineteenth-century America (*Wages of Whiteness*, 119). Shantytown broadsides may have served a similar function for Irish Americans.

42. Pro Basso (pseudo), *There's Monny a Shlip* (Cincinnati: John Church & Co., 1874), quoted in W. H. A. Williams, *'Twas Only an Irishman's Dream: The Image of Ireland and the Irish in American Popular Song Lyrics, 1800–1920* (Urbana: University of Illinois Press, 1996), 73; *The Emigrant's Farewell* (New York: J. Andrews, n.d.); W. J. Alexander, *Must We Leave Our Old Home* (San Francisco: John. P. Broder, 1890), quoted in Williams, *'Twas Only an Irishman's Dream*, 105; Tom McGuire, *Spare the Old Mud Cabin* (London: Felix McGlennon, 1903,), cited by Williams, 273 note 15; Eliza Cook and James G. Maeder, *Teddy O'Neale* (Boston: William H. Oakes, 1843), quoted in Williams, *'Twas Only an Irishman's Dream*, 73.

43. As emigrants would have known, the inhabitants of one-room mud huts in Ireland were not the poorest of the poor. Traveling in Ireland in the mid-1830s, French writer Gustave de Beaumont described a one-room rural "hovel" made of mud, straw, and sod, that housed a large extended family and "a dirty pig, the only thriving inhabitant of the place, for he lives in filth." Having let his readers assume that such living conditions indicated extreme poverty, de Beaumont corrects them: "This dwelling is very miserable, still it is not that of the pauper, properly so called; I have just described the dwelling of the Irish farmer and agricultural labourer." See de Beaumont, *Ireland: Social, Political, and Religious* (Cambridge, MA: Harvard University Press, 2006), 129. While no dates are listed on the broadside, the border was one De Marsan used frequently in the 1860s, and the address given at the bottom of the broadside is one the publisher occupied starting in 1864, allowing us to narrow the dates of publication to the second half of the 1860s. "Street Literature and Broadside Ballads: Definitions and Characteristics," *Broadside Ballads Catalog*, New York State Library, www.nysl.nysed.gov/msscfa/broadsides.htm.

44. George W. Osborn, *The Irishman's Shanty* (New York: H. De Marsan, n.d.).

45. Eric Lott address the use of blackface by Irish minstrels and its popularity with Irish working-class audiences mid-century, and argues for a connection between local struggles for working-class freedom and the politics of pleasure: "Minstrel comedy forces us to recognize the extent to which comic fun in America is bound up with intimate crises of racial demarcation" (*Love and Theft*, 149). Shantytown broadsides that poke fun at Irish Americans show that comic fun in America is also bound up with the subtleties of class (and intra-class) demarcation.

46. Again the composer is listed, as "'John Mackenzie,' of New York," which again hints that the song was currently being performed in New York. *The Dutch*

Ragpicker's Shanty (New York: H. De Marsan, 1864–1878). No date is listed on the broadside, but it includes De Marsan's address at 60 Chatham St., which he occupied between 1864 and 1878. For "Dutchman" and "Deichter," think "Deutsch-man" and "Deutscher"; both were slang for German immigrants. The quotation marks around the composer's name are in the original, suggesting an in-joke that invites further deciphering.

47. On the history of Irish immigration to the United States, see Hasia R. Diner, *Erin's Daughters in America: Irish Immigrant Women in the Nineteenth Century* (Baltimore: Johns Hopkins University Press, 1983); James R. Barrett, *The Irish Way: Becoming American in the Multiethnic City* (New York: Penguin Books, 2013); Jay P. Dolan, *The Irish Americans: A History* (New York: Bloomsbury Press, 2010); Kerby A. Miller, *Emigrants and Exiles: Ireland and the Irish Exodus to North America* (New York: Oxford University Press, 1988).

5. *Squatter Sovereignty:* Shantytown's Broadway Debut

1. "Amusements, Theatre Comique," *NYT,* January 10, 1882, 4; "An Elegant Playhouse," *NYT,* August 5, 1881, 8. On Tony Pastor's influence and the beginnings of musical theater generally in New York, see Armond Fields, *From the Bowery to Broadway: Lew Fields and the Roots of American Popular Theater* (New York: Oxford University Press, 1993). On Edward Harrigan's career, see Jon W. Finson, "Realism in Late Nineteenth-Century American Musical Theater: The Songs of Edward Harrigan and David Braham," in Finson, ed., *Collected Songs I,* Music of the United States of America 7 (Madison, WI: A-R Editions for the American Musicological Society, 1997), xv–xxxviii; Weldon B. Durham, ed., *American Theatre Companies, 1749–1887* (Westport, CT: Greenwood Press, 1986), 275–276. On patronage of the theater by the working and middle classes, see Richard Butsch, *The Making of American Audiences: From Stage to Television, 1750–1990* (Cambridge: Cambridge University Press, 2000), 45; Lewis A. Erenberg, *Steppin' Out: New York Nightlife and the Transformation of American Culture 1890–1930* (Chicago: University of Chicago Press, 1981), 15; and Mary C. Henderson, *Theater in America: 200 Years of Plays, Players and Productions* (New York: Harry Abrams, 1986), 237.

2. Edward Harrigan, *Squatter Sovereignty,* 1882, TS 1-13, Edward Harrigan Papers 1871–1984, Series III (Scripts), Box 2, Folder 8, Billy Rose Theatre Division, New York Public Library for the Performing Arts, New York, NY; all subsequent citations refer to this typescript using numerals to indicate act and page number. Mary A. Humphrey, *The Squatter Sovereign, or, Kansas in the '50s: A Life Picture of the Early Settlement of the Debatable Ground* (Chicago: Coburn & Newman, 1883); "The Squatter Sovereign of Manhattan," *BDE,* December 11, 1869, 2, advertised as "a humorous incident of metropolitan life."

3. By 1882 the street grid had been laid uniformly to about 138th Street, with some cross streets laid as far north as 159th. Streets also had been laid at 165th and

175th, and several avenues extended beyond that. For an interactive map of street openings, presented chronologically, see http://www.nytimes.com/interactive/2011 /03/21/nyregion/map-of-how-manhattan-grid-grew.html?ref=design.

4. *Squatter Sovereignty,* 1-53. The centrality of the goat as an icon of shantytown is summed up by Harrigan's mocking "Synopsis of Scenes" on the first page of the typescript: "ACT ONE. The Widow Nolan's Shanty. 'It's no bargain without the goat.' ACT TWO. Drawing room at Captain Ferdinand Kline's. 'The Capture of the Goat.' ACT THREE. Shantytown at night. . . . 'The Death of the Goat.'" The diminutive Hart, one of the first female impersonators on the American stage, was especially well-known for his blackface drag performance of the character Rebecca Allup in the *Mulligan Guard* skits; starting in 1882 he often performed opposite his wife, Gertie Granville, playing another female role. See Harry J. Elam Jr. and David Krasner, eds., *African American Performance and Theater History: A Critical Reader* (New York: Oxford University Press, 2001), 174; and Don B. Wilmeth and C.W. E. Bagsby, eds., *Cambridge History of American Theater* (Cambridge: Cambridge University Press, 1999), 464.

5. Brewers occupied a liminal social position in Great Britain as well as the United States. In *Great Expectations,* when Herbert Pocket explains Miss Havisham's status to Pip, he notes that her "father was a country gentleman down in your part of the world, and was a brewer. I don't know why it should be a crack thing to be a brewer; but it is indisputable that while you cannot possibly be genteel and bake, you may be as genteel as never was and brew."

6. *New York Clipper,* January 14, 1882, 710, quoted in Finson, *Collected Songs I,* 254.

7. Finson, *Collected Songs I,* xxiii; "A Dull Dramatic Season," *NYT,* June 11, 1882, 2.

8. Augustin Daly to Edward Harrigan, quoted with no citation in Richard Moody, *Ned Harrigan: From Corlear's Hook to Herald Square* (Chicago: Nelson-Hall, 1980), 125; William Dean Howells, "Editor's Study," *Harper's New Monthly*, July 1886, 315–316, quoted in Robert M. Lewis, *From Traveling Show to Vaudeville: Theatrical Spectacle in American, 1830–1910* (Baltimore: Johns Hopkins University Press, 2003), 104; Finson, *Collected Songs I,* xxiii; Edward Harrigan, "American Playwrights on the American Drama," *Harper's Weekly,* supplement February 2, 1889, 97–98.

9. *Squatter Sovereignty,* 1-5, 1-48, 3-1. Moody, *Ned Harrigan,* 125; Charles Witham box, New York City Theater and Broadway Collection, Museum of the City of New York. The box holds an assortment of Witham's set designs for Harrigan productions, including watercolors of the *Squatter Sovereignty* shantytown, and a block of tenements on Baxter Street, near Five Points, for Harrigan's Mulligan Guard skits.

10. *Squatter Sovereignty,* 1-23–1-47, 1-32.

11. Ibid., 1-25, 1-26, 1-27, 1-29. Romantic views of the Lakes of Killarney, none of them resident at the Louvre, were produced by several Irish landscape painters and etchers in the eighteenth and nineteenth centuries; the image New Yorkers may have been most familiar with was an 1857 painting by John Frederick Kensett, a member of the Hudson River School. In the script the overcoat is described as a

"prize" overcoat, but as there is no meaning apparent in that phrase, and since the typescript is riddled with typos, I have interpreted "prize" as a mistyping of "frieze" (which was pronounced in some quarters to rhyme with "prize"). Irish peasants wore frieze coats, known for their tight, tough weave, and in 1841 Daniel O'Connell, a beloved Irish Catholic parliamentarian who campaigned for the repeal of the Act of Union with Great Britain, famously assumed his seat in the House of Commons wearing one. After that they became popular more generally in the 1850s and 1860s; a longer version of the frieze overcoat manufactured in Ulster was known as an "Ulster coat," and it was something of a national fashion symbol, especially as the century wore on and Irish manufacturers competed with English mills for the American market in frieze. They were increasingly identified with Irish heritage; in a 1900 poem titled "My Coat of Irish Frieze" the narrator refers to his frieze coat as the "one friend / whose loyalty I prize."

12. *Squatter Sovereignty*, 1-27, 1-26, 1-25.

13. *Squatter Sovereignty*, 1-27, 1-25. On the Morning Glory stove see Timothy Starr, "Dennis Littlefield, Albany," in *Great Inventors of New York's Capital District* (Charleston, SC: History Press, 2010), unpaginated (inventors listed alphabetically); and D. G. Littlefield, "Theory of the Base-Burning Stove and Origin of the 'Morning Glory'" (Albany: Littlefield Manufacturing Co., 1870), 4–5. For an example of an 1869 ad, see "The Morning Glory of 1869," Library of Congress, Prints and Photographs Online Catalog, http://hdl.loc.gov/loc.pnp/cph.3a24728.

14. "Illustrated price-list for spring of 1881," W. S. Fogg & Sons catalog, 10–11 and 22–23, https://archive.org/stream/illustratedpriceoowsfo#page/n1/mode/2up. On immigrant furnishings, see Lizabeth Cohen, "Embellishing a Life of Labor: An Interpretation of the Material Culture of American Working-Class Homes, 1885–1915," *Journal of American Culture* 3, no. 4 (Winter 1980): 752–775.

15. *Squatter Sovereignty*, 1-26. Barbara Brackman, *Clues in the Calico: A Guide to Identifying and Dating Antique Quilts* (McLean, VA: EPM Publications, 1989), 26, 165; T. S. (Timothy Shay) Arthur, "The Quilting Party," *Sketches of Life and Character* (Philadelphia: J. W. Bradley, 1850), 364, quoted in Brackman, *Clues in the Calico,* 15–16; Sybil Lanigan, "Revival of the Patchwork Quilt," *Ladies Home Journal,* October 1894, 19. The oldest quilt designated as an "Irish chain" in the collections of the National Museum of American History was made between 1825 and 1832, but neither the maker nor her daughter called it that; see http://collections.si.edu/search/results.htm?q=record_ID%3Anmah_556266&repo=DPLA. In Ireland, once the practice of naming patterns was adopted, the same design was often called the "American chain." For more on the history of the Irish chain pattern in Ireland see Spike Gillespie, *Quilts around the World: The Story of Quilting from Alabama to Zimbabwe* (Minneapolis: Voyageur Press, 2010), 204–207. Gillespie suggests that the name was coined in response to the number of quilts of that pattern brought to America by Irish immigrants.

16. "Did the Irish Chain Pattern Really Come from the Irish?," September 23,

2003, *Quilt History* blog, http://www.quilthistory.com/2003/254.htm; Andro Linkla-
ter, *Measuring America: How an Untamed Wilderness Shaped the United States and
Fulfilled the Promise of Democracy* (San Clemente, CA: Tantor Media, 2003), 69. The
Irish chain was a collapsible chain of one hundred metal spikes measuring just over
ten inches each, for a total of eighty-four feet; there was also a Scotch chain and a
Gunter's chain, prized by American surveyors because it made measuring acres easy:
one acre equaled ten square Gunter's chains, and one New York City block—264 feet—
was equivalent to four Gunter's chains. Audience members at *Squatter Sovereignty*
were encouraged to consider the surveying allusion by the presence of Darius and
Salem, characters who are mistaken for surveyors early in the play.

    17. *Squatter Sovereignty,* 1-8, 1-6, 1-8, 1-3.

    18. Ibid., 1-19, 1-17, 1-23, 2-3, 2-5.

    19. Ibid., 3-19, 3-11.

    20. Ibid., 1-43.

    21. Ibid., 1-10, 1-13, 2-35, 3-10, 1-3. On ethnic humor in nineteenth-century
American theater, see Werner Sollors's discussion of the stage presentation of Native Americans in *Beyond Ethnicity: Consent and Descent in American Culture* (New
York: Oxford University Press, 1986), 131–140; Joseph Boskin and Joseph Dorinson,
"Ethnic Humor: Subversion and Survival," *American Quarterly* 37, no. 1 (Spring
1985): 81–97; Nancy A. Walker, ed., *What's So Funny? Humor in American Culture*
(Lanham, MD: Rowman and Littlefield, 1998); Hamm, *Irving Berlin Early Songs I,*
xx. Irving Howe argues that the popular arts of the late nineteenth century served
as "a sort of abrasive welcoming committee" for immigrants to the United States,
"[s]hrewd at mocking incongruities of manner, seldom inclined to venom" (Irving
Howe and Kenneth Libo, *World of Our Fathers* [New York: Galahad Books, 1994],
402). W. T. Lhamon Jr., *Raising Cain: Blackface Performance from Jim Crow to Hip
Hop* (Cambridge, MA, and London: Harvard University Press, 2000), 75, 91.

    22. *Squatter Sovereignty,* 1-8.

    23. *Squatter Sovereignty,* 1-2; Finson, *Collected Songs,* 271–273. All the music for
the songs in *Squatter Sovereignty* were written by Harrigan's longtime collaborator
and father-in-law, David Braham; Harrigan wrote the lyrics. Other songs from the
musical reprinted in Finson include "The Forlorn Old Maid," "Miss Brady's Piano
For-Tay," "Paddy Duffy's Cart," "The Maguires," and "The McIntyres." Original
sheet music for all but the last two are in the Sam DeVincent Collection of Illustrated Sheet Music, Series 4 (Songwriters, 1817–1982), Subseries 4.57, Box 121, Folder
E, Archives Center, National Museum of American History, Smithsonian Institution, Washington, DC.

    24. *Squatter Sovereignty,* 2-38, 3-13, 3-32, 3-21.

    25. *Squatter Sovereignty,* 3-25. David R. Roediger, *The Wages of Whiteness:
Race and the Making of the American Working Class* (London: Verso, 1991). In his
chapter titled "Class, Coons, and Crowds in Antebellum America," Roediger notes
the identification, starting in the middle of the nineteenth century, of Davy Crockett

with coonskin caps, and argues that the term does not have racist origins (*Wages of Whiteness*, 98). He also notes the association of coonskins in general with the Whig Party during the 1840 "log cabin and hard cider" campaign, which used them as another icon of the common man. Finally, he points to scholarship linking Crockett to the Black Seminole John Horse as the possible origination point of the coonskin connection. See Kenneth W. Porter, "Davy Crockett and John Horse: A Possible Origin of the Coonskin Story," *American Literature* 15 (March 1943): 10–15, cited in Roediger, *Wages of Whiteness*, 111 note 12. Stories linking coonskin caps to minstrel performer Noah Ludlow's 1822 performance as Daniel Boone are contradicted by Ludlow's autobiography, as others have pointed out.

26. Finson, *Collected Songs*, xx; "Squatter Sovereignty Revived," *NYT*, September 25, 1892, 13. The song "Harrigan" contains a memorably catchy chorus that spells out Harrigan's name: "H-A-double R-I-G-A-N spells Harrigan / Proud of all the Irish blood that's in me / Divil a man can say a word agin me / H-A-double R-I-G-A-N, you see."

27. "Second edition of the funniest farce in the world," (Cincinnati: U.S. Printing Co., 1898), Theatrical Poster Collection, Prints and Photographs Division, Library of Congress; "Shehan and Coyne in the Great Irish Comedy, *Grogan's Elevation*," *BDE*, December 18, 1887, 13; "Edmund Mortimer's Success, Comedy 'The Shanty Queen,'" *Pittsburgh Dispatch*, May 4, 1890, 16; "Music and the Drama, Fun in Shantytown," *Sacramento Daily Union*, June 21, 1896, 6; "At the Downtown Theaters . . . Tom Nawn," *Chicago Daily Tribune*, December 13, 1897, 5; *The Old Reliable McFadden's Flats: Everything New*, color lithograph, 46 cm. x 35 cm. (Cincinnati and New York: U.S. Lithograph Co., c.1902), Library of Congress Online Catalog, http://lccn.loc.gov/2014635442; Walter Ben Hare, *Mrs. Tubbs of Shantytown* (Chicago: T. S. Denison, 1914); "Plays and Players of the Advancing Season . . . 'Merry Wives of Gotham,'" *NYT*, January 27, 1924, 137.

28. "A Visit to Shantytown," *NYT*, July 11, 1880, 5.

6. Transformed by Art and Journalism

1. "A Visit to Shantytown," *NYT*, July 11, 1880, 5.
2. William H. Rideing, "Squatter Life in New York," *Harper's New Monthly Magazine*, September 1880, 568; H. C. Bunner, "Shantytown," *Scribner's Monthly Magazine*, October 1880, 855.
3. "A Visit to Shantytown," 5.
4. Ibid.
5. Rideing, "Squatter Life," 564, 568, 567.
6. Ibid., 569, 565, 567.
7. Ibid., 567.
8. Ibid., 567, 569, 563, 566, 569.
9. Ibid., 567–168.

10. Ibid., 566, 563, 564, 569.

11. "The New York Health Commissioners and the 'Shanty Towns,'" *American Architect and Building News* 13, no. 242 (November 20, 1880), quoted in Richard Plunz, *A History of Housing in New York City: Dwelling Type and Social Change in the American Metropolis* (New York: Columbia University Press, 1990), 55.

12. Bunner, "Shantytown," 861, 869, 862.

13. Ibid., 855. In the 1880s the ethnicity of immigrant groups arriving in New York City, largely Irish and German in earlier decades, shifted to Italians, European Jews, and (in smaller numbers) Chinese; Bunner's denunciation of "tenement-house people" may be related to this shift in ethnicity. On immigration patterns in New York City see Nancy Foner, *From Ellis Island to JFK: New York's Two Great Waves of Immigration* (New Haven: Yale University Press, 2000); Moses Rischin, *The Promised City: New York's Jews, 1870–1914* (Cambridge, MA: Harvard University Press, 1962); Stanley Nadel, *Little Germany: Ethnicity, Religion, and Class in New York City, 1845–1880* (Chicago: University of Illinois Press, 1990); Ronald H. Bayor and Timothy J. Meagher, eds., *The New York Irish* (Baltimore: Johns Hopkins University Press, 1996); and Rebecca Yamin, ed., *Tales of Five Points: Working-Class Life in Nineteenth-Century New York* (New York: John Milner Associates, 2000).

14. Bunner, "Shantytown," 856, 867, 868. Riis's famous book on tenements, *How the Other Half Lives: Studies among the Tenements of New York* (Charles Scribner's Sons, 1890), was published in 1890; his first photographs of tenement interiors appeared in 1888.

15. Bunner, 857, 856, 855, 859, 865, 858, 856, 857, 868, 855.

16. Ibid., 856.

17. Jerrold Seigel, *Bohemian Paris: Culture, Politics, and the Boundaries of Bourgeois Life, 1830–1930* (Baltimore: Johns Hopkins University Press, 1999), 11. As Seigel notes, one of the defining characteristics of Bohemia was an "orientation toward the lower parts of society" (11). H. C. Bunner, "New York as a Field for Fiction," *The Century* 27, no. 3 (January 1884); Bunner pursued the idea of laboring-class bohemias further with the short story "The Bowery and Bohemia," published in the April 1894 issue of *Scribner's*. Bunner, "Shantytown," 864, 856, 855; Seigel, 8; Bunner, "Shantytown," 856, 865.

18. Bunner, "Shantytown," 856, 859.

19. Ibid., 855.

20. Glyn Vincent, *The Unknown Night: The Madness and Genius of R. A. Blakelock, An American Painter* (New York: Grove Press, 2003), 84–85, 128–129.

21. For descriptions and reproductions of several of these images, see Abraham A. Davidson, "Shanty Pictures," *Ralph Albert Blakelock* (University Park: Pennsylvania State University Press, 1996), 118–121. Except for their massing, the house structures are not unlike the one in Blakelock's *Pioneer Home*, painted in 1867–1868—after Blakelock had started sketching shantytowns but before he had visited the frontier. The chronology raises the possibility that Blakelock's model for pioneer

homes was actually a Central Park shanty; the two were not, as the works of Thoreau and Cooper attest, so different from each other. In any case the similarity between the two structures underscores Blakelock's sympathetic interpretation of the shanty house form, which rises fortresslike from a daunting natural environment.

22. Albert Webster Jr., "A Strange Border," *Appleton's Journal*, May 20, 1871, 574.

23. On Blakelock see Vincent, *The Unknown Night*; Karen O. Janovy, ed., *The Unknown Blakelock* (Lincoln, NE: Sheldon Memorial Art Gallery, 2008); and Norman A. Geske, *Beyond Madness: The Art of Ralph Blakelock, 1847–1919* (Lincoln, NE: University of Nebraska Press, 2007). Critic Robert Vose wrote in 1982 that Blakelock's oil *Shanties in Harlem* was "the greatest Blakelock I have handled in my forty years."

24. "Red Hook Point: Thirty Years in the Slums," *BDE*, December 2, 1872, 4; the article documented five different Red Hook shantytowns, including Tinkersville, Slab City, Texas, and Sandy Bank—all Irish except for the last, which was German. Only Weeksville and Seneca Village, African American shantytowns discussed in the following chapter, had longer histories than Red Hook. Henry R. Stiles, *History of the City of Brooklyn, N.Y., Including the Old Town and the Village of Brooklyn, the Town of Bushwick and the Village of Williamsburgh* (Brooklyn: published by subscription, 1867–1870), 2:59; Stiles, *History*, 3:582.

25. On Falconer see Linda S. Ferber, "Our Mr. John M. Falconer," in *Brooklyn before the Bridge: American Paintings from the Long Island Historical Society* (Brooklyn: Brooklyn Museum, 1982), 16–23, 62; Sylvester Rosa Koehler, "Negro Huts Near Wilmington, N.C.," in *American Etchings: A Collection of Twenty Original Etchings* (Boston: Estes and Lauriat, 1879), not paginated, reprinted in H. Barbara Weinberg, ed., *American Etchings, American Art* (New York: Garland, 1978), not paginated.

26. F. B. (Frederick Burr) Opper, "A King of A-Shantee," *Puck*, February 15, 1882, 378.

27. "Backgrounds of Civilization," *New York Illustrated News*, February 11 1860, 195, ill. 200–201; "A Scene in Shantytown N.Y.," *New York Daily Graphic*, March 4, 1880, 4.

28. Middle-class women purchased stove polish in the second half of the nineteenth century, but its use was associated with servants, often African American women; see Phyllis Minerva Ellin, "At Home with the Range: The American Cooking Stove, 1865–1920" (MS thesis, University of Pennsylvania, 1985). Centaur Liniment was marketed for use on horses and humans starting in 1871 by New York City–based Centaur Co. (future proprietor of Fletcher's Castoria). Advertisements in the 1870s featured a drawing of a centaur and, sometimes, poems about the tonic's alleged myriad benefits ("What hear we now from West to East / Confounding man, befriending beast, / But Centaur Liniment?"); see Caroline Rance, "Centaur Liniment," on *The Quack Doctor* blog (http://quackdoctor.wordpress.com/category /rheumatism/, October 3, 2009). See a picture of a Centaur Liniment bottle and copies of print ads at http://www.centaur.com/.

29. On the etching revival, see Francine Tyler, ed., *American Etchings of the*

Nineteenth Century: 115 Prints (New York: Dover Publications, 1984); Eliza Pratt Greatorex, quoted without citation in Metropolitan Museum of Art, *Life in America, a Special Loan Exhibition of Paintings Held During the Period of the New York World's Fair, April 24 to October 29* (New York: Scribner's, 1939), 202. The quote was used to describe Blakelock's painting *Fifth Avenue at 89th Street in 1869;* Greatorex's print is also collected as *Some Shanties Opposite the Dakota* and dated 1885 at the Museum of the City of New York. On the picturesque, see Martin Price, *The Picturesque Moment* (New York: Oxford University Press, 1965); and Bermingham, *Landscape as Ideology,* 84–85. John Conron also addresses the multiplicity and variety of the picturesque in *American Picturesque* (University Park: Pennsylvania State University Press, 2000), especially in chapter 11, "The Picturesque City," but his theory of the movement as an expression of the American democratic spirit is incompatible with the evidence of shantytowns.

30. Sylvester Rosa Koehler, "Landscape—Portraiture," in *American Art* (New York: Cassell, 1886), 23, reprinted in Tyler, *American Etchings,* 23; Tyler, *American Etchings,* xii; Tim Barringer, *Art and Emancipation in Jamaica: Isaac Mendes Belisario and His Worlds* (New Haven: Yale Center for British Art in association with Yale University Press, 2007), 41. Art historian William R. Taylor argues that the growth of urban violence during the 1840s and 1850s, culminating in the New York Draft Riots of 1863, helps explain why city residents sought out picturesque distortions of reality. On the absence of realistic urban scenes in nineteenth-century art, and the resistance of New York artists to confront the darker sides of urban development, see Michele H. Bogart, "Art Scenes and the Urban Scene in New York City," in Jan Seidler Ramirez, ed., *Painting the Town: Cityscapes of New York: Paintings from the Museum of the City of New York* (New Haven, CT: Museum of the City of New York in association with Yale University Press, 2000), 37–67.

31. Henry Farrer, *Old Boat House,* 6¼ in. x 12 in. etching, 1882, Library of Congress Prints and Photographs Division, Washington, DC. Also collected privately as *A Seaside Residence.*

32. Charles A. Platt, *Shanties on the Harlem,* 4³⁄₁₆ in. x 7¾ in. etching, 1881, New-York Historical Society, Fine Art Prints of New York City, Print Room Collection 229, Box 2; "Sunday Along the Harlem," *NYT,* April 18, 1881, 5.

33. F. E. Fryatt, "The Navesink Highlands," *Harper's New Monthly Magazine,* September 1879, 541; Charles H. Moore, "Materials for Landscape Art in America," *Atlantic Monthly* 64 (November 1889), 678, quoted in Tyler, *American Etchings,* xiv; ibid., 671 and xii; Greatorex, *Life in America,* 202.

34. "Art Notes," *NYT,* December 25, 1881; Charles A. Platt, *Shanties on the Harlem,* in *American Etchings* 1, part 5 (New York: Art Interchange Publishing Company, 1881–1883), Library of Congress, Prints and Photographs Division.

35. Tyler, *American Etchings,* xv.

36. On refinement and the middle class, see Richard L. Bushman, *The Refinement of America: Persons, Houses, Cities* (New York: Vintage Books, 1993); Elisabeth

Donaghy Garrett, *At Home: The American Family, 1750–1870* (New York: H. N. Abrams, 1990); Katherine C. Grier, *Culture & Comfort: Parlor Making and Middle-Class Identity, 1850–1930* (Washington: Smithsonian Institution Press, 1997); and John F. Kasson, *Rudeness and Civility: Manners in Nineteenth-Century Urban America* (New York: Hill and Wang, 1990).

37. Moran's husband, Thomas Moran, wrote to art editor Sylvester Rosa Koehler on July 7, 1881: "Mrs. Moran has lately made a pretty large plate of *The Cliff Dwellers of New York*. Shanties on the rocks in our street which were removed a few days after she had finished her etching. As you can see, it is a good field, and would have an historic value in time to come"; quoted in Nancy K. Anderson, *Thomas Moran* (New Haven: Yale University Press, 1997), 232.

38. On the French flat craze in nineteenth-century Manhattan see Elizabeth Collins Crowley, *Alone Together: A History of New York's Early Apartments* (Ithaca, NY: Cornell University Press, 1990), 3.

39. Mary Welsh Baskett, *John Henry Twachtman, American Impressionist Painter as Printmaker: A Catalogue Raisonné of His Prints* (Bronxville, NY: M. Hausberg, 1999), 60. The setting for *Shanties and Factories* is sometimes incorrectly identified as Bridgeport, CT; on the correct location see Baskett, *John Henry Twachtman*, 60. The resettlement of Manhattan and Brooklyn shanty dwellers to Jersey City and Hoboken, NJ, deserves further study. A front-page *New York Times* article from November 13, 1889, headlined "Ousting Its Tenants," recounts the eviction of ground-rent-paying shanty dwellers—"so-called squatters"—from thirty shanties on land rented from the Central Railroad Co.: "The tenants of the shanties submitted quietly to the inevitable, and moved their household effects as rapidly as possible."

40. By 1871, Metzner, a leader of the American Turner movement, lived on East Fourth Street near Avenue B, about twelve blocks from the Free School building at 33 Orchard Street. In 1876 several drawings by Metzner's students and one of his own were exhibited in the International Exhibition in Philadelphia, in a gallery dedicated to the work of amateur artists working in pen, pencil, and crayon. The names and topics of the drawings are not known. "Free School of the New York Turnverein," in *Journal of Proceedings, New York Board of Estimate and Apportionment* (New York: New York Printing Co., 1871), 137; S. R. (Sylvester Rosa) Koehler, ed., *The United States Art Directory and Year-Book, A Chronicle of Events in the Art World, and a Guide for All Interested in the Progress of Art in America* (New York: Cassell, 1884), 125; "#67, Metzner, Henry, New York, NY—Drawings by the Pupils of the Free School of the New York Turnverein (Class) 420," *Official Catalogue of the U.S. International Exhibition* (Philadelphia: United States Centennial Commission, 1876), 66, 129; H. Metzner, "Sketchbook," H. Metzner Drawings, Container 139, item nos. 1951.637-.742, Works on Paper, Luce Center, New-York Historical Society. Metzner's numbering system is mysterious, as it is not chronological, topical, or geographic. The sketches of shantytowns are scattered throughout the volume.

41. Metzner, "Sketchbook"; *Shanties to Skyscrapers: Robert L. Bracklow's Photographs of Early New York, 15 December 1983–6 May 1984* (New-York Historical Society, 1983). One of the photographs reproduced in that exhibition catalog is a shanty and a large market garden taken in 1902, titled *West End Avenue and 89th Street.*

42. "The Shanties Must Go," *NYT,* May 31, 1896, 21; "Squatters Were Evicted," *NYT,* April 2, 1897, 2; Jacob Riis, Museum of the City of New York, ID numbers: 90.13.4.19, 90.13.1.303, 90.13.1.307, 90.13.2.137, 90.13.4.305, 90.13.2.229. There are also several photos, or illustrations based on photographs, of shanties built in downtown alleys, including an 1890 photograph of Mulberry Street (90.13.1.93) and an 1895 print of Wooster Street (90.13.1.312).

43. Bill Blackbeard and William Randolph Hearst, eds., *R. F. Outcault's the Yellow Kid: A Centennial Celebration of the Kid Who Started the Comics* (Northampton, MA: Kitchen Sink Press, 1995), plates 6 and 7.

44. Charles A. Vanderhoof, *A New York Shanty,* 10 in. x 8 ½ in. etching, 1887, Museum of the City of New York, 32.460; "Academy of Design," *NYT,* April 8, 1895, 5.

45. "The Shanties Must Go," 21; John M. August Will, *67th St. and 9th Av. Squatter Village,* 10.4 in x 7.5 in. pen and ink drawing, 1887, Museum of the City of New York; Will, *116th Str. 5-6 Av.,* 6 in. x 4 in. pen and ink drawing, 1890, Museum of the City of New York; Louis Oram, *Old Shanties, Corner of 11th Avenue and West 68th Street,* 9¼ in. x 8¾ in. watercolor, 1894, Luce Center, New-York Historical Society; Oram, *Bit on the Boulevard,* 9 in. × 8 in. watercolor, 1898, Luce Center, New-York Historical Society.

46. "True Story of an Eviction: Mrs. Jones Was a Squatter and Had Nine Months' Notice to Get Out," *NYT,* November 8, 1904, 8.

7. African-American Shantytowns 1860–1940

1. Margaret Mitchell, *Gone with the Wind* (1936; repr. New York: Scribner, 2011). My understanding of *Gone with the Wind (GWTW),* and of the race-making potential of post–Civil War space more generally, is informed by Grace Elizabeth Hale, *Making Whiteness: The Culture of Segregation in the South, 1890–1940* (New York: Vintage Books, 1999).

2. Mitchell, *GWTW,* 788, 769, 770.

3. In the film of *GWTW,* the shantytown scene starts at 2:29:51.

4. J. Eugene Grigsby, "Mentor and Nemesis," *International Review of African American Art* 22, no. 1 (2008), 62.

5. Affidavit of Barbara Price, May 15, 1867, Misc. Court Records, ser. 737, Atlanta, GA. Subasst. Comr., Bureau of Refugees, Freedmen, and Abandoned Lands, quoted in Tera W. Hunter, *To 'Joy My Freedom: Southern Black Women's Lives and Labors after the Civil War* (Cambridge, MA: Harvard University Press, 1997), 32.

6. Frederick Ayers to Rev. George Whipple, February 15, 1866, American Missionary Association Papers, quoted in Hunter, *To 'Joy My Freedom,* 37, italics in original.

7. On enslaved workers using space to signal political resistance, see Stephanie M. H. Camp, *Closer to Freedom: Enslaved Women and Everyday Resistance in the Plantation South* (Chapel Hill: University of North Carolina Press, 2004). On the use of space by enslaved workers more generally, see Clifton Ellis and Rebecca Ginsburg, eds., *Cabin, Quarter, Plantation: Architecture and Landscapes of North American Slavery* (New Haven: Yale University Press, 2010). On the cultural history of slavery and emancipation, see Edward E. Baptist and Stephanie M. H. Camp, eds., *New Studies in the History of American Slavery* (Athens: University of Georgia Press, 2006). On the transition from slavery to emancipation, Reconstruction, and its aftermath, see Edward L. Ayers, *The Promise of the New South: Life after Reconstruction* (Oxford and New York: Oxford University Press, 2007); Eric Foner, *Reconstruction: America's Unfinished Revolution, 1863–1877* (New York: Perennial Classics, 2002); Jane Elizabeth Dailey, Glenda Elizabeth Gilmore, and Bryant Simon, eds., *Jumpin' Jim Crow: Southern Politics from Civil War to Civil Rights* (Princeton, NJ: Princeton University Press, 2000); Steven Hahn, *A Nation under Our Feet: Black Political Struggles in the Rural South from Slavery to the Great Migration* (Cambridge, MA: Harvard University Press, 2005); and Hunter, *To 'Joy My Freedom*. On urban slavery see Howard N. Rabinowitz, *Race Relations in the Urban South, 1865–1890* (New York: Oxford University Press, 1978); Gregg D. Kimball, *American City, Southern Place: A Cultural History of Antebellum Richmond* (Athens: University of Georgia Press, 2000).

8. Rebecca Craighead to Rev. Samuel Grant, January 15, 1866, Georgia, American Missionary Association Papers, quoted in Hunter, *To 'Joy My Freedom*, 23.

9. On Atlanta shantytowns, see Allison Dorsey, *To Build Our Lives Together: Community Formation in Black Atlanta, 1875–1906* (Athens: University of Georgia Press, 2004); Matthew Potteiger, *Landscape Narratives: Design Practices for Telling Stories* (New York: J. Wiley, 1998); Franklin M. Garrett, *Atlanta and Environs: A Chronicle of Its People and Events* (Athens: University of Georgia Press, 1969), 740–741.

10. Joseph O. Jewell, *Race, Social Reform, and the Making of a Middle Class: The American Missionary Association and Black Atlanta, 1870–1900* (Lanham, MD: Rowman & Littlefield, 2007), 77–80.

11. *Atlanta Constitution,* June 19, 1868, quoted in Jewell, *Race,* 79.

12. Ernest Ingersoll, "City of Atlanta," *Harper's Monthly Magazine* 60, December 1879, 42.

13. Ibid.

14. Ibid. 43, 41; "The Washerwoman's Strike," *Atlanta Constitution,* July 21, 1881, 4. Additional stories appeared in the *Atlanta Constitution* on July 24, 26, and 29. On headdresses as resistance, see Steeve O. Buckridge, *The Language of Dress: Resistance and Accommodation in Jamaica, 1760–1890* (Kingston, Jamaica: University of the West Indies Press, 2004), 88–96.

15. Ingersoll, "City of Atlanta," 33. On laundresses in Atlanta, and African-American women domestic workers more generally, see Hunter, *To 'Joy My*

Freedom, 52–56, 85–89; and Carl Greenfeld, "The Identity of Black Women in the Post-Bellum Period, 1865–1885," *Binghamton Journal of History,* Spring 1999, https://www.binghamton.edu/history/resources/journal-of-history/article1.html.

16. Ingersoll, "City of Atlanta," 34.

17. Stephen B. Jordan, "Houses without Frames: The Uncommon Technique of Plank Construction," *Old-House Journal* 21, no. 3 (May–June 1993): 36–41; John Brinckerhoff Jackson, *Discovering the Vernacular Landscape* (New Haven: Yale University Press, 1984), 99; Michael Ann Williams, "Pride and Prejudice: The Appalachian Boxed House in Southwestern North Carolina," *Winterthur Portfolio* 25, no. 4 (Winter 1990): 217–230, 218, 229, 228. Williams found evidence of box houses from the early twentieth century in rural regions of North Carolina but concludes based on other evidence that they were a "common form of vernacular building across the rural U.S." in the late nineteenth and early twentieth centuries; illustrations like the one in the December 1879 *Harper's* places box houses in Atlanta following the war, as residences of African Americans. On box housing see also Walter R. Nelson, "Some Examples of Plank House Construction and Their Origin," *Pioneer America* 1, no. 2 (July 1969): 18–29. On vernacular housing styles more generally see Thomas Carter and Elizabeth C. Cromley, *Invitation to Vernacular Architecture: A Guide to the Study of Ordinary Buildings and Landscapes* (Knoxville: University of Tennessee Press, 2005); and Dell Upton and John Michael Vlach, eds., *Common Places: Readings in American Vernacular Architecture* (Athens: University of Georgia Press, 1986).

18. On urban slave housing see John Michael Vlach, "Evidence of Slave Housing in Washington," *Washington History* 5, no. 2 (1993–1994): 64–74; and on slave housing reforms, Vlach, "'Snug Li'l House with Flue and Oven': Nineteenth-Century Reforms in Plantation Slave Housing," *Perspectives in Vernacular Architecture,* vol. 5, *Gender, Class, and Shelter* (1995): 118–129. On housing built by emancipated slaves in rural areas, see Dylan C. Penningroth, *The Claims of Kinfolk: African American Property and Community in the Nineteenth-Century South* (Chapel Hill: University of North Carolina Press, 2003), 4, 6–7, 91, 95–96, 146–149, 153, 165, 179, 185.

19. On the social meanings of vernacular architecture, see Paul Erling Groth and Todd W. Bressi, eds., *Understanding Ordinary Landscapes* (New Haven: Yale University Press, 1997); and Chris Wilson and Paul Erling Groth, eds., *Everyday America: Cultural Landscape Studies after J. B. Jackson* (Berkeley: University of California Press, 2003). Williams, "Pride and Prejudice," 229.

20. Williams, "Pride and Prejudice," 218. On the mobility of labor following emancipation, see Ayers, *The Promise of the New South,* 157. On box housing, see Michael J. Obrien, "Load-Bearing Single-Wall Constructions from Shanties to SIPS," symposium paper, 13th Annual Texas A&M College of Architecture Research Symposium: Natural, Built, Virtual, October 24, 2010, http://mjobrien.com/Papers/Loa-Bearing-Single-Wall-Construction-from-Shanties-to-SIPS.pdf.

21. Hunter, *To 'Joy My Freedom,* 236.

22. Ibid., 228.

23. *Daily National Intelligencer,* July 25, 1865, 3, quoted in James Borchert, *Alley Life in Washington: Family, Community, Religion, and Folklife in the City, 1850–1970* (Urbana: University of Illinois Press, 1982), 13.

24. Kate Masur, *An Example for All the Land: Emancipation and the Struggle over Equality in Washington, D.C.* (Chapel Hill: University of North Carolina Press, 2010), 235; Zina Fay Peirce, "The Externals of Washington," *Atlantic Monthly,* December 1873, 701–716.

25. "Wretched Habitations," *Washington Post,* August 12, 1879, 4; John Burroughs, "Spring in Washington," *Atlantic Monthly,* May 1869, 580–590.

26. Robert Harrison, *Washington during Civil War and Reconstruction: Race and Radicalism* (Cambridge and New York: Cambridge University Press, 2011), 236; Masur, *An Example,* 49, 54–56.

27. Masur, *An Example,* 68–70. On the Freedmen's Village at Arlington, see Joseph P. Reidy, "'Coming from the Shadow of the Past': The Transition from Slavery to Freedom at Freedmen's Village, 1863–1900," *Virginia Magazine of History and Biography* 95, no. 4 (October 1987): 403–428.

28. General Oliver Otis Howard, *Autobiography,* vol. 2, part 1 (New York: Baker & Taylor Co., 1908), 417.

29. Ibid., 416–421.

30. Ibid., 418.

31. Harrison, *Washington,* 207.

32. *Daily National Intelligencer,* July 25, 1865, 3, quoted in Borchert, 28; J. V. W. Vandenburgh to W. W. Rogers, June 20, 1867, quoted in Harrison, *Washington,* 70; A. C. Richards to the Board of Police, March 6, 1866, enclosed in T. A. Lazenby to Maj. Genl. O. O. Howard, March 12, 1866, quoted in Sojourner Truth and Olive Gilbert, *Narrative of Sojourner Truth: A Bondswoman of Olden Time, with a History of Her Labors and Correspondence Drawn from Her Book of Life; Also, A Memorial Chapter,* Penguin Classics (New York: Penguin Books, 1998), 127–129.

33. *Constitutional Union,* June 16, 1863, quoted in Masur, *An Example,* 55. On the right to the city see Henri Lefebvre, *Le Droit à la ville* (Paris: Anthropos, 1968), and David Harvey, "The Right to the City," *New Left Review* 53 (September–October 2008): 23–40.

34. George Lathrop, "A Nation in a Nutshell," *Harper's New Monthly Magazine,* March 1881, 541–566. *Negro Shanties* is on p. 544.

35. On rural housing built by emancipated African Americans, see Penningroth, *Claims of Kinfolk,* 148; Earl Lewis, "Connecting Memory, Self, and the Power of Place in African American Urban History," *Journal of Urban History* 21 (March 1995): 347–371, 358; Barbara Burlison Mooney, "Looking for History's Huts," *Winterthur Portfolio* 39, no.1 (Spring 2004): 43–68, 47, 60–65.

36. On slave housing, see John Michael Vlach, *Back of the Big House: The Architecture of Plantation Slavery* (Chapel Hill: University of North Carolina Press, 1993), and Mooney, "Looking for History's Huts," 43–68.

37. Diane Tepfer, *Becoming the Capital City: DeLancey Gill's Washington, April 11, 1992 to January 1993*, exh. cat., (Washington: Historical Society of Washington, DC, 1992), 12.

38. Ibid., 14; DeLancey Walker Gill, *Meridian Hill*, 1883 (view 2), *Near 22nd and N Street*, 1883, pen and ink; *P St. near 18th*, 1883, pen and ink; *Near 18th & B, N.W.*, 1883, pen and ink; *Near 18th & D N.W.*, 1883, pen and ink; *22nd & O*, 1883, pen and ink; *Dupont Circle*, 1883, pen and ink; *R St. Near 23rd*, 1883, pen and ink; *I Street Near 12th Street*, 1883, pen and ink; *Near Boundary, 1st St. N.E.*, 1883, pen and ink; all in Historical Society of Washington, DC, Gill collection, Box 2; Gill, *26th & N Streets NW*, 1883, watercolor, Elden D. "Josh" Billings Collection, Digital Library and Archives, Virginia Polytechnic Institute and State University, Blacksburg, VA.

39. On vernacular architecture in the Caribbean, see Jerome S. Handler and Stephanie Bergman, "Vernacular Houses and Domestic Material Culture on Barbados Sugar Plantations, 1650–1838," *Journal of Caribbean History* 43, no. 1 (July 2009): 1–36; T. J. Barringer, *Art and Emancipation in Jamaica: Isaac Mendes Belisario and His Worlds* (New Haven, CT: Yale University Press, 2007); and Louis P. Nelson et al., eds., *Falmouth, Jamaica: Architecture as History* (Kingston, Jamaica: University of West Indies Press, 2014).

40. Names and census figures quoted in Tepfer, *Becoming the Capital City*, 8.

41. Christopher Martin, "'Hope Deferred': The Origin and Development of Alexandria's Flounder House," *Perspectives in Vernacular Architecture* 2 (1986): 111–119, 118; Tepfer, *Becoming the Capital City*, 8.

42. On the importance of family life in African-American households, see Earl Lewis, "Connecting Memory, Self, and the Power of Place in African American Urban History," *Journal of Urban History* 21 (March 1995): 347–371, 351–352, 358–359; Penningroth, *Claims of Kinfolk*, 146–148, 179, 185.

43. "The New Washington," *Century Magazine* 27, March 1884, 646, 641.

44. Frank "Carp" Carpenter, "The Season Opens," *Cleveland Leader*, 1883, exact date unknown, quoted in Carpenter, *Carp's Washington* (New York: McGraw-Hill, 1960), 5.

45. Most famously, Winslow Homer, Eastman Johnson, and William Aiken Walker painted scenes of emancipated life that recalled enslaved conditions, either as a means of critique (Homer and Johnson) or an expression of nostalgia (Walker).

46. On Gill and photography, see James R. Glenn, "DeLancey W. Gill: Photographer for the Bureau of American Ethnology," *History of Photography* 7, no. 1 (October 2013): 7–22.

47. Booker T. Washington, "A Speech at the Memorial Service for Samuel Chapman Armstrong, Hampton, Va., May 25, 1893," in Louis R. Harlan, ed., *Booker T. Washington Papers, Volume 3, 1889–1895* (Urbana: University of Illinois Press, 1974), 317.

48. Booker T. Washington, *The Story of My Life And Work* (Toronto: J. L. Nichols, 1901), 5. For a thorough analysis of Washington's rhetorical use of the cottage, see Barbara Burlison Mooney, "The Comfortable Tasty Framed Cottage: An African

American Architectural Iconography," *Journal of the Society of Architectural Historians* 61, no. 1 (March 2002): 48–67.

49. Washington, *Story of My Life,* 13, 15–16. On materials used in the construction of slave cabins see Vlach, *Back of the Big House,* 157.

50. Vlach, *Back of the Big House,* 162–163. Mooney argues for including cabins in a larger category of outbuildings that also includes kitchens, tool sheds, etc., rather than as intentional domestic spaces. See Mooney, "Looking for History's Huts," 47, 60–61, 65.

51. Washington, *Story of My Life,* 22.

52. Ibid., 57, 64–65, 361.

53. On Scott and this painting see William E. Taylor, *A Shared Heritage: Art by Four African Americans* (Bloomington: Indiana University Press, 2000), 22–24.

54. Alfred O. Phillipp, "Robbins, Ill.—A Folklore in the Making," April 6, 1939, 2–4, in *American Life Histories: Manuscripts from the Federal Writers' Project 1936–1940,* Library of Congress, Washington, DC, http://www.loc.gov/item/wpalh000078/; Thomas J. Kellar, "History of the Village of Robbins, Ill.," (December 17, 1921), unpublished essay, https://edocs.uis.edu/mleon1/www/Texts/village.htm; Phillipp, "Robbins," 4.

55. Ibid., 1.

56. Ibid., 1, 3, 4, 5.

57. Ibid., 10.

58. John Michael Vlach, e-mail interview by author, October 6, 2003. Vlach pointed out that his own efforts to collect more than cursory information on southern shantytowns had proven frustrating. "Beneath the Underground: The Flight to Freedom and Communities in Antebellum Maryland," Maryland State Archives electronic publication, December 19, 2002, http://slavery.msa.maryland.gov/html/antebellum/fr.html.

59. Katherine Duncan Morse, "Shanty," *Poetry* 31, no. 2 (November 1927): 72.

60. Hale Aspacio Woodruff produced murals called *Shantytown* and *Mudhill* in 1934, and in subsequent years prints possibly based on those murals. The 10 in. x 8 in. linocut from 1935, collected privately as *Shantytown,* is also in the collections of several museums under different titles, including *Returning Home* (National Gallery of Art) and *View of Atlanta* (Metropolitan Museum of Art). Woodruff, *Sunday Promenade,* linocut, 15 in. × 11¼ in., 1935, Metropolitan Museum of Art.

61. Ralph McGill, "Quiet, Modest Negro Hailed as One of Modern Masters," *Atlanta Constitution,* December 18, 1935, n.p., quoted in Taylor, *A Shared Heritage,* 131; Woodruff, *Relics,* linocut, 8 in. × 11 in., 1935, Metropolitan Museum of Art. Other black artists referred to these Atlanta shantytowns in their work. In 1927, Piedmont blues musician Peg Leg Howell recorded "Beaver Slide Rag" for Columbia Records; jazz saxophonist Marion Brown included "Buttermilk Bottom," commemorating another Atlanta shantytown, on the 1973 *Geechee Recollections* for the Impulse! label.

8. Depression-era Shantytowns

1. Joe Young, John Siras, and Little Jack Little, *In a Shanty in Old Shanty Town* (New York: M. Witmark & Sons, 1932), in the Sam DeVincent Collection of Illustrated Sheet Music, Col. #300, Series 4, Box 190, Folder H, National Museum of American History, Smithsonian Institution, Washington, DC.

2. *Relief for Unemployed Transients: Hearings Before a Sub-Committee of the Committee on Manufactures, U.S. Senate,* 72nd Congress (1933), statement of Nels Anderson, quoted in David Levinson, *Encyclopedia of Homelessness* (New York: Sage Publications, 2004), 1:183.

3. Harry Woods, *In the Shanty Where Santy Claus Lives* (New York: M. Witmark & Sons, 1931); Leon Schlesinger, "The Shanty Where Santy Claus Lives," Merrie Melodies, Warner Bros. Pictures, 1933; https://www.youtube.com/watch?v=eVM17U96d3c.

4. "Hard Times are Still Hoovering," Underwood and Underwood, in collection of Presidential Library and Museum of Herbert Hoover, National Archives and Records Administration, http://www.ecommcode2.com/hoover/research/photos/1932–97.html.

5. On the Bonus March see Paul Dickson and Thomas B. Allen, *The Bonus Army: An American Epic* (New York: Walker, 2006), and their article based on the book, "Marching on History," *Smithsonian Magazine,* February 2003, http://www.smithsonianmag.com/history/marching-on-history-75797769/?no-ist; and Jeremy Scott White, "The Presence and Protest of the 1932 Bonus March in Washington: A Case Study of Spatial Inversion" (PhD diss., University of California, 1998).

6. John Dos Passos, "Washington and Chicago," *New Republic,* June 29, 1932, 177–178.

7. *Fire, Set by U.S. Army, Consuming Camp of Bonus Expeditionary Forces; Washington Monument in Background,* Associated Press, 1932, http://www.loc.gov/pictures/item/96500469/.

8. On hoboes and homelessness, see Todd DePastino, *Citizen Hobo: How a Century of Homelessness Shaped America* (Chicago: University of Chicago Press, 2003); on the Bonus March specifically, see 194–197. See also Lynne Adrian, "'The World We Shall Win for Labor': Early Twentieth-Century Hobo Self-Publication," *Print Culture in a Diverse America,* James P. Danky and Wayne A. Wiegand, eds. (Urbana: University of Illinois Press, 1998), 101–128; and Adrian's forthcoming archive, *Hobo News Digital Archive,* University of Alabama, http://www.lib.ua.edu/digitalhumanities/hobonews.

9. Russell Lee, *Rear of House Occupied by Buckboard Charlie, Squatter Near Iron River, Michigan,* 1937, FSA/OWI Photograph Collection, Library of Congress Prints and Photographs Division, Washington, DC; Barbara Berry Darsey and Stetson Kennedy, "Florida Squatters," 1938, Folklore Project, WPA Federal Writers' Project, in *American Life Histories: Manuscripts from the Federal Writers' Project, 1936–1940* (Washington, DC: Library of Congress, National Digital Library Program, 1998); David Ward, *Poverty, Ethnicity, and the American City, 1840–1925: Changing*

Conceptions of the Slum and Ghetto (Cambridge: Cambridge University Press, 1989), 35; Russell Lee, *House in Shantytown on Nueces Bay, Corpus Christi, Texas, 1939*, FSA/OWI Photograph Collection, Library of Congress Prints and Photographs Division, Washington, DC; Dorothea Lange, *One of Forty Houses Adjoining Arvin (Kern County) Camp for Migrants, California*, 1938, FSA/OWI Photograph Collection, Library of Congress Prints and Photographs Division, Washington, DC; *Minimal House*, no photographer or date given, in New Deal Network Photo Gallery, Franklin and Eleanor Roosevelt Institute, Teachers College/Columbia University, http://newdeal.feri.org/library/r74.htm.

10. *Interstate Migration: Report of the Select Committee to Investigate the Interstate Migration of Destitute Citizens, House of Representatives, 76th Congress, Pursuant to H. Res. 63, 491, 629* (1941; repr., New York: Da Capo Press, 1976), 385 n.13; Jacob Fisher, *The Response of Social Work to the Depression* (Cambridge, MA: Schenkman, 1980), 145, quoted in Joan M. Crouse, *The Homeless Transient in the Great Depression: New York State 1929–1941* (New York: State University of New York Press, 1986), 216. Crouse notes titles among those Fisher may never have read: *Depression Pioneers, The Transient Unemployed*, and *Migrant Families*.

11. Crouse, *Homeless Transient*, 99–100; Matthew Josephson, "The Other Nation," *New Republic*, May 15, 1933, 14–16, quoted in Crouse, *Homeless Transient*, 72–74.

12. Reginald Marsh, *Soup Kitchen [East River Shanties]*, 1937, watercolor, 20.5 in. x 5.625 in., Museum of the City of New York; Crouse, *Homeless Transient*, 100.

13. Crouse, *Homeless Transient*, 101–102.

14. Francis G. Blair for the National Association of Travelers Aid Societies, *A Brief Report on Transient Families in Arizona* (New York: President's Organization on Unemployment Relief, 1931), 5, 4. This account and others made by relief workers show a complex mix of compassion, repulsion, and helplessness, but all shared a determination to keep migrants moving: "The old cars in which the transient families are traveling often break down entirely on the [steep] grades, so that much of the relief money has to go for repairing cars, furnishing new parts or tires," Blair reported (9).

15. Crouse, *Homeless Transient*, 171, 167, 165; Boyden Sparkes, "The New Deal for Transients," *Saturday Evening Post*, October 19, 1935, 90–95; Crouse, 171.

16. Crouse, *Homeless Transient*, 167, 169, 170.

17. Carleton Beals, "Migs: America's Shantytown on Wheels," *Forum and Century*, January 1938, 10–15.

18. Ibid., 11, 13.

19. Henry Hill Collins Jr., *America's Own Refugees: Our 4,000,000 Homeless Migrants* (Princeton: Princeton University Press, 1941), 259, 258, 260, 259.

20. Ellery F. Reed, *Federal Transient Program: An Evaluative Survey, May to July, 1934* (New York: Committee on Care of Transient and Homeless, 1934), 19, 20, 22, 24.

21. *Interstate Migration*, 52.

22. The term "culture of poverty" was introduced by anthropologist Oscar Lewis

in his book *La Vida: A Puerto Rican Family in the Culture of Poverty, San Juan and New York* (New York: Panther, 1966).

23. On historical amnesia see Michael Kammen, *Mystic Chords of Memory: The Transformation of Tradition in American Culture* (1991; repr., New York: Vintage, 1993), 531–536; Harvey Warren Zorbaugh, *Gold Coast and Slum* (Chicago: University of Chicago Press, 1929), 11; ibid., 128; *Final Reports of the President's Conference on Home Building and Home Ownership III., Slums, Large-Scale Housing and Decentralization,* Appendix III, 30–33, quoted in Ford, *Slums and Housing,* 9.

24. James Ford, *Slums and Housing, Volume I: With Special Reference to New York City History—Conditions—Policy* (January 1936): 10, 14; *Interstate Migration,* 385.

25. George C. Stoney, "A Valley to Hold To," *Survey Graphic: Magazine of Social Interpretation,* July 1940, 391.

26. *Little Old Sod Shanty on the Claim,* arr. by Mort. H. Glickman, with a Hawaiian guitar solo arr. by Nick Manoloff (Chicago: Calumet Music Co., 1935), Sam DeVincent Collection of Illustrated Sheet Music, Col. #300, Series 4, Box 222, Folder C, National Museum of American History, Smithsonian Institution, Washington, DC. The song is reminiscent in name only of the 1898 "Little Sod Shanty on the Plains: A Trans-Mississippi Song," written by Morte Parsons; and the 1880s folk song of the same name, written by Oliver Edwin (Dr. O.E.) Murray of South Dakota, which was sung to the tune of the 1871 minstrel hit by Will Hays, "Little Old Log Cabin in the Lane." Laura Ingalls Wilder, *On the Banks of Plum Creek* (New York: Harper & Bros., 1937), 11. Inexact replicas of the dugout house and the claim shanty are on view at the Ingalls Homestead tourist attraction in De Smet, http://www.ingallshomestead.com/virtualvisit/dugout.html.

27. Laura Ingalls Wilder, *By the Shores of Silver Lake* (New York: Harper & Bros., 1939), 235–236.

28. "The Year in Hollywood," *NYT,* December 30, 1934, 5. The movie *My Man Godfrey* was based on a short novel by Eric Hatch, *1101 Park Avenue,* published the year before; it was later reissued under the name of the film.

29. See Andrew Bergman's analysis of screwball films as fantasies of social unity—as "implosive" rather than explosive—in *We're in the Money: Depression America and Its Films* (New York: New York University Press, 1971), 133, 140. On the film as a promotion of class reconciliation, see Terry Donovan Smith, "Mixing It Up in the Depression," in *Journal of Popular Film and Television* 24, no. 3 (Fall 1996): 124–133. See also William Brigham, "Down and Out in Tinseltown: Hollywood Presents the Dispossessed," in Paul Loukides and Linda K. Fuller, eds., *Beyond the Stars: Studies in American Popular Film, Vol. 5: Themes and Ideologies in American Popular Film* (Bowling Green, Ohio: Bowling Green State University Press, 1996), 168. See also Morris Dickstein, *Dancing in the Dark: A Cultural History of the Great Depression* (New York: W. W. Norton, 2010), 399–401; and Gwendolyn Audrey Foster, *Class-Passing: Social Mobility in Film and Popular Culture* (Carbondale: Southern Illinois Press, 2005), 26. Foster argues that Godfrey's contact with the poor in

shantytown, and his opportunity to view the rich through the eyes of a servant at the Bullock household, awakens his political conscience and inspires him to make change happen.

30. On the Hooverville montage in *Sullivan's Travels,* see Sonnet Retman, *Real Folks: Race and Genre in the Great Depression* (Durham, NC: Duke University Press, 2011), 219–227.

31. For a brief but trenchant discussion of *Sullivan's Travels* and *Let Us Now Praise Famous Men,* see Julia L. Foulkes, "Politics and Culture in the 1930s and 1940s," in Karen Halttunen, ed., *A Companion to American Cultural History* (New York: Wiley-Blackwell, 2008), 223–224.

32. Washington, "A Speech at the Memorial Service for Samuel Chapman Armstrong," *Papers* 3:317; Barbara Burlison Mooney, "The Comfortable Tasty Framed Cottage: An African American Architectural Iconography," *Journal of the Society of Architectural Historians* 61, no. 1 (March 2002): 56–57. Examples of housing photographs in *The Crisis* include "The Old Type of Negro Alley," and "The New Type of Negro Home," November 1911, 28–29; untitled photograph of a bungalow, August 1913, 194; and "The Old Cabin," October 1920, 26, all reproduced in Mooney, "Comfortable Tasty Framed Cottage," 56–58.

33. W. E. B. Du Bois, *The Philadelphia Negro* (1899; repr., Philadelphia: University of Pennsylvania Press,1996), 293–294, quoted in Mooney, "Comfortable Tasty Framed Cottage," 62–63; Du Bois, "The Negro American Family," *Atlanta University Publications* 13 (1908): 51–52, quoted in Mooney, "Comfortable Tasty Framed Cottage," 62; ibid., 53. Over the years Du Bois's positions moved sharply left and by the 1930s he had embraced Marxist and socialist views to become a critic of consumer capitalism.

34. On black musicians and white audiences in the early twentieth century, see Karl Hagstrom Miller, *Segregating Sound: Inventing Folk and Pop Music in the Age of Jim Crow* (Durham: Duke University Press, 2010), chapters 6–7, 187–240.

35. "Shantytown," Johnny Cash and June Carter, from *Carryin' On with Johnny Cash and June Carter,* Columbia CS 9528, August 1967, 33⅓ rpm.

36. Janice Perlman, *The Myth of Marginality: Urban Poverty and Politics in Rio de Janeiro* (Berkeley: University of California Press, 1976), 242–243, quoted in Peter Hall, *Cities of Tomorrow: An Intellectual History of Urban Planning and Design in the Twentieth Century* (New York: Wiley-Blackwell, 2002), 277.

37. John F. C. Turner, "Lima's Barriadas and Corralones: Suburbs vs. Slums," *Ekistics* 19 (1965), 152, quoted in Hall, *Cities,* 252; ibid.; Turner, "Uncontrolled Urban Settlement: Problems and Policies," in *International Social Development Reviews I: Urbanization: Development Policies and Planning* (New York: 1968), 360, quoted in Hall, *Cities of Tomorrow,* 252. Recent scholarship suggests Lewis was misinterpreted, perhaps willfully so; see Orlando Patterson, "How Sociologists Made Themselves Irrelevant," *Chronicle of Higher Education,* December 1, 2014, https://chronicle.com/article/How-Sociologists-Made/150249/.

38. Ward, *Poverty, Ethnicity,* ix; Paul Groth, *Living Downtown: The History of Residential Hotels in the United States* (Oakland, CA: University of California Press, 1999), 10, xi.

Epilogue

1. Alejandro Silva and Howard Campbell, "*Colonia*-ism and the Culture of the Normals," *Latin American Issues* 14 (1998): 91–106. On *colonias* see also Angela J. Donelson and Adrian X. Esparza, *The Colonias Reader: Economy, Housing, and Public Health in U.S.-Mexico Border Colonias* (Tucson: University of Arizona Press, 2010). On the contemporary international debate over urban "informal" housing, see Ananya Roy, "Urban Informality: Toward an Epistemology of Planning," *Journal of the American Planning Association* 71, no. 2 (Spring 2005): 147–158.

2. Philip True, "Shanty Town, U.S.A.," *The Progressive* 60, no. 1 (1996): 25–26.

3. Ibid., 25–27.

4. Charles Stokes famously coined the term "slums of hope" for Third World shantytowns in 1962 in "A Theory of Slums," *Land Economics* 8, no. 3 (August 1962): 187–197. For a more recent assessment of Third World shantytowns past and present, see Peter Lloyd, *Slums of Hope? Shanty Towns of the Third World* (Manchester: Manchester University Press, 1979), and Peter Hall, "The City of Sweat Equity," in *Cities of Tomorrow,* 241–273; ibid., 26. On recent developments in Brownsville's *colonias,* see Alina Simone, "On the Texas Border, They're Fighting for the Right to Have Street Lamps," PRI, April 3, 2015, http://www.pri.org/stories/2015-04-03/texas-border-theyre-fighting-right-have-street-lamps; and Lynn Brezosky, "Texas Still Looking for a Solution for Colonias," *Houston Chronicle* online, July 28, 2012, http://www.chron.com/news/houston-texas/article/State-still-seeks-solu-tion-for-colonia-communities-3743612.php.

5. "Take Back the Land: Miami Grassroots Group Moves Struggling Families into Vacant Homes," *Democracy Now,* December 19, 2008, http://www.democracynow.org/2008/12/19/take_back_the_land_miami_grassroots; Max Rameau, *Take Back the Land: Land, Gentrification and the Umoja Village Shantytown* (Miami, FL: Nia Interactive Press, 2008).

6. Ben Ehrenreich, "Tales of Tent City," *The Nation,* June 22, 2009, http://www.thenation.com/article/tales-tent-city. Recent scholarship on shantytowns in the developing world includes Robert Neuwirth, *Shadow Cities: A Billion Squatters, a New Urban World* (New York: Routledge, 2005); Doug Saunders, *Arrival City: How the Largest Migration in History Is Reshaping Our World* (New York: Pantheon, 2010); and Mike Davis, *Planet of Slums* (London and New York: Verso, 2006). On theories of urban informal housing and globalization, see Ananya Roy and Nezar AlSayyad, eds., *Urban Informality: Transnational Perspectives from the Middle East, Latin America, and South Asia* (Lanham, MD: Lexington Books, 2004).

Acknowledgments

Grace Elizabeth Hale guided this project, and its author, from seminar paper to published manuscript, becoming along the way a colleague and friend as well as a mentor. Dell Upton, Edward Ayers, Eric Lott, and Peter Onuf provided the early input and feedback that formed the intellectual foundation for this book. Anna Brickhouse's incisive critiques inspired me to make it better, even as my deadline neared. And Bruce Holsinger's final reading gave me confidence that, indeed, I was done.

Several grants provided the access to archives that are essential to completing projects dependent upon primary documents, and the time to write. I am grateful to the Smithsonian Institution for a Predoctoral Fellowship; the Mellon/ACLS for a Dissertation-Year Completion Grant; and the Gilder-Lehrman Institute of American History for a research fellowship that took me to the New-York Historical Society, where with the help of their crack staff I found several crucial pieces of evidence. I also have been fortunate to work in the archives of the National Museum of American History, the Smithsonian American Art Museum, the Historical Society of Washington, DC, the New York Public Library, the Museum of the City of New York, and the Library of Congress, all of which yielded up, with a bit of digging, artifacts illuminating the largely forgotten history of shantytowns in this country.

I thank my editor, Joyce Seltzer, for her shrewd editing and her unflinching devotion to the author's voice; and her assistant, Brian Distelberg, for making everything go smoothly.

I am deeply grateful to my husband, Stephen Arata, whose acuity as a scholar is matched by his loving-kindness as a spouse. This book is about forgotten landscapes, but our life together has blossomed with the discovery of new ones.

Credits

Background photograph on title page: "Homeless shantytown known as Hooverville, foot of S. Atlantic St.," ca. 1937. Seattle Photograph Collection, UW2129. University of Washington Libraries, Special Collections Division.

Page 37: "1. A Hut or Wigwam; 2. A Shade or Shantie; 3. A Cottage." Robert Lamond, *A Narrative of the Rise and Progress of Emigration from the Counties of Lanark and Renfrew,* Chalmers & Collins, 1821.

Page 70: "View from School House in 42nd Street, Between 2nd & 3rd Avs. Looking North." Manual of the Corporation of the City of New York, Common Council, Lith. W.C. Rogers & Co., 1868. Mid-Manhattan Picture Collection, New York Public Library Digital Collections.

Page 81: "The Squatters of New York—A Scene Near Central Park." Sketch by D.E. Wyand. *Harper's Weekly,* 26 June 1869. Library of Congress Prints and Photographs Division, LCUSZ62106378.

Page 96: "Backgrounds of Civilization: Establishment of Mr. Glennan and his Full-Headed Family," *New-York Illustrated News,* J. Warner Campbell & Co., 1860. Neg #90969d. Photography © New-York Historical Society.

Page 111: "The Irishman's Shanty: A Favorite Comic Song with Imitations as sung by Matt Peel." New York: Firth, Pond & Co., 547 Broadway, 1859. Engraved by Greene & Walker, Boston. Firth, Pond & Co., 1859. Francis G. Spencer Collection of American Sheet Music, American Melting Pot Collection, Baylor University Libraries.

Page 122: "Squatter Sovereignty." Program. Buffalo, N.Y. Courier Lith. Co., c1882. The Harris Collection of American Poetry and Plays. John Hay Library, Brown University.

Page 147: "On the Border of Central Park." Lithographic print. Albert B. Shults (1868–1913). *Harper's Weekly,* September 1880. Mid-Manhattan Picture Collection, New York Public Library Digital Collections.

Page 157: Ralph Albert Blakelock (American, 1847–1919). *Old New York: Shanties at 55th Street and 7th Avenue,* ca. 1875. Milwaukee Art Museum, Gift of Eliot Grant Fitch, in memory of his son, John Grant Fitch, W1948.I. Photo by P. Richard Eells.

Page 161: "Puck's Gallery of Celebrities—The King of A-Shantee." Frederick Burr Opper (1857-1937). *Puck,* February 15, 1882. Library of Congress Prints and Photographs Division, LC-USZ62-118627.

Page 168: "The Cliff Dwellers of New York," 1881. Mary Nimmo Moran, (1842–1899). Image © The Metropolitan Museum of Art. Source: Art Resource, NY.

Page 172: Heinrich Metzner. "1st Ave., bet. 39–40 str.", from a sketchbook. Object #1951.708. Photography © New-York Historical Society.

Page 186: "Shermantown" in "The City of Atlanta" by Ernest Ingersoll. *Harper's New Monthly Magazine,* Vol. LX, No. CCCLV, December 1879.

Page 199: "Meridian Hill," De Lancey Walker Gill, 1883. De Lancey Gill Papers (MS 735), The Historical Society of Washington, DC.

Page 204: "22nd and N Streets," De Lancey Walker Gill, 1883. De Lancey Gill Papers (MS 735), The Historical Society of Washington, DC.

Page 206: "Dupont Circle," De Lancey Walker Gill, 1883. De Lancey Gill Papers (MS 735), The Historical Society of Washington, DC.

Page 217: "Going Home. 1935. Linocut." Hale Aspacio Woodruff, (1900–1980). Art © Estate of Hale Woodruff / Licensed by VAGA, New York, NY. Image © The Metropolitan Museum of Art. Gift of Reba and Dave Williams, 1999. Image source: Art Resource, NY.

Pages 222-223: "Homeless shantytown known as Hooverville, foot of S. Atlantic St.," ca. 1937. Seattle Photograph Collection, UW2129. University of Washington Libraries, Special Collections Division.

Pages 226-227: "Shacks, put up by the Bonus Army on the Anacostia flats, Washington, DC, burning after the battle with the military, 1932." War Department, Army War College, Historical Section. The U.S. National Archives and Records Administration, 531102.

Pages 230-231: Figures (a)-(b): "A shanty built of refuse near the Sunnyside slack pile, Herrin, Illinois, 1939." FSA/OWI Photograph Collection, LC-DIG-fsa-8a10723. Library of Congress, Prints and Photographs Division. Figure (c): "Hooverville/ Snooseville, Elliott Avenue West." Photograph by James Lee, February 6, 1933. Seattle-King County Department of Public Health photograph files, Series 275, Box 7, item 090.2.680; King County Archives, Seattle, Washington.

Index

Reference to illustrations are indicated by *italic* page numbers.